Microsoft Dynamics NAV 2009: Professional Reporting

Discover all the tips and tricks for Dynamics NAV report building

Steven Renders

BIRMINGHAM - MUMBAI

Microsoft Dynamics NAV 2009: Professional Reporting

Copyright © 2011 Packt Publishing

All rights reserved. No part of this book may be reproduced, stored in a retrieval system, or transmitted in any form or by any means, without the prior written permission of the publisher, except in the case of brief quotations embedded in critical articles or reviews.

Every effort has been made in the preparation of this book to ensure the accuracy of the information presented. However, the information contained in this book is sold without warranty, either express or implied. Neither the author, nor Packt Publishing, and its dealers and distributors will be held liable for any damages caused or alleged to be caused directly or indirectly by this book.

Packt Publishing has endeavored to provide trademark information about all of the companies and products mentioned in this book by the appropriate use of capitals. However, Packt Publishing cannot guarantee the accuracy of this information.

First published: September 2011

Production Reference: 1160911

Published by Packt Publishing Ltd.
Livery Place
35 Livery Street
Birmingham B3 2PB, UK.

ISBN 978-1-84968-244-2

www.packtpub.com

Cover Image by Vinayak Chittar (vinayak.chittar@gmail.com)

Credits

Author
Steven Renders

Reviewers
Alex Chow
Eric "waldo" Wauters
Matt Traxinger
Daniel Rimmelzwaan

Acquisition Editor
Dhwani Devater

Development Editor
Alina Lewis

Technical Editor
Ajay Shanker

Project Coordinator
Shubhanjan Chatterjee

Proofreader
Aaron Nash

Indexer
Rekha Nair

Graphics
Valentina D'silva

Production Coordinator
Shantanu Zagade

Cover Work
Shantanu Zagade

About the Author

Steven Renders is a Microsoft Certified Trainer (MCT) with a wide range of skills spanning business and technical domains. He later specialized in Microsoft Dynamics NAV and Microsoft SQL Server.

He has more than 15 years of business and technical experience and provides training and consultancy focused on Microsoft Dynamics NAV, Microsoft SQL Server, Business Intelligence Solutions, Microsoft SQL Server Reporting Services, and Database Performance Tuning.

Furthermore, he is also an expert on Microsoft Dynamics 2009, on which he has already delivered many training sessions. Steven was an author of some of the official Microsoft training materials on Dynamics NAV Reporting, Dynamics NAV SQL Server performance tuning, and development. Steven was also a reviewer of the book: Programming in Microsoft Dynamics NAV 2009.

Steven was also a presenter at various Microsoft MSDN and TechNet evenings, conferences, communities, events, and the MCT Summit in Prague.

Steven has been awarded the Microsoft Certified Trainer (MCT) status since 2007, and is a Microsoft Certified Technology Specialist (MCTS) in Microsoft SQL Server, Microsoft Certified IT Professional Developer for Microsoft Dynamics NAV (MCITP), and Microsoft Certified IT Professional Installation and configuration for Microsoft Dynamics NAV (MCITP).

Recently, Steven started his own company, Think About IT, which is specialized in training and consultancy, helping companies learn, implement, understand, and solve complex business requirements related to IT, in Belgium and abroad.

Specialties:

- Microsoft Dynamics NAV
- Microsoft SQL Server
- Business Intelligence & Management Reporting

E-mail: steven.renders@thinkaboutit.be

LinkedIn: http://be.linkedin.com/in/stevenrenders

Acknowledgement

First of all I would like to express how lucky I am to have found such a fantastic soul mate in Marie Christine. The last few months, when I spent a lot of evenings, weekends, and free time on the book and in starting up a new company, Think About IT, she was the one person that always supported, motivated, and inspired me to continue. She stood by me, and without her it would have been impossible to achieve this result.

Also a special thanks to my parents, parents in law, brother, sister, nephews, godchildren, and friends, who always stood behind me and allowed me to spend so much time apart from them.

The team from Packt Publishing also deserves a lot of gratitude. It was really a pleasure working with them. They helped me a lot and guided the book into the good direction. I'm very thankful and appreciative for their help and guidance.

A big thank you also for the team of reviewers, who volunteered their time, knowledge, and experience reviewing every chapter, guarding the quality, accuracy, and flow of the book. They had a very big contribution in getting this book to become a great piece of work that is agreeable to read and understand.

In Belgium, we have a very good community with lots of events helping to share the knowledge, making sure everyone keeps up-to-date with the latest news and developments in the Dynamics NAV and SQL Server world. Going to the events, sometimes as a participant, sometimes as a speaker, helped me a great deal in broadening my view and subject matter expertise.

A special thanks also for my previous employer, Plataan. Five years ago, they motivated me to become a Microsoft Certified Trainer and allowed me to deepen my knowledge and experience in the Dynamics community.

Special thanks also to Microsoft and their employees in making fantastic products like Dynamics NAV and SQL Server come closer together. Both of them are great applications on their own, but combining them was one of the best achievements of the last few years. The way that Dynamics NAV is getting more and more integrated with other Microsoft technologies has shaped the future and opened up an almost unlimited window of possibilities and opportunities.

To all the above individuals and to several colleagues, whose names I cannot continue listing and who have assisted me one way or another, especially, in challenging me with alternative views, I feel very much indebted.

I would like to thank you all!

About the Reviewers

Alex Chow has been working with Microsoft Dynamics NAV since 1999. He has done hundreds of implementations across multiple industries. The size of businesses Alex has works with range from $2 million a year mom and pop-shops to $500 million a year multi-national corporations.

Throughout his Dynamics NAV career, he is frequently designated as the primary person responsible for the successful and failure of a Dynamics NAV implementation. The fact that Alex is still in the Dynamics NAV business means that he's been pretty lucky so far.

Alex has done implementation in all functions and modules in Microsoft Dynamics NAV (Navision) with practical and impractical requirements and business rules. From this experience, he has learned that sometimes you have to be a little crazy to gain a competitive edge.

Alex keeps a blog at `www.dynamicsnavconsultant.com` to share his experiences in Dynamics NAV (Navision). He is also the founder of AP Commerce, Inc. (`www.apcommerce.com`), a full service Dynamics NAV (Navision) service center.

Alex lives in Southern California with his beautiful wife and two lovely daughters. He is the luckiest man in the world.

Eric "waldo" Wauters is one of the founding partners of iFacto Business Solutions(www.ifacto.be). With his 10 years of technical expertise, he is an everyday inspiration to its development team. As development manager, he continually acts upon iFacto's technical readiness and guarantees that he and iFacto are always on top of the latest Microsoft Dynamics NAV developments.

Apart from that, Eric is also very active in Microsoft Dynamics NAV community-life, where he tries to solve technical issues and strives to share his knowledge with other Dynamics NAV enthusiasts. Surely, many among you will have read some of Eric's posts on Mibuso.com, Dynamicsusers.net, or his own blog www.waldo.be, which he invariably signs with waldo. In 2008, he co-founded the Belgian Dynamics Community, a platform for all Belgian Dynamics NAV users, consultants, and partners, enabling knowledge sharing and networking. His proven track record entitled him to be awarded as MVP (Microsoft Most Valuable Professional) every year since 2007.

Matt Traxinger graduated from the Georgia Institute of Technology in 2005 with a B.S. in Computer Science, specializing in Human Computer Interaction and Cognitive Science. After college he took a job as an add-on developer using a language he was unfamiliar with for a product he had never heard of: Navision. It turned out to be a great decision.

In the years following, Matt learned all areas of the product and earned MCITP certifications in both technical and functional areas of NAV. He continues to stay current with new releases of the product and is certified in multiple areas for versions 4.0, 5.0, and 2009. Currently, Matt works as a developer for ArcherPoint, one of the most experienced NAV partners in the United States, and helps companies model NAV to their business processes.

Matt is also the author of another book in Packt's Dynamics NAV series: Microsoft Dynamics NAV 2009 Programming Cookbook. It is a collection of short, easy to read recipes or tutorials about writing code for NAV.

In his spare time you can find him on the online communities Mibuso.com and DynamicsUser.net under the name MattTrax, helping others learn more about the Dynamics NAV software, or writing free solutions for the I Love NAV community (www.ILoveNAV.com).

Daniel Rimmelzwaan was born and raised in the Netherlands, and moved to the USA at the end of 1999 to be with his new American wife. In Holland, he worked as a Microsoft Access and VBA developer. When looking for a job as a VB developer in the USA, he was introduced to Navision by a "VB Recruiter", and was intrigued by the simplicity of its development tools. He decided to accept a job offer as a Navision Developer, with the firm intention to continue looking for a 'real' developer job. More than 10 years later, Daniel is still working with NAV. He currently works for Archerpoint, one of the largest and most experienced Microsoft Dynamics NAV partners in the USA, and he is enjoying his career more than ever.

Daniel has had the opportunity to work in a wide variety of roles such as Developer, Analyst, Designer, Team Lead, Project Manager, Consultant, and more. Although he has a very versatile experience with all things related to NAV, his main focus is custom development, with a bias towards helping his customers solve NAV performance issues on SQL Server.

Ever since he started working with NAV, Daniel has been an active member of the online communities for NAV, such as `mibuso.com`, dynamicsuser.net, and the online forums managed by Microsoft. For his contributions to these online communities, Daniel received his first of seven consecutive Microsoft Most Valuable Professional Awards in July 2005, which was just the second year that the MVP Award was given out for NAV. The MVP Award is given out by Microsoft to independent members of technology communities around the world, and recognizes people that share their knowledge with other members of the community.

Daniel has also served as a reviewer for "Microsoft Dynamics NAV 2009 Application Design" by Mark Brummel.

Daniel lives with his wife and two kids in Michigan in the USA.

www.PacktPub.com

Support files, eBooks, discount offers and more

You might want to visit www.PacktPub.com for support files and downloads related to your book.

Did you know that Packt offers eBook versions of every book published, with PDF and ePub files available? You can upgrade to the eBook version at www.PacktPub.com and as a print book customer, you are entitled to a discount on the eBook copy. Get in touch with us at service@packtpub.com for more details.

At www.PacktPub.com, you can also read a collection of free technical articles, sign up for a range of free newsletters and receive exclusive discounts and offers on Packt books and eBooks.

http://PacktLib.PacktPub.com

Do you need instant solutions to your IT questions? PacktLib is Packt's online digital book library. Here, you can access, read and search across Packt's entire library of books.

Why Subscribe?

- Fully searchable across every book published by Packt
- Copy and paste, print and bookmark content
- On demand and accessible via web browser

Free Access for Packt account holders

If you have an account with Packt at www.PacktPub.com, you can use this to access PacktLib today and view nine entirely free books. Simply use your login credentials for immediate access.

Instant Updates on New Packt Books

Get notified! Find out when new books are published by following @PacktEnterprise on Twitter, or the *Packt Enterprise* Facebook page.

Table of Contents

Preface	**1**
Chapter 1: Charts and Dimensions	**7**
Role Centers	**8**
Charts	**9**
Chart panes	10
Limitations of chart panes	11
Chart parts	12
Chart security	17
Chart performance	18
Reports	**18**
List reports	21
Test reports	21
Posting reports	21
Transaction reports	22
Document reports	23
Other reports	23
Printing reports	**23**
Determining print report settings	26
Printer selection	27
Report selections	30
Creating reports without development tools	**31**
What are dimensions?	31
Global	33
Shortcut	33
Budget	34
Where are dimensions set up?	34
Dimensions and dimension values	36
Dimension values	37
Dimension combinations	40

Default dimensions	42
View posted dimension information	43
Analysing financial information using dimensions	43
Dimension-based reports	49
Summary	**49**
Chapter 2: Creating a Report in the Classic Client	**51**
The Report Designer	**51**
Using the report wizard	52
Form type report	53
Tabular type report	54
Label type report	54
Creating a simple List report	**55**
Sorting and grouping data in a report	60
Sections in a classic report	68
Controls	70
Triggers	71
What happens when a report runs?	72
How is a data item processed?	73
Properties in a report	74
Adding color to a classic report	77
What is a ProcessingOnly report?	**77**
Creating an Excel-like layout for a report	**78**
Printing a report to Excel	80
What is so special about the Excel Buffer table (370)?	81
Report functions	**84**
Summary	**86**
Chapter 3: Creating Role Tailored Reports	**87**
The optional enhanced layout	**88**
Why you cannot call it Reporting Services	**88**
Difference between RDL and RDLC?	89
Printed reports versus online reports	**90**
Creating your first enhanced report	**91**
What's happening?	**102**
Adding formatting, grouping, sorting, and filtering to a report	107
Report creation workflow	115
Using multiple data items	**116**
Using the Create Layout Suggestion option	**118**
Changing the template	**123**
Making a report available in the Role Tailored client	**127**
Limitations of enhanced report design in Dynamics NAV 2009	**128**
Summary	**130**

Chapter 4: Visualization Methods — 133
Report items — 134
Common report item properties — 135
Text box — 138
List data regions — 139
Document Outline — 147
What is the List control used for? — 149
Undo/Redo — 150
Matrix boxes — 151
More advanced matrix techniques — 154
  Using colors in a matrix — 155
  Green bar matrix — 158
Chart data regions — 161
Adding images to your report — 164
Expanding/collapsing report sections — 168
Interactive sorting — 171
Using the document map — 172
Linking reports — 175
Bookmark links — 176
Hyperlinks — 180
  Filtering a report — 182
  Filtering a page — 182
Multi-column reports — 184
Headers and footers — 186
Expressions — 188
The Fields collection — 191
The Globals collection — 192
The ReportItems collection — 192
The User collection — 193
Functions — 193
Useful tips and techniques — 195
Use a title, page numbers, and show applied filters — 196
Using rectangles, lines, and images — 197
Adding a report border — 197
Tracking report usage — 197
Checking on empty datasets — 199
Using a report layout setup table — 199
Blanking properties — 199
Pagination — 200
Use rectangles — 200
Give everything a proper name — 200

Test, test, and test	200
Summary	**201**
Chapter 5: Developing Specific Reports	**203**
Document reports	**203**
The number of copies option	204
Displaying data-bound information in the header	209
Working with addresses in reports	224
Displaying the current page and copy number	226
TOP X reports	**227**
Creating a TOP X table	229
Creating a TOP X chart	234
Using the wizard	**238**
Adding KPIs and conditional formatting	**240**
Simulating data bars	244
Simulating spark lines	251
Implementing conditional formatting	**257**
Choosing the right colors	260
Summary	**261**
Chapter 6: Other Reporting and Business Intelligence Tools	**263**
Knowing your data and database	**264**
Dynamics NAV database design	264
How is the Dynamics NAV database created in SQL Server?	269
Relations and foreign keys	274
Using an Entity Relationship model	275
Reporting Services	**277**
Using Report Builder	278
Using BIDS	289
Comparing RDL and RDLC	**292**
Using Microsoft Excel with Dynamics NAV	**294**
Excel Data Mining Add In	298
PowerPivot	301
Business Intelligence and NAV	**306**
Business Analytics	310
The advantage of having a BI solution	313
Summary	**314**

Chapter 7: A View of the Future	**315**
Dynamics NAV 7 and beyond	**315**
Jet Reports Express	316
RDLC mandatory and 2008 integration	316
Section designer replaced with an extended data item designer	317
Dynamics NAV and SharePoint	318
Dynamics NAV in the cloud	318
What will SQL Server do?	**319**
Project Crescent	320
BISM	322
Summary	**323**
Index	**325**

Preface

Microsoft Dynamics NAV gives you direct access to real-time, business-critical information, and a wide range of analytical tools to help you manage budgets, create and consolidate reports, and look for trends and relationships.

What's more, Microsoft Dynamics NAV is built on industry-standard Microsoft technology and integrates with other Microsoft Business Intelligence (BI) products and technologies. So, you can start with the basic modules and Microsoft Office Excel and then add functionality and tools as you need them.

This is how Microsoft describes the Business Intelligence capabilities of the Dynamics NAV product. As we will see in this book, this description is not far from the truth. The only problem is that most people don't have a clear idea of how much is available in the box and what's available out of the box.

Implementers are usually very good in setting up the application so that users can input their data into the system according to the processes and flows in their organization / company. A lot of time and effort is spent on adapting the application to the flows and processes of the organization. But, after the data is then finally inside the database, how do we then get it out again? That's a question I get a lot from customers. In this book, I will give you an answer to this question.

After reading this book it should be clear how to manipulate Dynamics NAV for it to produce the reports and analytical data that you want, when you want it, and in the format you want it!

Preface

What this book covers

Chapter 1, *What's Available in the Box?*, gives an overview of the types of reports available in the application, where to find them, and how to use them. You can create your custom reports without the need for a developer or report designer. This can be done by making use of dimensions, analysis views, and account schedules and so on. It's important to know what's already available for free in the application, before you start spending time, money, and resources on developing custom reports.

Chapter 2, *Creating a Classic Report*, explains the classic layout, how to create it, and all the capabilities of the good old classic report designer. The creation aspect of the classic report will be kept to a minimum, with more focus on new reporting possibilities of the Role Tailored Client. You will need this information to design reports for the Role Tailored Client, as development of reports starts with a classic report and knowledge about the classic designer is still required.

Chapter 3, *Creating a Role Tailored Client Report*, dives into the Role Tailored Report designer, or the RDLC report layout as it is called. It starts with an introduction to Visual Studio, its different flavors (versions), the toolbars, the environment, and useful shortcuts. It will explain the different ways to create a report from scratch using the Create Layout suggestion feature. You will see different kinds of problems you may encounter when developing reports for the Role Tailored Client and how to troubleshoot them.

Chapter 4, *Visualization Methods*, explains that creating reports is not just extracting and formatting data from the database and dropping it onto a layout. The way you visualize the information is equally important. The report will stand or fall depending on the way the information is rendered and presented to the user. That's why a big portion on the chapter will be about data visualization techniques and how to apply them in RDLC.

Chapter 5, *Developing Specific Reports*, explains how the RDLC report layout for documents, such as a sales invoice, is full of workarounds. We will explore it in detail with the most important workarounds, how and why they are required, and explore some alternative solutions. Creating dashboards and top x reports are also covered in this chapter.

Chapter 6, *Other Reporting Tools and Business Intelligence*, explains the database behind the Dynamics NAV application. How can you create an ER model? How are the tables related to each other? This chapter will address all these questions. The chapter then dives into SQL Server Reporting Services and explains how you can create an SSRS report. Other BI tools from the Microsoft stack, like for example PowerPivot, Excel Data Mining and Business Analytics, are also covered in this chapter. The purpose is to get a good overview on the other tools that are out there and the added value they have to offer on top of a Dynamics NAV database.

Chapter 7, A View to the Future, shows the future panorama of reporting in Dynamics NAV. Besides the Dynamics NAV application, the other BI applications are also evolving and becoming more integrated. This chapter will try to give you an overview on what will or might happen and the kind of impact or added value it might offer for Dynamics NAV.

Who this book is for

Basically, this book is for everyone who is using Microsoft Dynamics NAV or has an interest on the reporting capabilities of NAV 2009. The book does not have heavy prerequisites, although it is mainly focused on Dynamics NAV 2009, RDLC, and Business Intelligence.

This does not mean that this book has no technical depth and you don't require any technical skills. On the contrary, many parts of the book will cover in great detail the technical aspects and development techniques and reporting tools for Dynamics NAV.

If you want to get an impression on what's possible inside and outside the box of Dynamics NAV 2009 then this book will give you a great overview. If you are interested to know how to attach other Reporting or Business Intelligence products to Dynamics NAV then this book will also give you an overview of these possibilities.

You might be an application developer, a power user, or a technical decision maker. Regardless of your role, I hope that you can use this book to discover the reporting features in Dynamics NAV 2009 that are most beneficial to you.

Conventions

In this book, you will find a number of styles of text that distinguish between different kinds of information. Here are some examples of these styles, and an explanation of their meaning.

Code words in text are shown as follows: "`Relative` can be used to compare values on a scale between 0 and 1."

A block of code is set as follows:

```
Public Function BlankZero(ByVal Value As Decimal)
if Value = 0 then
        Return ""
end if
    Return Value
```

```
End Function

Public Function BlankPos(ByVal Value As Decimal)
if Value > 0 then
        Return ""
end if
    Return Value
End Function
```

Any command-line input or output is written as follows:

DynamicsNAV:////runreport?report=xxxxx

New terms and **important words** are shown in bold. Words that you see on the screen, in menus or dialog boxes for example, appear in the text like this: "A chart is added by using the **Customize This Page** feature in the RTC".

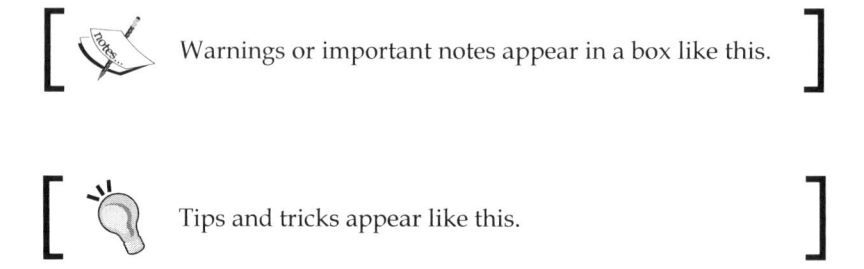

[Warnings or important notes appear in a box like this.]

[Tips and tricks appear like this.]

Reader feedback

Feedback from our readers is always welcome. Let us know what you think about this book—what you liked or may have disliked. Reader feedback is important for us to develop titles that you really get the most out of.

To send us general feedback, simply send an e-mail to feedback@packtpub.com, and mention the book title via the subject of your message.

If there is a book that you need and would like to see us publish, please send us a note in the **SUGGEST A TITLE** form on www.packtpub.com or e-mail suggest@packtpub.com.

If there is a topic that you have expertise in and you are interested in either writing or contributing to a book, see our author guide on www.packtpub.com/authors.

Customer support

Now that you are the proud owner of a Packt book, we have a number of things to help you to get the most from your purchase.

Downloading the example code

You can download the example code files for all Packt books you have purchased from your account at http://www.PacktPub.com. If you purchased this book elsewhere, you can visit http://www.PacktPub.com/support and register to have the files e-mailed directly to you.

Errata

Although we have taken every care to ensure the accuracy of our content, mistakes do happen. If you find a mistake in one of our books—maybe a mistake in the text or the code—we would be grateful if you would report this to us. By doing so, you can save other readers from frustration and help us improve subsequent versions of this book. If you find any errata, please report them by visiting http://www.packtpub.com/support, selecting your book, clicking on the **errata submission form** link, and entering the details of your errata. Once your errata are verified, your submission will be accepted and the errata will be uploaded on our website, or added to any list of existing errata, under the Errata section of that title. Any existing errata can be viewed by selecting your title from http://www.packtpub.com/support.

Piracy

Piracy of copyright material on the Internet is an ongoing problem across all media. At Packt, we take the protection of our copyright and licenses very seriously. If you come across any illegal copies of our works, in any form, on the Internet, please provide us with the location address or website name immediately so that we can pursue a remedy.

Please contact us at copyright@packtpub.com with a link to the suspected pirated material.

We appreciate your help in protecting our authors, and our ability to bring you valuable content.

Questions

You can contact us at questions@packtpub.com if you are having a problem with any aspect of the book, and we will do our best to address it.

1
Charts and Dimensions

In most implementations, the focus is set on customizing the Dynamics NAV application to meet the needs of the current processes in the organization and sometimes the future needs are also considered. The effort that is required for reporting in general is often underestimated and unfortunately assigned to the least experienced consultants, who have to create/adapt the document reports conforming the look and feel of the customer.

Personally, I believe reporting is one of the most important aspects of an implementation. And so, it should be considered from the beginning, in the analysis phase of the project. The kind of information you want to be able to retrieve from your ERP system and the way you want to retrieve this information has a deep impact on the implementation of the system. Doing this correctly from the beginning of a project can and will save a lot of time, money, and frustration. The unfortunate reality is that many prospects and/or customers look at reporting first when they want to reduce the budget of an ERP implementation project.

In this chapter, we will learn:

- The usage and difference between chart panes and chart parts in the Role Tailored Client
- Types of reports that are available in Dynamics NAV 2009
- Printing reports
- Creating reports without the development tools
- What dimensions are and their setup

Charts and Dimensions

Role Centers

Dynamics NAV 2009 is all about the Role Tailored Client and the Role Tailored Client always opens with a Role Center page. A Role Center is like a dashboard. It is the starting page in Dynamics NAV 2009 and on it you will find the links to all the kinds of information you are looking for.

This is an example of the Role Center for the Order Processor role:

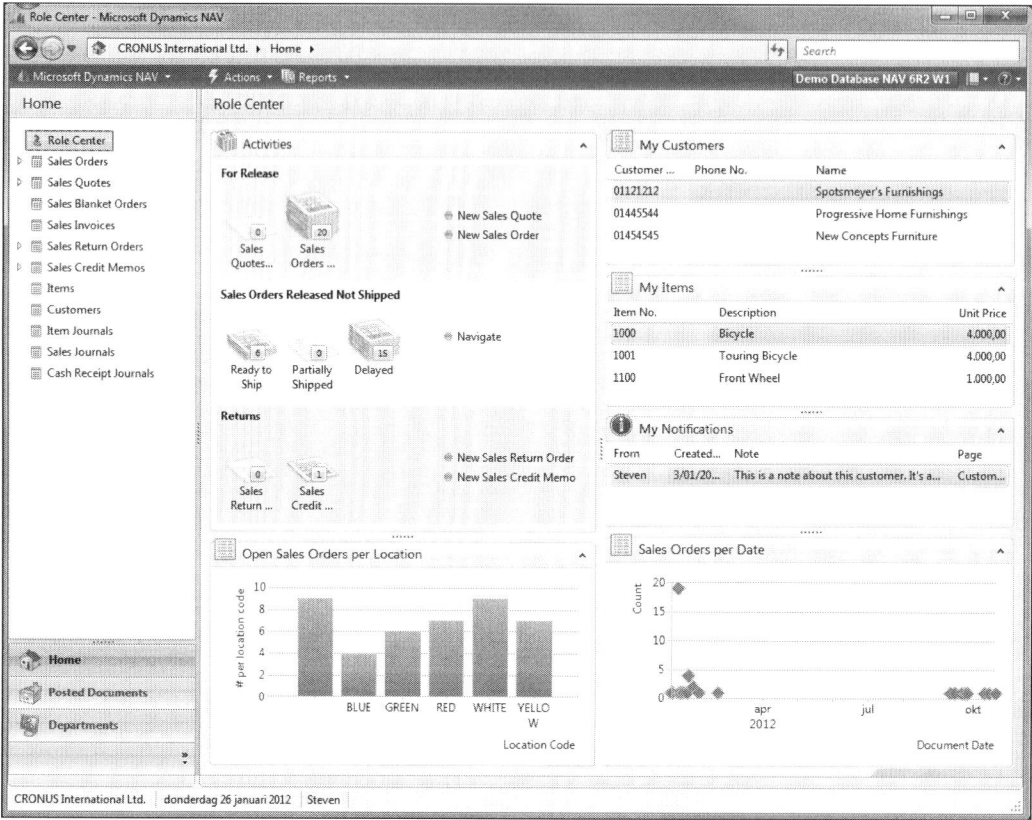

As you can see, the Role Center contains several panes of information. There's an activity pane that contains cues. Each of these cues represents a pile of documents and the height of the pile and the number on the pile represent the number of documents behind the pile. When you click on the pile, or cue icon as it is called, you are redirected to the corresponding page. On the Role Center page, you can have several other types of panes, but the ones that are interesting from the reporting point of view are the charts. On this Role Center, we can see two charts: the Open Sales Orders per Location chart and the Sales Orders per Date chart.

As a user, you can customize your Role Center. This way, you can, for example, visualize other charts and so customize your Role Center as a personal dashboard page.

For example, the next screenshot shows the Role Center for the President of a small business. Of course, this page can also be customized by the user, for example to include charts:

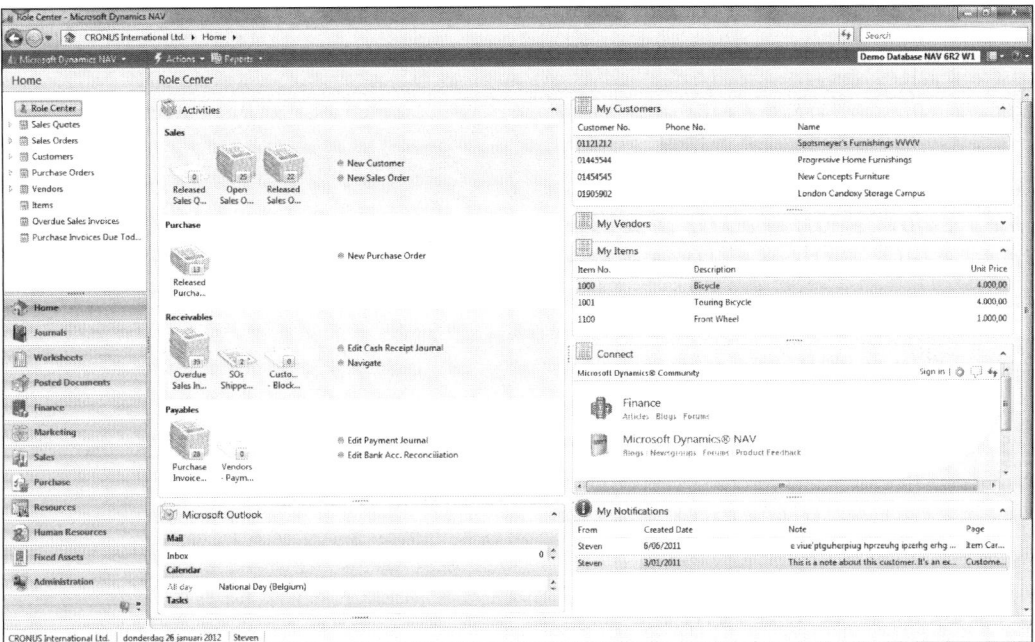

Charts

In the Role Tailored client there are two kinds of charts that can be added to any page by the user. To do this, the user can add chart parts and/or charts panes to a page. But there are some restrictions:

- A chart pane is only available on a List page
- A chart part has to be available in the design of the page

These charts that can be added to the Role Tailored Client at runtime give the user the perception of self service business intelligence in the Role Tailored Client.

Charts and Dimensions

 You can also add other types of charts to the RTC, for example via Control Addins. These types of charts are not covered in this chapter.

Chart panes

In any List page of the Role Tailored client a user can go to **Customize This Page** and add a chart pane to the page. When you do this, a chart pane is added that can be used to design a chart at runtime. The following screenshot presents these customization options. Enable the **Chart Pane:**

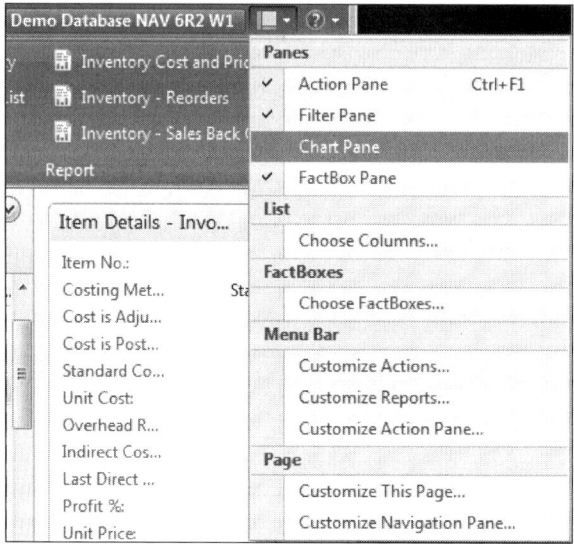

When you do this, a blank chart is added to the List page, below the list of fields. In this chart, the user can select one measure and one or two dimension fields:

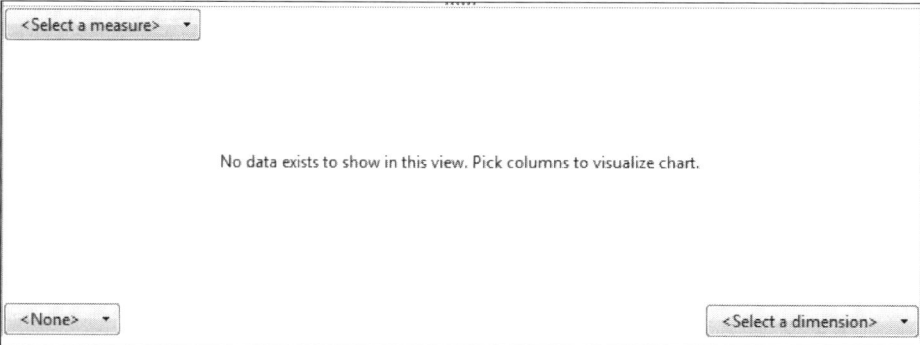

Chapter 1

The measure and dimension fields are all fields from the underlying table of the list page. Flowfields are also available to choose from:

- The measure represents a numerical value you want to visualize in the chart.
- The dimensions represent the axes you want to use to analyse the selected measure.

For example, in the Item List page, the user can create this kind of chart:

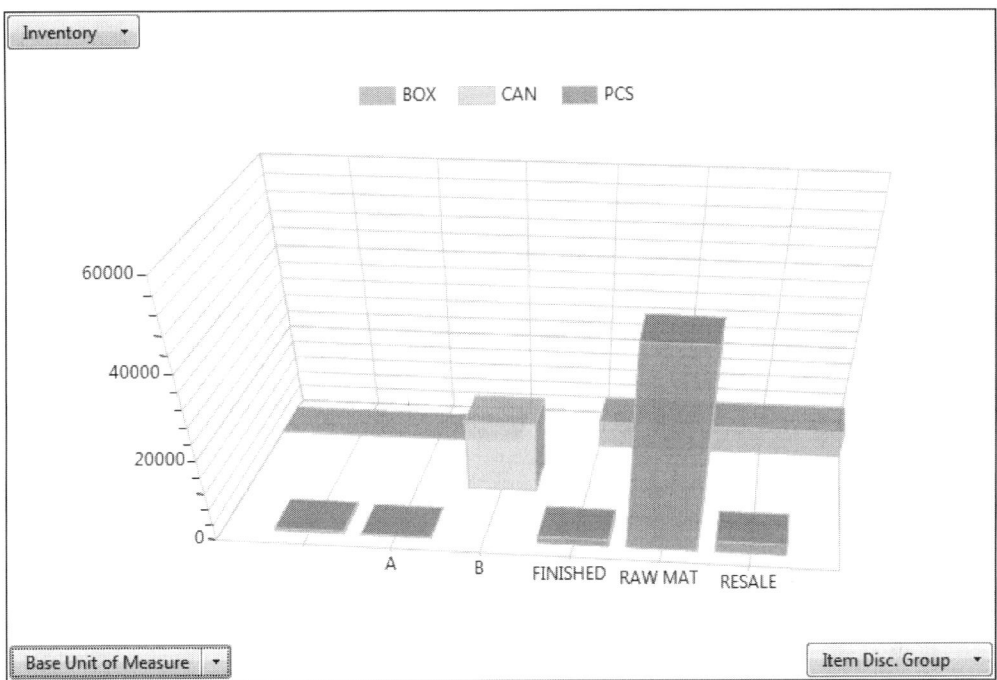

By selecting the Inventory flowfield as the measure and the Item Discount Group and Base Unit of Measure fields as dimensions, you have now visualized the inventory in a three dimensional bar chart. This provides you with an easy to understand graphical representation of the Inventory.

When you right-click on the chart, you can either copy or export it as a bitmap.

Limitations of chart panes

Chart panes are added by the user at runtime, and they are limited to the user only. Chart panes are a part of the user personalization features of the Role Tailored Client. Furthermore, after you stop and restart the Role Tailored Client, the chart pane is removed.

Charts and Dimensions

Chart panes can be demanding on performance. Chart panes are combinations of one measure field and one or two dimension fields, without filters. As you can probably imagine, when there are many records in the underlying table, running these chart panes can become very demanding on server resources. That's probably why they are removed after you restart the RTC.

Chart parts

A chart is added by using the **Customize This Page** feature in the RTC. Click on the Customize button at the top right of the window in the RTC as follows:

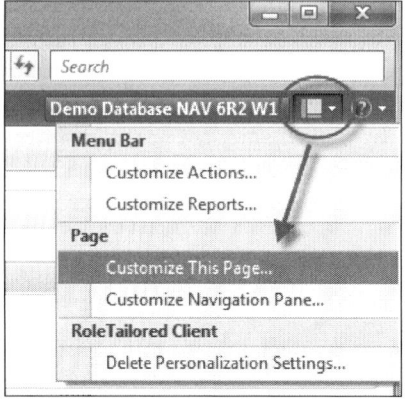

Now, you can add a chart to the page as follows:

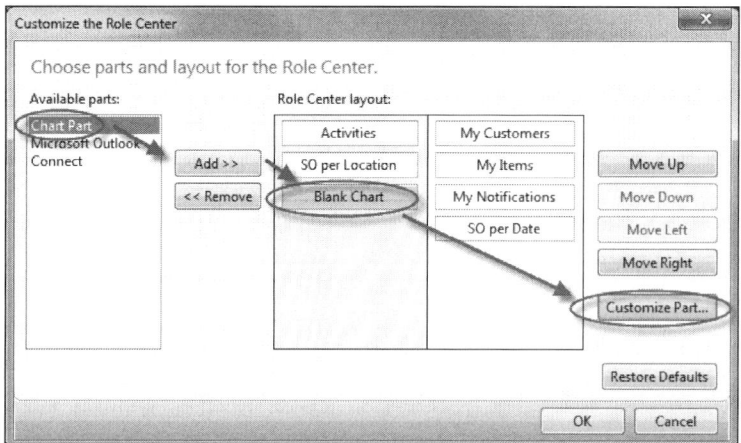

When you then click on **Customize Part**, after selecting **Blank Chart**, you can select the chart you want to show in this chart part from the list of chart parts.

[12]

Now, where are these chart parts coming from? Actually, the chart parts are stored in the table: 2000000078 Chart.

You can create a new chart by importing it into this table. To help you in this process you can use the Classic Client (CC) or the Role Tailored Client (RTC):

- To use the Classic Client, navigate in the CC to Administration/Application Setup/RoleTailored Client and click on Charts
- To use the RTC, navigate in the RTC to Departments/Administration/Application Setup/RoleTailored Client and click on Charts

A window opens that you can use to import a new chart into the Chart table. Give the chart a unique ID, and a name. Then, you must import an XML file, which will contain the definition of the chart. Furthermore, you can enter none, one, or more companies, to limit the chart to become only available in certain companies of the database.

There are some limitations when creating a chart:

- A chart must be based on exactly **one table**. You can't combine data from multiple tables.
- You have two basic chart types: **Point** or **Column**.
- **Green** is the only color currently supported.
- Charts can use one of two operators: **Sum** or **Count**.
- You can only apply **static filters** in charts, that is, you must type in (hardcode) the filter when you generate the chart.

A chart has a simple layout. You choose the table to base it on, then a field from that table to show along the X-axis, and, if needed, a filter on this table. Then, you select what data from the table to show on the Y-axis (also called a measure). A measure can be based on Sum or Count. You can display multiple measures in the same chart. Charts are defined by XML documents that are stored as BLOB fields. You can export a chart to an XML document, then modify the XML document, and import it back as a new chart.

The table, measures, and dimensions on which you base your chart are entered in the XML document.

This is an example of a chart definition:

```xml
<ChartDefinition xmlns="urn:schemas-microsoft-com:dynamics:NAV:MetaObjects" xmlns:xsd="http://www.w3.org/2001/XMLSchema" xmlns:xsi="http://www.w3.org/2001/XMLSchema-instance" Type="Column">
    <Title>
        <Text ID="ENU">Items by location</Text>
```

Charts and Dimensions

```
      </Title>
      <Table ID="32">
         <Filters>
            <Filter>
               <Field Name="Item No." />
               <Value>70000|70001|70002|70003</Value>
            </Filter>
         </Filters>
      </Table>
      <XAxis ShowTitle="true">
         <Title>
            <Text ID="ENU">Location Code</Text>
         </Title>
         <Field Name="Location Code" />
      </XAxis>
      <YAxis ShowTitle="false">
         <Measures>
            <Measure Operator="Sum">
               <Field Name="Quantity" />
            </Measure>
         </Measures>
      </YAxis>
</ChartDefinition>
```

A chart automatically becomes a 3D chart by adding a Z-axis to the chart definition, for example like this:

```
<ZAxis ShowTitle="false">
   <Field Name="Item No." />
</ZAxis>
```

The presence of a Z-axis will automatically make the user able to rotate the chart:

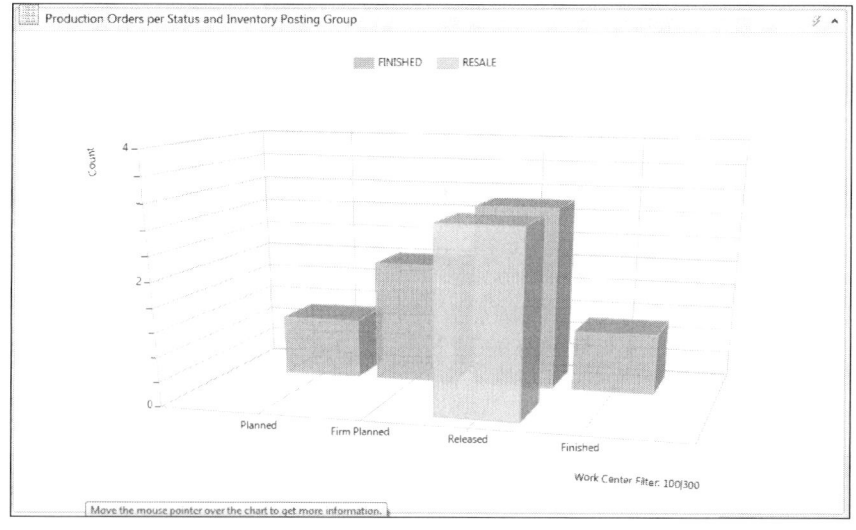

> This XML file is an example coming from this website: `http://blogs.msdn.com/b/nav/archive/2008/08/20/nav-2009-how-to-generate-charts-kpis.aspx`.
>
> On this blog, you can also download a Chart Generator tool. This tool contains objects that can make it easier to generate charts using the Classic Client and not by editing the XML file directly, which is very error sensitive. The tool contains the following objects:
>
> | Type | ID | Name |
> | --- | --- | --- |
> | 1 | 72000 | Chart Generator |
> | 1 | 72001 | Chart Generator Filter |
> | 1 | 72003 | Chart Generator YAxis |
> | 2 | 72000 | Chart Generator List |
> | 2 | 72001 | Chart Filters |
> | 2 | 72003 | YAxis List |
> | 2 | 72004 | Chart Generator Card |
> | 5 | 72000 | Chart Generator Mgt |
>
> Charts can be generated from form 72004 "Chart Generator Card". The Chart Generator tool is only supplied as an example of how such a tool could be made. It is completely un-supported and to be used at your own risk and responsibility.

A definition of the XML file can be found in an XSD file that you can find on the installation DVD of the Dynamics NAV application. It has been added on this DVD in version NAV 2009 R2. Before the R2 release, there was no `.xsd` file available.

This XSD file can be found in this location on the DVD: `DVD\Documentation\Utility\ChartMetaData.xsd`.

This `.xsd` schema describes the possible building blocks of the XML definition for a chart. A schema is a blueprint of an XML document that defines the elements, data types, and nesting structure of the page.

Charts and Dimensions

The following is a screenshot of the XSD file, when you open it in Visual Studio and display it in the XML Schema Explorer:

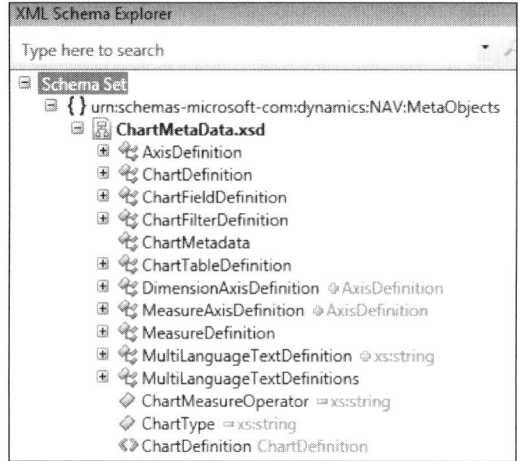

What can we conclude after investigating the .xsd file?

Well, first of all, some of the limitations we had before on charts are removed in NAV 2009 R2.

The ChartType is limited to Column, Point, and Line, as you can see here:

```
<xs:simpleType name="ChartType">
<xs:restriction base="xs:string">
<xs:enumeration value="Column" />
<xs:enumeration value="Point" />
<xs:enumeration value="Line" />
</xs:restriction>
</xs:simpleType>
```

The ChartMeasureOperator is now limited to the following operations:

- None
- Count
- Sum
- Min
- Max
- Avg
- Relative
- RelativePct

And the default is Sum, as you can see here:

```
<xs:simpleType name="ChartMeasureOperator">
<xs:restriction base="xs:string">
<xs:enumeration value="None" />
<xs:enumeration value="Count" />
<xs:enumeration value="Sum" />
<xs:enumeration value="Min" />
<xs:enumeration value="Max" />
<xs:enumeration value="Avg" />
<xs:enumeration value="Relative" />
<xs:enumeration value="RelativePct" />
</xs:restriction>
</xs:simpleType>
```

Compared to the previous release of Dynamics NAV, there are new options—`Relative` and `RelativePct`:

- `Relative` can be used to compare values on a scale between 0 and 1.
- `RelativePct` will do the same on a scale between 0 and 100%.

Secondly, the `ChartTableDefinition` now has an extra attribute: Key. This will I think determine the sort order when possible, but also have an impact on performance.

Chart security

A question you might ask yourself is: What about charts and security? Can I make sure only specific users will be able to add a chart to their Role Center page?

Well, the answer to this question is: no and yes. No, because there's no specific feature that was added to NAV 2009 to set up chart security. The way to set up security for these charts is by using security filters. As you might have seen, the existing charts all have a specific naming convention in their ID's. It is the Table Number followed by an index. This means that if you also follow this naming convention, you can use the chart ID as a security filter value when setting up roles and security in NAV 2009.

Record level security is a system that allows you to limit the access that a user has to the data in a table by specifying that the user only has permission to access certain records in the table. Record level security is implemented by applying security filters to the tables and the table data that a user has access to. You can specify, for example, that a user can only read the records that contain information about a particular customer and cannot access the records that contain information about any of the other customers.

Charts and Dimensions

>
> Record level security is only available in the SQL Server Option for Dynamics NAV. But because the RTC only works on a SQL Server database this should not be a problem.
>
> Record level security filters do not support wildcards. This means that you cannot use * and ? in the filters. You can use the other symbols, delimiters, and operators, such as, <, >, |, &, .. and =.
>
> The maximum length of a security filter is 250 characters, but all of the delimiters, symbols, and operators such as, <, >, |, &, .. and = also count as characters and can considerably reduce the length of the security filters that you can enter.
>
> Furthermore, security filters are concatenated and therefore the sum of all the security filters applied to a user or a role cannot exceed 250 characters.

Chart performance

When you are a developer who designs the XML for a chart object, or when you are a user who's adding a chart to a page in the Role Tailored Client, you should consider the performance impact of the chart. In a chart object, although the data comes from one table, this table could contain thousands, tens of thousands, or even more records. Doing calculations on such huge amounts is normally not a problem for SQL Server, but for Dynamics NAV it might be.

That's why you should carefully design the chart. You can do this by selecting the appropriate key in the chart definition, and by supplying the appropriate filters.

The user should also be aware that the more charts he or she adds to a page, the bigger the impact on performance.

Reports

Besides charts, the Role Center also provides access to reports:

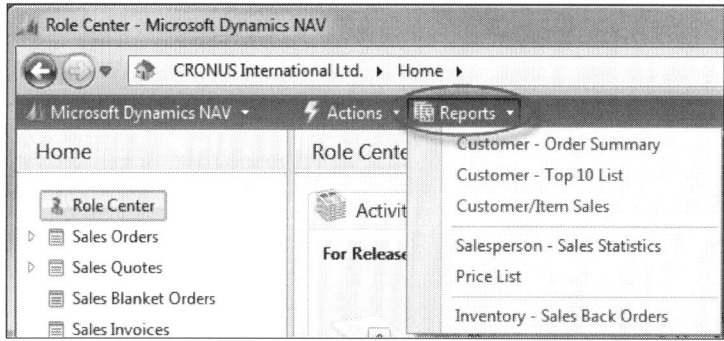

Depending on the Role Center you are on, the list will contain different reports. Also, on the other types of pages you will be able to access reports. For example, from the Customer Card page you can access reports in the menu at the top of the window:

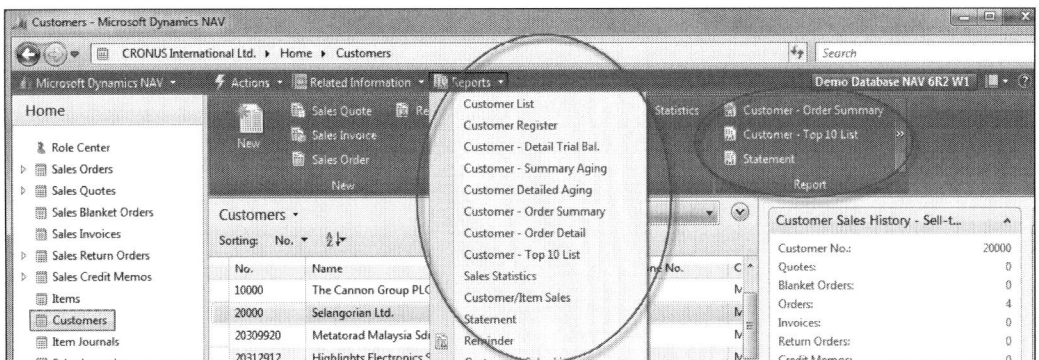

When you go to the Departments in the RTC, you can go to any department, for example Sales & Marketing. When you click the Department, in the content window different categories will appear.

Click on **Reports and Analysis**: here, you will get an overview of all the reports that are related to Sales and Marketing. The reports are divided into different groups:

- Analysis & Reporting
- Sales
- Order Processing
- Marketing
- Inventory & Pricing

Charts and Dimensions

These groups correspond to the groups defined in the Menu Item when the Sales and Marketing Menu was designed in the MenuSuite designer. In each group, you will find links to reports:

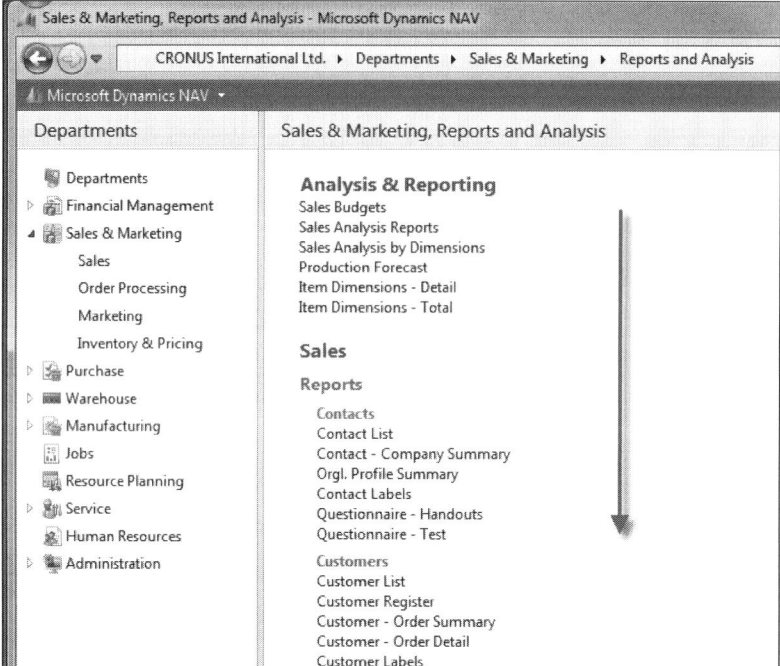

This kind of classification of reports is available in every section of the Departments suite in the RTC.

Reports have several purposes in Dynamics NAV:

- Reports are used to print information from a database in a structured way. For example, you can create a report that lists all the customers and all the orders placed by each customer.
- Every application document must be created as a report. For example, to print an invoice, you must create a report that is automatically filled out with the relevant information.
- Reports can also be used for other tasks and not just for printing. A report can be used to automate many recurring tasks such as updating all the prices in an item list. This could be achieved by writing C/AL code in a Codeunit, but using a report is much easier because you can take advantage of the powerful data modeling facilities available in the report designer.

There are different types of reports available in Dynamics NAV.

List reports

A List report prints a list of records from a table. A List report usually contains a single data item. This data item represents the table being listed. The table is either a Master table or a Supplemental table. Each column contains a field from the table. Most data are printed from that table and sometimes brought in or calculated from other tables. The name of the List report is usually the name of the table followed by the word List.

The following are examples of List reports:

- Report 101, Customer – List
- Report 301, Vendor - List

> Some of the reports mentioned here might not be available in all localizations of Dynamics NAV 2009. For example, the Customer List report is not a part of the US version of Dynamics NAV.

Test reports

A test report is printed from a Journal Table. Its purpose is to test each Journal Line according to certain criteria that are used for posting so that all the errors can be found and fixed before posting. As soon as an error is found during posting, processing stops and the error must be fixed before posting can be tried again. Therefore, a test report is a good way to find errors in a journal that has multiple errors. The name of the Test report is usually the name of the corresponding Journal, followed by the word Test.

The following are examples of Test reports:

- Report 2, General Journal – Test
- Report 1005, Job Journal – Test

Posting reports

A Posting report prints from the Register table. It lists all the transactions (ledger entries) that are posted into that Register. This allows the accountant to detect exactly who posted the transaction, on what date, and in what sequence. This kind of report can be very useful for auditing. A Posting report can be printed as part of the Post and Print option in a Journal. The name of the Posting report is usually the name of either the Register table or the Master table of the corresponding ledger entries.

Charts and Dimensions

When you post a document in Dynamics NAV, for example a sales or purchase order, the system creates entries in the General Ledger. At the same time, specific ledger entries are created in separate tables, like for example the customer ledger entry, item ledger entry, resource ledger entry, VAT ledger entry, and so on. The specific ledger entry tables that are affected by a posting will depend on the type of information on the document. For example, if there were no items involved then no item ledger entry needs to be created.

When the posting routine posts a document, multiple entries may need to be created in the same specific ledger entry table. This is then stored and summarized in the register table. For example, in the item register table a record will be created by the posting routine with the starting number and ending number of the generated item ledger entries. Also, the user involved and the date are stored.

That way the register table can be used to analyze the transactions that took place concerning specific documents. The ledger entry tables will contain more detailed information and are used a lot when creating transactional reports.

The following are examples of Posting reports:

- Report 3, G/L Register
- Report 103, Customer Register
- Report 1015, Job Register

Transaction reports

A Transaction report has the following characteristics:

- It lists all the ledger entries for each record in the Ledger table.
- It contains a subtotal for each Master table record, and a grand total for all tables printed.
- It is used to view all transactions for a particular Master record.
- It has no standard naming convention. A Transaction report usually has one or more data items, including the Master table and the corresponding Ledger table.

The following are examples of Transaction reports:

- Report 4, Detail Trial Balance
- Report 104, Customer – Detail Trial Bal.
- Report 1007, Job – Transaction Detail

Document reports

A Document report prints a document. Document reports differ from most other reports, in that, many of the fields are not displayed in columns. An example of this type of report is the Sales Invoice. The header information in a Sales Invoice is printed as if filling out an invoice document. This header information is repeated at the top of each page, and no page has information from more than one header.

The lines for the invoice print more like an ordinary report in rows and columns. The lines correspond to the header on the same page, and lines from other invoices are not displayed on the same page.

The following are examples of Document reports:

- Report 206, Sales—Invoice
- Report 116, Statement
- Report 405, Order

Other reports

Reports are more loosely defined than other application objects because they are frequently customized for a particular client. However, most reports consist of a tabular listing with records listed horizontally and each field displaying in its own column. Many times, there is a group heading or total to split the lines among various categories and to subtotal the lines by the categories.

The following are examples of other reports:

- Report 113, Customer/Item Sales
- Report 313, Vendor/Item Purchases
- Report 1012, Jobs per Customer

Printing reports

How can reports be printed? What are the options to select a printer (printer selections) and which properties can be set when printing a report? What's the difference between printing reports from the Classic Client and from the Role Tailored Client, and how can you use the report viewer? These are all questions I will answer in this section.

To print a report:

1. Open the report you want to print.
2. Click **File | Print**, or click the **Print** button on the toolbar.
3. You can also print a report by clicking **Print** in the report windows.

You can print the contents of any window that has a **Print** button. When you choose **File**, **Print**, the system opens a window where you can enter details about how the printing will be done.

In the uppermost field, you can see the name of the printer that is selected in the Windows Control Panel as your default printer. The printer selection will be valid for all of Microsoft Dynamics NAV until you choose a different one, or unless you associate a certain printer with a certain user and/or report in the Printer Selections window.

When you print a report and you have specified print and layout settings in the design of the report layout, you can also specify print and layout settings in the request page, in the printer properties of the selected printer, and in the print layout view of the report viewer at runtime. So then, which print settings will get priority?

You can specify page settings and page orientation for a printed report from the following UI locations:

- The **Report Properties** dialog box on the client report definition (RDLC) report layout in Visual Studio
- The **Properties** dialog box for the printer
- The **Print** dialog box that is displayed immediately before you print
- The **Page Setup** dialog box from the **Print Preview** page in the `RoleTailored` client

The page settings that are used for the printed report depend on the mode in which you print the report.

Chapter 1

You can use the following modes to print a report from the `RoleTailored` client:

- Run a report that has the `UseReqForm` property set to No, and therefore, does not display a request page
- Print a report from the request page without previewing the report
- Print a report from the **Print Preview** page

The printer that you use determines how to handle the case in which the actual paper size in the printer is different from the page size that is specified.

The following table describes how you access each of the dialog boxes in which you can specify page settings and orientation:

Print mode	To access the Report Properties dialog box	To access the Properties dialog box for the printer	To access the Print dialog box	To access the Page Setup dialog box
Run a report that does not have a request page	When you design the report layout in Visual Studio, on the **Report** menu, click **Report Properties**.	In **Control Panel**, double-click **Printers**. Right-click the selected printer and then click **Properties**.	Cannot access.	Cannot access.
Print a report from the request page without previewing	When you design the report layout in Visual Studio, on the **Report** menu, click **Report Properties**.	In **Control Panel**, double-click **Printers**. Right-click the selected printer, and then click **Properties**.	On the request page, click **Print**.	Cannot access.
View a preview of a report	When you design the report layout in Visual Studio, on the **Report** menu, click **Report Properties**.	In **Control Panel**, double-click **Printers**. Right-click the selected printer and then click **Properties**.	In the **Print Preview** window, click the Print icon.	In the **Print Preview** window, click the Page Setup icon.

Determining print report settings

When you are printing a report without a request page, then the following table applies:

If	Then the printed report paper size and margins are determined by	And the printed report orientation is determined by
The settings in the **Report Properties** dialog box on the layout of the report specify a standard paper size.	The settings in the **Report Properties** dialog box on the RDLC layout.	The settings in the **Properties** dialog box for the printer.
The settings in the **Report Properties** dialog box on the layout of the report specify a custom paper size.	The settings in the **Properties** dialog box for the printer.	The settings in the **Properties** dialog box for the printer.

When you are printing a report from the request page, the following table applies:

If	Then the printed report paper size and margins are determined by	And the printed report orientation is determined by
The settings in the **Report Properties** dialog box on the layout of the report specify a standard paper size.	The settings in the **Report Properties** dialog box on the RDLC layout, but is overridden if you change the settings in the **Print** dialog box.	The settings in the **Report Properties** dialog box on the RDLC layout, but is overridden if you change the settings in the **Print** dialog box.
The settings in the **Report Properties** dialog box on the layout of the report specify a custom paper size.	The settings in the **Properties** dialog box for the printer, but is overridden if you change the settings in the **Print** dialog box.	The settings in the **Report Properties** dialog box on the RDLC layout, but is overridden if you change the settings in the **Print** dialog box.

> The values in the **Print** dialog box are initially set to the values from the **Report Properties** dialog box on the RDLC report layout.

When you are printing a report from the print preview page, the following table applies:

If	Then the printed report paper size and margins are determined by	And the printed report orientation is determined by
The settings in the **Report Properties** dialog box on the layout of the report specify a standard paper size.	The settings in the **Report Properties** dialog box on the RDLC layout, but is overridden if you change the settings in the **Page Setup** dialog box.	The paper size settings in the **Report Properties** dialog box on the RDLC layout, but is overridden if you change the settings in the **Page Setup** dialog box.
The settings in the **Report Properties** dialog box on the layout of the report specify a custom paper size.	The settings in the **Report Properties** dialog box on the RDLC layout, but is overridden if you change the settings in the **Page Setup** dialog box.	The paper size settings in the **Report Properties** dialog box on the RDLC layout, but is overridden if you change the settings in the **Page Setup** dialog box.

> The values in the **Page Setup** dialog box are initially set to the values from the **Report Properties** dialog box on the RDLC report layout.

Printer selection

When you print invoices, credit memos, and so on, it is important to choose the correct printer. You use the Printer Selection table to control this. In this table you can assign certain printers to certain users and/or reports so that the invoice report, for example, is always printed on printer X. You can also specify that only user Y will always print credit memos on printer X, for example.

Charts and Dimensions

Once you have set up the connections among users, reports and printers, the program will automatically use the information to direct future printouts.

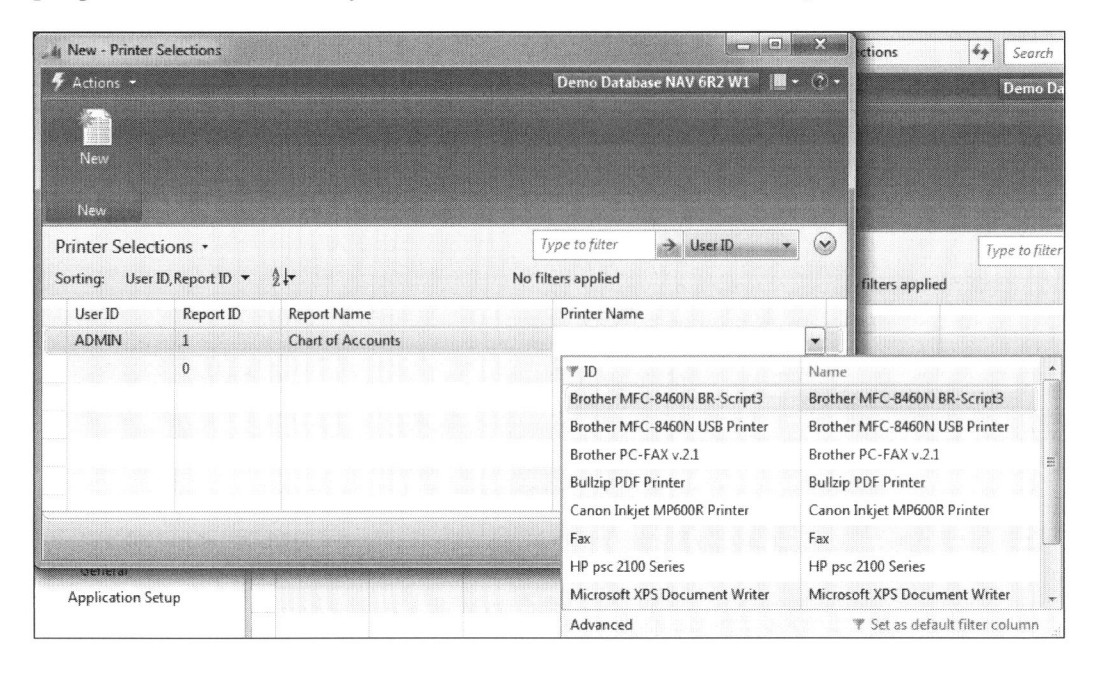

You can set up reports so that they must be printed on a specific printer from the Role Tailored client. For example, you can print reports on a special company letterhead or on different paper sizes, or you can print reports on the default printer of a specified employee.

You can set different values to obtain different outputs. If you set a specific printer selection, then it takes precedence over a more general printer selection. For example, you can set a printer selection that has values in the **User ID**, **Report ID**, and **Printer Name** fields. This printer selection takes precedence over a printer selection that has blank entries in the **User ID** or **Report ID** fields.

The following table describes the combination of values to specify when you set up printer selections for a report:

To	Set these values
Print a report to a specific printer for all users	Specify values in the **Report ID** and **Printer Name** fields and leave the **User ID** field blank
Print all reports to a specific printer for a specific user	Specify values in the **User ID** and **Printer Name** fields and leave the **Report ID** field blank
Set the default printer for all reports	Specify a value in the **Printer Name** field and leave the **User ID** and **Report ID** fields blank
Print a specific report to a specific printer for a specific user	Specify values in all three fields

To set up printer selections for a report:

1. In the Role Tailored client, in the navigation pane, click **Departments**, click **Administration**, click **IT Administration**, click **General**, and then click **Printer Selections**.
2. In the Action Pane, click **New** to add a printer selection for a specific report.
3. In the **User ID** field, select whether the printer selection applies to a specific user.
4. In the **Report ID** field, select the ID of the report to print. The **Report Name** field is automatically populated with the report name.
5. In the **Printer Name** field, select from the list of available printers. The list of available printers is generated from the printers that are currently installed. Different users on different computers may see different options.
6. Click **OK** to close the page.

The specified report is now set up to print to the selected printer. You can always change the printer selection in the **Print** dialog box.

> In Codeunit 1 Application Management there's a function FindPrinter that makes use of Printer Selection table:
>
> ```
> FindPrinter(ReportID : Integer) : Text[250]
> CLEAR(PrinterSelection);
>
> IF NOT PrinterSelection.GET(USERID,ReportID) THEN
>   IF NOT PrinterSelection.GET('',ReportID) THEN
>     IF NOT PrinterSelection.GET(USERID,0) THEN
>       IF PrinterSelection.GET('',0) THEN;
>
> EXIT(PrinterSelection."Printer Name");
> ```
>
> **Note**
>
> The printer selection functionality of Dynamics NAV was broken when Dynamics NAV was released. It was fixed again in version Dynamics NAV R2.

Report selections

When you work with the various documents for sales and purchases (orders, quotes, invoices, credit memos, and so on), you can print different reports. For example, you print a sales invoice when you click the **Posting** button on an invoice in a sales application area and select **Post and Print**.

The program has preselected which report will be printed when you click the **Print** button on various types of purchase and sales headers. For example, when you click the **Print** button on an order, the Order Confirmation report is automatically printed.

The **Report Selections** table contains the specification of which report will be printed in different situations. The **Report Selection** table also contains the report ID and report name for the report that will be printed when you work with a given document type.

You can, of course, choose to have the program print a different report than the preselected one. You can also add reports to the **Report Selection** table to have the program print more than one report per document type.

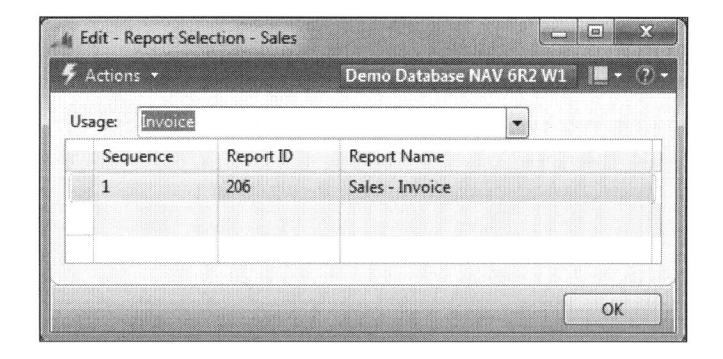

> The advantage of **Report Selections** is to have one location where you manage which reports will be executed when a user selects an action in the RTC. When you create a new report that will replace an existing document report, like for example the Sales Invoice, then you do not need to redesign the page objects linking to the old report. All you have to do is make one change in the **Report Selection** table.

Creating reports without development tools

A functional consultant, usually someone without technical or development skills, has the ability to set up dimensions in Dynamics NAV. With these dimensions, reports can be created and customized: Chart of Accounts Analysis, Account Schedules, Analysing Financial Information Using Dimensions, and Exporting Analysis Views. Some of these reporting tools provide functionality to export information to Microsoft Excel. You could say that this is Dynamics NAV's built-in Business Intelligence tool.

What are dimensions?

Basically, a dimension is data added to an entry so that entries with similar characteristics can be grouped and easily retrieved for analysis purposes. Dimensions can be used throughout Microsoft Dynamics NAV on entries in journals, documents, ledgers, and budgets.

You must allocate adequate time when setting up the dimensions in Microsoft Dynamics NAV. The dimensions structure must be determined in combination with the chart of accounts and posting group structure. Additionally, using dimensions and simplifying the chart of accounts provides a better analysis of financial information. Getting this right in the beginning of an implementation is important because, changing the ways that dimensions are set up a long time after Go Live is not an easy job...

Technically, dimensions are values added to an entry to act as markers for the program, which allows entries with similar dimension values to be grouped for analysis purposes.

Metadata is data about your data, like attributes that you define and link to your data (entries). You can then use these dimensions for reporting purposes.

Many different types of entries in the program can have dimensions, including the following:

- Master records
- Transaction document headers and lines
- Journal lines
- Ledger entries
- Posted documents and their lines

Each dimension can have an unlimited number of dimension values. For example, a dimension called Department can have dimension values of Sales, Administration, Purchasing, and so on. Users define and tailor these dimensions and values to their company's needs.

> **Dimension setup**
>
> Setting up dimensions in Dynamics NAV should be considered a job for experienced consultants. Just because Dynamics NAV allows you to create an unlimited amount of dimensions, that does not mean that you should. When you create dimensions without proper understanding of the business process and the reporting requirements of the customer, that will lead to Dynamics NAV collecting a massive amount of information and in the end it might bring confusion instead of a better understanding. The key is to keep it simple.

In Dynamics NAV, there are three types of dimensions:

- Global
- Shortcut
- Budget

Global

Global dimensions are the most used and important dimensions because of their availability throughout Microsoft Dynamics NAV. Two dimensions can be specified as global dimensions.

Global dimensions can be used as filters for the following:

- G/L entries
- Reports
- Account schedules
- Batch jobs

Both global dimensions are also available as Shortcut Dimensions 1 and 2 for use on the following:

- Document headers
- Entry lines

When setting up dimensions in the G/L Setup, two of them can be global dimensions. These dimension types can be used throughout the program as a filter for G/L entries and on reports, account schedules, and batch jobs. Global dimensions are the only dimensions that are stored as part of the tables they describe. For instance, the G/L Entry table has two fields for the global dimensions.

Shortcut

Shortcut dimensions are used to enter dimensions and dimension values directly on the lines in the following:

- Journals
- Sales and purchase documents

There are a total of eight shortcut dimensions available. The first two shortcut dimensions are automatically defined as global dimensions. The remaining six shortcut dimensions are selected from the dimensions previously set up and can be changed regularly, as needed.

Use either of the following methods to assign dimensions to document entry lines:

- Enter dimension values for a dimension directly on the line by using the Choose Column function to add shortcut dimensions to the lines.
- Enter dimensions information in the Document Dimensions page by clicking the Actions menu (lightning bolt icon) on the Lines Fast Tab, pointing to Line, and then clicking Dimensions.

When you enter shortcut dimensions on journal and document lines, these lines have eight fields that are designated for dimensions. The first two are always the global dimensions, but the remaining six can be selected from those set up as shortcut dimensions in the G/L Setup. Dimensions that are not set up as shortcut dimensions can also be specified, but these must be set up in a separate Dimensions window for the header or line. Shortcut dimensions that are not set up as global dimensions are not stored as actual fields of the tables they describe. Instead, they are stored in a separate table.

Budget

For each budget, four dimensions can be defined, in addition to the two global dimensions. These budget-specific dimensions are called budget dimensions.

Budget dimensions are assigned to each budget from among the dimensions previously set up and can be used to:

- Set filters on a budget
- Add dimension information to budget entries

Where are dimensions set up?

Where dimensions are stored depends on the type of entry. The following table shows different tables that contain dimensions with the types of entries with which they are associated:

Dimension Table	Type of Entry
352 Default Dimension	Master records
355 Ledger Entry Dimension	Ledger entries
356 Journal Line Dimension	Journal lines
357 Document Dimension	Document headers and lines
358 Production DocumentDimension	Production orders, lines, and components
359 Posted Document Dimension	Posted document headers and lines
361 G/L Budget Dimension	Budget entries

Dimensions are set up under the Administration area in the Departments, under `Administration\Application Setup\Financial Management\Dimensions`. For each dimension, a code, a name, a code caption, and a filter caption are defined.

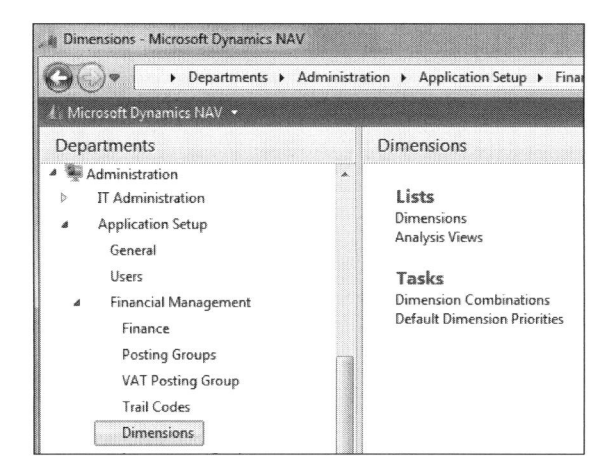

Global dimensions and shortcut dimensions are set up under General Ledger Setup, under the Dimensions Fast Tab. For the standard CRONUS International Ltd. demonstration database, the global dimensions have been set to the **Department** and **Project** dimensions, as shown here:

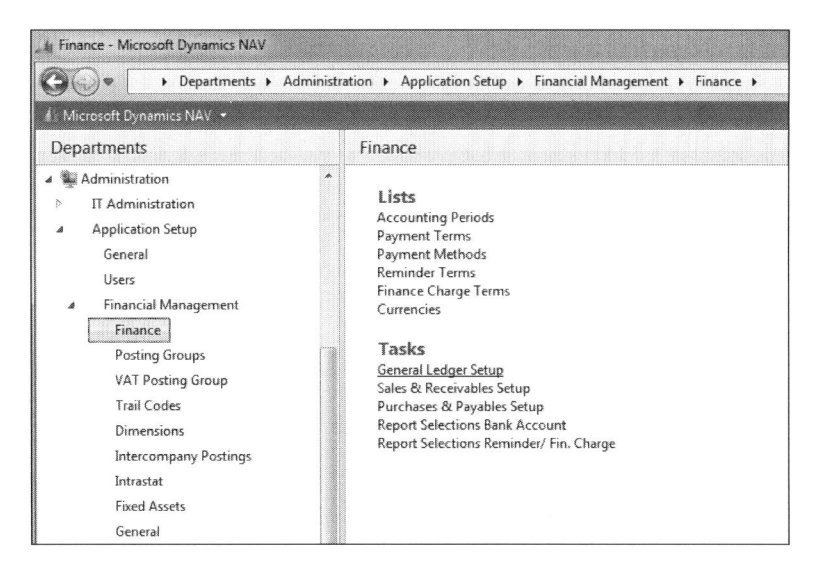

Charts and Dimensions

When you click on **General Ledger Setup**, the following window opens:

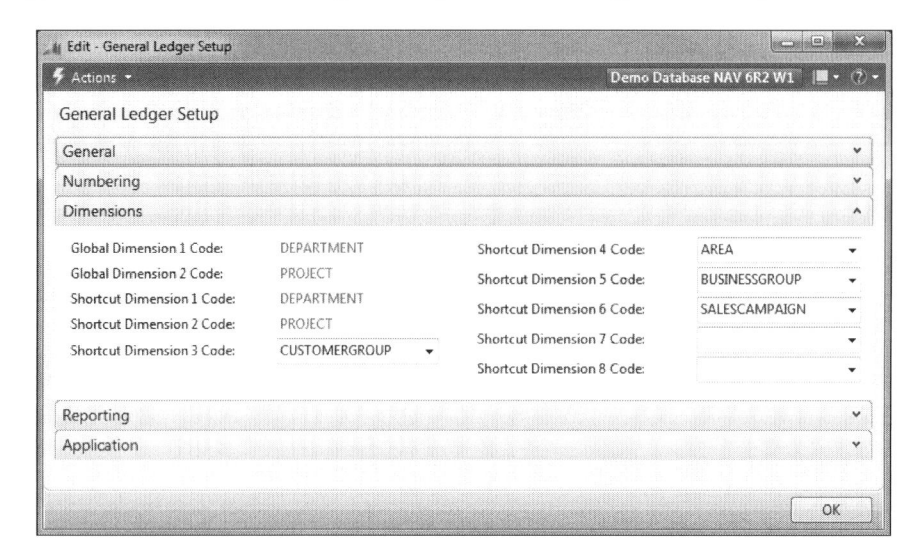

Global Dimensions 1 and 2, if set up in the system, will now link to these two dimensions. For example, the **Global Dimension 1 Code** field in the Customer table will now have a caption of **Department Code**, because this dimension is set up as the **Global Dimension 1 Code** in **General Ledger Setup**.

The aspects of defining and setting up dimensions include:

- Dimension values
- Dimension combinations
- Default dimensions
- Default dimension priority

Dimensions and dimension values

Dimensions are an integral aspect of Microsoft Dynamics NAV and are used throughout the product. The ability to set up the various types of dimensions and dimension values helps companies tailor their reporting needs to their business, and through the use of dimension defaults, combinations, and priorities, companies can retain control of how dimension entries are posted. Setting up and using dimensions properly initially assists in achieving better financial analysis results later.

Each dimension can have an unlimited series of dimension values. For example, a dimension called Department can have the dimension values Sales, Administration, and so on, as department names.

Dimensions and dimension values are user-defined and unlimited, which means dimensions are tailored for each company.

> **Too many dimensions cause performance issues**
>
> Be careful not to create too many dimensions and dimension values. The more dimensions that you allow and use, the more dimension information that will be stored in the database and this might have a very negative impact on performance. In most cases it is recommended not to use more than four or six dimensions.

To access the dimension setup, click on the link in the Departments suite as shown in the previous screenshot. If you do not find the link in the Departments suite then as an alternative you can type the name into the search box at the top right of the RTC. The following window will open:

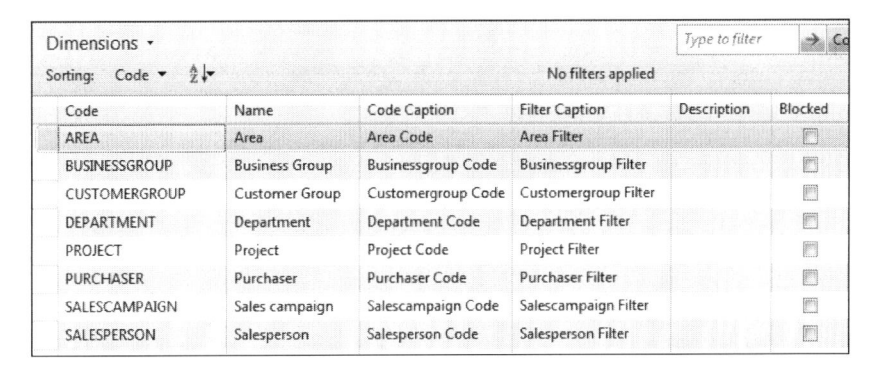

Code	Name	Code Caption	Filter Caption	Description	Blocked
AREA	Area	Area Code	Area Filter		☐
BUSINESSGROUP	Business Group	Businessgroup Code	Businessgroup Filter		☐
CUSTOMERGROUP	Customer Group	Customergroup Code	Customergroup Filter		☐
DEPARTMENT	Department	Department Code	Department Filter		☐
PROJECT	Project	Project Code	Project Filter		☐
PURCHASER	Purchaser	Purchaser Code	Purchaser Filter		☐
SALESCAMPAIGN	Sales campaign	Salescampaign Code	Salescampaign Filter		☐
SALESPERSON	Salesperson	Salesperson Code	Salesperson Filter		☐

Dimension values

A dimension value:

- Is a subset within a dimension.
- Can have an infinite number of values, with unique value codes within a dimension.

Dimensions and dimension values make it possible to:

- Gain an accurate picture of a company's activities
- Analyse relationships between dimensions and dimension values

Users can create a hierarchical relationship between dimension values so that Microsoft Dynamics NAV will consider some dimension values as subsets of another dimension value. This relationship is achieved using dimension value types.

Charts and Dimensions

Dimension values are set up in the **Dimension Values** page, located on the Dimensions page by clicking the **Related Information** menu, pointing to **Dimension**, and then clicking **Dimension Values**.

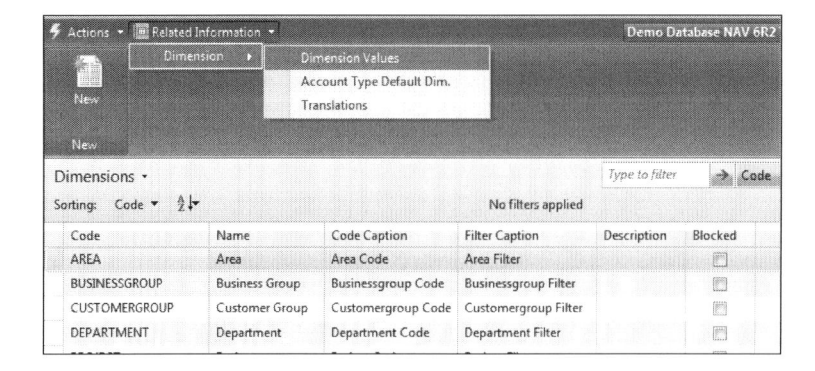

When you select the option **Dimension Values**, as shown in the screenshot above, then the following window opens:

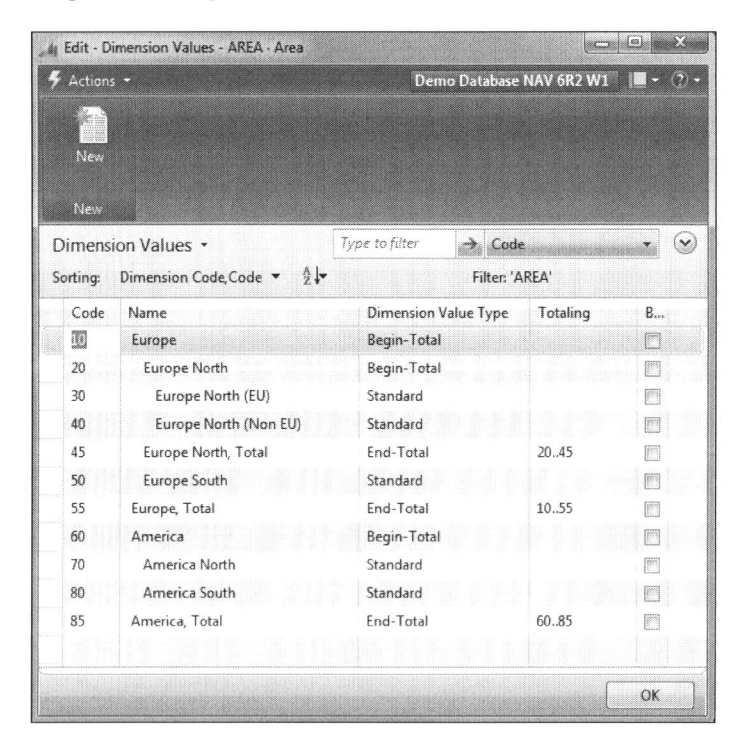

The explanations of how to use the fields are in the following table:

Field	Description
Code	Unique code for the dimension value.
Name	Descriptive name for the dimension value.
Dimension Value Type	Determines the manner in which a dimension value is used when posted. The options are: • Standard • Heading • Total • Begin-Total • End-Total
Totalling	Identifies a dimension value interval or a list of dimension values, used to total the entries for the dimension values displayed in the field to give a total balance.
Blocked	Used to block the posting of journals containing specific dimension values.

The Dimension Value Type and Totalling fields together create the hierarchical relationship in dimension values:

Option	Description
Standard	Used for standard posting of dimension values
Heading	Heading for a group of dimension values
Total	Used to total a series of balances on dimension values that do not immediately precede the Total dimension value
Begin Total	Marker for the beginning of a series of dimension values to be totalled and ends with an End-Total dimension value type
End Total	Total of a series of dimension values that starts with the dimension value type Begin-Total

The Totalling field is completed based on the selection made in the Dimension Value Types field:

- If the dimension value type is Standard, Heading, or Begin-Total, the Totalling field must be blank
- If Total is selected, the Totalling field must be manually populated to indicate which dimension values will be totalled
- If End-Total is selected, the Totalling field is automatically populated when the Indent Dimension Values function is run

The Indent Dimension Values function:

- Indents all dimension values between a Begin-Total and the matching End-Total by one level
- Totals all dimension values within the same range and updates the Totalling field for each End-Total

You can access the Indent Dimension Values function from the Dimension Values page by clicking the **Actions** menu, pointing to **Functions**, and then clicking **Indent Dimension Values**.

Dimension combinations

Dimension combinations provide the ability to prevent (block) particular dimensions from being combined on a journal or in a document, and under what circumstances. The blocking may be, for example, that a specific project team cannot post certain expense types or that a certain item cannot be sold in a particular area.

In addition, the use of a particular dimension combination can be restricted, depending on which dimension value combination is being used for the two dimensions.

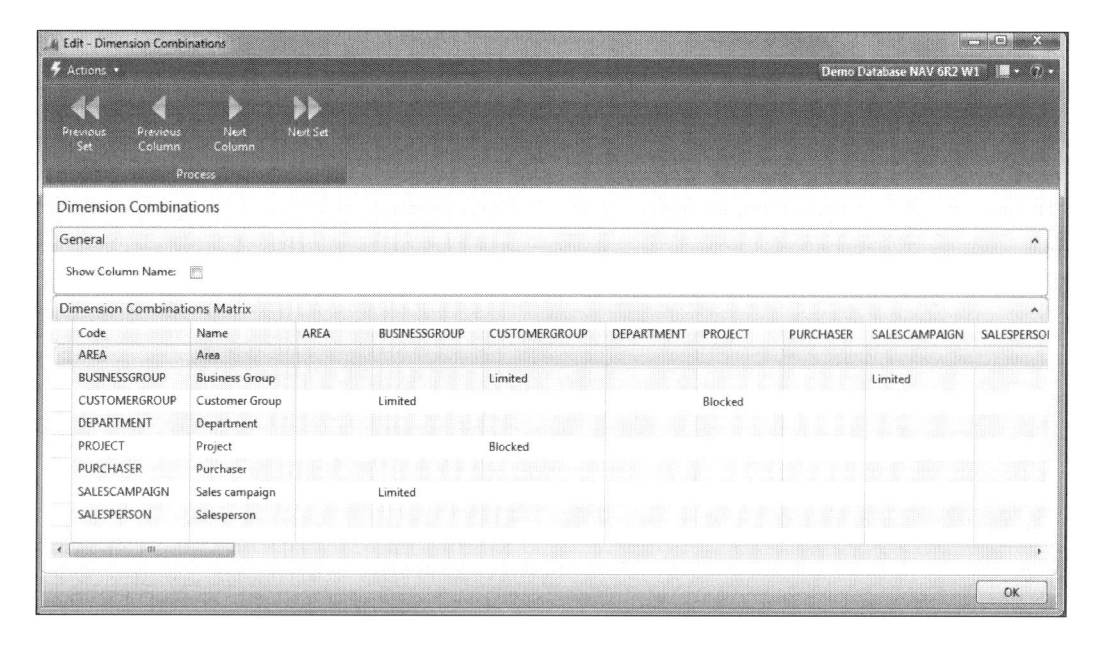

This page displays a matrix of all combinations of dimensions created in Microsoft Dynamics NAV. The dimensions displayed in the rows of the matrix are also represented as dimension columns.

The columns in the Dimension Combinations Matrix are called combination restriction fields. The combinations for these fields are accessed by clicking the field, and include the options shown in the following table:

Option	Description
No Limitations	The dimension combination is always allowed on entries. This is the default setting for dimension combinations.
Limited	The dimension combination is only allowed in certain circumstances, depending on which dimension values are selected when you are creating an entry.
Blocked	The dimension combination is excluded from use on entries.

> If the Limited option is selected, the restricted dimension value combinations must be specified. Dimension value combinations are only applicable to the Limited option.

Dimension value combinations are set up by drilling down in the relevant restriction field on the Dimension Combinations Matrix to define restrictions in the Dimension Value Combinations Matrix page.

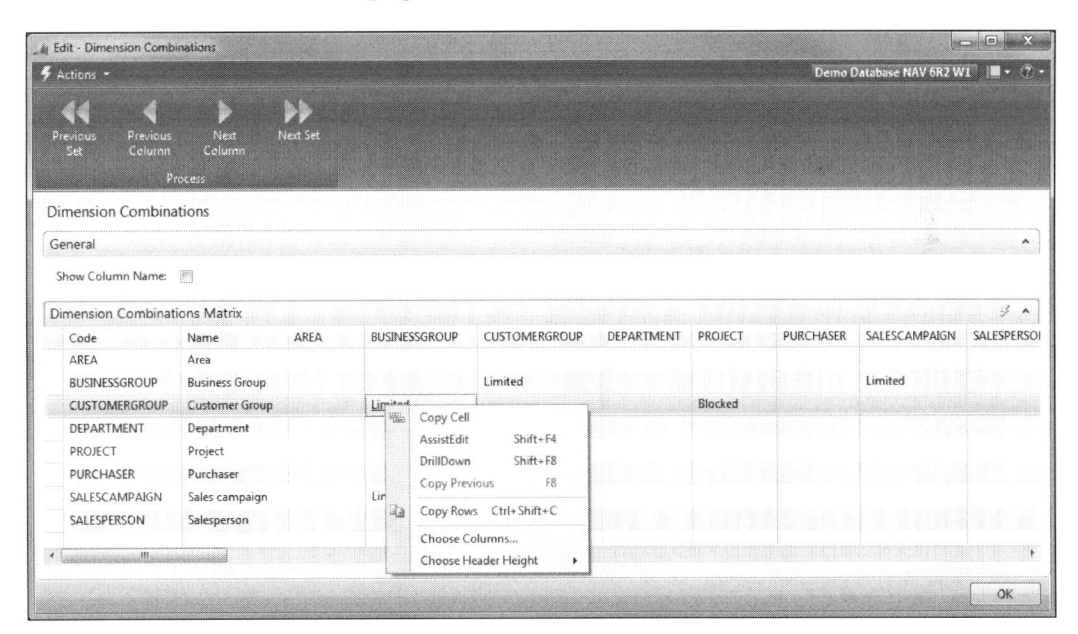

When you click on **Drilldown**, the following window opens:

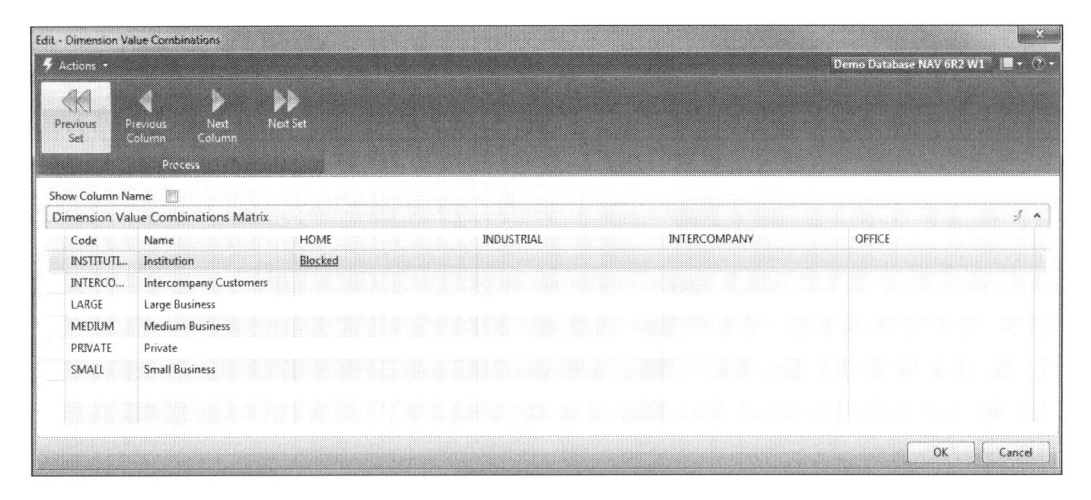

The Dimension Value Combinations Matrix page is a matrix of all combinations of dimension values for a particular dimension combination. The rows represent the dimension values of the dimension selected in the rows of the Dimension Combinations Matrix page. The columns represent the dimension values of the dimension selected in the column of the Dimension Combinations Matrix page. The dimension value combination restrictions are set up by clicking the relevant field and selecting Blocked. If Blocked is not selected, the combinations are allowed for these dimension values.

Default dimensions

You can minimize the data entry involved in recording dimension information by assigning default dimensions to accounts, customers, vendors, items, and other objects in Microsoft Dynamics NAV. Once you have set up default dimensions for an account, those dimensions and related values will automatically be filled in whenever the account is used, but the dimension values can still be changed if required.

Users can specify default dimensions in various ways:

- For an individual account on the relevant account card
- For a particular group of accounts within an account type by using the Default Dimension—Multiple menu item on an account list, such as the Vendor List
- For an entire account type, such as the customer account type, in the Account Type Default Dim. Page

Account type default dimensions can be used, for example, to ensure that a company-defined dimension called Customer Group is always used for customer accounts. Default dimensions can suggest conflicting dimension values. For example, if a user has set up different default dimensions for two accounts used on a journal line, different dimension values might be recommended, causing a conflict. Users can set default dimension priorities that will resolve these potential conflicts. In cases where conflicting default dimension values are of the same account type, the last entered account is favored.

View posted dimension information

You can access all the dimension information relating to a specific entry, improving traceability and inquiry response. When a journal or document containing global dimension information is posted, the dimension information is stored in two areas:

- Directly in ledger entries
- In a separate table

Shortcut dimensions are stored in a separate table, not in ledger entries.

The posted global dimensions and other dimensions are also recorded in a separate table, depending on whether they relate to a posted document or ledger entry.

Storing posted dimensions in a separate table allows for an unlimited number of dimensions. If dimensions are only recorded on the entries, for each new dimension created, a new field must be added to every table that contains the entries. This cannot be done without having a license with solution developer permissions.

Remember that all posted dimension values will be stored in this one table. Global dimensions are also available in the ledger entry tables.

Analysing financial information using dimensions

Account Schedule analysis capabilities are primarily based on the G/L accounts and their structure in the Chart of Accounts. The analysis view is a means of viewing data from the general ledger for particular output needs based on criteria specified within a business. For an analysis view, G/L entries are grouped by criteria such as:

- G/L accounts
- Period
- Business units
- Up to four dimensions

In other words, if a G/L entry has been posted to a particular account with one of the four dimensions selected for an analysis view, this G/L entry information will be included in the analysis view as an analysis view entry. You can include detailed dimension information in an analysis view using the Analysis View Filter.

You can for example include G/L budget entries in an analysis view to compare actual figures with expectations. The analysis view can be continually updated with new G/L entries using the following methods:

- Clicking Update on a specific Analysis View Card
- Running the Update Analysis Views batch job
- Placing a check mark in the Update on posting check box on the Analysis View Card

Use the analysis view in the Analysis by Dimensions page, where it is possible to:

- Filter amounts
- Manipulate the presentation of amounts
- Compare actual amounts with budgeted amounts

> Automatically updating an Analysis View each time a G/L entry is posted might create a performance issue. It is actually recommended to turn off automatic updates to prevent issues with performance.

Budget entries included in an analysis view can only be updated using the first two methods.

The **Analysis View Card** contains the criteria for creating the Analysis View entries for the Analysis by Dimensions page.

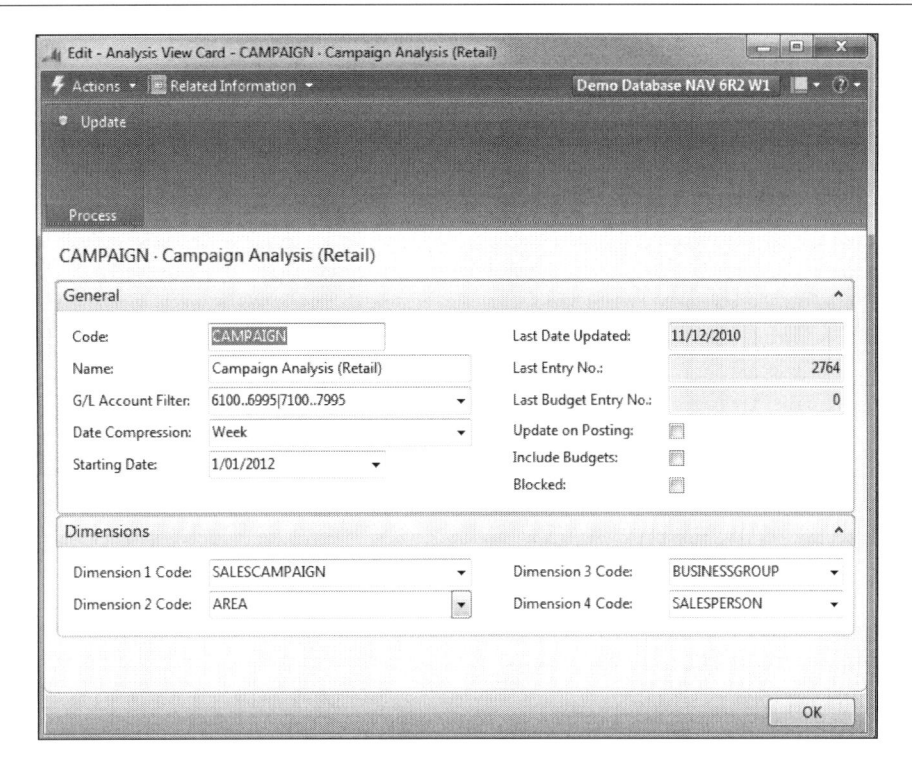

![Edit - Analysis View Card - CAMPAIGN - Campaign Analysis (Retail) window screenshot]

In the following table, there's a brief explanation of the fields in this window:

Field	Description
Code and Name	A unique identifier and description of the analysis view.
G/L Account Filter	The G/L accounts that are included in an analysis view. Setting filters also specifies that only entries posted to the filter accounts are included when an analysis view is updated.
Date Compression	By using date compression, the level of detail for an analysis view is determined. For example, to analyse financial information for an analysis view on a monthly basis, use the Month date compression to sum all entries in a given month and create one single entry for the entire month.

Charts and Dimensions

Field	Description
Starting Date	All G/L entries posted on or after the entered Starting Date will be compressed to the level selected in the Date Compression field and included in the analysis view. The Posting Date for the compressed entries will be the first date of the related period.
	For example, if compressing by month with a Starting Date of 1/1/10, the compressed entries for each month will have a Posting Date of 1/1/10, 2/1/10, 3/1/10, and so on.
	All entries prior to the Starting Date are compressed into one entry for each G/L account, for each dimension combination. The Posting Date of these prior entries is the day before the Starting Date.
Last Date Updated	Displays the date on which the analysis view was last updated.
Last Entry No.	Contains the number of the last G/L entry posted prior to when you update the analysis view. If G/L entries have been posted since the analysis view was last updated, the analysis view will not include these entries.
Last Budget EntryNo.	Contains the number of the last budget entry entered prior to when you update the analysis view. If additional budget entries have been entered since the analysis view was last updated, the analysis view will not be up-to-date.
Update on Posting	If selected, Microsoft Dynamics NAV automatically updates the analysis view every time an entry is posted.
Include Budgets	If selected, analysis view budget entries are included when updating an analysis view. Updating both analysis view entries and analysis view budget entries simultaneously ensures that up-to-date information is used in the comparison of actual and budgeted figures.
Blocked	If selected, the analysis view cannot be updated. Neither the Update on Posting function nor the Update Analysis View batch job can be used to update an analysis view while it is blocked.
Code and Name	A unique identifier and description of the analysis view.

The Dimensions Fast Tab contains the four dimensions that can be used as filters in the Analysis by Dimensions page. These dimensions provide the ability to investigate and monitor relationships between entries and the dimension information attached to them.

To create an analysis view, follow these steps:

1. In the navigation pane, click the **Administration** department.
2. Click **Application Setup** and then click **Financial Management**.
3. On the **Financial Management** page, click **Dimensions**, and then click **Analysis Views**.
4. Click **New** to insert an analysis view.
5. In the **Code** field, type a unique identifier for the analysis view.
6. In the **Name** field, type a short description.
7. In the **G/L Account Filter** field, enter the accounts to be included in the analysis view.
8. If compressing analysis view entries, do the following:
    - In the **Date Compression** field, enter the period to use
    - In the **Starting Date** field, enter the date on or after which posted entries will be compressed
9. Select the **Include Budgets** check box to update budget entries when the analysis view is updated.
10. Expand the Dimensions Fast Tab.
11. Enter the dimensions to be included in the analysis view.

> **Attention**
> If an analysis view is deleted, Microsoft Dynamics NAV deletes all associated analysis view entries.

You can further filter the G/L entries used to make the Analysis View entries using dimension value filters. Setting a dimension value filter establishes that only entries with the dimension values set in the filter are to be included in an analysis view.

For example, an analysis view is set up for the purposes of analysing the sales activity of particular departments. The Analysis View Filter is then used to specify that only entries with the company-defined dimension called Department and with the specified dimension values can be included in that analysis view.

Charts and Dimensions

To add dimension value filters, follow these steps:

1. On the **Analysis View Card** page, click the **Related Information** menu, go to **Analysis**, and then click **Filter**.
2. In the **Dimension Code** field, enter the dimension to filter.
3. In the **Dimension Value Filter** field, enter the dimension value to be included in the analysis view.
4. Repeat steps 2-3 for additional dimension value filters.
5. Click **OK** to close the **Analysis View Filter** page.
6. In the Action Pane, click **Update**.
7. Click **Yes** to update the Analysis View.
8. Click **OK** to close the **Analysis View Card** page.

In the Analysis by Dimensions Matrix page, you can view and analyse amounts derived from analysis views that they have created. You can analyse entries from various perspectives by selecting dimensions on each axis in the matrix. Entries can also be filtered to create a highly specific picture of a company's activities.

You can access the Analysis by Dimensions page on the General Ledger page by clicking **Analysis by Dimensions** under **Analysis & Reporting**, selecting the relevant analysis view, and clicking **Edit Analysis Update**.

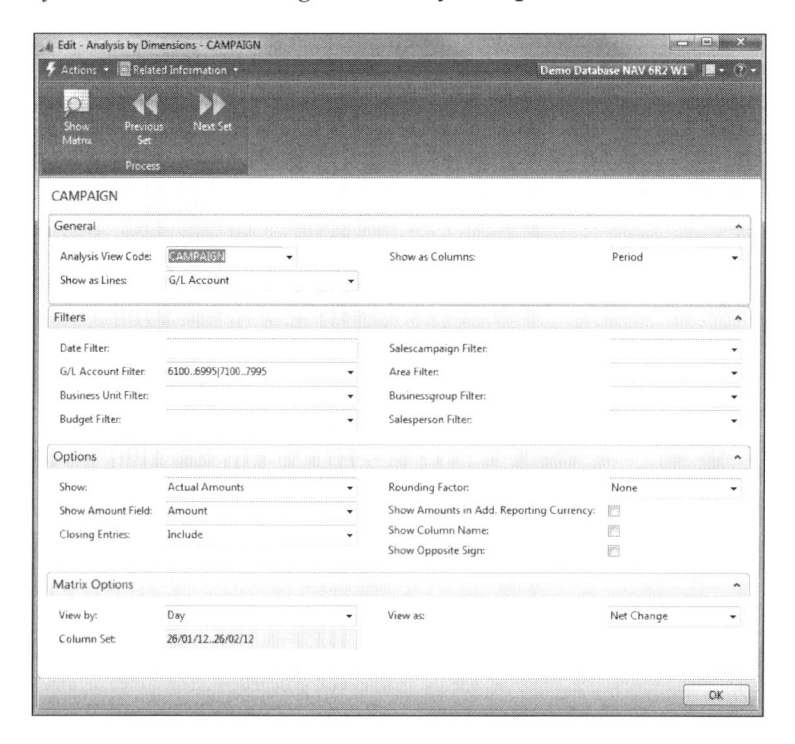

Dimension-based reports

It is not possible to print an analysis view directly from the Analysis by Dimensions page. However, dimension information can be printed by combining analysis view entries with Account Schedule column layouts in the reports called Dimensions—Total and Dimensions—Detail.

Analysis views can be exported to Excel. When running an analysis view, you can use the menu at the top of the window, as you can see in the next screenshot:

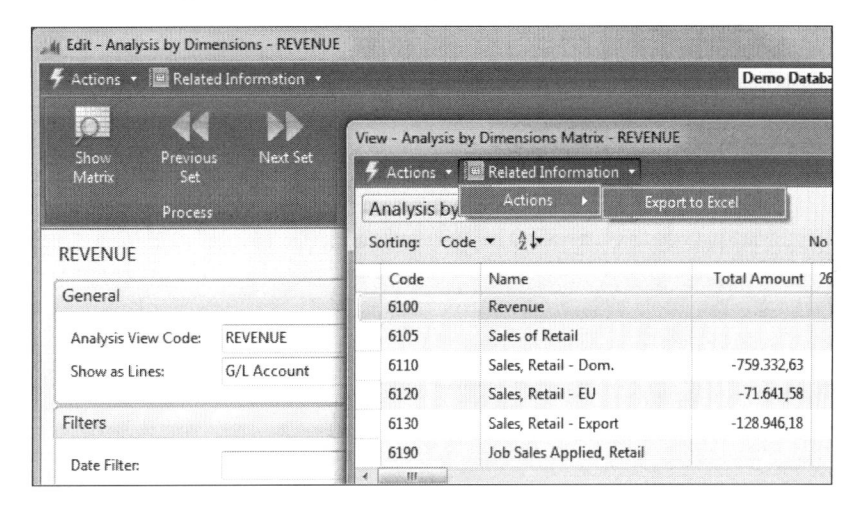

Doing this exports the data into Excel and from there you can print it or use it for further analysis.

Summary

Microsoft Dynamics NAV 2009 provides an intuitive and customizable user interface called the Role Tailored client, which developers, partners, administrators, and super users can customize to support the job functions of different work roles in an organization.

The Role Center is the user interface in Microsoft Dynamics NAV 2009 and is like a homepage to the system. It displays the specific tasks, activities, and information that each role needs to do their job, providing them with an overview of what they've done and what is next. It enables them to focus on their tasks and organize their time.

One of the key advantages of Role Center is that it's so easy to personalize. Parts can be added, removed, or customized by users to show the information or view that suits individual needs, without the need for a programmer.

The various types of dimensions available in Microsoft Dynamics NAV (global, shortcut, budget, and default) provide companies with an effective method of analyzing information. Through the use of analysis views, companies can access financial and budget information based on specific G/L criteria. Together, dimensions and analysis views allow companies to analyze trends and compare various characteristics across a range of entries.

We have seen that Dynamics NAV comes with a lot of built-in functionality that provides different types of reports and analysis tools without having to do any customizations or development. Setting up dimensions and dimension-based reports requires some expertise, but doing it right will result in a lot of added value. You can say that the dimension functionality of Dynamics NAV is its own internal business intelligence system. Having it in place provides you with the added value of being able to create more types of analyses and reports.

Besides dimensions, Dynamics NAV comes with many reports already available, out of the box, tailored to the localization that you are using. Reports can be divided into types, to make it easier to understand why and when to use them.

The charts parts and chart panes of the Role Tailored Client provide you with an extra added value compared with other products or previous versions of Dynamics NAV. Furthermore, you can customize every page and data visualization has been built into the application, making it easier to see and understand the information you require on a daily basis, so you can make informed business decisions with confidence.

When printing a report there are a couple of settings that come into play to determine how the report will be printed and understanding that can avoid a lot of frustration.

In the next chapter, we will learn to create a simple report using the Report Designer.

2
Creating a Report in the Classic Client

When Dynamics NAV 2009 was introduced, it also came with the capability to add a Role Tailored Layout for a report. The previous version had only the Classic Layout. This chapter is all about the Classic Layout, how to create it, and all of the capabilities of the good old Classic Report Designer.

The knowledge obtained in this chapter is required for when you migrate towards the Role Tailored Client or when you are already using the Role Tailored Client with the new report layout. This is because the Classic Report Designer is, currently, the starting point for the development of all types of reports in Dynamics NAV. First, we learn how to walk, then how to run and win the race.

In this chapter, we will learn about:

- Using the report wizard
- Creating a simple list report
- Creating an Excel-like layout for a report
- Printing a report to Excel
- Report functions

The Report Designer

Reports are used to present information from the database, structure and summarize information, and print documents such as invoices. Reports can also be used to process data without printing anything.

Reports can be created or customized via the **Report Designer**, which can be found in the **Object Designer**.

Creating a Report in the Classic Client

The Report Designer is the development environment that is available in the Dynamics NAV Classic Client to create or customize report objects. It contains a data item designer to define the data model for the report, a section designer to design the layout of the report for the Classic Client, and a request form designer to create an optional request form in which the user can select options when running the report.

The workflow for designing a Classic report in Dynamics NAV 2009 can be visualized with the following diagram:

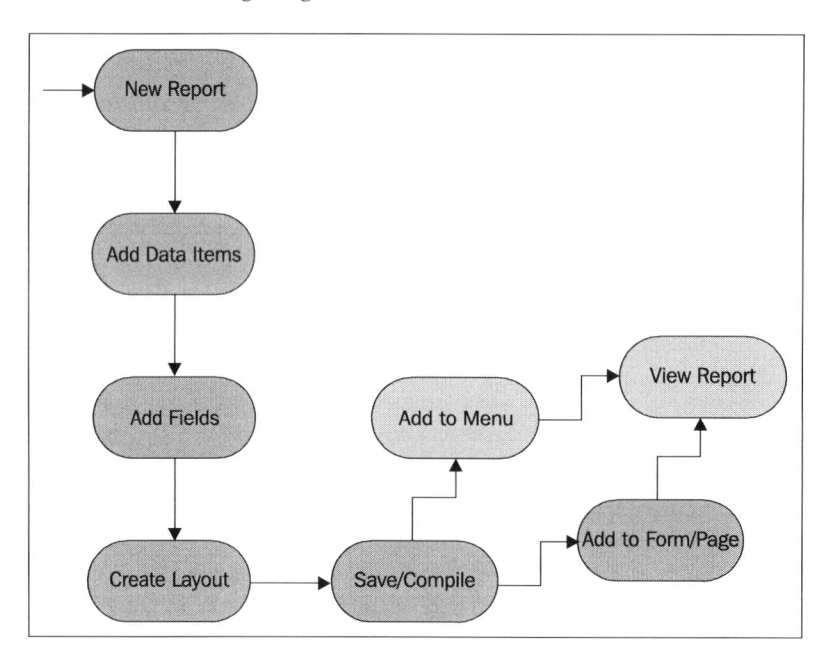

There are two ways to create a new report: from scratch or by using the wizard. I will start with an explanation of the report wizard and then dive into the process of manually creating a report from scratch.

Using the report wizard

Dynamics NAV has a built in report wizard that you can use to automatically create a report with just your mouse. The report wizard can create three types of reports:

- Form Type Reports: Use this template to create a form type report. The report will have multiple columns of information and the look and feel of the report resembles the look and feel of a Card type form.
- Tabular Type Reports: Use this template to create a list type report. The report will resemble the look and feel of a list type form.

- Label Type Reports: Use this template to create a report used to print labels. You can use these labels from the report for example on letters or on envelopes.

You launch this wizard by clicking on the **New** button in the **Object Designer** window, after selecting the Report objects button on the left side of the Object Designer.

This will open the following window:

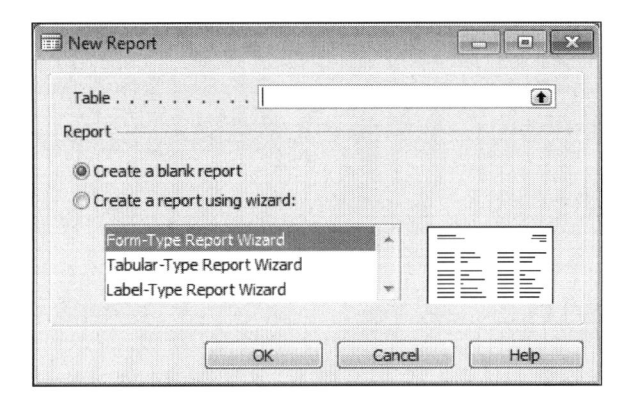

> When you select a report type in this window, then the image to the right of the report type will change to reflect the layout of the chosen report type.

Form type report

At this stage, you have to enter the name or number of the table you want to display information from in the textbox at the top of the report wizard window.

Then, click on the **next** button to open the next window in the report wizard. Here, you can select the fields from the table. You can select a field from the list on the left and use the buttons in the middle to add a field (or multiple fields at once) to the report. At the right-hand side, there are two buttons: **Separator** and **Column Break**. You can use these buttons to add columns to the report and to insert a separator.

In the next window, you can optionally select the sorting order or the **Key** the report will use.

When you click on the **Finish** button, the report is ready and opens in the report designer. In here, you can save the report or modify it further.

Tabular type report

When you select Tabular Type Report, the next two windows are the same as the one for the Form Type Report. You select the fields you want to be available on the report and then the Key to use to sort them.

When you then click on the **Next** button, a window opens in which you can select the fields to use to group the data of the report. This is an option, it's not mandatory. In the next window, you can select a report style: List or Document. This will change the look and feel. Clicking on either of these options will change the preview image at the right of the window.

When you click on the **Finish** button, the report is ready and opens in the report designer. Here, you can save the report or modify it further.

Label type report

When you select Label Type Report, the next two windows are the same as the one for the Form Type Report. You select the fields you want to be available on the report and then the Key to use to sort them.

In the next window, you can specify the size of the labels, as you can see in the following screenshot:

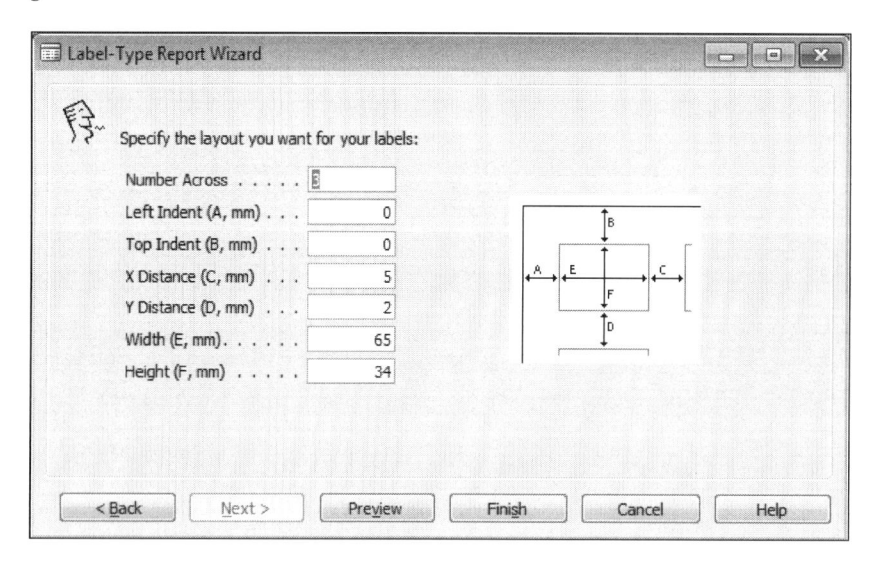

Creating a simple List report

The first thing you have to do when you want to design a new custom report is create the data model. Where is the data coming from that I want to show in the report? Is it all in one table or do I need multiple tables? If there are multiple tables, how will I connect the records from the different tables? A good suggestion that I can give is to first make a draft drawing on a piece of paper of the layout of the report you want to create. Write down the fields that need to be visible on the report and then find out which table they are coming from. After that, if there are multiple tables find out how the tables are related and write that down.

This way, when you open the designer you already know what you need to do. Many novice and experienced developers make the mistake of not thinking before they begin. And then it can get confusing very quickly in the report designer.

Now that we have a good idea of the tables that we will require, it's time to open the report designer. The first thing that you will see is the **Data Item Designer**. This is where you define the Data Model of the report.

Let's start with a simple example of a **List report**. Suppose you would like to create a list of customers. Then, the table from which the data is coming out of is the **Customer table (18)**. This will be our **DataItem**, as you can see in the following screenshot:

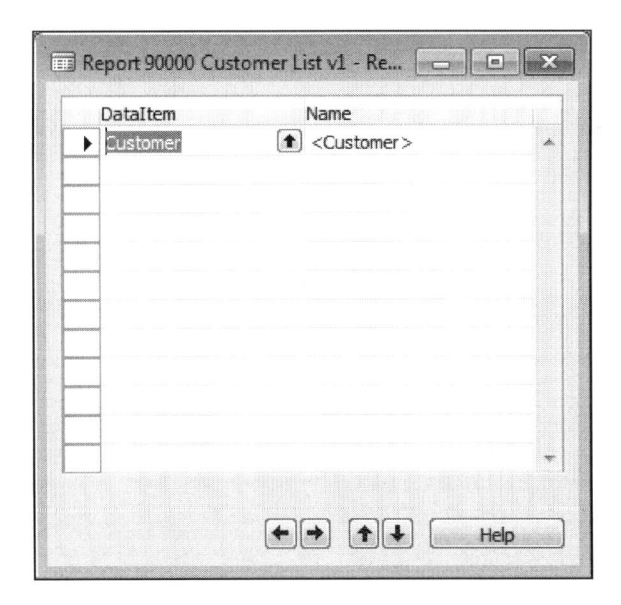

Creating a Report in the Classic Client

Now, it's time to design the actual layout of the report. For this, we need to open the Section Designer. There's no shortcut for this, so you will need to click on the menu and select **View | Sections**. When the **Section designer** opens, you will notice a **Body** section with the same name as your data item, like in the following screenshot:

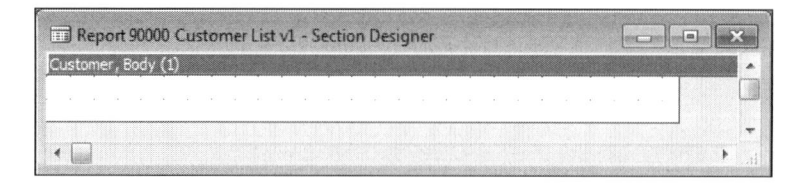

Sections are linked to data items. A body section will repeat itself for every record of the data item. When you click the *F3* function key, the **Insert New Section** window will open.

Here, you can select to add a section to the report:

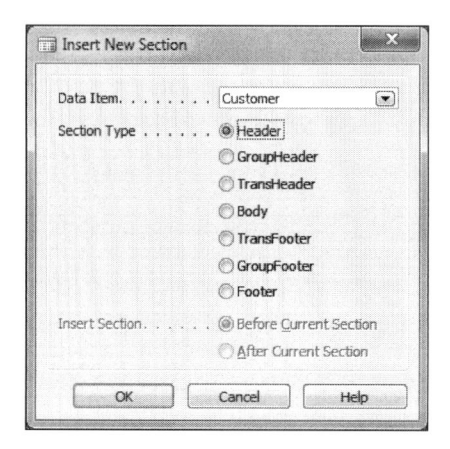

A **Header** section will be shown only once, before the **Body**. A **Footer** section will be shown only once, below the **Body** section. A header section is usually used to display column labels and a footer section is usually used to display totals. You can add as many sections as you like. For example, you can create multiple Header (and/or Body, Footer…) sections for a Data Item.

We will insert a header and footer section for our Customer Data Item as follows. Then, click on the **Field Menu** button on top of the screen. The **Field Menu** window will open. This will list all of the fields of the **Customer table**, our Data Item. In here, you select the fields that you want to add to the report using the mouse in combination with the *Ctrl* or *Shift* key. Then, click two times inside the **body** section, like in the following screenshot:

[56]

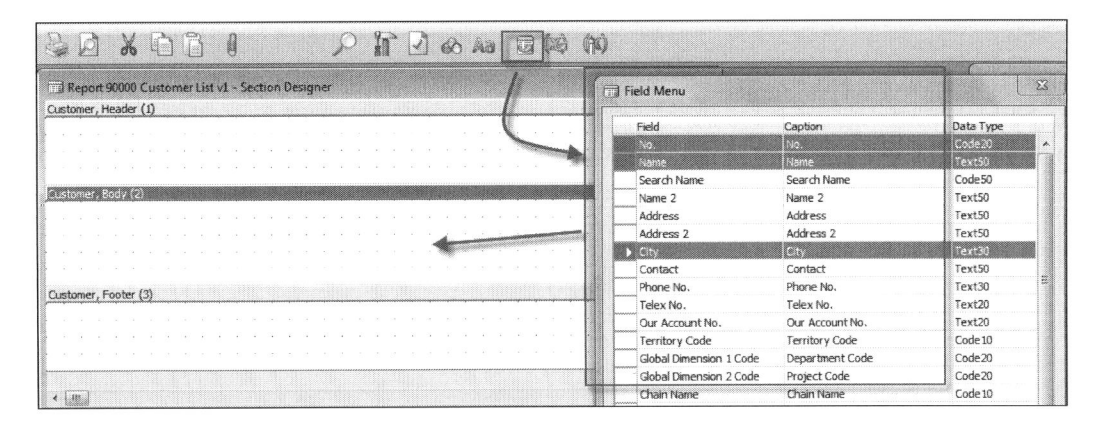

The selected fields will now be added to the body section. Every field will have a label and a textbox. Drag and drop the labels onto the header section, as in the following screenshot:

> The field picker in the field menu puts the labels together with the textboxes in the same section. You have to move the labels manually to a header section. To move a report item, hover over it with the mouse and wait until the mouse pointer changes into a hand. Then, you can grab and drag-and-drop the fields into another section.

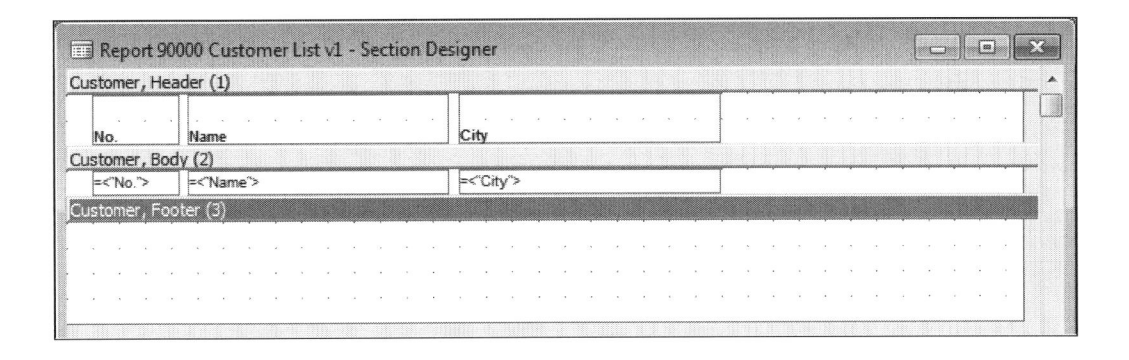

Creating a Report in the Classic Client

To run the current report, type *Ctrl-R*, or click on **File** and then on **Run**. The report viewer will open. After you select **Preview** in the **Request Form** the following Customer List will display:

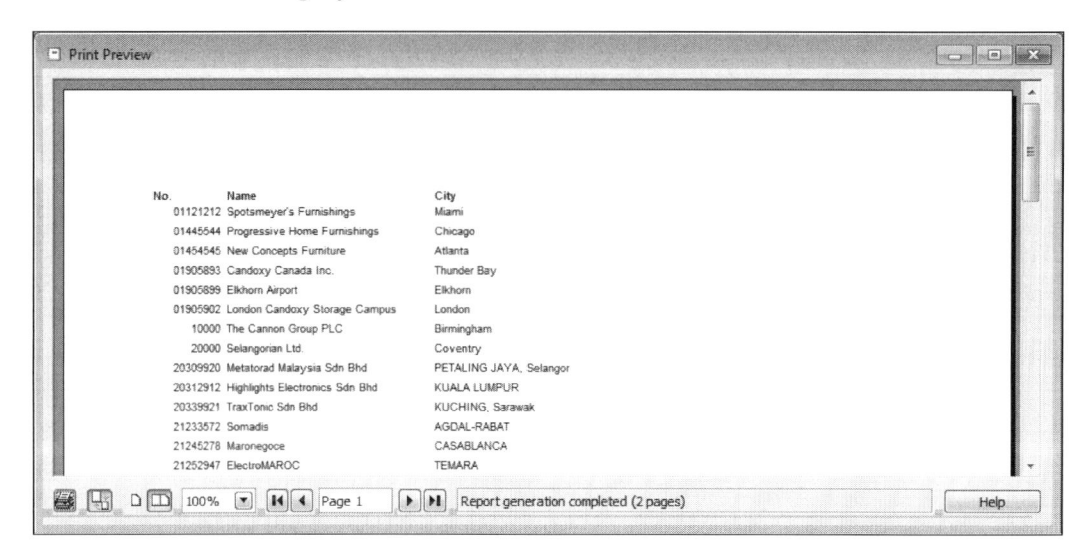

[screenshot of Print Preview window showing a Customer List with columns No., Name, City — listing entries such as 01121212 Spotsmeyer's Furnishings Miami, 01445544 Progressive Home Furnishings Chicago, 01454545 New Concepts Furniture Atlanta, 01905893 Candoxy Canada Inc. Thunder Bay, 01905899 Elkhorn Airport Elkhorn, 01905902 London Candoxy Storage Campus London, 10000 The Cannon Group PLC Birmingham, 20000 Selangorian Ltd. Coventry, 20309920 Metatorad Malaysia Sdn Bhd PETALING JAYA, Selangor, 20312912 Highlights Electronics Sdn Bhd KUALA LUMPUR, 20339921 TraxTonic Sdn Bhd KUCHING, Sarawak, 21233572 Somadis AGDAL-RABAT, 21245278 Maronegoce CASABLANCA, 21252947 ElectroMAROC TEMARA. Status bar: Report generation completed (2 pages).]

Let's now add something in the footer section, for example a numerical field like Sales (LCY), to see a total of what has been sold to the customers in the list. Make sure you add the Sales (LCY) field to the body and the footer sections and put the label on the header section as in the following screenshot:

To do this, you can follow these steps:

1. Open the field menu.
2. Find the Sales (LCY) field and click on it in the list.
3. Click in the body section; this will add the label and textbox.
4. Move the Label to the header section.
5. Select the Sales (LCY) textbox in the body.
6. Type: *Ctrl-C* and *Ctrl-V* to do a copy/paste of the textbox. You now have two textboxes containing the Sales (LCY) in the body.
7. Copy and paste a Sales (LCY) textbox from the header to the footer section.
8. Select the label in the header and make it bold.

You can do this with the **Aa** button in the menu bar. When you click on the **Aa** button, a popup window opens that you can use to format a textbox on the report.

After following these steps, the report will look like the next screenshot:

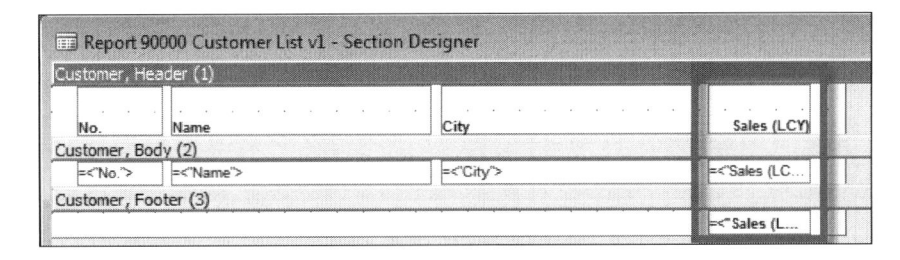

Now, run the report again to see the result. Scroll towards the last page of the report and have a look at the total. It's not correct. The total is the same as the value of the last Sales (LCY) in the body Section. Why is that?

Well, this is because you have to explain to Dynamics NAV for which fields you want to calculate totals. You can do this in the data item properties by using the property: `TotalFields`.

You can open the properties window via the button in the menu at the top of the screen, or via **Menu** | **View** | **Properties**, or via the shortcut *F4*.

When you enter the field Sales (LCY) in this property, Dynamics NAV will calculate totals for this field. When this field is then added to a footer section, the calculated total will be shown. Instead of using the `TotalFields` property, you could also obtain the same effect via C/AL code using the function `CreateTotals()`. This C/AL code should go into the `OnPreReport` trigger of the report.

No.	Name	City	Sales (LCY)
01445544	Progressive Home Furnishings	Chicago	1.499,02
10000	The Cannon Group PLC	Birmingham	17.100,96
20000	Selangorian Ltd.	Coventry	6.510,64
30000	John Haddock Insurance Co.	Manchester	6.142,90
32656565	Antarcticopy	Antwerpen	2.582,81
35451236	Gagn & Gaman	Hafnafjordur	877,32
35963852	Heimilisprydi	Reykjavik	2.024,21
40000	Deerfield Graphics Company	Gloucester	1.063,10
42147258	BYT-KOMPLET s.r.o.	Bojkovice	1.602,90
43687129	Designstudio Gmunden	Gmunden	2.498,10
46897889	Englunds Kontorsmöbler AB	Norrköbing	673,71
47563218	Klubben	Haslum	11.772,20
49633663	Autohaus Mielberg KG	Hamburg 36	281,40
50000	Guildford Water Department	Guildford	533,40
			55.162,67

Sorting and grouping data in a report

Now, we are ready to group this report. Actually, we want to group the data according to salesperson. So for every salesperson we want to see his/her customers, with a subtotal of the total sales by salesperson and a grand total per customer. To do this you need to include a group section in the report. A group header section can be used to show the salesperson and a group footer section can then be used to display the subtotal(s):

1. Type *F3* to open the Insert New Section window.
2. Select the **GroupHeader** option.
3. Click on **Ok** to add the **GroupHeader** section to the report.
4. Repeat these steps to add a **GroupFooter** section to the report.
5. Now, use the Field Menu to add the salesperson field to the **GroupHeader** section.
6. Now, use the Field Menu to add the Sales (LCY) field to the **GroupFooter** section.
7. You can use the **Aa** button to underline the Sales (LCY) field in the **GroupFooter** and to make the salesperson bold in the **GroupHeader** section.

You should now have this result in the **Section Designer**:

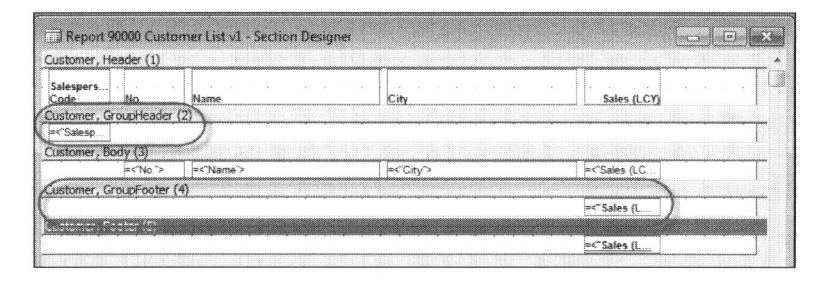

And when you run the report, this is the layout:

But wait, this is not what we expected. There's no salesperson group or subtotal. Why is that?

Well, that's because you also have to explain to Dynamics NAV that a grouping needs to be calculated when the data item is executed.

You do this via the property: `GroupTotalFields`. In this property, you need to include the field on which we are grouping: Salesperson Code. It is a property of the data item. To change it, click on the data item and then on *F4*.

When you do this and then run the report again, you will still see no difference. Well, that's because Dynamics NAV is only capable of calculating group totals when the key that is used to sort the data item contains the field on which you are grouping. So you also need to include the salesperson in the `Key` property of the `DataItemView` property. And if there's no key in the table, then you will need to create one. The following is what the property list of the data item should look like:

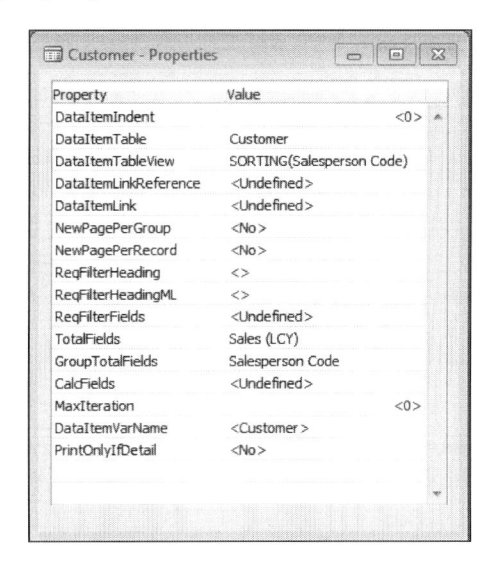

Property	Value
DataItemIndent	<0>
DataItemTable	Customer
DataItemTableView	SORTING(Salesperson Code)
DataItemLinkReference	<Undefined>
DataItemLink	<Undefined>
NewPagePerGroup	<No>
NewPagePerRecord	<No>
ReqFilterHeading	<>
ReqFilterHeadingML	<>
ReqFilterFields	<Undefined>
TotalFields	Sales (LCY)
GroupTotalFields	Salesperson Code
CalcFields	<Undefined>
MaxIteration	<0>
DataItemVarName	<Customer>
PrintOnlyIfDetail	<No>

Creating a Report in the Classic Client

And then, you get this result when you run the report:

Salesperson Code	No.	Name	City	Sales (LCY)
JR				
	01445544	Progressive Home Furnishings	Chicago	1.499,02
	32656565	Antarcticopy	Antwerpen	2.582,81
	35451236	Gagn & Gaman	Hafnafjordur	877,32
	35963852	Heimilisprydi	Reykjavik	2.024,21
	42147258	BYT-KOMPLET s.r.o.	Bojkovice	1.602,90
	43687129	Designstudio Gmunden	Gmunden	2.498,10
	46897889	Englunds Kontorsmöbler AB	Norrköbing	673,71
	47563218	Klubben	Haslum	11.772,20
	49633663	Autohaus Mielberg KG	Hamburg 36	281,40
				23.811,67
PS				
	10000	The Cannon Group PLC	Birmingham	17.100,96
	20000	Selangorian Ltd.	Coventry	6.510,64
	30000	John Haddock Insurance Co.	Manchester	6.142,90
	40000	Deerfield Graphics Company	Gloucester	1.063,10
	50000	Guildford Water Department	Guildford	533,40
				31.351,00
				55.162,67

What is that, a **Key**?

Well, a **Key** is defined in a table. Basically, in Dynamics NAV there are two types of keys:

- A primary key
- Secondary key(s)

When you open a table in design, by clicking on the **Design** button in the object designer after selecting the table objects, you can open the key window via the Menu: **View** | **Keys**. In this window, you can see and define the keys for the table.

The very first key in this list of keys will always become the primary key of the table (most of the time abbreviated as **Pk**). The other keys in the list become secondary keys.

A primary key defines what makes a record unique. For example in the customer table the primary key is "No.". This means that every record in that table, in other words every customer, must have a unique "No.".

> **Unique keys**
>
> In fact in Dynamics NAV all keys are unique, including secondary keys. This is because when you create a secondary key, the fields from the primary key are automatically added at the end of all secondary keys. Because the Pk is unique, the secondary keys also become unique. You cannot see this in the key window in the Classic Client, but if you open the database design in the SQL Server Management Studio, then you can see this.

Keys are used for mostly three purposes in Dynamics NAV:

- Sorting
- Finding records faster
- Sum Index Fields

When you open a form or a page in Dynamics NAV and you want to change the sorting order of the data displayed on screen, then you click on a sort button and a popup window opens that shows a list of keys from the underlying table. The key you select will then determine the sort order.

For example, if you want to be able to sort the customer list page by city, then you need to select a key that contains (or begins with) the city field. If there is no such key available, then it will have to be created in the table.

When you fetch data from a table, via C/AL code or via the user interface, selecting a good key will result in faster search results. For example, imagine that you have a big encyclopedia containing thousands of pages of information about painters and you are looking for the information of all painters living in your city. If you do not have an index in city in your encyclopedia, then the only way to find the information you request is to read every single page.

Having a good index results in faster results and less scanning of tables. This is of course also the case in reports. I should say that especially in reports it is very important to select good keys because it can make the difference between a very slow reports causing lots of frustration to the end users, and a very fast report everyone is pleased with.

Keys are also used in reports for grouping purposes. When you want to apply sorting or grouping in a report, you will need to select the appropriate key in the data item, as described in the section here above.

As you can imagine, when using multiple **data items**, reports get more interesting. For example, you might want to include information about the Customer Ledger Entries on the report. To do this, you can create a second data item below the **Customer** data item, like in the following screenshot:

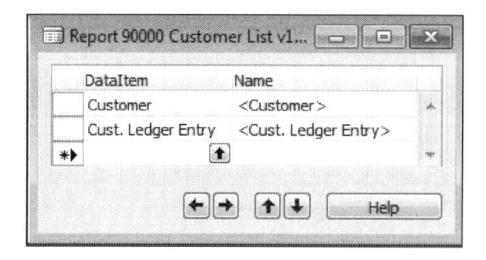

When two data items are below each other in the **data item designer**, at runtime Dynamics NAV will first process all the records from the first data item (Customer) and then the second data item (Customer Ledger Entry) and so on. In some reports this is exactly what is required. But in this report we want the Customer Ledger Entries by customer. To accomplish this we will need to reflect this in the DataItem designer by indenting the second data item one level to the right. You can do this by clicking on the arrow → at the bottom of the data item designer:

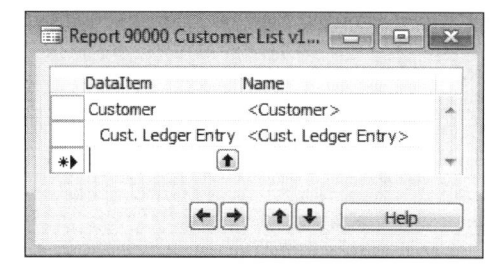

The next thing we need to do is explain to Dynamics NAV how to connect the two tables. This can be achieved via the `DataItemLink` property on the indented data item:

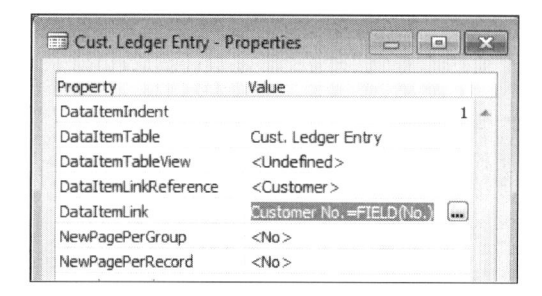

If there are multiple fields that connect the two data items, then you can enter multiple connections on the `DataItemLink` property.

If you have a look now at the **Sections** of this report you will see this:

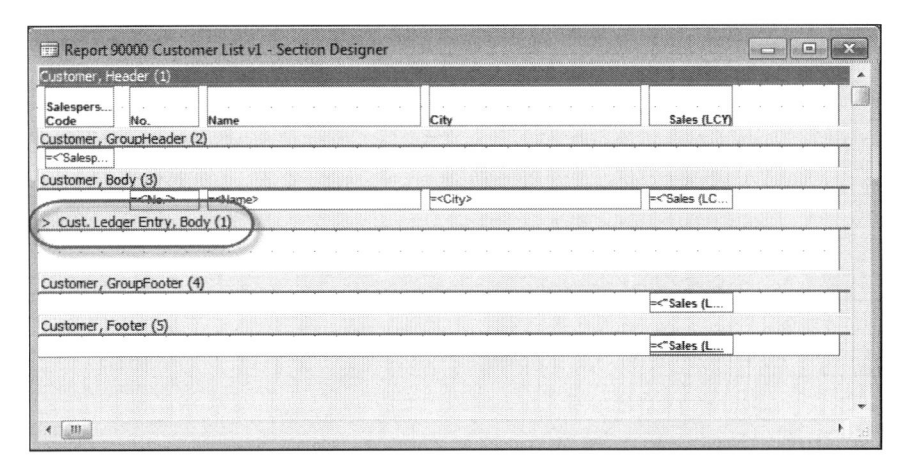

As you can see, there's now also a section for the **Customer Ledger Entry** data item, and the **>** sign indicates the level of indentation. If required, you can use the *F3* shortcut to add extra sections for the Customer Ledger Entry data item, like for example a Header and Footer. You can now put the fields from the Customer Ledger Entry Section(s), like in the following screenshot:

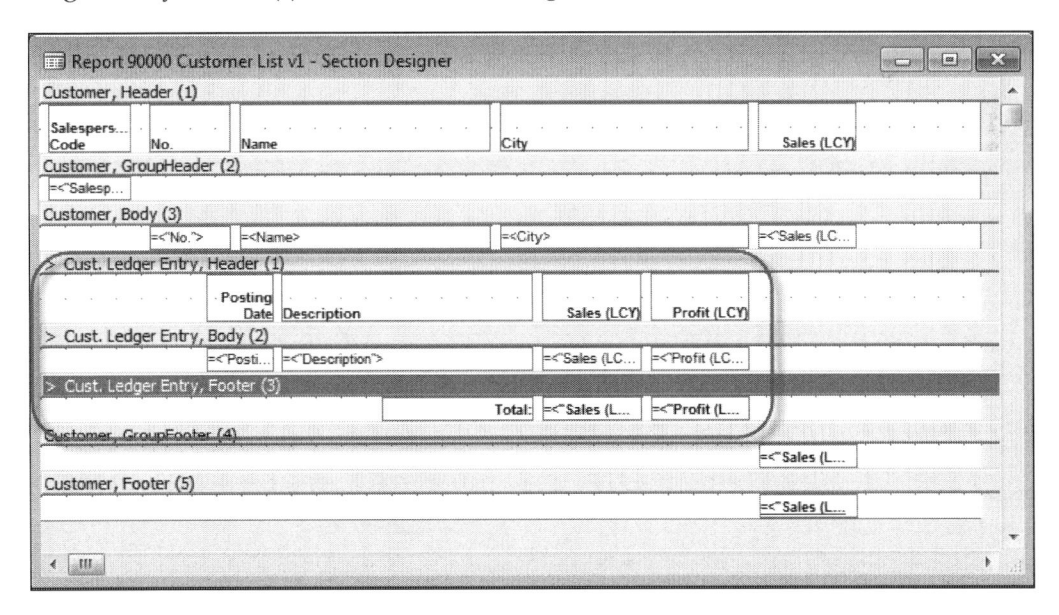

The same rules apply to the indented data item(s) as for the first data item regarding Totalling and/or Grouping. In this example, this means that for the Totals for Sales (LCY) and Profit (LCY) to be calculated, the `TotalFields` property needs to be filled in as in the following screenshot:

And if you would like to group the Customer Ledger Entries by Posting Date you will need to:

- Put the Posting Date in the `GroupTotalFields` property of the Customer Ledger entry data item
- Add a `GroupHeader` and/or `GroupFooter` section to the layout of the report to display the Posting Date and/or Group Totals
- Select a Key in the `DataItemTableView` property of the Customer Ledger entry data item

This is shown in the following screenshot:

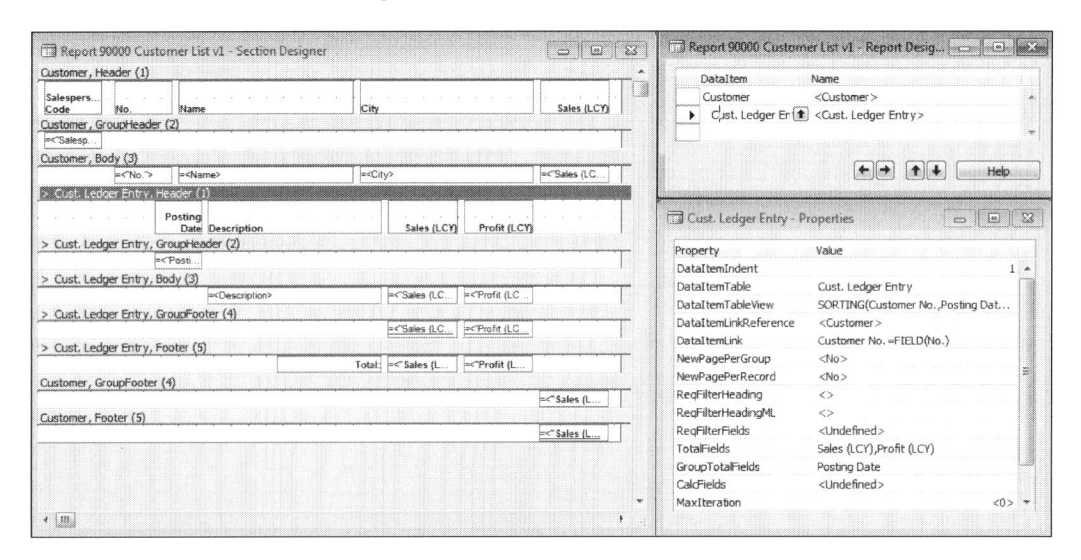

After which you will get this result when you run the report:

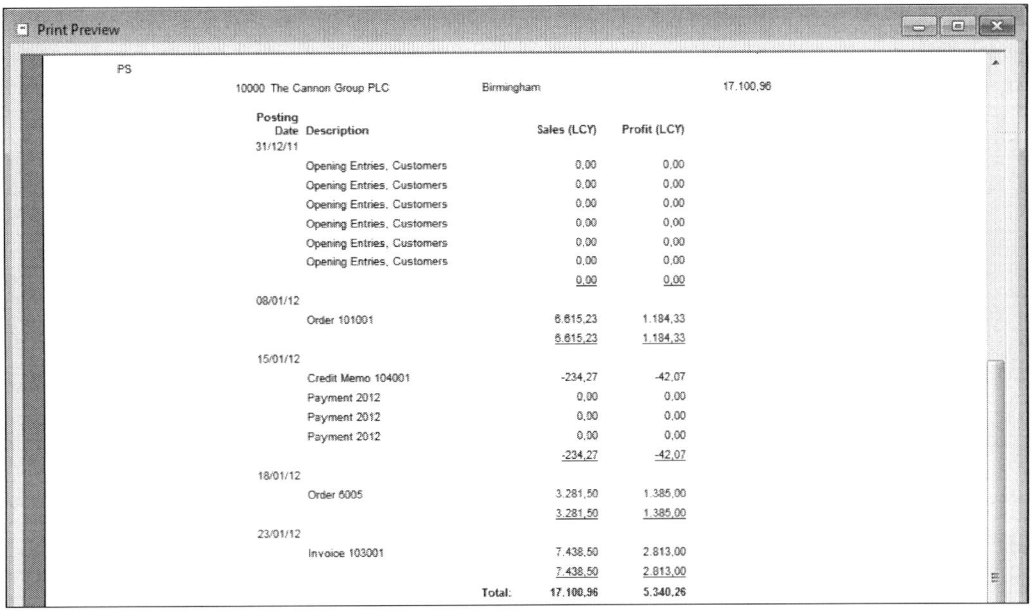

What we have now is a simple report with two indented data items, groupings, totals, and subtotals.

To improve the layout of the report, you could now add some formatting, company logo, company information, labels, rectangles, and so on. To do this, you have a toolbox at your disposal. It's the same toolbox that is used when designing a Form, but not all of the controls are enabled for Reports, as you can see in the next screenshot:

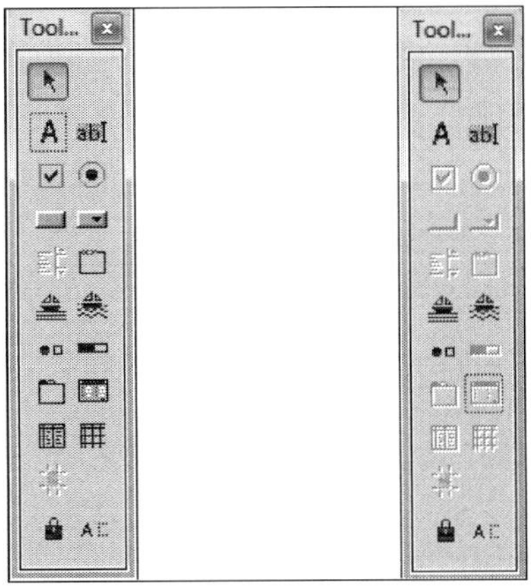

An example of a report where you can see the usage of the Line and Rectangle controls is report 752 Work Order. When you run the report, this is what it looks like:

As you can see, there's a header section containing general information like the name of the report, the company, date, page number, username, and so on. Then, you can see three tables containing information about Sales Orders. The actual content of the report is not our interest right now; let's focus on how it is designed.

More information about how to create the Excel look and feel of this report can be found in this chapter in the section: *How can you create an Excel-like layout for a report?*

Sections in a classic report

You might have noticed in the Work Order report, in the sections, the occurrence of a TransFooter section for several data items. The purpose of adding a TransHeader or Transfooter section for a data item is that when, during the execution of the report, a page break occurs during the data item loop, the TransHeader/TransFooter sections are printed. If there's no page break during the processing of the data item, then the TransFooter and/or TransHeader sections will not be printed.

> **Running totals**
>
> Another common usage for TransHeaders and TransFooters is to show running totals.

This is a screenshot of the **TransFooter** section(s) for the Work Order report:

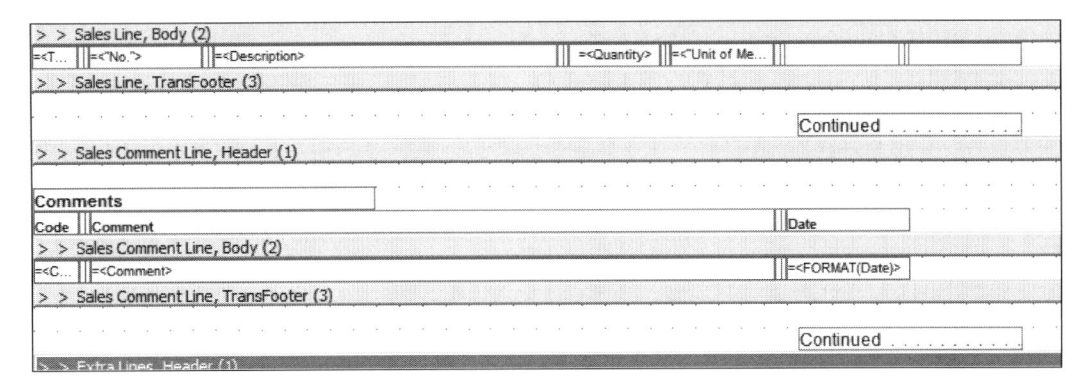

And this is the result at runtime:

To summarize, the following table lists the different report sections and their purpose:

Section Type	Description
Body	Prints for each iteration of the data item loop. When there is an indented data item, the complete loop for this data item begins after the body section of the higher level data item has been printed.
Header	Prints before a data item loop begins. If the `PrintOnEveryPage` property of the section is set to Yes, the header is also printed on each new page.
Footer	Prints after the loop has ended. If the `PrintOnEveryPage` property of the section is set to Yes, the footer is also printed on each new page. If the `PlaceInBottom` property of the section is set to Yes, the footer section is printed at the bottom of the page, even if the data item loop ends in the middle of a page.
GroupHeader	Beginning of a new group.
GroupFooter	Ending of a group.
TransHeader	Prints if a page break occurs during a data item loop; the header is printed at the top of the new page. This section is printed after any header section of the data item.
TransFooter	Prints if a page break occurs during a data item loop, the header is printed before the page break. This section is printed before any footer section of the data item.

Controls

The information that is printed in the sections is made of controls. The available controls are as follows:

- **Text boxes** – These are used for printing the results of the evaluation of any valid C/AL expression, such as the contents of a table field. They are also used for printing the results of complex calculations.
- **Labels** – These are used for printing static text, such as a caption for a column of data.
- **Shapes, images, and picture boxes** – These are used for printing bitmap pictures and graphical elements, such as lines and circles.

Controls are also available in the **request form** and the **request page**.

Triggers

In reports, triggers are typically used to perform calculations and to control whether or not to output sections. This depends, for example, on the value in a field, or a choice the user made in the request form. But the most important point about triggers is that they allow you to control how data is selected and retrieved in a more complex and effective way than you can achieve by using properties.

Reports can contain the following types of triggers:

- Report triggers
- DataItem triggers
- Section triggers
- Control triggers (Request Form/Page)

Report triggers apply to the report itself:

Trigger	When is it executed?
OnInitReport	When the report is loaded.
OnPreReport	Before the report is run but after the request form has been run.
OnPostReport	After the report has run, but not if the report was stopped manually or by the Break function.
OnCreateHyperlink	After the user creates a URL to a form or a report.
OnHyperlink	After the OnInitReport trigger is executed for a report. The trigger executes a URL string.

DataItem triggers apply to each data item of the report:

Trigger	When is it executed?
OnPreDataItem	Before the data item is processed, but after the associated variable has been initialized.
OnAfterGetRecord	When a record has been retrieved from the table.
OnPostDataItem	When the data item has been iterated for the last time.

Section triggers apply to each of the sections of a data item:

Trigger	When is it executed?
OnPreSection	Before processing a section.
OnPostSection	After processing a section but before printing it.

What happens when a report runs?

When you run any report, the `OnInitReport` trigger is called first. This trigger performs any processing that is necessary before the report is run.

Next, the request form for the report is run if it is defined. Here, you select the options that you want for this report.

If you decide to continue, the `OnPreReport` trigger is called. At this point, no data has yet been processed. You can use this trigger for example to initialize variables or fetch information from the database via C/AL code. In this trigger, usually the Company Information table is queried to retrieve company information like the name, vat number, company logo, and so on.

When the `OnPreReport` trigger has been executed, the first data item is processed. When the first data item has been processed, the next data item, if there is any, is processed in the same way.

When there are no more data items, the `OnPostReport` trigger is called to do any necessary post processing.

The following is a visual representation of the Report Execution Flow:

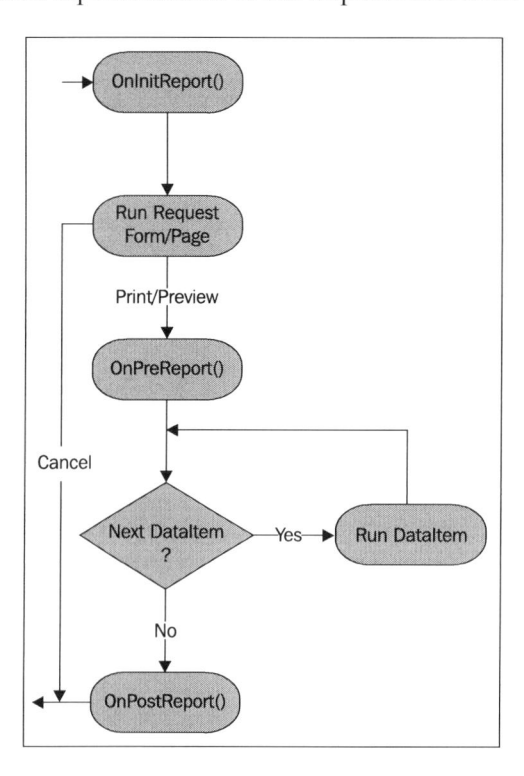

How is a data item processed?

Before the first record is retrieved, the `OnPreDataItem` trigger is called, and after the last record has been processed, the `OnPostDataItem` trigger is called.

Between these two triggers, the data item records are processed. Processing a record means executing the record triggers and outputting sections. C/SIDE also determines whether the current record should cause the outputting of a special section, such as a header, footer, group header, or group footer.

If there is an indented data item, a data item run is initiated for this data item. These are processed for each record in the parent data item. (Data items can be nested 10 levels deep.)

When there are no more records to be processed in a data item, control returns to the point from which processing was initiated. For an indented data item, this means the next record of the data item on the next highest level. If the data item is already on the highest level indentation, control returns to the report.

The following is a visual representation of the DataItem Execution Flow:

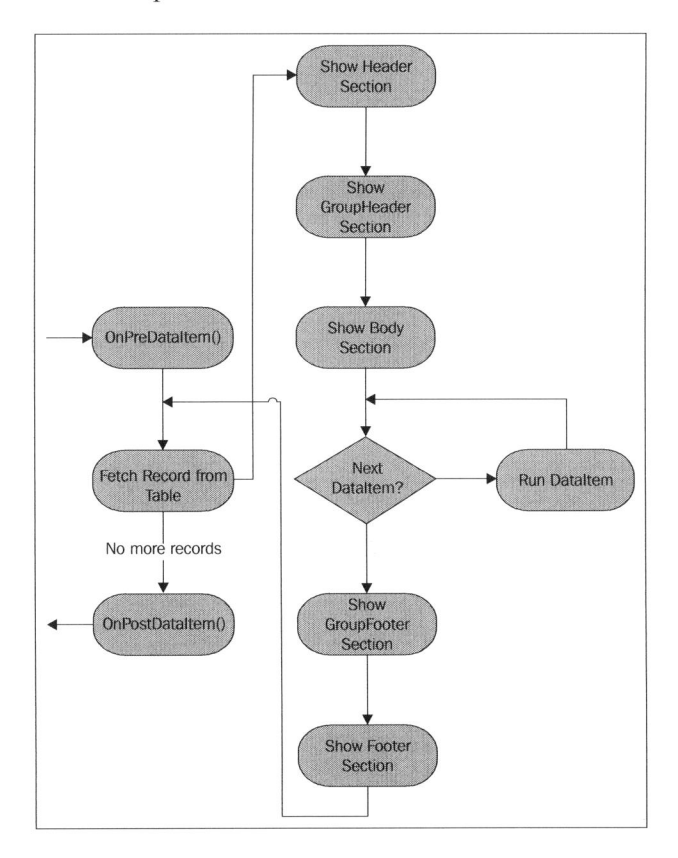

Understanding the flow of the report triggers and data item triggers is crucial to decide where to put C/AL code. The idea should always be not to execute C/AL code when it is not necessary. For example, if you can choose between the `OnAfterGetRecord` trigger or the `OnPreDataItem` trigger you should choose the `OnPreDateItem` trigger. This is because the `OnAfterGetRecord` trigger will execute for every single record that is retrieved from the database.

Properties in a report

Every object in a report has properties, including:

- The report itself
- Data items
- Sections
- Controls in the section
- Request forms
- Controls on a request form

> **How to see the properties**
>
> To see the properties of a textbox or data item, or section, you have to first select it. Make sure it is selected by clicking on it with your mouse. Then, you can click on the properties button at the top of the screen, or press *Shift* and the *F4* function key. Now, the property window opens and displays the appropriate properties.

The following table briefly describes the report properties. The C/SIDE Reference Guide Online Help contains more detailed information about these properties and you can get context-sensitive Help for a property by opening the Properties window for the report, selecting the property in question, and pressing *F1*.

Property	Description
ID	ID of the report. Must be unique among reports.
Name	Name of the report.
Caption	Caption (shown on the Request Form window, for example). The default is the same as Name.
CaptionML	The translation of the caption.
ShowPrintStatus	Determines whether the printing status window should be displayed during printing (with the opportunity to cancel printing).

Property	Description
UseReqForm	Determines whether the request form should be run before the report.
UseSystemPrinter	If Yes, then the system default printer is used to print the report. If No, then the printer defined for the combination User/Report in the setup is used.
ProcessingOnly	If No, the report is a processing only report. If Yes, the report cannot have sections.
TransactionType	The behavior of a transaction takes effect from the beginning of a transaction. There are four basic transaction type options: Browse, Snapshot, UpdateNoLocks, and Update. There is a Report option that maps to one of the basic options and enables a report to use the most concurrent read-only form of data access.

When you use Classic Database Server, it maps to Snapshot. When you use SQL Server, it maps to Browse. |
Description	For internal purposes.
TopMargin	Top margin in 1/100 mm.
BottomMargin	Bottom margin in 1/100 mm.
LeftMargin	Left margin in 1/100 mm.
RightMargin	Right margin in 1/100 mm.
HorzGrid	Distance between horizontal gridlines (1/100 mm).
VertGrid	Distance between vertical gridlines (1/100 mm).
Permissions	The permissions of the report to access database objects. (The report can have wider permissions than the individual user, thereby enabling the user to print reports that retrieve information from tables which normally cannot be accessed.)
Orientation	Sets the page orientation for the report, Portrait or Landscape.
PaperSize	Sets the paper size for the report.
PaperSourceFirstPage	Specifies the paper source to use for printing the first page of the report. This is useful if the report has a cover.
PaperSourceOtherPage	Specifies the paper source to use for the remaining the pages in the report.
DeviceFontName	Use this property for reports that are designed specifically for dot matrix printers, to prevent the printer from switching into graphics mode when printing text. Specify the name of a device font (a font that is built into a printer).

The next table briefly describes the data item properties.

Property	Description
DataItemIndent	The indentation level, which can be set in the designer when creating data items.
DataItemTable	The table that the data item is based on, which can be set in the designer when creating data items.
DataItemTableView	The key, sort order, and filters to apply.
DataItemLinkReference	The DataItemVarName of a less-indented data item that this data item will be linked to.
DataItemLink	Link between the current data item and the data item specified by DataItemLinkReference.
NewPagePerGroup	Determines whether each group should be printed on a separate page.
NewPagePerRecord	Determines whether each record should be printed on a separate page.
ReqFilterHeading	The caption for the request form tab that relates to this data item. The default is the name of the table that the data item is based on.
ReqFilterHeadingML	Translation of the caption for the request form tab.
ReqFilterFields	Name of the fields that will be included in the request filter form.
TotalFields	Name of the fields for which totals will be calculated.
GroupTotalFields	Name of the fields that will be used for grouping data.
CalcFields	Name of the fields that will be calculated after a record has been retrieved.
MaxIteration	Maximum number of data item loop iterations.
DataItemVarName	Name of record as a variable. The default is the name of table that the data item is based on.
PrintOnlyIfDetail	Print item only if sublevels generate output.

The next table briefly describes the section properties:

Property	Description
PrintsOnEveryPage	Determines whether the header and footers should be printed on every page.
PlaceInBottom	Determines whether the footer should be placed below the last line or at the bottom of the page.
SectionWidth	Width in 1/100 mm.
SectionHeight	Height in 1/100 mm.

Controls in reports have the same properties as controls on forms. The Properties window of a control shows the properties, and they are described in the C/SIDE Reference Guide Online Help.

Adding color to a classic report

When you are designing a report, in the menu bar there's a button to assign colours to a control, as you can see in the following screenshot:

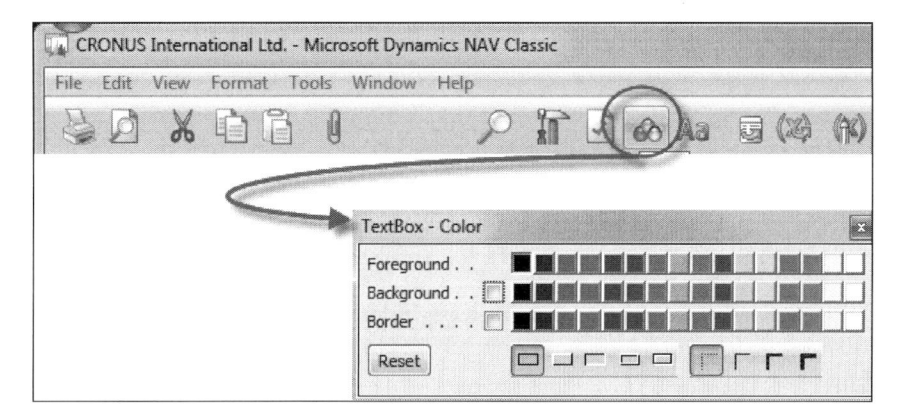

> In the designer the object for which you set a color will get the selected color, but when you run the report the color is not shown. Although colors are visible for controls that are set in the **Section Designer**, these colors do not print when the report is run. The only way to print colors is to use **Image** or **PictureBox** controls.
>
> When you create an RDLC layout for a report and run it in the Role Tailored Client, then colors will be visible. It is only one advantage of an RTC report over a Classic report, but it is sometimes considered as a good enough reason to switch from a Classic report to an RTC report.

What is a ProcessingOnly report?

A processing-only report is a report that does not print but instead only processes data or C/AL code. Processing table data is not limited to processing-only reports. Reports that print can also change records. This section applies to those reports as well.

It is possible to specify a report to be "Processing Only" by changing the ProcessingOnly property of the Report object. The report functions as it is supposed to (processing data items), but it does not generate any printed output.

When the `ProcessingOnly` property is set, the request form/page for the report changes slightly, as the **Print** and **Preview** buttons are replaced with an **OK** button. The **Cancel** and **Help** buttons remain unchanged.

When the `ProcessingOnly` property is set you also cannot create any sections.

There are advantages to using a report to process data rather than a code unit:

- The request page functionality that allows the user to select options and filters for data items is readily available in a report, but difficult to program in a code unit
- Using the features of Report Designer ensures consistency
- Instead of writing code to open tables and to retrieve records, report data items can be used

Creating an Excel-like layout for a report

This is how the sections look like when you take the Work Order report into design mode:

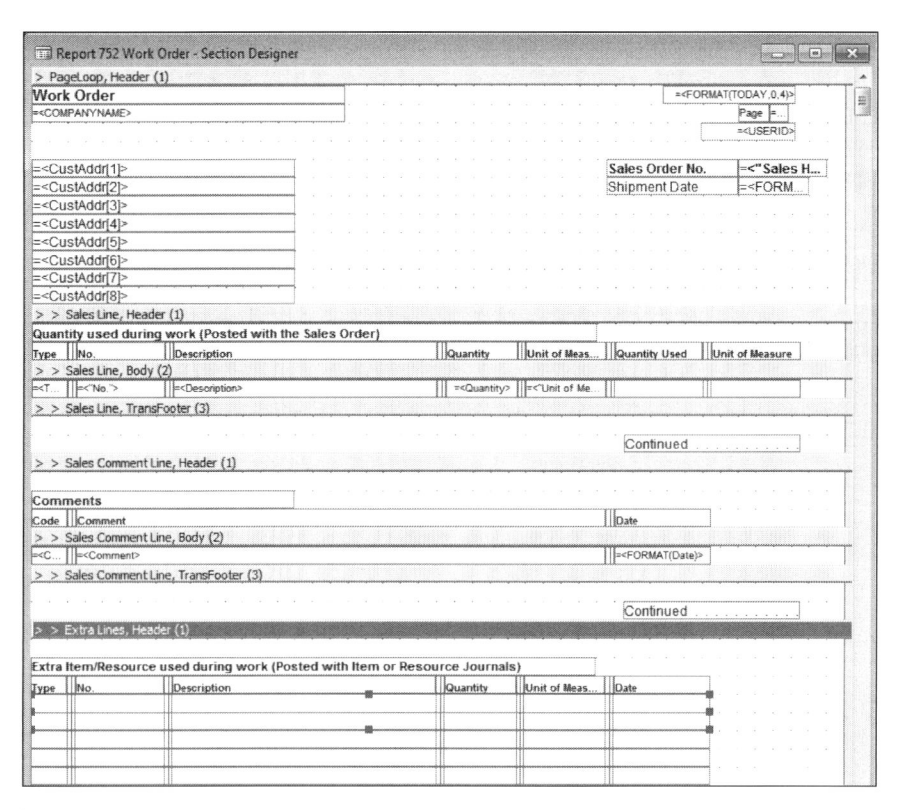

When you look a little closer and click on one of the cells, you will notice that when you have a look at its properties, they are the properties of a **Shape** control. When you select a **Shape** control in the toolbox and put it on a section you can decide via the property ShapeStyle which type of **Shape** you are adding.

These are the possible values for the ShapeStyle property of a Shape control:

- Rectangle
- Rounded Rectangle
- Oval
- Triangle
- NWLine
- NELine
- HorzLine
- VertLine

You have to put the **Shape** control on top of the other controls (labels, textboxes) that contain the actual data. To do this you can select a Shape and bring it to front or send it to back using the **Format** menu on top of the report designer like this:

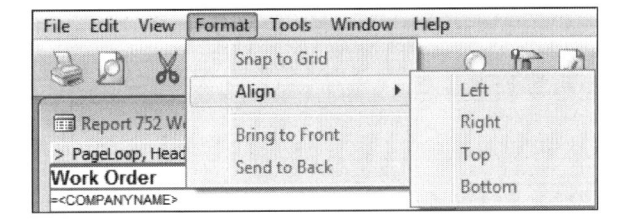

Overlapping controls

As you can see, putting two controls on top of each other can provide an added value. Another example of when this technique is applied is when you want to give a **textbox** a **backgroundcolour**. We already know that colours are never printed, but when you use a **Picturebox** or **Image** control you can overcome this issue. That is why in some reports a **Picturebox** control or an **Image** control is put behind a **Textbox or Label**.

This menu can also be used to align multiple controls to the Left, Right, Top, or Bottom.

So by using the **Shape** Control, you can draw the rectangles or lines that will make up the Excel look and feel of the report. But there are a few disadvantages:

- When you put a Shape on top of another control, you can no longer select the control unless you move or resize the Shape control
- To be able to produce an Excel look and feel for a report, it will take a long time to draw the Shapes and put them in the correct position
- Anytime you need to make a change to this kind of report, you will need to take time into account to check whether the Shapes have not moved so the layout at runtime still resembles the Excel look and feel

Actually, when someone asks me to create this kind of report with an Excel look and feel I would estimate it taking about twice the amount of time than without the Excel look and feel.

Also, when this kind of report that uses a lot of **Shape** controls is exported to HTML, it will usually cause unwanted effects and sometimes even an unusable layout.

When you run this report and the **Request Form** opens, there's also an **Options** tab in there. In here you can see an option box—**Print to Excel**:

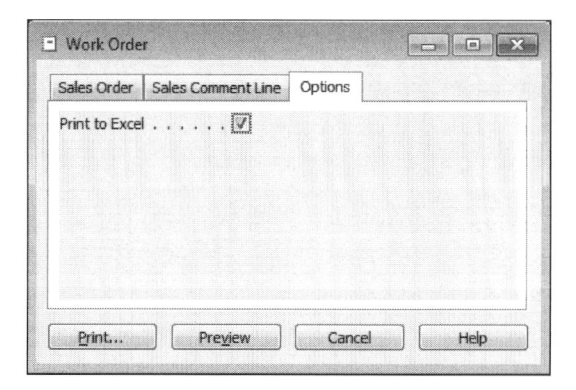

Let's have a look now at how this can be achieved.

Printing a report to Excel

Behind the **PrintToExcel** option box on the **Request Form** there's a Boolean variable PrintToExcel, which will be true if the user selects the option and false otherwise.

If you have a look at the Report triggers, you will see the following code in the `OnPreReport` and `OnPostReport` trigger:

```
Report - OnPreReport()
IF PrintToExcel THEN
  ExcelBuf.CreateBook;

Report - OnPostReport()
IF PrintToExcel THEN BEGIN
  ExcelBuf.CreateSheet(Text000,Text000,COMPANYNAME,USERID);

  IF NOT "Sales Header".ISEMPTY THEN BEGIN
    IF NOT "Sales Line".ISEMPTY THEN
      ExcelBuf.AutoFit('WorkOrderLineRange');
    IF NOT "Sales Line".ISEMPTY THEN
      ExcelBuf.BorderAround('WorkOrderLineRange');
    IF NOT "Sales Comment Line".ISEMPTY THEN
      ExcelBuf.BorderAround('WorkOrderCommentLineRange');
    IF NOT "Sales Line".ISEMPTY THEN
      ExcelBuf.BorderAround('WorkOrderExtraLineRange');
  END;

  ExcelBuf.GiveUserControl;

  ERROR('');
END;
```

To be able to send information into Microsoft Office Excel, a variable `ExcelBuf` is used. This is a record variable that points towards the **Excel Buffer table**. When you run the Excel Buffer table in the object designer, you will see that the table is empty. That is because it is always used as a temporary table. In the Work Order report, you will see in the properties of the `ExcelBuf` variable that **Temporary** has been put set to Yes.

What is so special about the Excel Buffer table (370)?

These are the fields of the Excel Buffer table:

E..	Field No.	Field Name	Data Type	Length	Description
✓	1	Row No.	Integer		
✓	2	xlRowID	Text	10	
✓	3	Column No.	Integer		
✓	4	xlColID	Text	10	
✓	5	Cell Value as Text	Text	250	
✓	6	Comment	Text	250	
✓	7	Formula	Text	250	
✓	8	Bold	Boolean		
✓	9	Italic	Boolean		
✓	10	Underline	Boolean		
✓	11	NumberFormat	Text	30	
✓	12	Formula2	Text	250	
✓	13	Formula3	Text	250	
✓	14	Formula4	Text	250	

Creating a Report in the Classic Client

But the fields are not the most interesting part of the Excel Buffer table. Let's have a look at the C/AL functions of the table. This is the list of some of the functions of this table:

- Name
- CreateBook
- OpenBook
- CreateSheet
- ReadSheet
- FilterToFormula
- SumIf
- AddToFormula
- NewRow
- AddColumn
- AutoFit
- BorderAround

The Excel Buffer table contains no data, some fields, and a lot of functions. These functions can be used to work with Microsoft Excel. For example, the function `CreateBook` will create a new empty Excel workbook; the function `CreateSheet` will create an Excel sheet in the current workbook, and so on…

How is this possible? Well, let's have a closer look at one of the functions of the Excel Buffer table, for example the `CreateBook` function:

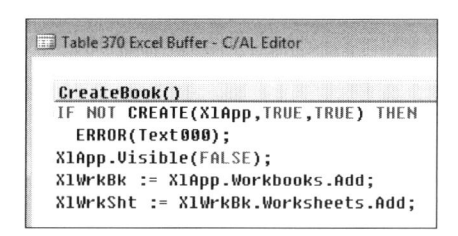

```
Table 370 Excel Buffer - C/AL Editor

CreateBook()
IF NOT CREATE(XlApp,TRUE,TRUE) THEN
  ERROR(Text000);
XlApp.Visible(FALSE);
XlWrkBk := XlApp.Workbooks.Add;
XlWrkSht := XlWrkBk.Worksheets.Add;
```

This function makes use of variables like `xlApp`, `xlWrkBk`, `xlWrkSht`, and so on…

![Screenshot of Table 370 Excel Buffer - C/AL Globals window showing Variables tab with the following entries:

Name	DataType	Subtype	Length
InfoExcelBuf	Record	Excel Buffer	
XlApp	Automation	Unknown Automation Server.Application	
XlWrkBk	Automation	Unknown Automation Server.Workbook	
XlWrkSht	Automation	Unknown Automation Server.Worksheet	
XlWrkshts	Automation	Unknown Automation Server._Worksheet	
XlRange	Automation	Unknown Automation Server.Range	
FormulaUnitErr	Text		250
RangeStartXlRow	Text		30
RangeStartXlCol	Text		30
RangeEndXlRow	Text		30
RangeEndXlCol	Text		30
CurrentRow	Integer		
CurrentCol	Integer		
UseInfoSheed	Boolean		
]

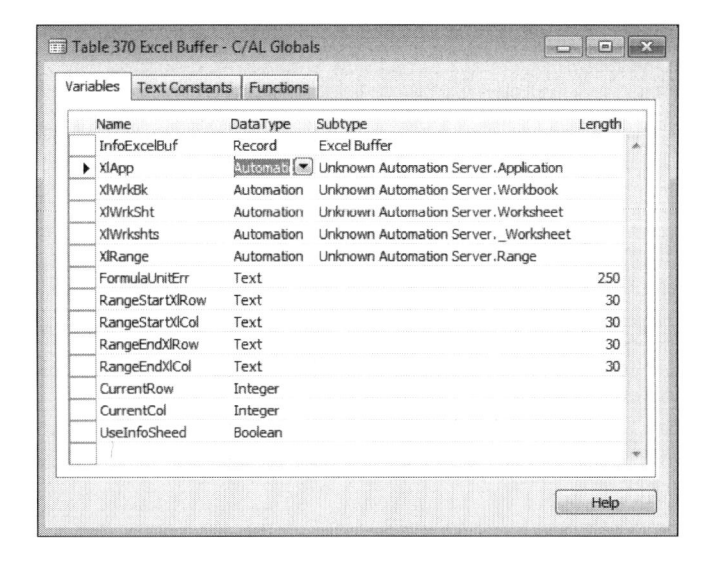

As you can see in the screenshot, these variables are of type `Automation`.

> **What is Automation?**
>
> Automation is a client/server infrastructure that allows one application to access and communicate with another application. With Automation, an application, such as Microsoft Office Word, exposes its internal functions and routines as Automation objects that Microsoft Dynamics NAV 2009 can access through an Automation controller in C/SIDE. The application that exposes the Automation object, such as Word, acts as the Automation server, and the C/SIDE Automation controller acts as the client.

So basically, by using an automation variable we can control Excel and use the Microsoft Excel Object Library to do it, and do this from within Dynamics NAV.

Because there might be multiple reports, or other objects, that need to be able to export/print information towards into Excel, the functions used to control the Excel automation server have been created in the Excel Buffer table. Now, all one needs to do is put some data in the temporary table and then use the 'built in' functions of the Excel Buffer table to send the data towards into Excel.

Of course, the real work is then in the report, to call these functions in the report and data item triggers, so that the date data is sent.

The Excel Buffer table is an example on how you can use a table to centralize functions, much like a codeunit does, but with the advantage of also having fields to store information.

Now, you do not have to use the Excel Buffer table if you don't want to. Of course you could create automation variables in the report and write all of the automation code in the report.

> **Warning**
>
> Be careful if you make customizations or modifications on the design and/or C/AL code of the Excel Buffer table. This table is being used by a lot of reports and other objects in the Dynamics NAV application to manage Excel via automation. Changing the Excel Buffer table might result in changing the behaviour in all of these objects.

The idea here is not to go into detail but to give you an overview on what's involved when you want to export towards Microsoft Office applications from within a Dynamics NAV Classic report.

Report functions

Certain functions can only be used in reports. These functions can be useful for complex reports:

- CurrReport.SKIP

  Use this function to skip the current record of the current data item. If a record is skipped, it is not included in totals and it is not printed. Skipping a record in a report is much slower than never reading it at all, so use filters as much as possible.

  A good trigger to use this function in is the `OnAfterGetRecord` trigger of a data item.

- CurrReport.BREAK

  Use this function to skip the rest of the processing of the data item currently being processed. The report resumes processing the next data item. All data items indented under the one that caused the break are also skipped.

  A good trigger to use this function in is the `OnAfterGetRecord` trigger of a data item.

- CurrReport.QUIT

  This function skips the rest of the report. It is not an error, however. It is a normal ending for a report. Also, the `OnAfterReport` trigger will not be executed if you use this function in the `OnAfterGetRecord` or `OnPreDataItem` trigger.

- CurrReport.PREVIEW

    Use this function to determine whether a report is being printed in preview mode.

    This function can be useful when you want to execute C/AL code when a report runs, but not when it is executed in preview mode. For example if you want to keep track of how many times a report has actually been printed on paper.

    > As soon as you use the CurrReport.Preview function in a report, then at runtime in the preview mode, you lose the option to print the report. Either you print the report from within the request form/page or you preview it.

- CurrReport.PAGENO

    Use this function to return the current page number of a report and/or to set a new page number.

- CurrReport.CREATETOTALS

    Use this function to maintain totals for a variable in the same way as totals are maintained for fields by using the TotalFields property. This function must be used in the OnPreDataItem trigger of the data item in the sections where the totals are displayed.

- CurrReport.TOTALSCAUSEDBY

    Use this function to determine which field caused a break to occur. The return value is the field number of the field that the data item is grouped on that changed and caused a Group Header or GroupFooter section to print. This function is usually used in the OnPreSection trigger of Group Header and Group Footer sections. This function must always be used when grouping more than one field for a single data item.

- CurrReport.NEWPAGE

    Use this function to force a page break when printing a report. This is usually found in the data item triggers.

- CurrReport.SHOWOUTPUT

    Use this function to return the current setting of whether a section should be outputted or not, and to change this setting. This function should only be used in the OnPreSection trigger of a section. If TRUE is passed to the function, nothing changes and the section prints as normal. If FALSE is passed to the function, the section is not printed for this iteration of the data item.

Summary

In this chapter, we have covered the basics on how to create a simple report. We've seen how to implement sorting, grouping, totalling, and how to indent data items. You also have an idea on what's involved to be able to print a report to Microsoft Excel. And when you want to make changes or customizations to these kinds of reports it can quickly become complicated.

Furthermore, you should also have an idea by now of the limitations of the Classic report designer. A good example is the lack of colors at runtime. Also, the steps that need to be performed to have an Excel look and feel can become very tedious. Regarding the interactivity features of Classic reports, those are limited to what you can do with the request form.

A lot, if not all, of the shortcomings or difficulties that are inherent to the Classic report designer are solved, more intuitive and more user and developer friendly in RDLC reports for the Role Tailored Client.

The idea of this chapter was to give you a good introduction to classic report design and a view on some of the difficulties.

In the next chapter, we will have a look at the steps involved in creating a report for the Role Tailored client and the advantages the new report designer and Reporting Services technology has to offer.

3
Creating Role Tailored Reports

When Dynamics NAV 2009 (version 6) was finally released it came with the possibility for reports to have a different layout in the Role Tailored client than in the Classic client. This new layout differs from the 'old' classic layout in many ways. The technology behind the scenes of this new layout comes from SQL Server Reporting Services. For this reason many people, whitepapers, and manuals, call it the Reporting Services Layout, but actually, this is not correct. There's a difference between the layout used in Dynamics NAV 2009, which I will call the enhanced layout, and the report definition language used in SQL Server Reporting Services. This is what I will begin by explaining in the first section of this chapter.

After that I will give you an overview of Visual Studio and the development of these enhanced reports. We will start with a simple report, like we did in the previous chapter. Then, we will dive into more technical details as we move along.

Don't expect to see a lot of examples about visualization methods in this chapter, because that is what the next chapter will be all about.

In this chapter you will learn:

- The optional Role Tailored Layout
- Why you cannot call it Reporting Services
- Printed reports versus online reports
- Creating your first enhanced report
- Using multiple data items
- Using the Create Layout Suggestion
- Changing the template
- Making a report available in the Role Tailored client
- Limitations of enhanced report design in Dynamics NAV 2009

The optional enhanced layout

This chapter is all about the enhanced layout for reports. One thing I would like you to remember is that at the moment of writing, the enhanced report layout is only an option, it's not mandatory.

This means that a report with only a classic layout will be executed by the Role Tailored client. If the report object also contains an enhanced layout, then that will be used instead of the classic layout.

In future versions of Dynamics NAV, probably as of version 7, the enhanced layout will become mandatory, but until then you have time to convert your classic reports into enhanced reports.

Now, for the Role Tailored client to be able to run a classic report, it will use the classic client. This means of course that the classic client needs to be installed on the machine where the Role Tailored client is running.

Why you cannot call it Reporting Services

SQL Server has been around for many years now and has evolved over its different versions. Reporting Services was introduced with the release of SQL Server 2000.

When Reporting Services was released, Microsoft offered a free webcast explaining the features of this new reporting technology. Rumor says that until today this webcast was the second most popular webcast ever from Microsoft and the number of downloads for Reporting Services increased exponentially.

The reason for its popularity cannot be explained just because of its 'free' license model. Reporting Services is fully integrated with SQL server and has evolved with every new version of SQL server. It contains a complete set of tools to manage, create, and consult reports, based upon any type of database that can be accessed via OLE DB, ODBC, or the .NET data provider. It can also be fully integrated within any custom application that is developed with Visual Studio by making use of the Report Viewer control, which you may freely distribute together with your solution.

Reporting Services allows for the creation of many different types of reports: starting from simple lists up to very interactive business intelligence reports containing key performance indicators and stunning data visualizations. Any report has the out-of-the-box functionality to be exported towards a number of formats such as Excel, Portable Document Format, Tiff, HTML, XML, Word and in the latest version even as an RSS feed.

All Reporting Services reports are created using Report Definition Language (RDL) or using Report Definition Language for Clients (RDLC). RDLC is not the same as RDL. I would suggest that RDLC contains a subset of the features of RDL.

Because RDL and RDLC are XML-based languages, you could use good old Notepad or any text editor to develop reports, although I would strongly advice using Microsoft Visual Studio.

The enhanced report layout for the Role Tailored client uses the RDLC format.

Difference between RDL and RDLC?

Basically, RDL means Report Definition Language and RDLC stands for Report Definition Language for Client applications. Thus, the C stands for Client-side processing.

RDL reports require a report server to execute the report. RDLC reports do not. To run a RDLC-based report, all you need is the Reporting Services report viewer control.

Report viewer is a freely redistributable control that enables embedding reports in applications developed using the .NET Framework. It is available for download here: `http://www.microsoft.com/download/en/details.aspx?displaylang=en&id=6442`

For example, if you use Microsoft Visual Studio to develop a Windows forms application or an ASP.Net website, you can use the report viewer control to embed reports into your custom developed application. The report viewer control is freely distributable, which means that when you sell your application to a potential customer, you don't have to pay a license fee towards Microsoft for the report viewer control.

> Reporting services reports that you develop with the SQL Server report designer use the RDL format.
>
> Reports that you develop with the Visual Studio report designer use the RLDC format.

RDL and RDLC reports are both based upon the same XML schema, but there are differences. Although it is technically possible to change an RDLC file into an RDL file and vice versa, it is usually not done. The effort required to do this kind of conversion is greater than simply creating a new report from scratch.

To summarize, you can say that a host application is required to trigger and manage the execution of an RDLC report, while for an RDL report this is managed by the report server.

This host application in our case will of course be Dynamics NAV. Because Dynamics NAV will be responsible for providing data to the report viewer control, the development of reports is split up in two parts.

The Classic report designer is used to define the data model; the Visual Studio report designer is used to define the layout of the report.

The execution of enhanced reports will be managed by the Role Tailored client. It is the RTC that will use the report viewer to run reports. No report server is required to be able to run these enhanced reports.

More information about the limitations of the RDLC implementation in Dynamics NAV and the different RDL schemas can be found at the end of this chapter.

Printed reports versus online reports

An attention point that I would like to mention in this section is that there can be a big difference in what you see and experience when you print an enhanced report on screen and what you see, and expect, when you actually print it on paper or export it to Excel or PDF.

When you run a report in the report viewer then it is fully functional. What I mean by this is that all interactive features the report contains are available to the end user. An enhanced report can for example contain hyperlink actions, expand/collapse functionality, drilldown(s), and so on. When the user decides to print the report on paper of course that interactivity is lost. If the main usage of a report is to print it, like for example document reports usually are, then don't spend much time adding interactivity to the report, because it will almost never be used and so will not have a very good return on investment.

> **Don't enhance too much**
>
> From personal experience I have seen it happening many times when customers migrate towards enhanced reports they are eager to implement a lot of interactive features in reports, because it looks like a good thing to do. It is possible, so why not implement it?
>
> Remember that adding functionality to reports should be based upon business requirements and not only because it looks nice. The more functionality you implement in reports, the more difficult it will be to maintain these reports.

Besides these functional reasons why online reports are sometimes better than printed reports, there's of course also the financial aspect. By using online reports you will spend less on paper, ink, storage, binding, and distribution.

The ability of RDLC to export a report to PDF and/or Excel can help, but you must also remember that not all of the interactive features will still work in PDF and/or Excel. For example, drill down is available in Excel, but not in the PDF format.

> **Print the report**
> Some reports can look very different in online mode and printed on paper or exported to Excel or PDF. For example, totals at the bottom, page breaks, running totals, headers and footers are items to pay attention to. That's why it's very important to test all of these scenarios and explain if necessary to the end user how to use the report.

Creating your first enhanced report

It's time now to create our first enhanced or RDLC report. As I did in the previous chapter, I'll start with a simple Customer List, and then enhance it with grouping, sorting, and interactive features.

I will not focus on the classic report designer. The focus in this chapter is on the enhanced report design. The classic report designer was already covered in *Chapter 2*.

To start the development of our first enhanced report, I will create a new report, based upon the Customer table and put some fields on the body section of the Customer data item: **No, Name, City, Country Region Code, SalesPerson, Currency, Sales (LCY)**, and **Profit (LCY)**, as you can see in the next screenshot:

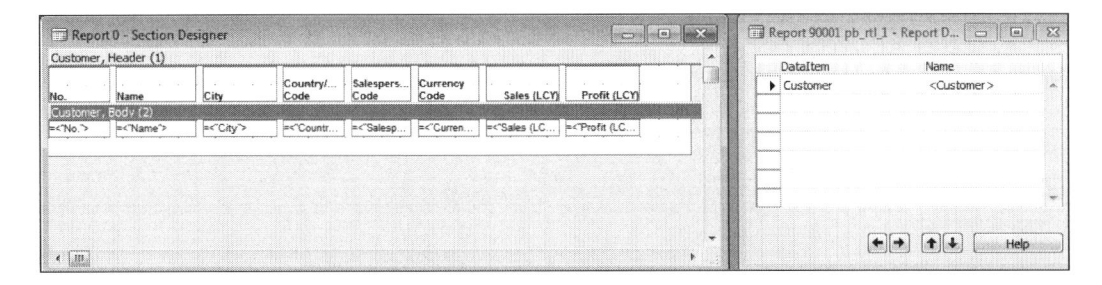

Creating Role Tailored Reports

When you run this report from within the Classic client, this is what you see:

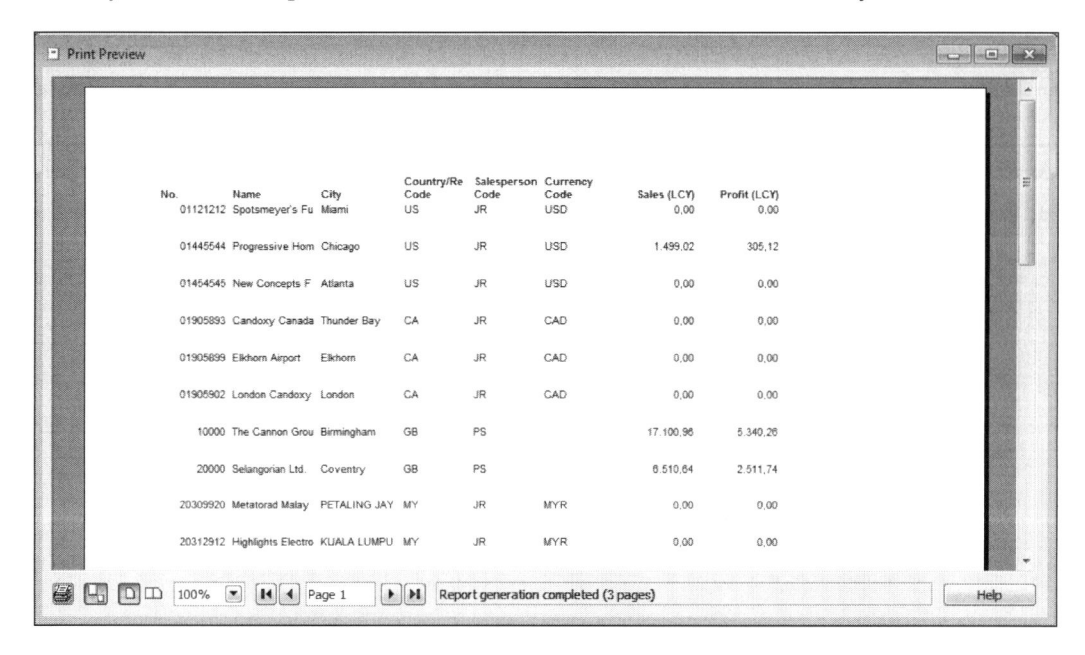

To be able to run this report in the RoleTailored client, we need to add this report to the menu structure or as an action in a page. Because we don't want to do this at this stage of the development of the report, we will use another way to run this report.

The trick is to open a command window. You can use the shortcut: `Windows-Key + R` for this, or click on the **Start** button and then the **Run** command. In the window that opens you can use the following command:

`DynamicsNAV://server/service/company/runreport?report=xxxxx`

For example, my report has the id: **90001** so the command is:

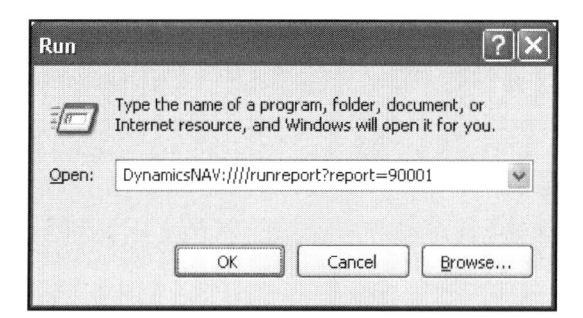

As soon as you run this command, it will open the Role Tailored client (if it's not already open) and run report 90001:

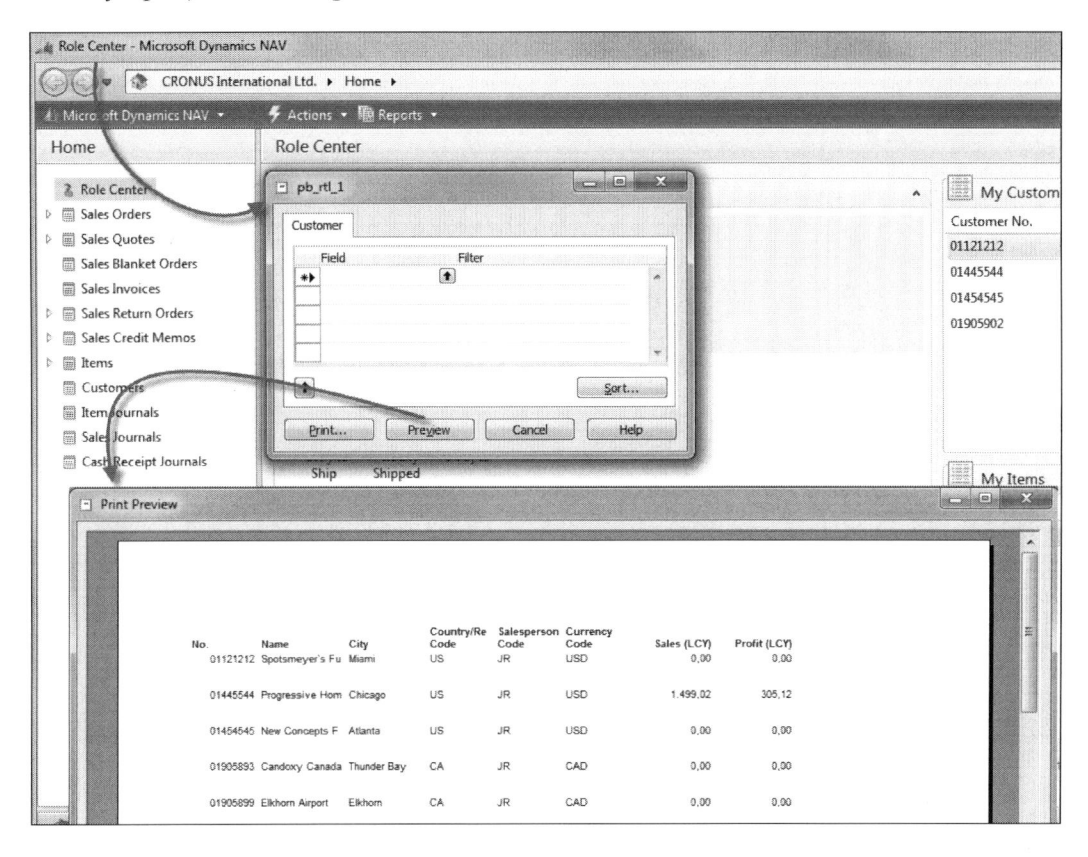

![Screenshot of Role Tailored client running report 90001 with Print Preview showing customer data]

> **Classic client required!**
>
> The Role Tailored client only uses the report viewer from the Classic client to run the report. It will not show the Classic client itself. But if there's no Classic client installed on your machine, then it will not work.
>
> When the Role Tailored client connects to the database it will consume a session and when it uses the Classic client to run a report this will consume an extra session. Make sure that you have plenty of sessions available in your license file when pursuing this scenario.

So, now we have the Role Tailored client running the classic report.

Creating Role Tailored Reports

> **Run command**
>
> You could also use this command to run a report: `DynamicsNAV:////runreport?report=xxxxx`
>
> By omitting the server, service, and company parameters from the run command the system will look for a local service tier to execute the report. If you don't have this installed on your local machine, as is the case with most end users, then you should use the full command.

This is nice to know, but it's not what we want for this report. We want to create an enhanced (RDLC) layout. To do this, we will go back to the Classic report designer for this report. To generate an enhanced layout, there are, at this moment, two options. Either you use **Tools | Create Layout Suggestion** or you use **View | Layout**.

Both of these options will create an RDLC file and open it with Visual Studio. The difference is that with the option: **View | Layout** it will be empty and with the option **Tools | Create Layout Suggestion**, the layout will be partly already generated.

Right now, we will use the **View | Layout** option, because we would like to do everything from scratch. Later, I will discuss the **Create Layout Suggestion**.

This is a screenshot of the two available options:

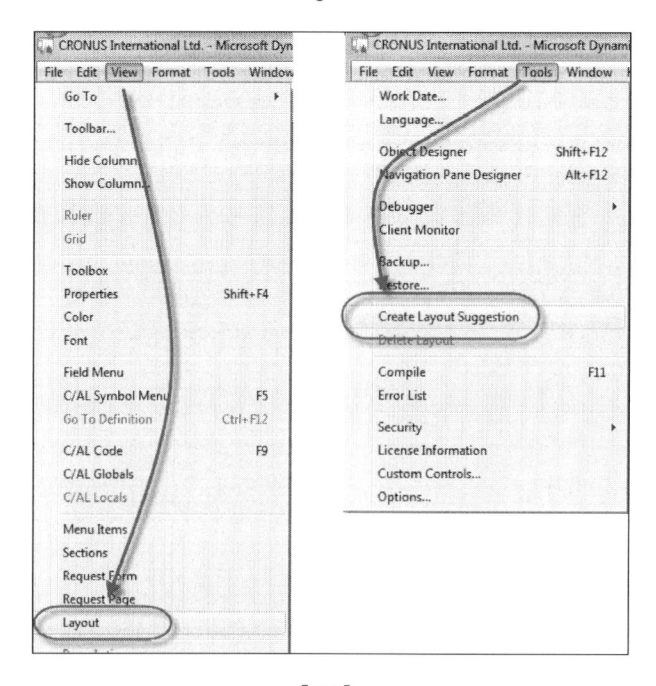

When you click on the **View | Layout** option, Visual Studio will open, as presented in the following screenshot:

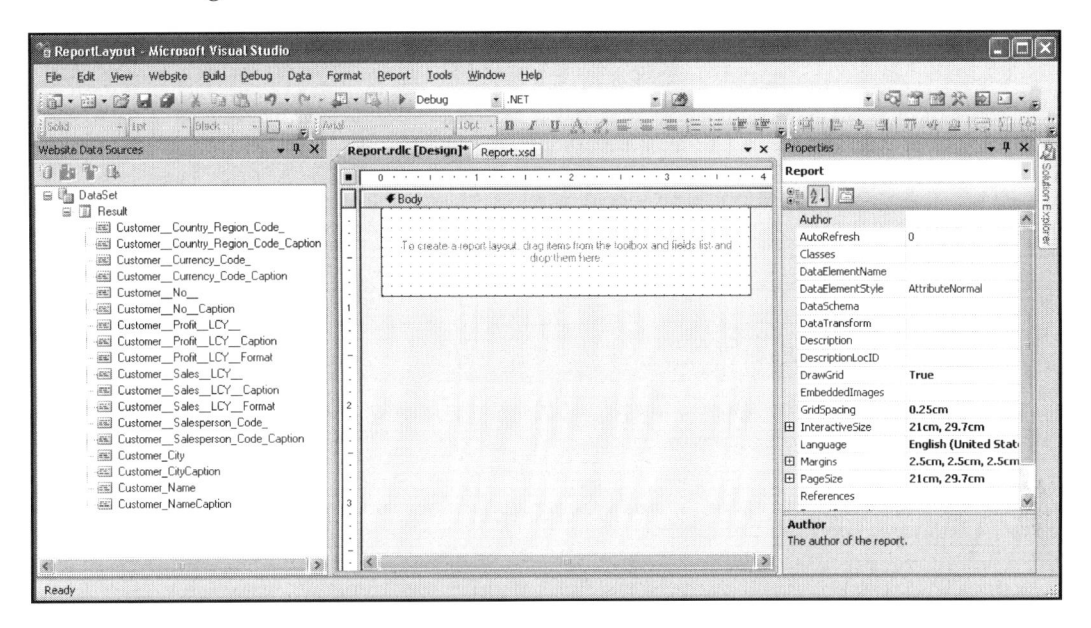

As you can see, Visual Studio is displaying several windows:

- Website Data Sources
- RDLC Layout
- Properties

A nice feature, in comparison with the Classic report designer, is the possibility to rearrange the location, appearance, and behaviour of the windows in Visual Studio. You can even group or sort the properties in the property window. There are also other windows that you can show or hide. You can find them in the View menu. Not all of them can be used for enhanced report design. This is because Visual Studio is a multifunctional or multipurpose development environment and is not limited to RDLC projects.

In the centre, we can see the **Body** of our report. It's actually the **Report.rdlc** file from the **Solution Explorer**, which is in fact an XML file, but represented in a visual designer.

The **Solution Explorer** might not be displayed by default. It can be made visible via the menu **View | Solution Explorer** or the shortcut *Ctrl +W, S*.

The solution explorer contains the following files:

- `ReportLayout.sln`
- `ReportLayout.suo`
- `Web.config`
- `Report.xsd`
- `Report.rdlc`

The enhanced layout of our report is actually the `Report.rdlc` file.

> **Note**
> Although you can make changes to the other files in the solution and/or you can add files to the solution, Dynamics NAV will only import the Report.rdlc file back into the database. All other changes/modifications/additions are lost.
>
> Because you are not supposed to make changes to the solution explorer, I usually hide it, to make room for the other windows, for example the property window.
>
> **Strange Report.rdlc visualisation**
> If you are using Visual Web Developer Express 2008 sp1, then it is possible that the report.rdlc file is represented in its xml layout instead of the visual layout. To solve this you will need to install an add-on for Visual Studio that you can download here: http://www.microsoft.com/downloads/en/details.aspx?FamilyID=b67b9445-c206-4ff7-8716-a8129370fa1d&DisplayLang=en

On the left side, you can see the **Toolbox** and the **Website Data Sources**. I'll come back to the **Toolbox** later. The **Website Data Sources** window contains the **dataset**. The **dataset** contains a **Result** and below the **Result** you can see some fields.

When you take a closer look at the **dataset**, you can see that most of the fields in there have two versions and some of the fields even more. For every field you can see a version that contains the value and a version that contains the caption. For decimal fields there's also a format version.

This is an example of an advantage of Dynamics NAV RDLC reporting over SQL Server side Reporting Services. Dynamics NAV RDLC reporting is multilanguage out of the box. Whenever you would like to name a column in the RDLC layout, you can use the caption fields. The content of the caption fields will be translated at runtime, depending on the language of the user.

The first time I created an enhanced report, I was a bit surprised that I could not see all the fields of the **data item** in the **dataset result**. Only the fields that have been put on a section in the classic layout will become available as fields in Visual Studio. This means that if you require another field in the **dataset**, you will first have to put it on a section in the **Section Designer** in C/SIDE.

A report can contain a classic layout and an enhanced layout. If you are going to maintain both layouts for a report, this might require putting a field on a section because you need it in the enhanced layout, but you might not want to show it in the classic layout of the report. To solve this issue, you can put the `Visible` property of the **textbox** to `False`. Even then, the field is still available in the enhanced layout. To make it easier for the developer to spot these fields, you can give them a color. For example, when you open report 111 **Customer Top 10**, you will see some small, yellow textboxes with their `Visible` property set to `False`, like in the following screenshot:

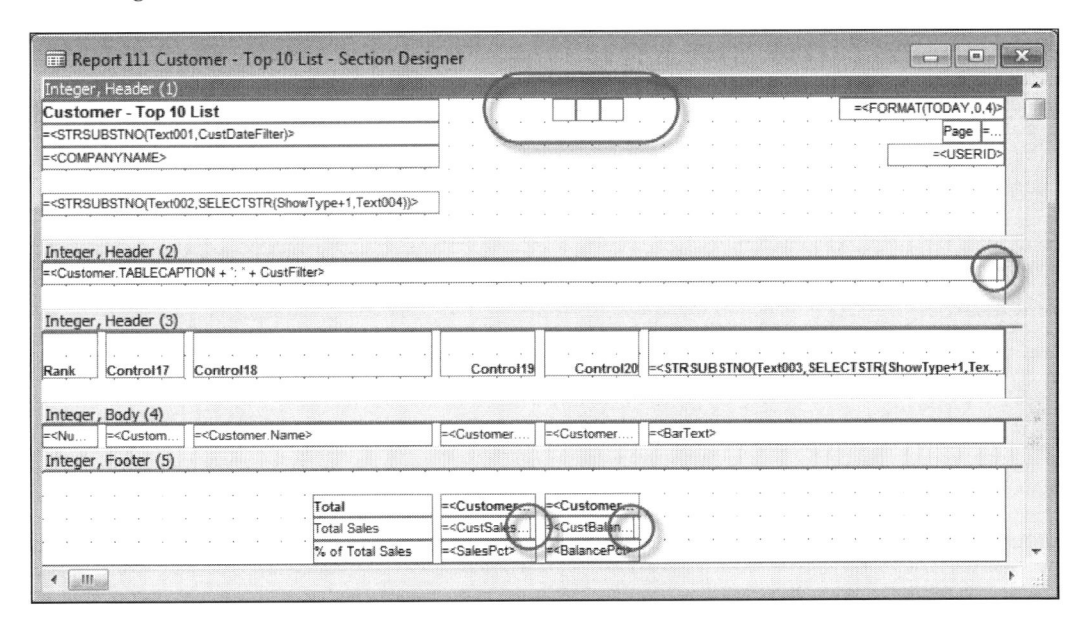

The color used to mark these textboxes can sometimes be yellow, red, or blue. It depends on the developer who created the report. It's a good idea to also agree upon an internal guideline in your company for these kinds of modifications.

Creating Role Tailored Reports

Let's go back to Visual Studio and drag some fields from the **dataset** onto the **Body**. When you drag and drop a field onto the **Body**, the field is actually put inside a **Textbox** control. This is very similar then to the Field Menu in the Classic report designer. You can see this in the following screenshot:

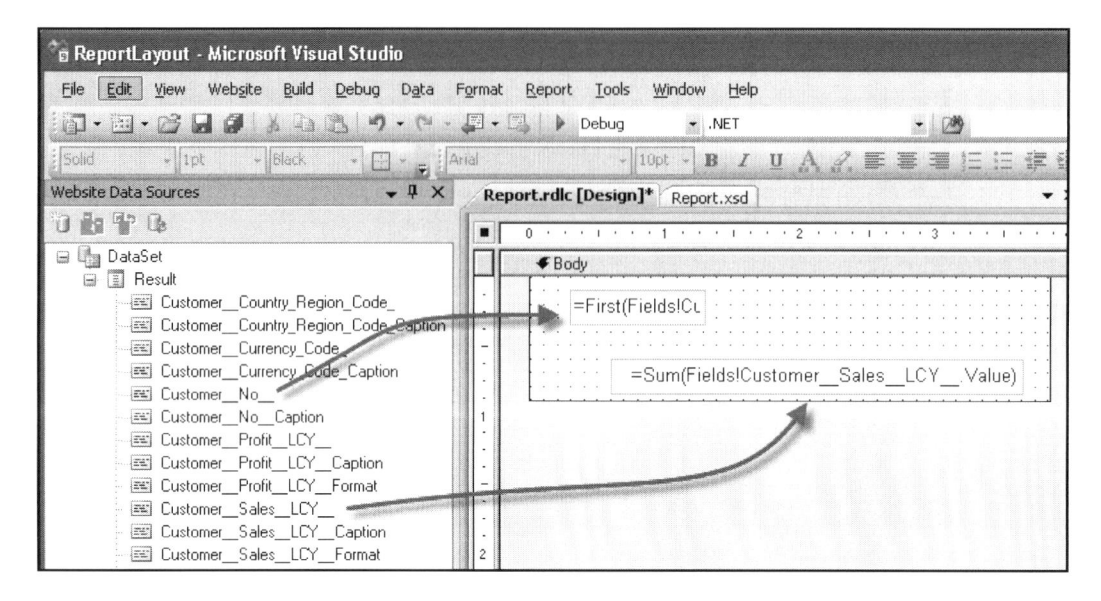

After adding the fields we now want to have a look at the results. An enhanced report cannot be run or previewed from within Visual Studio. You need to save the changes in Visual Studio and then minimize or close Visual Studio.

After that you have to click somewhere in the **data items** in the Classic report designer. As soon as this happens, Dynamics NAV will ask the following question, as you can see in the next screenshot:

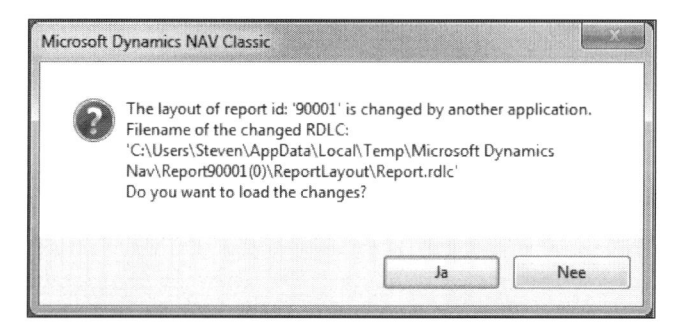

You should answer **Yes**, otherwise the changes you made in the RDLC file are lost. When you answer **Yes**, then the RDLC file is imported into the report object. During the import of the RDLC file, the file will also be parsed for errors by Dynamics NAV.

To save your changes to the database, you will need to manually save the report. When you save the report, the RDLC file is parsed again by Dynamics NAV. Some errors will only be detected during this second parsing. All other errors, not detected when parsing the report will be detected at runtime.

> **Building in Visual Studio**
> To detect errors earlier, you can build or compile the enhanced report in Visual Studio. You can do this via the menu **Build | Build Solution** or via the shortcut *F6*.

Now that the RDLC is imported and saved in the Dynamics NAV database, you can run the report. Running the report can be done via the same command as before: `DynamicsNAV:////runreport?report=90001`

You will notice that the Role Tailored client now shows a **Request Page**, as in the following screenshot:

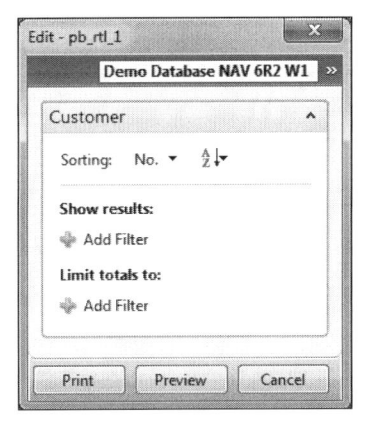

The **Request Page** is the counterpart of the **Request Form** of the Classic report. For every **data item** in the **data item designer** of the report you will see a **FastTab** in the **Request Page**. When you click on **Preview**, the report will run in the Report Viewer, as you can observe in the following screenshot:

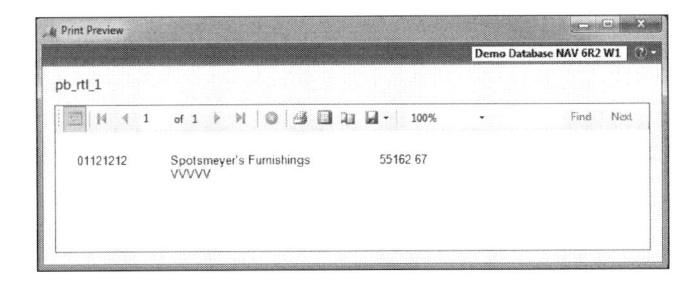

In the report viewer, you can use the toolbar to manipulate the report. The toolbar consists of the following buttons:

- Document Map:

  The Report Viewer toolbar includes an icon used to toggle a document map on a report. A document map is a navigation area that is attached to the left side of the report view area. It contains a list of links that users can click to navigate to a specific area of the report. Not all reports have a document map; you must define one in the report definition if you want to use this feature.

- First, Previous, Current Page, Total Pages, Next, Last, Stop Execution: The Report Viewer toolbar includes buttons to navigate the records and pages in the report.

- The Report Viewer toolbar includes a variety of page navigation functions. You can select a specific page or navigate directly to the first or last page. Pages are determined by pages breaks that are explicitly defined in the report definition. Page breaks can also be calculated automatically, depending on the report output format you are using.

- Print, Print Layout, Page Setup:

  Use these buttons to print the report. Before printing you can preview the actual print layout with the page margins via the **Print Layout** button.

- Save As:

  The Report Viewer toolbar provides export formats so that you can save a report as an Excel or PDF application file.

- Zoom:

  The Report Viewer toolbar provides standard zoom functionality so that you can enlarge or shrink the zoom in and out.

- Search – Find – Next:

  The Report Viewer toolbar includes a search field so that you can find specific text within a report. Search for content in the report by typing a word or phrase that you want to find. The search is case-insensitive and begins at the page or section that is currently selected. Wildcards and Boolean search operators are not supported. Only visible content is included in a search operation. If the report uses show/hide functionality, hidden content is not exposed through search operations. To search for subsequent occurrences of the same value, click **Next**.

Let's go back to our report. When we executed the report in the report viewer, did you notice something strange about the layout? Did you see only one record was shown in the report? Is there something going wrong?

Chapter 3

To answer these kinds of questions, you should be aware that basically things can go wrong in two locations. Either something goes wrong in the enhanced layout, or something is wrong in the classic layout of the report. We should check to verify if the enhanced layout receives all of the required records. We should check the **dataset** generated at runtime. And this is something you can do via the **About this Report** feature. This feature can be enabled by clicking on the **Help** button at the top right of the report viewer window, as shown in the following screenshot:

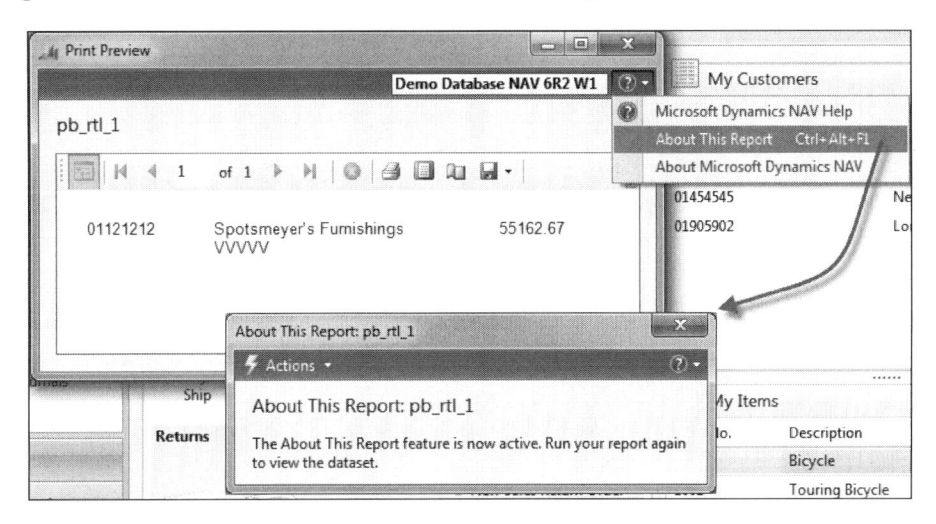

Actually, the first time you enable the feature, and then the second time you run the report, it can be visualized. This means of course that you have to run your report twice, just to be able to see the contents of the **dataset**. The following screenshot shows the content of the **About this Report** feature:

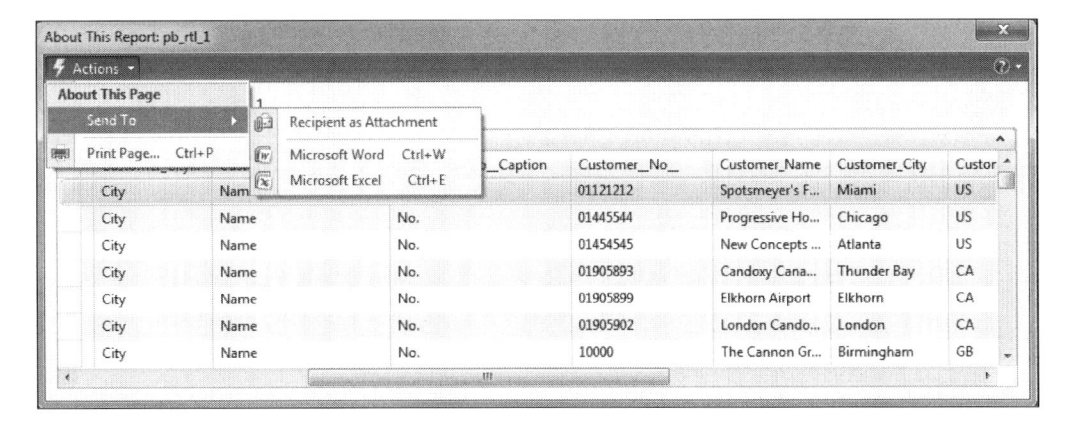

As you can see, the window contains a row for every record shown in the **dataset** and a column for every field in the **dataset**. The columns that contain captions are, of course, the same for every record.

The information in the **About this Report** page can also be exported to Microsoft Word or Excel or towards a new email in Microsoft Outlook. This way, a user can forward this information to the person providing support or the helpdesk.

> **Tip**
> If you click on the **About this report** feature in the **Request Page** of the report, then it is also enabled. After that, at runtime you can click on **About this report** and the **dataset** will contain data. This way, you don't have to run the report twice to be able to see the **dataset**.

As you can clearly see, our dataset contains multiple records, so as a consequence our error must be caused in the enhanced layout.

The enhanced layout can be considered as a layer that is put around the **dataset** to represent it. It seems that in this RDLC layer we are filtering the **dataset** somehow.

To verify this, let's open the enhanced layout for this report in Visual Studio, using the `View,Layout` option in the menu of the Classic report designer.

Looking at the **Body** of the report in Visual Studio, you might notice that the word `First` is inside the textboxes we put there, as shown in the next screenshot:

You might think that this is the reason why when we run the report we only see the first record from the **dataset**. But actually, even when you remove the `First` function in the value expression for the textboxes, the report will still only show 1 record from the **dataset**.

What's happening?

The reason for this behaviour is that the **Body** of the report isn't capable to repeat itself for every record in the **dataset**. To be able to show multiple records, we need to put the **dataset** fields inside a **Data Region** container. These containers can be found in the **toolbox**.

With a data region, you can also group, sort, filter, and aggregate data from a single dataset. You can arrange more than one data region in a report. Data regions can be placed side by side in the report body or in a rectangle container, or can be nested in other data regions. Multiple data regions can provide different views on the same dataset or similar views of different datasets.

The data regions are the following:

- **List**

    A list displays data in a free-form format. For example, you might use a list to design a form or display both a table and a chart. Arrange text boxes anywhere in the list to create your layout. The list row repeats one time for each value in the dataset.

- **Table**

    A table displays detail data or data grouped by row. A table has a fixed number of columns. The table expands down the page as needed. You can display all the detail data, row by row, or group the data by creating row groups. Row groups can be nested or adjacent. A row group displays a dynamic row down the page for each value in the group, which is determined at runtime. You can also add static rows for labels or totals. You can add totals to the table or to a specific group.

- **Matrix**

    A matrix displays data grouped by row and column. A matrix provides similar functionality to cross-tabs and PivotTable dynamic views. A matrix has at least one row group and one column group. The matrix expands across the page for column groups and down the page for row groups. The matrix cells display summary and aggregate values scoped to the intersections of the row and column groups. You can create additional nested groups and adjacent groups. The number of rows and columns in a matrix depend on the values for each group, determined at runtime. You can also add static rows for labels or totals. You can add totals to the table or to a specific group.

- **Chart**

    A chart displays data graphically. Charts help visualize summary and aggregate data.

As an example let's use a table data region. Drag a table from the toolbox onto the body of the report. When you put a table on a report, it will show three rows and three columns. Each cell of the table is a textbox. The three rows of the table start with a **Header** row, then a **Details** row, and then a **Footer** row. These **Header**, **Detail**, and **Footer** levels in a **Table Data Region** will behave like a **Header**, **Body**, and **Footer** section in the **Section Designer** of the Classic client. Each type of row in a table is marked with a symbol, as you can see in the following figure:

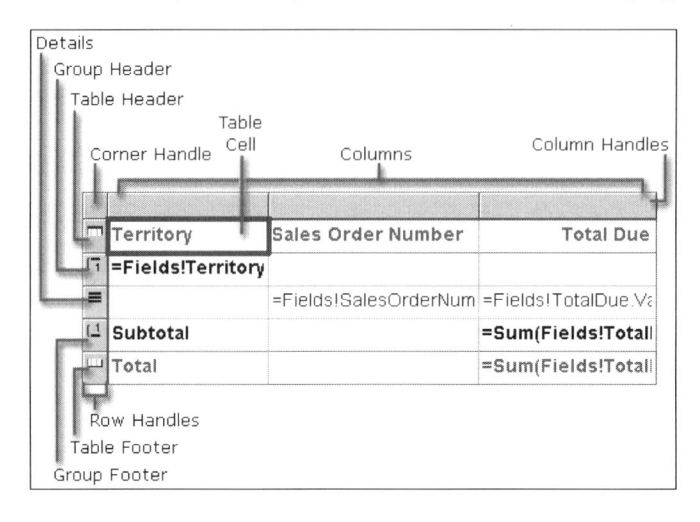

In report designer, you work with columns, rows, and the table by interacting with handles. Handles are grey boxes that appear above and next to the table when it is selected:

- The handles that run across the top of the table are column handles
- The handles that run down the side of the table are row handles
- The handle where the column and row handles meet is the corner handle

You can perform most actions with columns, rows, and the table by right-clicking on column handles, row handles, or the corner handle, respectively. To select the table, click the corner handle.

You can add fields to a table by dragging them from the **dataset** and dropping them in the table. When you do this and for example drag and drop the **Customer Name** from the **dataset** on a detail cell in the table, you will notice that the detail cell and also its corresponding header cell will get data. This is default behaviour from the table data region. In server side reporting services that's a good thing, but in Dynamics NAV RDLC reporting it might not be. Why? Well, the header row in the table will contain the names of the columns. In our case, sometimes we would like these names (captions) to be multilanguage. By dragging and dropping a field from the **dataset** on the table detail row, the header cell's value will become static text and will not be translated at runtime to the language of the user. For it to become multilanguage enabled, you should select the corresponding caption field from the **dataset** and drag it onto the header cell. Then, the header cell will be linked to the caption field in the **dataset**, and so also translated at runtime, because the captions in the **dataset** will be filled in by Dynamics NAV.

> **Multi Language**
>
> My advice would be to use the caption fields. That way, when the customer decides they want the report to become multilanguage enabled in the future you will have less work. Or you could inform the customer in the beginning of the implementation of the consequences and let them decide.

The footer level in the table can be used to calculate totals. When you drop a numerical field on a footer row, the Sum function is used to calculate the value. The same kind of behaviour is used in the Classic report designer, but for the total to be calculated you also have to use the TotalFields property of the corresponding **data item**. In an enhanced report this is not required. The total is calculated based upon the dataset, and not by Dynamics NAV. The same is valid for sorting and grouping. RDLC is capable of sorting, filtering, and grouping the dataset directly. Of course, depending of your report and the way the query is sent to the SQL Server database, the query performance might still benefit from the existence of an index on the table, but it's not a requirement.

To create the report in Visual Studio, follow these steps:

1. Click on **Table** in the **Toolbox.**
2. Click on the **Body**: a **Table** is now added to the **Body**.
3. Select the **Customer No** field in the dataset and drag and drop it in the table at the detail level.
4. Select the **Customer Name** field in the dataset and drag and drop it in the table at the detail level.
5. Select the **Customer Sales (LCY)** field in the dataset and drag and drop it in the table at the detail level.
6. Select the **Customer Sales (LCY)** field in the dataset and drag and drop it in the table at the footer level.
7. Select the **Customer No Caption** field in the dataset and drag and drop it in the table at the header level.
8. Select the **Customer Name Caption** field in the dataset and drag and drop it in the table at the header level.

9. Select the **Customer Sales (LCY) Caption** field in the dataset and drag and drop it in the table at the header level.
10. Select the header row and the footer row using the corresponding row handlers and click on the *B* button in the **Report Formatting** toolbar. This will make the rows bold.

Now, after having added the fields from the **dataset** to the table's rows you get a table like that shown in the following screenshot:

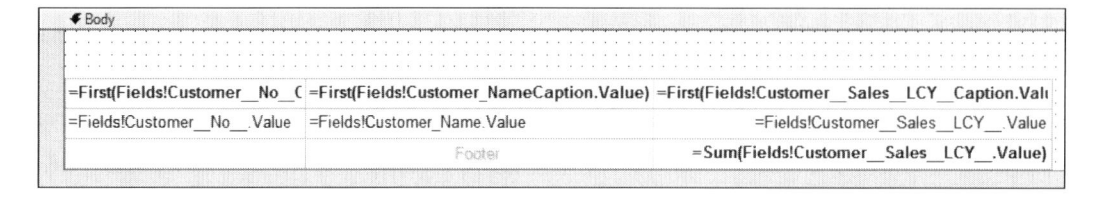

=First(Fields!Customer__No_C	=First(Fields!Customer_NameCaption.Value)	=First(Fields!Customer__Sales__LCY__Caption.Valu
=Fields!Customer__No__.Value	=Fields!Customer_Name.Value	=Fields!Customer__Sales__LCY__.Value
	Footer	=Sum(Fields!Customer__Sales__LCY__.Value)

11. Save the report in Visual Studio.
12. Click on the **data items** in the Classic report designer to trigger the import, and answer **Yes**.
13. Save the report in the Classic report designer and run the report.

This is what you will see at runtime:

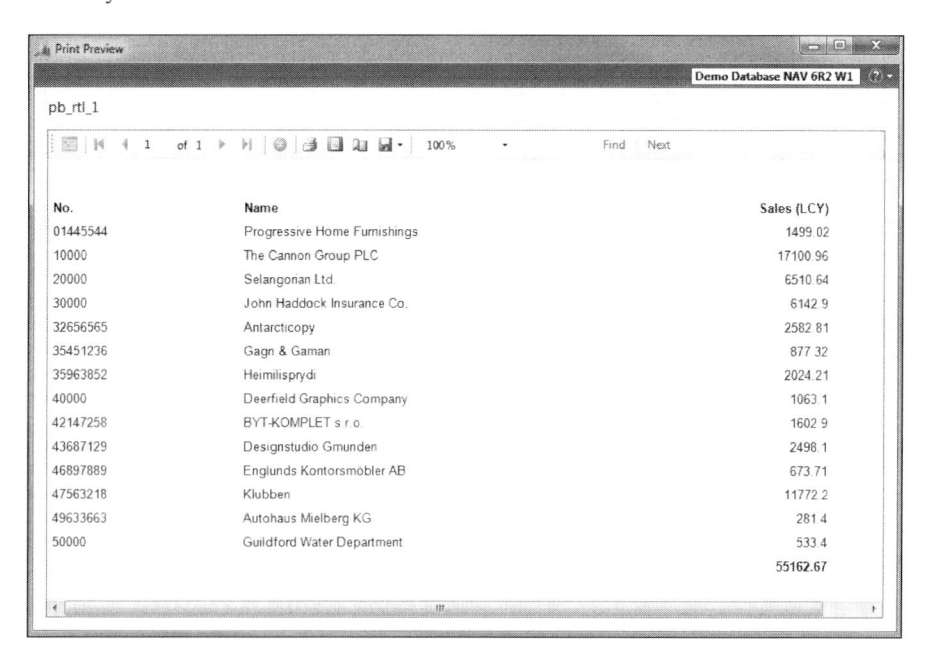

No.	Name	Sales (LCY)
01445544	Progressive Home Furnishings	1499.02
10000	The Cannon Group PLC	17100.96
20000	Selangorian Ltd.	6510.64
30000	John Haddock Insurance Co.	6142.9
32656565	Antarcticopy	2582.81
35451236	Gagn & Gaman	877.32
35963852	Heimilisprydi	2024.21
40000	Deerfield Graphics Company	1063.1
42147258	BYT-KOMPLET s.r.o.	1602.9
43687129	Designstudio Gmunden	2498.1
46897889	Englunds Kontorsmobler AB	673.71
47563218	Klubben	11772.2
49633663	Autohaus Mielberg KG	281.4
50000	Guildford Water Department	533.4
		55162.67

You see a list of customers, with **No**, **Name**, and **Sales (LCY)** and a grand total of the **Sales (LCY)** at the bottom. Via the toolbar, you can also export the report to PDF or Excel.

When you run the report you might notice a lot of rows having customers with zero in Sales (LCY). Usually, we filter out these rows in a report. There are different ways to filter out records. The next section will explain how to do that.

Adding formatting, grouping, sorting, and filtering to a report

Let's go back to the Visual studio report designer for this report and group our list of customers by Salesperson. To group data in a table data region, there are several options.

One option is to right-click on the detail row handle. A menu appears, as shown in the next screenshot:

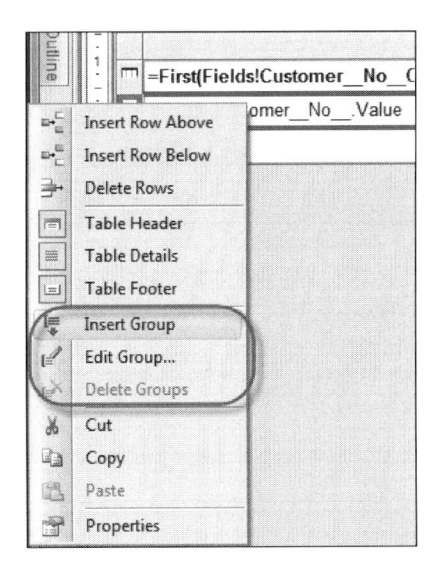

By clicking on **Insert Group**, a popup window will open allowing you to select the field on which to group. You can group on any field from the **dataset**. It's also possible to group on a calculated field. One of the options in the dropdown for the grouping field is **Expression**. Selecting this option will open the **Expression Designer**. In here, you can create an expression. The result of this expression will then be used for grouping.

> **Grouping/sorting and captions**
>
> A mistake I have seen many times is that by accident the caption fields is used as the field in the grouping, sorting, or filtering expression. As a result the report might behave very unexpectedly at runtime. (This is because caption fields are the same for every record in the **dataset**.)
>
> When this happens, one of the first things you should check is whether you made this kind of mistake.

Select the **Salesperson Code** field for the group expression. In the popup window there are also several other options. For example, if you enable the **Include group header/footer** then a group header/footer row will be added to the table. By default they are enabled, as you can see in the following screenshot:

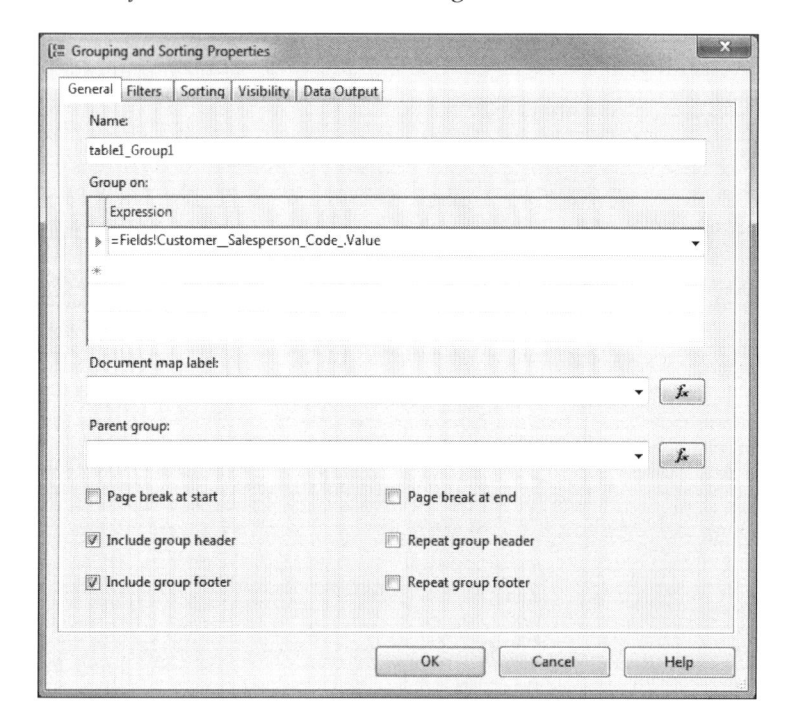

> **Note**
>
> The location of the new group row is determined by the row that is selected. Selecting a detail row places the new group just outside the detail row also described as a parent grouping. It means that the details will be grouped. Selecting an existing group row places the new group inside the selected group row, also described as a child grouping.

When you click on Ok, the table is changed. A group header and a group footer row are added. You can now add a column to the left of the first column to display the Salesperson code, as shown in the next screenshot:

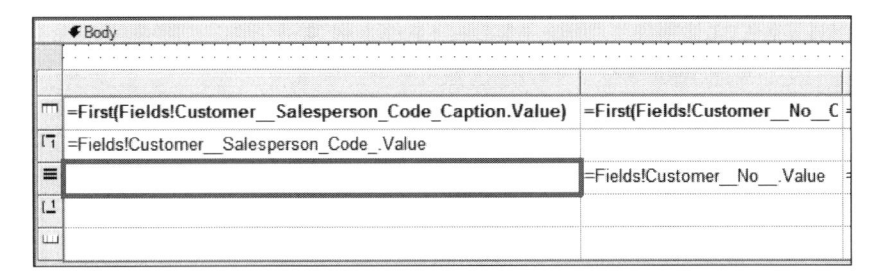

The group footer can be used to display subtotals. For example, in this report it would be good to add the **Sales (LCY)** field to the group footer row in the table. This way, the **Sales (LCY)** total per **Salesperson** will be calculated. You can have a look at the next screenshot to see how:

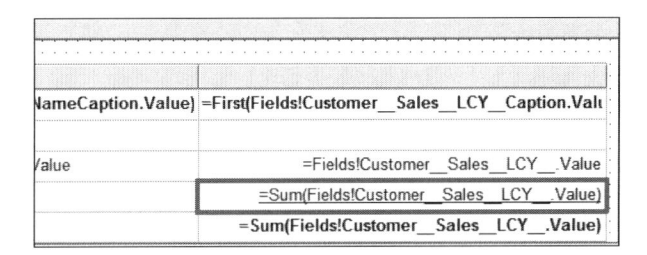

To see the difference between the subtotal and the grand total I have made the subtotal cell underlined, using the **U** button of the **Report Formatting** toolbar.

To sort the table you can select the table properties, open the **Sort** tab, and add the field you would like to use for sorting.

To open the table properties, you first need to select the table:

1. You can select it with the mouse or select it in the dropdown box in the property list.
2. When the table is selected you can right-click and select **Properties** in the dropdown menu that appears.

Creating Role Tailored Reports

3. You will then see the table properties in a popup window as shown in the next screenshot:

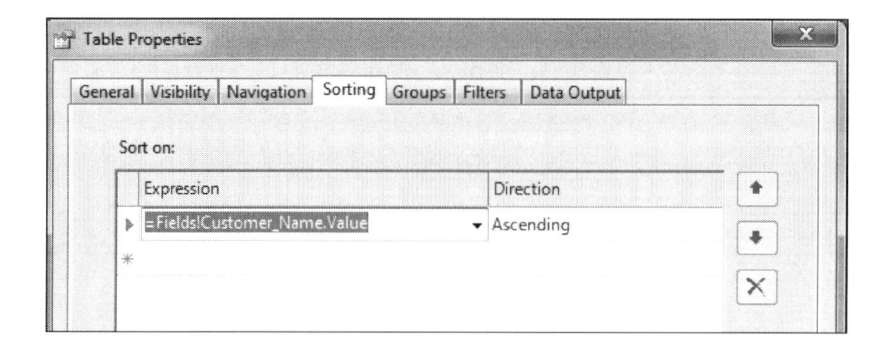

To sort the table:

1. Select the **Sorting** tab in the **Table Properties** popup.
2. Select the field you want to sort on in the dropdown box in the column named **Expression.**
3. Select a **Direction**, ascending or descending.
4. Click on the **Ok** button to apply the sorting.

When you save/import/save and run the report, this would be the result:

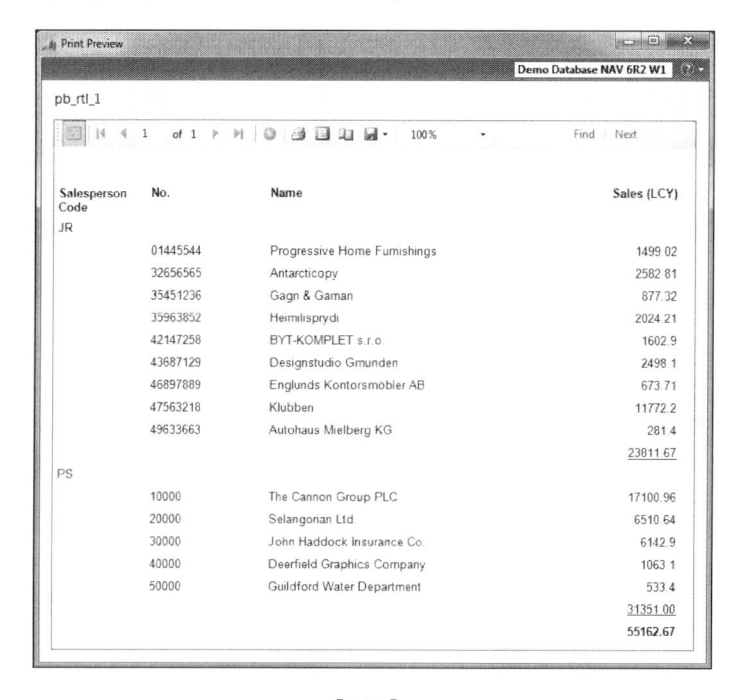

> **Page width causing page breaks**
>
> Sometimes when you run a report you notice that at runtime it gets very wide and when you print it on paper it has blank pages in between every page. Usually, this is because of the size of the **Body** in Visual Studio. By resizing the body's width and making it smaller you can make your report fit on one page. Sometimes, it can even be a matter of millimetres.

To effectively limit the data used for calculations after retrieving data from a data source, you can set filters on datasets, data regions, and data groupings.

To set a filter:

1. Open the report item's properties dialog box and select the **Filter** tab.
2. Select a field on which to apply the filter in the **Expression** column.
3. Select an **Operator**.
4. Select or type a **Value**.

You can create a simple expression or use the **Edit Expression** dialog box to create a complex expression. Each expression can be combined with the expression in the next row through an And or Or operator.

The following screenshot shows an example of how to filter out zero rows in our report:

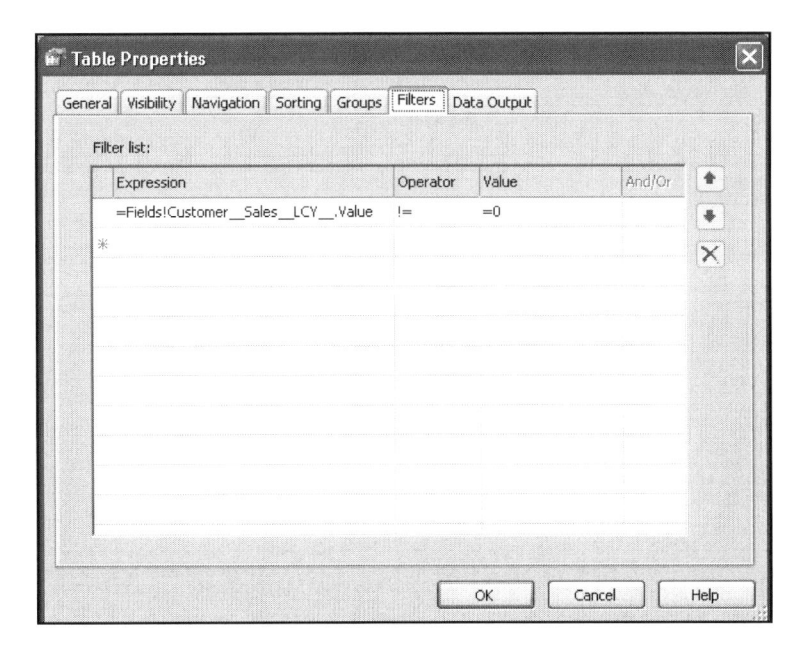

All property pages with a **Filter** tab present the same choices. You can set **Expression**, **Operator**, **Value**, and **And/Or** values. The following table shows the actions you can take on each column in the **Filter** list table:

Column	Action
Expression	From the dropdown list, choose a valid field for this filter to create a simple expression, or choose `<Expression>` to use the **Edit Expression** dialog box to create a complex expression.
Operator	Choose one of the valid operators for this filter expression.
Value	Enter a value directly, or, from the dropdown list, choose `<Expression>` to use the **Edit Expression** dialog box to create a complex expression. If Expression contains a field reference, the default type for Value matches the default type for the field. If Expression is not a field reference, the default type is `System.String`. See the following note about comparing a string type with other data types.
And/Or	Choose the Boolean operator to use to combine this expression with the expression in the next row. This cell activates after you begin to enter an expression in the next row.

> **Filtering on values**
>
> If you type the character "0" in the **Value** cell, by default, this evaluates to the string "0". To compare a numeric expression with the number 0, use the expression syntax which begins with an equal sign: `=0`.
>
> When previewing a report, you may see a runtime error from data type mismatches is similar to:
>
> `"The processing of FilterExpression for the [data set name] cannot be performed. Cannot compare data of types System.Int32 and System.String. Please check the data type returned by the FilterExpression."`

Be careful adding filters to a report. The reason is performance. In a Dynamics NAV 2009 role tailored report, you can put a filter in the RDLC layout but you can also create filter on a data item via its properties or by using C/AL code. If you have the choice then I would advise to create the filter in the classic part of the report, because this will filter the dataset that will be generated and sent to the RDLC layout.

For example, if you want to create a top ten customer list, you can use a table filter in the table data region in the RDLC layout. Let's presume you have about 100000 customers in the customer table. Then, at runtime, all of them will be fetched from the customer table, sent to the dataset, and then filtered in the RDLC layout. I think it's better to only fetch the rows that you will actually use from the database and send them to the dataset.

When is it better to filter in the RDLC layout? I would answer, when you don't know the filter value and/or filter field. Because the filter value and also the filter field can be expressions in RDLC, you can use that for dynamic filtering.

The same is valid in SQL Server side reporting services. If you filter your query you will get better performance than when you filter your dataset.

Another reason to filter in RDLC might be if you are using multiple data regions and not all of them need to be filtered.

Until now, we have always used the caption and the value fields from the dataset. But numerical fields have a `Format` property. This `Format` property will be populated by Dynamics NAV and will contain, at runtime, an rdl format code that you can use in the `Format` property of a textbox in Visual Studio.

When you right click on a textbox, a menu appears in which you can select the properties of the textbox, as shown in the next screenshot:

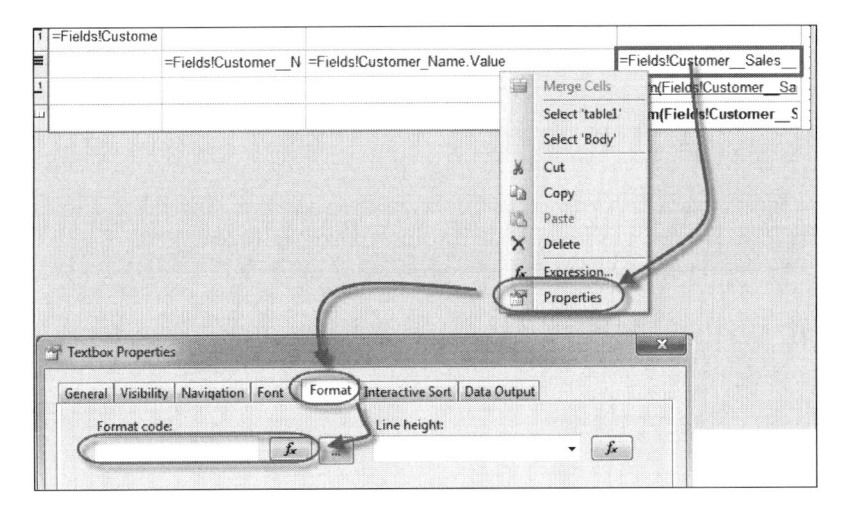

Here you can click on the **Fx** button. This will open the **Expression Designer**. In here you can type an expression. The result of the expression will be the value of the property. In this case, our expression should fetch the value from the format field from the **Sales (LCY)** field. The expression will be:

```
=Fields!Customer__Sales__LCY__Format.Value
```

Instead of using the **Expression Designer**, you can also just type this expression directly into the **Format Code** textbox or in the **Format** property in the properties window of the textbox, as shown in the following screenshot:

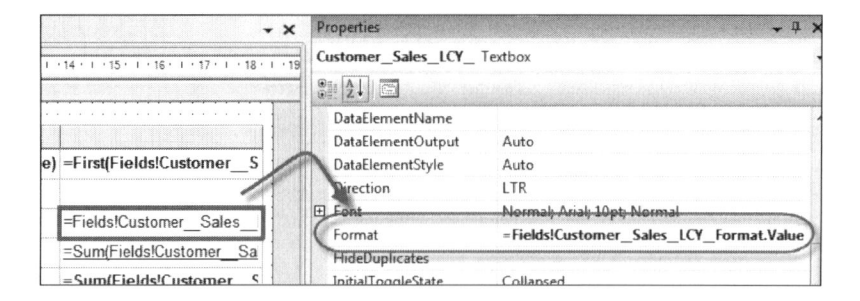

Reporting Services and RDLC use .NET Framework formatting strings for the Format property. The following is a list of possible format strings:

- C: Currency
- D: Decimal
- E: Scientific
- F: Fixed point
- G: General
- N: Number
- P: Percentage
- R: Round trip
- X: Hexadecimal

After the format string, you can provide a number representing the amount of digits that have to be shown to the right of the decimal point.

For example:

- F2 means fixed point with 2 digits: **1.234,00** or **1,234.00**
- F0 means fixed point without any digits: **1.234** or **1,234**

The thousand and comma separators (. and ,) that are applied, as also the **currency symbol**, depend on the Language property of the report.

> **More information about .NET Framework formatting strings can be found here:**
> Custom Numeric Format Strings:
> http://msdn.microsoft.com/en-us/library/0c899ak8.aspx
> Standard Date and Time Format Strings:
> http://msdn.microsoft.com/en-us/library/az4se3k1.aspx

As an alternative, you can use custom format strings to define the format value. This is actually how Dynamics NAV populates the Format fields in the dataset. The syntax is:

`#,##0.00`

You can use this to define the precision for a numeric field.

> **Why does the `Format` property sometimes have no effect?**
> To apply formatting to a text box, the text box must contain an expression, for example, `=Fields!LineTotal.Value` or `=1000`.
> When the text in the text box does not begin with the = sign, then the text is interpreted as a string and formatting does not apply.

Report creation workflow

Let's summarize what we have learned until now on how to create a Role Tailored report layout:

The steps required to create an RDLC report are:

1. Create a new report in the Object Designer.
2. Add a data item in the data item designer.
3. Add fields from the data item to the Section Designer.
4. Use the View/Layout menu to open Visual Studio and create the RDLC file.
5. Make changes to the layout in Visual Studio, and add new controls from the toolbox.
6. Save the changes in Visual Studio.
7. Go back to the data item designer and click on one of the data items.
8. Answer Yes to importing the RDLC file.

9. Save your report.
10. Run your report via a command or by adding it to the menu in a page.

These steps can be visualised in the following diagram:

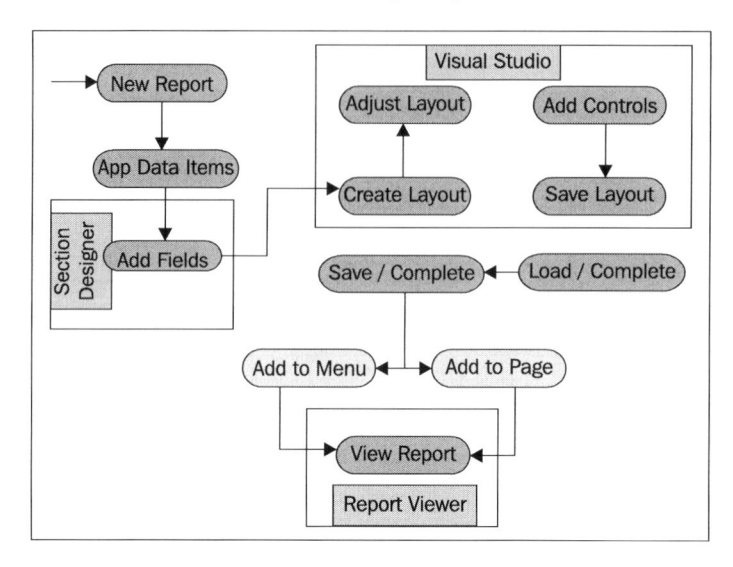

Using multiple data items

In our first report, we used the Customer table as the data item. In many reports you will want to use multiple data items. For example in document reports like the sales invoice, there will be multiple data items. It's important to understand the effects of using multiple data items, especially how the dataset is constructed.

At runtime the data items are processed, like they are processed in a classic report. After the data items are processed, a dataset is created containing the results of the combination of data items. This dataset is always a flat dataset. It consists of columns and rows. The columns correspond to the fields used on the section(s) and the rows correspond to the records from the database.

While processing the data items, properties like DataItemTableView are applied. Also, any C/AL code in the data item triggers is also applied. You can use these properties and triggers to filter the data item or make calculations.

As an example, let's use two data items: customer and customer ledger entry. Let's assume that there are three customers in the customer table and three ledger entries. Customer 10 has one ledger entry, customer 20 has two ledger entries, and customer 30 has no ledger entries.

Customer table			Customer Ledger Entry table		
No	**Name**		**CustomerNo**	**Posting Date**	**Amount**
10	Bill		10	07/01/2011	1245
20	Tom		20	10/12/2011	5587
30	Rose		20	21/02/2011	100

Example 1:

Let's add these data items in the data item designer, but don't indent or link them.

In the body section of the report, we will add the **No** and **Name** from the customer table and the **Posting Date** and **Amount** from the customer ledger entry table.

The dataset will contain four columns: **No, Name, Posting Date and Amount**. The order of the columns is according to the order of the data items.

Because the data items are not indented, and not linked, they will be processed one by one: First the three customer records and then the six ledger entry records. The dataset will look like the following table:

dataset				
No	Name	Customer No.	Posting Date	Amount
10	Bill			
20	Tom			
30	Rose			
		10	07/01/2011	1245
		20	10/12/2011	5587
		20	21/02/2011	100

Example 2:

Now, let's indent the data items and link them using the **No** field as the link between the two tables. After this the dataset will change into the following table:

DataSet

No	Name	Customer No	Posting Date	Amount
10	Bill	10	07/01/2011	1245
20	Tom	20	10/12/2011	5587
20	Tom	20	21/02/2011	100
30	Rose			

Notice that the customer information is repeated for each of its ledger entries. This is called a flat dataset. You can imagine that if you use more data items, the dataset will become bigger, but it is always a flat dataset.

At runtime this dataset will be populated with data by Dynamics NAV and the enhanced layout will work on the generated dataset.

Code behind section triggers have no effect on the creation of the dataset, and so this has no effect on the enhanced layout of the report. The same is valid for layout properties, like for example textbox properties that determine the look and feel: `Font`, `Format`, `BlankZero`, `BlankNumbers`. To simulate the same kind of behavior in the enhanced layout we will use workarounds or expressions or properties in Visual Studio. In the following chapters, I will explain some of these workarounds.

In the second example here above, customer 30 does not have any ledger entries. Sometimes, you want to filter out these unrelated records. You can do this in RDLC, but remember, filtering is better in the classic part. To do this, you can use the `PrintOnlyIfDetails` property on the parent data item (Customer). This property has an effect on the dataset and so it will also work for enhanced layout reports.

Using the Create Layout Suggestion option

Until now we have created the enhanced layout of our report completely manually in Visual Studio. To automatically generate the enhanced layout you have to use the **Tools | Create Layout Suggestion** option in the menu, as shown in the next screenshot:

Chapter 3

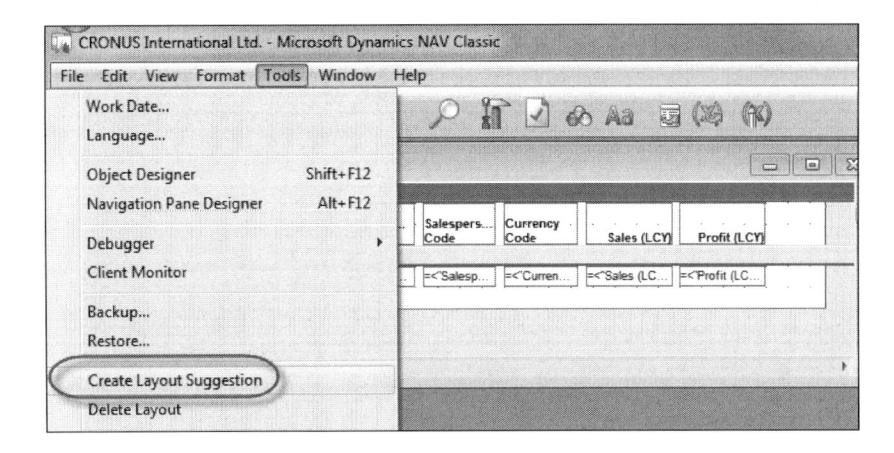

Selecting this option will create a new layout for our report. If there was already a layout created, it will overwrite the existing layout with a new one, after asking for validation:

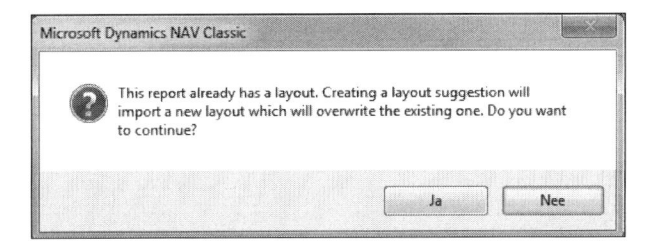

Visual studio will be opened and the report will have a layout generated, as displayed in the next screenshot:

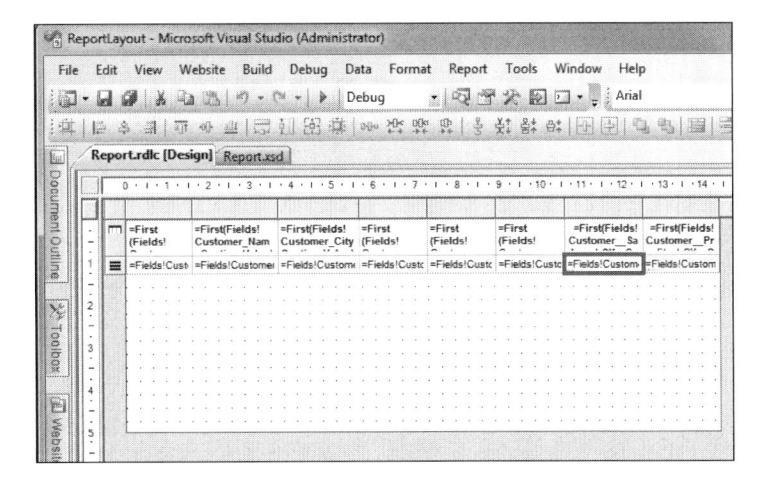

[119]

Creating Role Tailored Reports

The create layout suggestion will create an RDLC file. As a data region, it will always use a table. The way that the table is created will depend on the way information is laid out in the sections. The following screenshots might shine some light on this mechanism:

Example 1:

This classic layout:

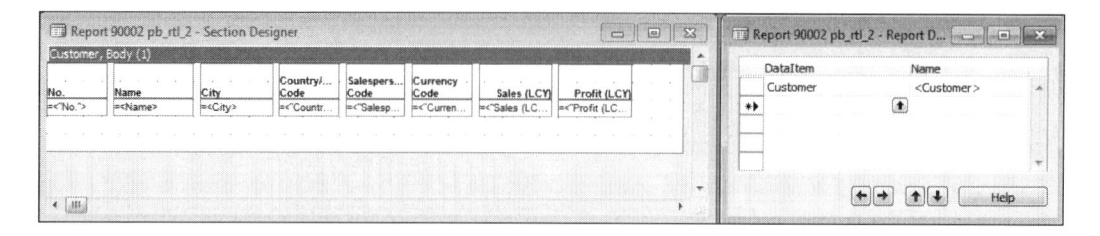

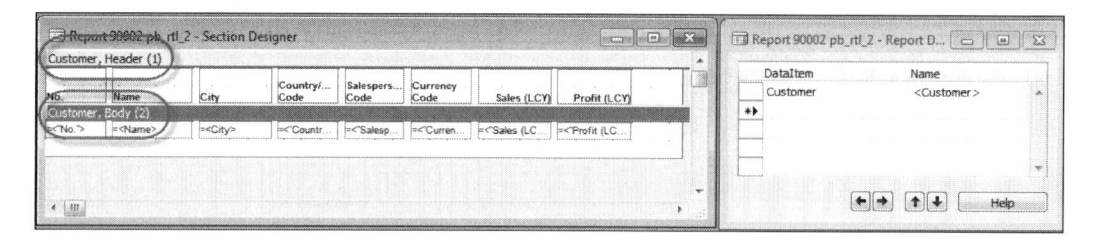

Is converted into this enhanced layout:

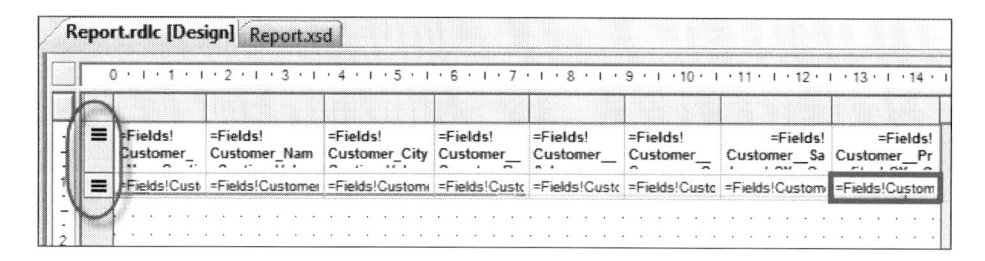

Example 2:

This classic layout:

Is converted into this enhanced layout:

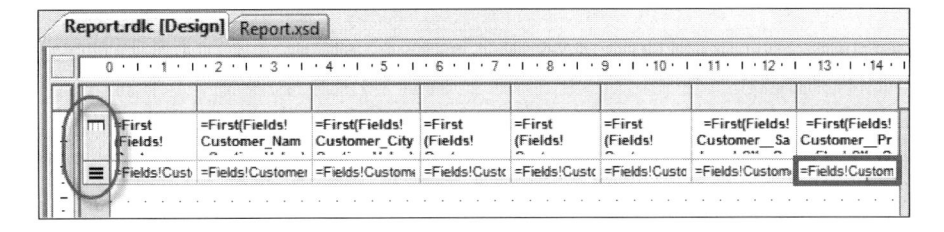

Example 3:

This classic layout:

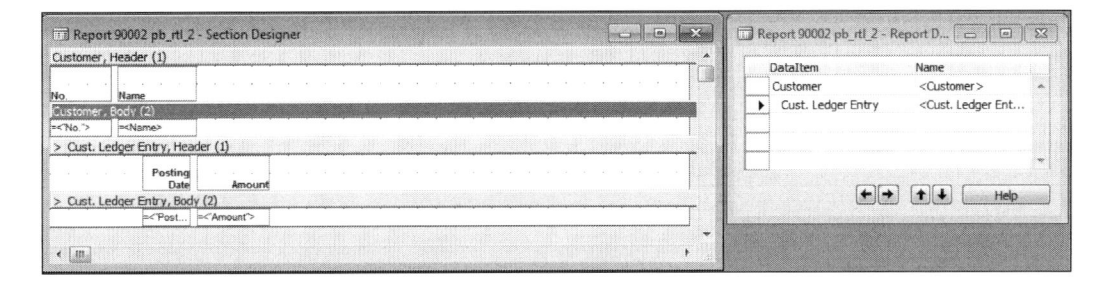

Is converted into this enhanced layout:

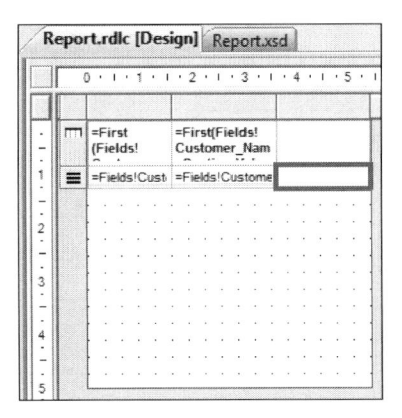

Creating Role Tailored Reports

Example 4:

This classic layout:

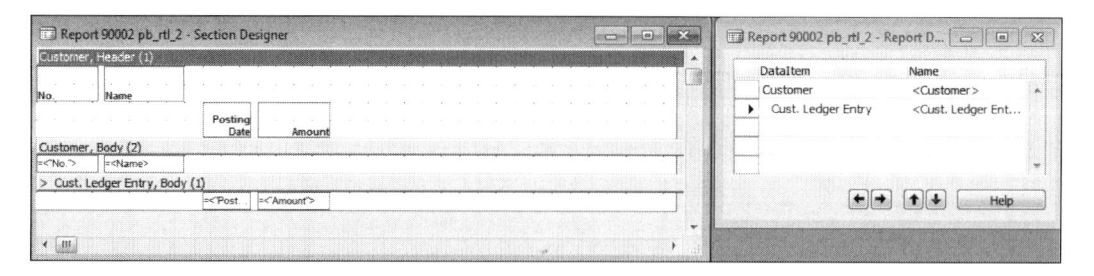

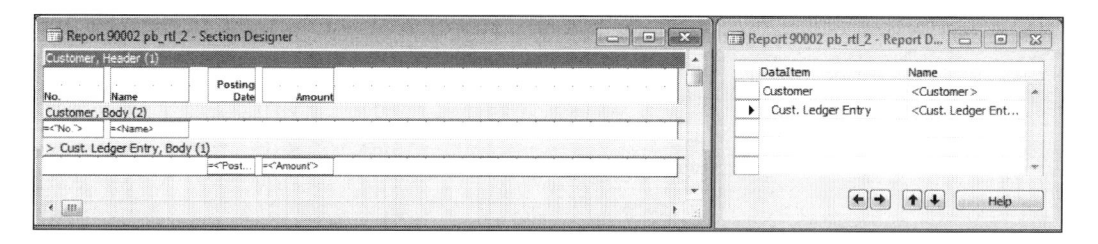

Is converted into this enhanced layout:

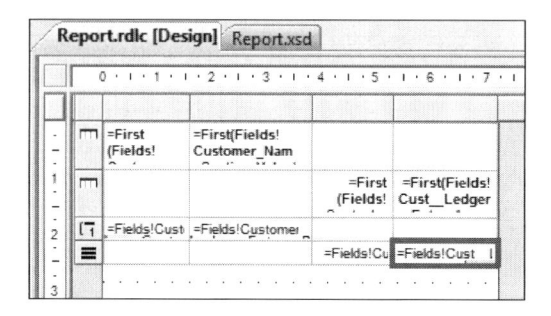

Example 5:

This classic layout:

Is converted into this enhanced layout:

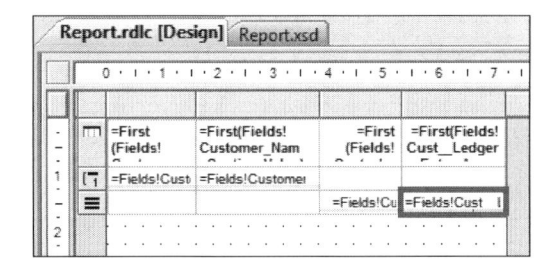

As you can see, the algorithm that generates the RDLC looks at the sections and tries to build something similar.

As you can see between example 1 and example 2, a body section is translated into a detail row and a header section is translated into a header row.

The trick with indented data items is to put the labels of the indented data items on the header section of the first data item. Otherwise the fields from the indented data items are not put in the table data region. See the difference between examples 3 and 4 for this behaviour.

The algorithm also seems to take into account the vertical alignment of fields, as you can see in the difference between examples 4 and 5.

Changing the template

When you click on the **View** | **Layout** option for a report that does not have an enhanced layout, then an empty enhanced layout is created. But, did you now know that Dynamics NAV uses a template for this, and that you can make changes to this template?

The template can be found in the installation directory of the Dynamics NAV 2009 Classic client. The default location is:

`C:\Program Files\Microsoft Dynamics NAV\60\Classic`

As you can see in the following print screen, there are actually two templates:

- ReportLayout2005
- ReportLayout2008

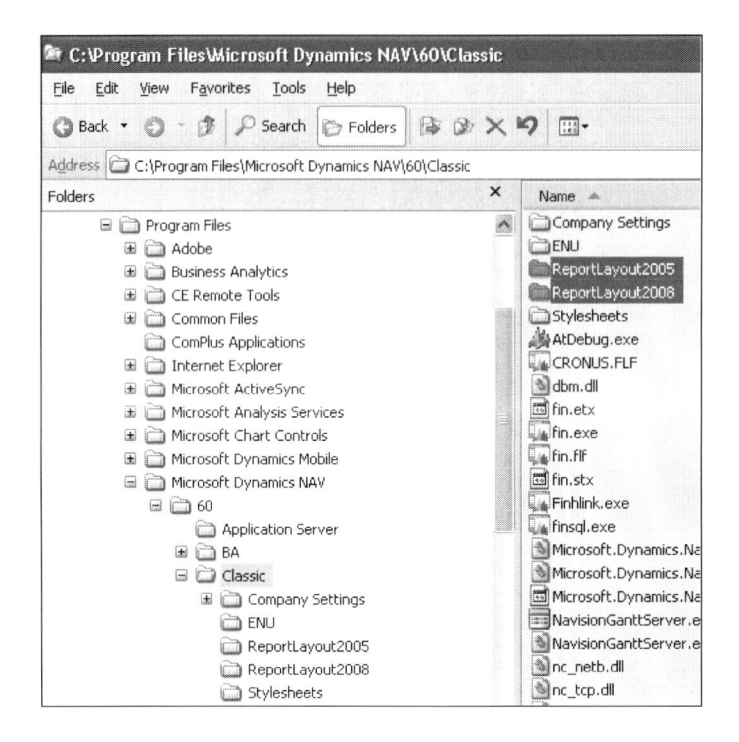

When you are using Visual Studio 2005 then Dynamics NAV will use ReportLayout2005 and when you use Visual Studio 2008 then Dynamics NAV will use ReportLayout2008.

Inside the ReportLayout2008 folder, you can see the following files:

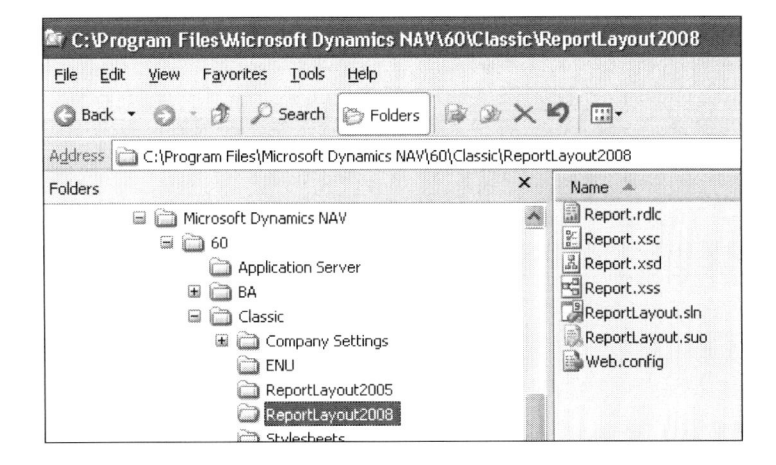

You can open this template by double-clicking on the file: **ReportLayout.sln**. Visual Studio will open and you will see an empty report layout, as you do when you create a new report from within Dynamics NAV.

You can make changes to the RDLC file as long as they don't include any database bound information. This is because the template solution does not have a result set.

For example, you can add a header and/or footer, textboxes with static information, embed images, change properties, and so on.

When you open **Report** | **Properties** and have a look in the tab **Code**, you will see the following functions:

```
Public Function BlankZero(ByVal Value As Decimal)
if Value = 0 then
        Return ""
end if
    Return Value
End Function


Public Function BlankPos(ByVal Value As Decimal)
if Value > 0 then
        Return ""
end if
    Return Value
End Function


Public Function BlankZeroAndPos(ByVal Value As Decimal)
if Value >= 0 then
        Return ""
end if
```

```
            Return Value
    End Function

    Public Function BlankNeg(ByVal Value As Decimal)
    if Value < 0 then
            Return ""
    end if
        Return Value
    End Function

    Public Function BlankNegAndZero(ByVal Value As Decimal)
    if Value <= 0 then
            Return ""
    end if
        Return Value
    End Function
```

These functions were put into the template because they represent functionality (properties) that was available in the Classic report designer but not in Visual Studio report designer. With these functions you can simulate the same behaviour in RDLC.

As you probably understand, any useful function that might be useful in future reports that you will develop can be put in here so they will be available whenever you create a new report via **View | Layout**.

> **Important**
>
> When you create a new report with the **Create Layout Suggestion** feature, as explained in this chapter, then the template solution is not used to generate the report. **Create Layout suggestion** generates an RDLC that is not based upon this template.

Let's make an example and change the background colour of the body to red and add a textbox with the value **test**, as displayed in the next screenshot:

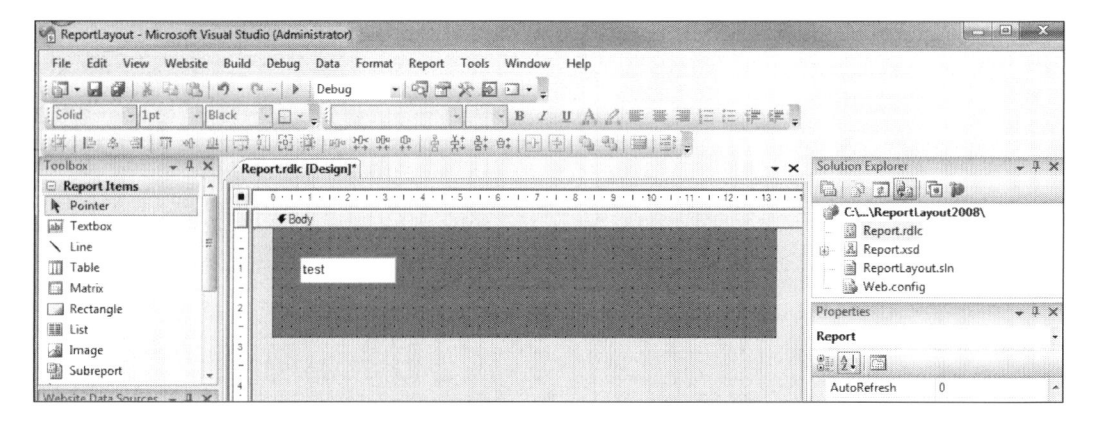

Now, save and close Visual Studio. Go into the Classic client, and create a new report or open an existing report that does not have an enhanced layout. Next, click on **View Layout** and you will see that your template is used to create the RDLC.

After you have created and designed a report using Visual Studio, you must also add the report to the interface of the Role Tailored client. The following procedure explains how to make a report available in the Role Tailored client by adding the report to the promoted actions pane in the customer list page.

Making a report available in the Role Tailored client

Once you have developed and tested your report you want the end user to be able to run the report. For this you will have to make your report available in the Role Tailored client. To do this, carry out the following steps:

1. In the Classic client, open **Object Designer**, and then click **Page**.
2. Select the page to display the report, for example, Page 22, Customer List.
3. Click **Design** to open the page in **Page Designer**.
4. Select an empty line in the designer. Click **View**, and then **Actions** to open **Action Designer**.
5. Scroll down to the **ActionContainer** that has Reports as its subtype.
6. Add an action to the list; in the Caption field enter a name for the action, and in the Type field, select Action.
7. Click **View**, and then **Properties** to open the **Properties** window for the new action.
8. In the Value field of the RunObject property, , click the drop-down arrow and select the new report in the **Object List** window.
9. Set the PushAction property to RunObject, set the **Promoted** property to Yes, and set the PromotedCategory property to Report.
10. Compile and save the page.
11. Open the Role Tailored client and then open the customer list page.
12. The report is added to the list of promoted actions.
13. Click the action to run the report.

> More information about page design is available in the **C/Side reference guide** in the help menu of the Classic client or can be found on this website:
> `http://msdn.microsoft.com/en-us/library/dd338806.aspx`

Limitations of enhanced report design in Dynamics NAV 2009

Dynamics NAV 2009 is currently using the 2005 version of the RDLC implementation. This means that all that has been added after SQL Server Reporting Services 2005 is not available for Dynamics NAV 2009 RDLC reports. This limits the amount of features currently available in Dynamics NAV 2009 report design and also the version of Visual Studio that can be used to develop reports.

For example, ReportViewer 2010 supports RDL 2008 features such as:

- Tablix
- Rich Text
- Gauges
- Maps
- Sparklines and databars
- Indicators
- Rendering reports to RSS feeds

Other enhancements include support for ASP.NET AJAX. The following table lists the available RDL schema versions:

Version	Schema Version
RDL 2010	`http://schemas.microsoft.com/sqlserver/reporting/2010/01/reportdefinition`
RDL 2008	`http://schemas.microsoft.com/sqlserver/reporting/2008/01/reportdefinition`
RDL 2005	`http://schemas.microsoft.com/sqlserver/reporting/2005/01/reportdefinition`
RDLC 2005	`http://schemas.microsoft.com/sqlserver/reporting/2005/01/reportdefinition`
RDL 2000	`http://schemas.microsoft.com/sqlserver/reporting/2003/10/reportdefinition`

At this time, Dynamics NAV 2009 does not support these features. Recently at Directions 2011, Microsoft has confirmed that the next release, Dynamics NAV version 7, will support the 2008 RDLC schema.

Until then, we will need to use Visual Studio version 2005 or 2008 as explained on the Microsoft Dynamics NAV Team Blog: `http://blogs.msdn.com/b/nav/archive/2010/04/29/visual-studio-2010-and-ssrs-rdlc-reports-in-nav-2009.aspx`

Here, you will find the following statement about future report design and RDLC 2008/2010:

> *To view an "RDL 2008" format report you will need to have the "Microsoft Report Viewer 2010" installed on all RoleTailored client (RTC) machines, currently the "Microsoft Report Viewer 2008" is installed by the NAV 2009 installation program.*
>
> *If we opened up for Visual Studio 2010 you will convert the reports you design to "RDL 2008" format, and leave the unopened reports in "RDL 2005" format. So, to develop an add on and share this with other partners you will need to inform these partners that Report Viewer 2010 is a requirement for all RTC machines. And if these partners are to modify any of your reports, Visual Studio 2010 is a requirement as well.*
>
> *We need change our code to now compile to "RDL 2008" format when importing the RDLC layout back to NAV.*
>
> *So, to avoid this confusion we will not open up for Visual Studio 2010 support before our next major version of Dynamics NAV.*
>
> *If you for other reasons want to use Visual Studio 2010, you can easily have Visual Studio 2008 and Visual Studio 2010 installed on the same machine. We will just open the Visual Studio 2008 version when you select* **View** | **Layout** *in the Object Designer.*
>
> *If you only have Visual Studio 2010 installed you will see this message:*
>
> *"An error occurred when opening Report Designer. A supported version of Visual Studio could not be found."*
>
> *This is the same message you get when you have no Visual Studio installed, because we search for the following Visual Studio versions and in prioritized order. So in case you have both Visual Studio 2005 and 2008 installed, we will use the 2008 version:*

1. Microsoft Visual Studio 2008
2. Microsoft Visual Web Developer 2008 Express edition with SP1
3. Microsoft Visual Studio 2005 with SP1
4. Microsoft Visual Web Developer 2005 Express edition with SP1

Visual Studio is not installed when you install Dynamics NAV 2009. It has to be installed manually. If you don't want to buy a version of Visual Studio I recommend you download and install Visual Web Developer Express 2008.

Here's where you can download it:

http://www.microsoft.com/express/Downloads/#2008-Visual-Web-Developer

You will also need to install a plugin for Visual Studio 2008 sp1, which you can download here:

http://go.microsoft.com/fwlink/?linkid=74666

Another consequence of using the RDLC 2005 implementation is that to be able to display database information on the header or footer of an enhanced report a number of workarounds have to be implemented. Depending on the layout of the report these workarounds can become complex. When we migrate to the RDLC 2008 implementation, these workarounds will most probably no longer be required.

Summary

In this chapter, we created our first enhanced report, using the Visual Studio report designer. The chapter provides you with a good understanding of the steps required to create enhanced report layouts.

We can conclude that the enhanced layout is a very big step forward in regards to report design functionality. It has an enormous potential of added value and features that we can now use and apply when designing reports in Dynamics NAV.

Right now, the enhanced layout is optional, meaning reports without an enhanced layout will render in the Role Tailored client with their classic layout. As of version 7, an enhanced layout will probably become mandatory for all reports.

Because RDLC is different from RDL and Dynamics NAV 2009 is using the 2005 version of the RDLC specification, we cannot apply all the controls and features that are currently available in server side SQL Server Reporting Services. Of course there are workarounds that can be applied to overcome this issue and in the following chapters we will go into more detail on that. Very probably in the next version(s) of Dynamics NAV, we will evolve towards RDLC 2008.

The create layout suggestion has the advantage that it can automatically generate an enhanced layout. In the cases where you don't want to use a table data region, you will need to create the report from scratch and create the content yourself.

In the next chapter, we will explore some data visualisation techniques that we can apply to enhanced reports. Until now we have always used the table data region; in the next chapter we will dive into the details of other data regions like the **List**, **Matrix**, and **Chart**.

We will learn to make reports more interactive, using for example display/collapse, interactive sorting, document maps, and key performance indicators (KPIs), and start using the RDLC technology to its full potential.

Last but not least, we will learn about the usage of headers and footers and ways to enable data bound information to be displayed in them.

4
Visualization Methods

When it comes to choosing how to visualize the data, the RDLC report designer provides a variety of options. Some of these are available as controls in the toolbox in Visual Studio Report Designer; others can be implemented using expressions and properties.

In this chapter, we will start off with a look at other Data Regions besides the table, which we used in the previous chapter: list, matrix, and chart. Each of them serves a specific purpose and can provide added value when visualizing data in Dynamics NAV 2009.

We will move on to understand the use of images, and how to make a report more interactive using document maps, interactive sorting, hyperlinks, and expressions.

Last but not least, you need to stand still and think about how the report viewer will render data. This is important because it will influence the way you design a report. Everything depends on the requirements of the user. Will they run the report in the report viewer or will the report mainly be printed or exported to PDF and Excel?

Before you learn to implement data visualisation techniques, let's go through the available report items and report data regions one by one. In the previous chapter, we mainly focussed on using the table data region but there are other controls available in the toolbox and understanding their purpose and knowing how and when to use and or combine them will assist you when thinking about a way to visualize the data on your reports.

In this chapter we will cover:

- Reports items
- List data regions
- Matrix boxes
- Chart data regions

- Adding images to reports
- Expanding/collapsing report sections
- Interactive sorting
- Using the Document Map
- Linking reports
- Expressions
- Useful tips and techniques

Report items

When designing the enhanced layout of a report in Visual Studio, there's the toolbox in which you will find all the controls you can use on your report. It's via the toolbox, by clicking on a control and dropping (or via drag and drop or drag and draw), that you can add it to the report. In the next version, as it is in RDLC 2008, you can also right click on the layout (body, header, or footer) and insert a control.

The controls in the toolbox can be divided into report items and data regions. Report items are the controls that appear in the toolbox. Report items can be containers too for data from the dataset. Some report items however only help in creating format styles in the report itself. These report items are independent of the dataset and their values cannot be changed. Examples of these types of report items are lines and rectangles. Images and text boxes are independent report items that can be connected to a field from the dataset, but it's not mandatory.

Static report items are items on a report that are not connected to a dataset. A text box for example represents a text constant for labels or comments in a report. The static report items are the following:

- Pointer
- Text box
- Line
- Rectangle
- Image

Data regions are areas on a report that contain data from the dataset that is repeated. The data regions are:

- List
- Table
- Matrix
- Chart

Common report item properties

Except for the Line report item, which has only color, style and line width properties, there are common properties between all report items, and they are as follows:

Property Name	Description
BackgroundColor	Sets the color for the background.
BackgroundImage	Sets an image as a background for a control or for the complete report. Can be used as a watermark.
BorderStyle	Sets the style of the border (solid, dotted, dashed, double-lined, and so on)
BorderColor	Sets the color of the border around the report item
BorderWidth	Sets the width of the report item. (points, inches, and so on).
Padding	Sets the size of the padding against the border and text (left, right, top, bottom).

Apart from these common properties, all controls in the toolbox have design properties and layout properties to specify location, size, page breaks, tooltips, bookmarks, and so on.

Except for the image, line and rectangle, all controls have international properties like language, calendar, and direction, and so on to determine how text should be displayed or formatted.

> **International properties**
> International properties are properties that define how information should be presented to the user, keeping in mind the regional settings of the user. For example, in Belgium a date is formatted as dd/mm/yyyy and in the USA or UK it might be mm/dd/yyyy. You can decide to select a fixed value for the property or use an expression. Especially for international or language-related properties, I would advise to use an expression so a value can be generated dynamically for every type of user.

As an example, let's explore the BackgroundColor property. Actually, the following information is valid for all of the Color properties.

A Color property needs to be an expression that evaluates to the name of an existing color or a hexadecimal HTML color string with this format: #HHHHHH.

> **The color table**
>
> On this Microsoft website you can find more information about color coding: http://msdn.microsoft.com/en-us/library/ms531197(v=vs.85).aspx
>
> And on this website you will find a color coding table: http://samples.msdn.microsoft.com/workshop/samples/author/dhtml/colors/ColorTable.htm.
>
> This is a very practical table containing a list of colors with examples, names, and hex values.

These are a few examples of colors:

- ="Maroon"
- ="Firebrick"
- ="#596ae3"

When you want to assign a value to a Color property then you can do this in several ways:

- You can select the Color from the list of colors in the Color property dropdown box
- You can type the expression directly into the Color property text box
- You can select Expression in the dropdown box of the Color property

If you use the last option then the expression designer window opens and you can create the expression in there, as you can see in the next screenshot:

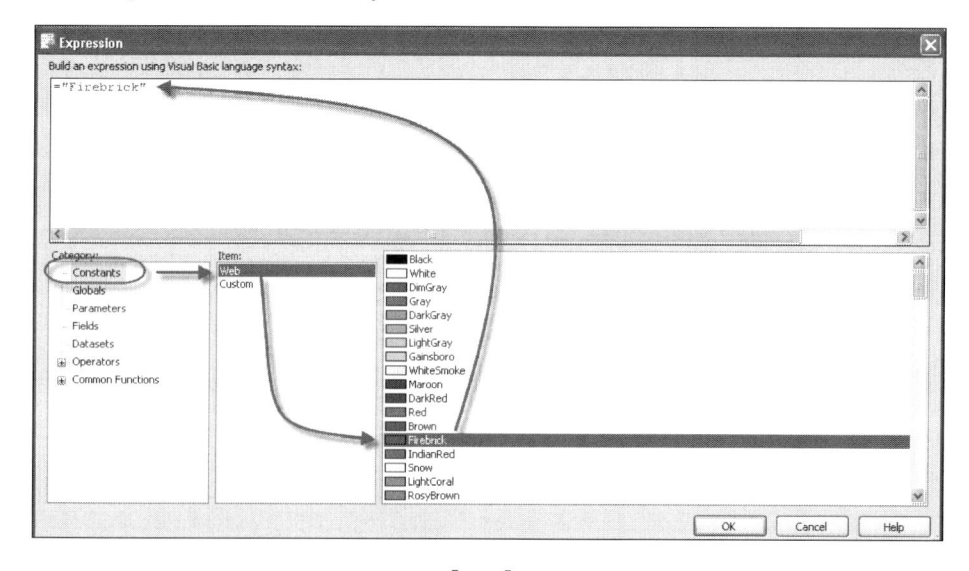

Chapter 4

In the expression designer for a Color property, you could also select the Custom option and so select a color directly from a color chart.

To do this, follow these steps, as demonstrated in the following screenshot:

1. Click on the **Custom** option.
2. Click on the **Edit Colors** button.
3. Select a `Color` in the **color chart**.
4. Click on or select the **Custom Color** in the **Custom colors** boxes.
5. Click on the **Ok** button.
6. The `Color` is now available in the **Color** boxes of the **expression designer**.
7. Double click on this box and the expression for the selected `Color` is now generated in the **expression designer**.

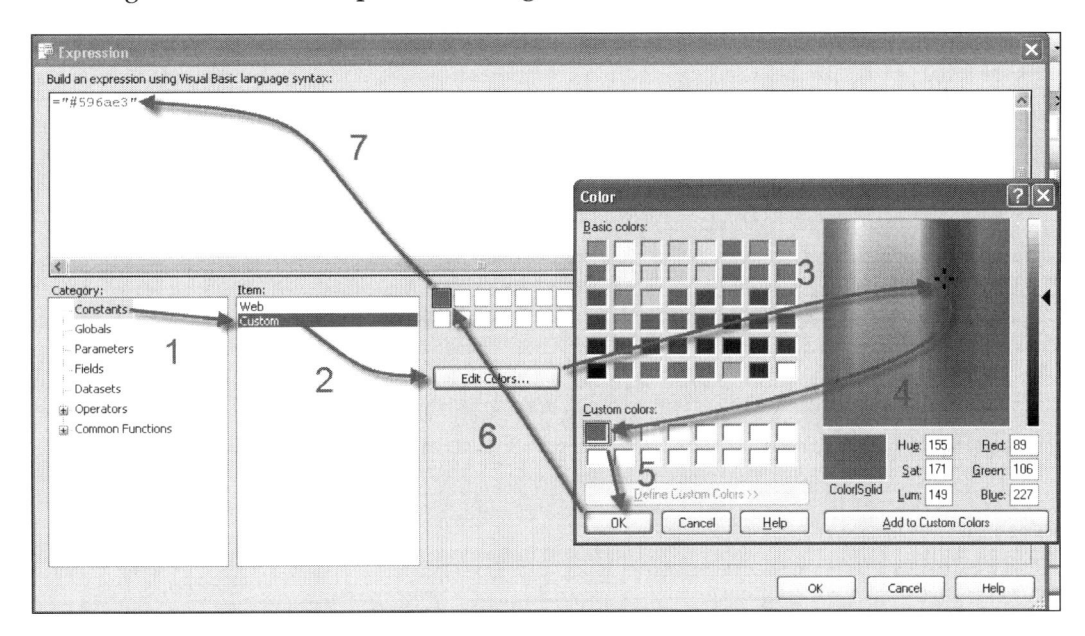

As you can see in the above screenshot, in the **Color** chart window you can also type in the RGB or HSL values instead of picking the color manually.

Visualization Methods

You will have noticed that in a `Color` property, the **Constants** collection on the left side of the expression designer window contains the available colors. This list of constants will always contain the allowed values associated with the property. For example, when you do this in the `FontFamily` property, you will see the following list:

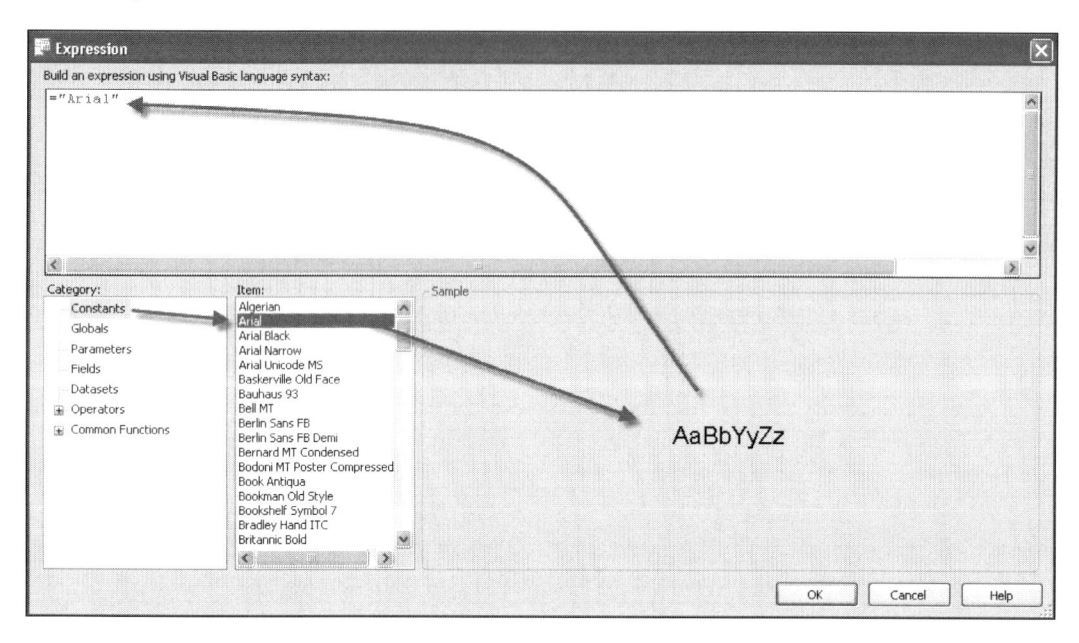

Text box

A text box is used to display text in a report. You can place a text box anywhere in the report and it can contain different values. Actually, a text box will always contain an expression that will result at runtime as the value of the text box.

This expression can contain static text, for example to display labels, it can connect to a field from the dataset and it can be a calculated value.

An example of the expression could be one of the following:

- Static text:
  `="Hello World"`
- The value of the field Salesperson:
  `=Fields!Salesperson.Value`
- The value of the field Quantity multiplied by the value of the field Amount:
  `=Fields!Quantity.Value * Fields!Amount.Value`

- The calculated sum of the field Sales across all rows in the dataset or group:
  `=Sum(Fields!Sales.Value)`

> **Is a text box a data region?**
>
> When you use a list, table, or a matrix, the data region contains text boxes and the text boxes might show information coming out of the dataset. That might be confusing and look like the text box is also a data region.
>
> In the previous chapter in the first report we created, we dragged a field from the dataset onto the body of the report. A text box was created showing only the first value for that field.
>
> Still, the text box control is not a data region, because it doesn't have the capability to repeat itself for rows in the dataset. Also, data regions have a property: Dataset_Name that will connect it to the dataset.
>
> In other words, you can use a text box for a variety of purposes and if you want to display database information in them, you have to use an expression. When you use a text box inside a data region, like for example a list, table, matrix, or chart, then the expression is created automatically when you drag a value in the text box from the dataset.

More information and examples of expressions can be found later in this chapter, in the section called expressions.

List data regions

The definition of a List data region, which can be found in the SQL Server Books Online help, is specified as follows:

> *A list data region repeats with each group or row in the dataset. A list can be used for free-form reports or in conjunction with other data regions. Using Report Designer, you can define lists that contain any number of report items. A list can be nested within another list to provide multiple groupings of data.*

> The SQL Server Books Online can be found here: `http://msdn.microsoft.com/en-us/library/ms130214.aspx`. It is the official documentation from Microsoft about SQL Server.

A list is a free form data region that can contain multiple items, freely arranged, and linked to a dataset. You can arrange report items to create a form, with text boxes, images and other data regions, placed anywhere within the list. A list is like a rectangle that repeats for each row in the dataset, since it's free-form.

Visualization Methods

Free form means that you have complete control or freedom over the positioning of the control. When you design the report, you decide exactly where the control should be on screen. This can be a requirement for reports that need to be printed on pre-printed paper.

Let's have a look at an example of using the List control. The following screenshot is the report that we will develop:

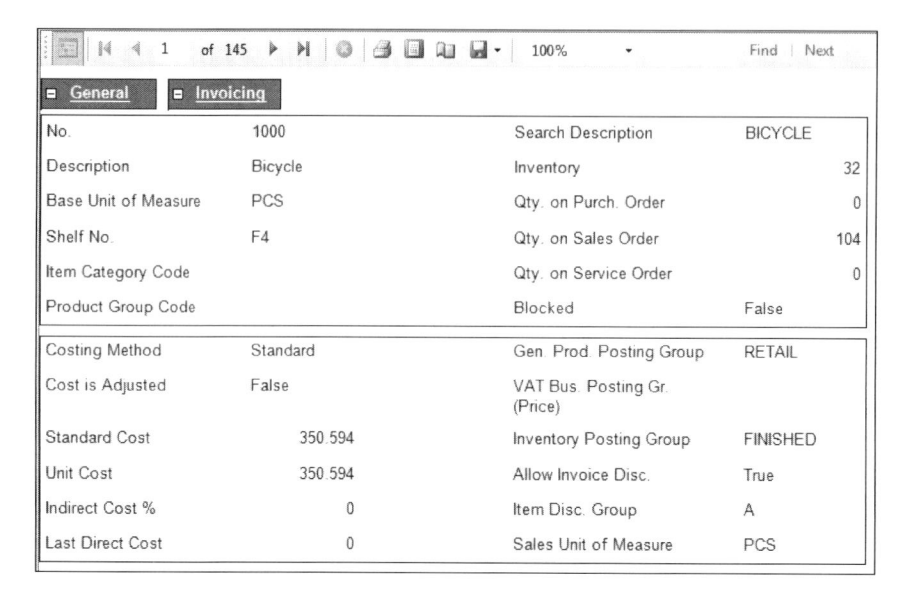

No.	1000	Search Description	BICYCLE
Description	Bicycle	Inventory	32
Base Unit of Measure	PCS	Qty. on Purch. Order	0
Shelf No.	F4	Qty. on Sales Order	104
Item Category Code		Qty. on Service Order	0
Product Group Code		Blocked	False
Costing Method	Standard	Gen. Prod. Posting Group	RETAIL
Cost is Adjusted	False	VAT Bus. Posting Gr. (Price)	
Standard Cost	350.594	Inventory Posting Group	FINISHED
Unit Cost	350.594	Allow Invoice Disc.	True
Indirect Cost %	0	Item Disc. Group	A
Last Direct Cost	0	Sales Unit of Measure	PCS

Presume that we have already created a new report, with a data item: "Item" and some fields on the section(s). We have opened Visual Studio Report Designer and now we drop a List control from the toolbox onto the body of the report as shown in the following screenshot:

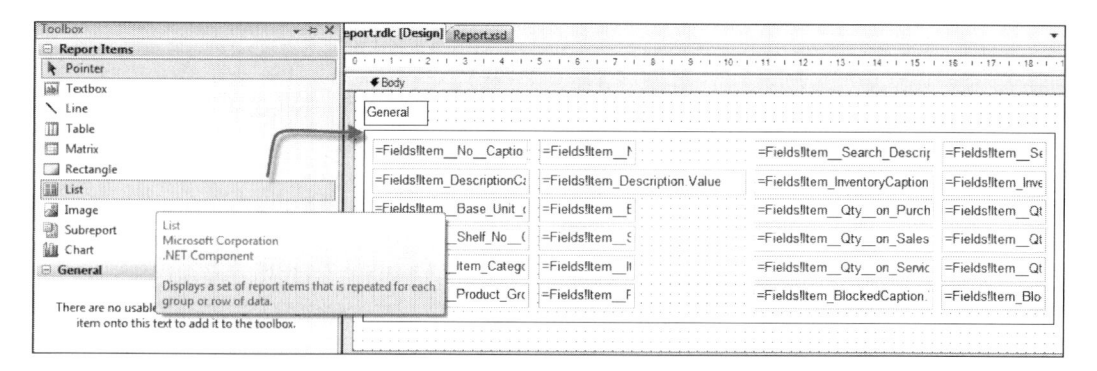

In the list you drag and drop fields from the dataset. For example, use the layout from the screenshot above. To do this, follow these steps:

1. Begin by inserting an empty text box on the **list**, and type in the text General. This text box should be placed inside the list. If it isn't, then the text box will only be visible on the first page of the report.
2. Select a **Rectangle** from the toolbox and add it to the list, below the general text box. The reason why we use a rectangle is for layout purposes. We will give it a Solid border. The rectangle will act as the container for the fields. For every tab, we will use a new rectangle.
3. Select the rectangle, open the property list, and set the BorderStyle, Default property to Solid.
4. Next, add fields from the dataset onto the rectangle. Begin with a caption field and its corresponding value field. You can use the existing **Item Card** page or form as an example.
5. Then, right-click on the List control and open its properties. The following window will open:

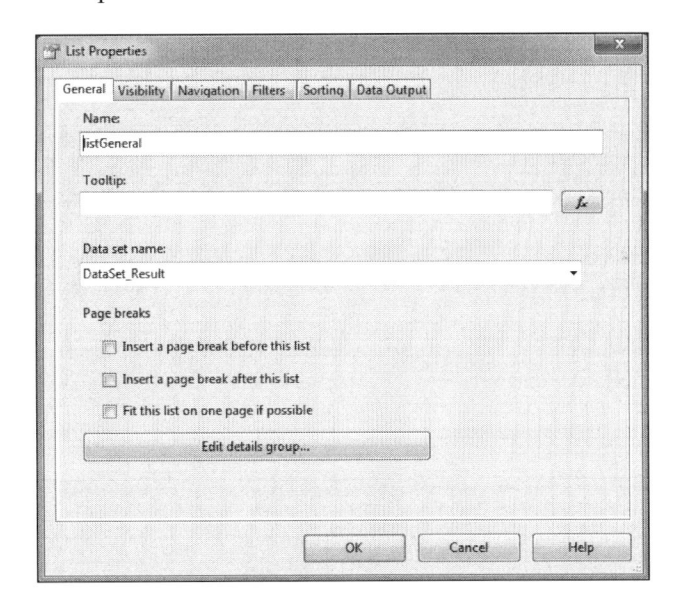

In the **List Properties** window, you might notice the **Data set name** field contains Dataset_Result, which is the dataset of the report. When you add a List control to a report, by default the **Data set name** is empty. You can select one manually via the corresponding dropdown box. When you drag and drop a field from the dataset on the list, the list is automatically connected to the dataset and the property will be filled in by the system.

Visualization Methods

The report that we are creating will show item information and we want to create a page break for every item. To achieve this goal we need to first group the list according to the item number and then generate a page break for every different item.

In the **List Properties** window, click on the **Edit details group** and use the primary key from the table as the grouping expression. In this case, for the Item table, it's the Item Number, as shown in the next screenshot:

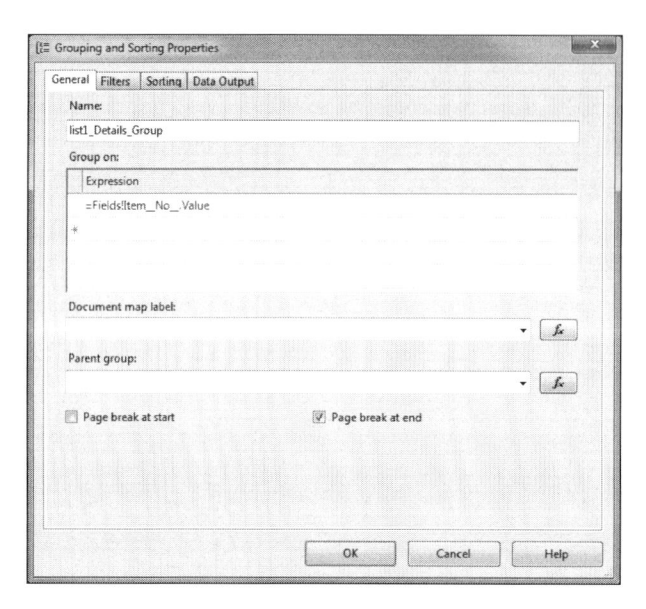

Notice also the checkbox: **Page break at end**. It will make sure that after every record, a new page will start. Then, to further accessorize the report, you can set some additional layout properties like fonts, sizes, foreground colors, background colors, borders, and so on. The final result is now the same as what is shown in the screenshot we started with in the beginning.

It looks a little like the Item Card Form in Dynamics NAV, and that was exactly my intention. A List control is the control to use when building a Card type report.

Let's take this idea to the next level and include another tab from the Item Card Form. This will become the Invoicing tab and will contain invoice related information from the Item table. To do this we will make some changes to our report:

1. First, add the extra fields in the Dataset.
2. Then, in the List, add an extra rectangle control, below the existing rectangle.
3. In the second rectangle, drop the fields you added to the dataset.
4. Above the first rectangle, drag and drop two text boxes

5. Put the text General in the first text box
6. Put the text Invoicing in the second text box
7. Use the Border properties from the rectangle controls to add an outside border to each rectangle.
8. Use the Backgroundcolor and Font properties from the two text boxes to give them a grey background and make them underlined.

> **Borders:**
>
> To add a border to a control you can use the "Report Borders" toolbar, as shown in this screenshot:

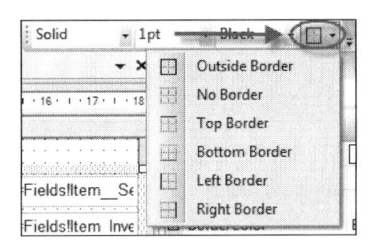

Your report should now look like the following screenshot:

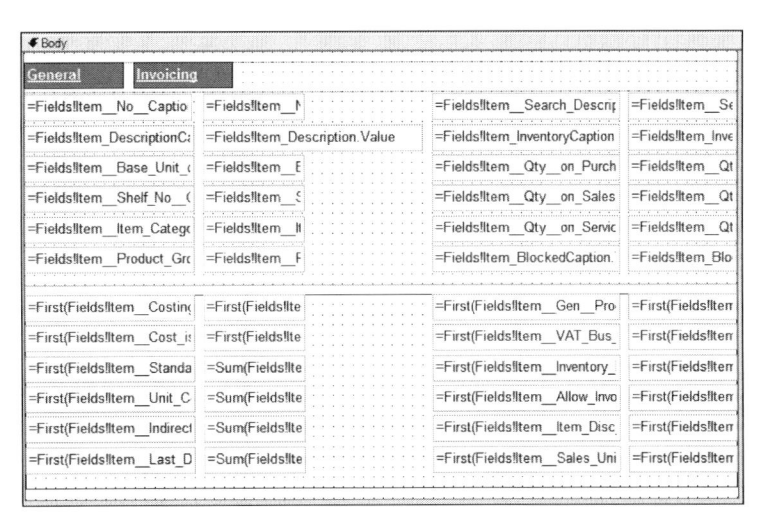

You might notice that when you try this out yourself, some text boxes contain the `First()` or `Sum()` function, around the Fields coming from the dataset. This is because of the grouping of the List control:

- When you add a dataset field onto a list and the list contains no grouping, then the expression will be: `Fields!FieldName.Value`.
- When you add a dataset field onto a list and the list contains a grouping, then the expression will be: `Sum(Fields!FieldName.Value)`, `First(Fields!FieldName.Value)`, or just `Fields!FieldName.Value`, depending on the datatype of the field that you are adding.

The reason for this behavior is the group. When a group is applied to a list and you add a field, the system will aggregate the field according to the scope of the group the field is in. This is very similar in a table where you have a header, detail, and footer level. In this example, we are grouping on the **Item No**, which is the primary key of the table. Because a primary key is unique, every group will have exactly one value and as a consequence the Sum, First, or Field expressions have the same result. If you change the group to a field for which there are multiple values, as for example the costing method field, then `Sum(Fields!FieldName.Value)` will not have the same result as `Fields!FieldName.Value`.

In the screenshot above you can see the different effects in the two rectangles. The first rectangle contained fields before the group was set to the list. On the second rectangle fields were added, after the list was grouped.

> To avoid possible issues you should first apply the grouping to the list, before you put any dataset fields on the list.

To summarize, the following steps give the best results:

1. Add a list to the body of the report.
2. Set the grouping and sorting properties of the list on the Pk of the table and generate a page break for every record.
3. Add a text box onto the list.
4. Add a rectangle onto the list, below the text box and give it a solid border.
5. Add fields (captions and values) from the dataset onto the rectangle.

Following these steps should produce the following report design:

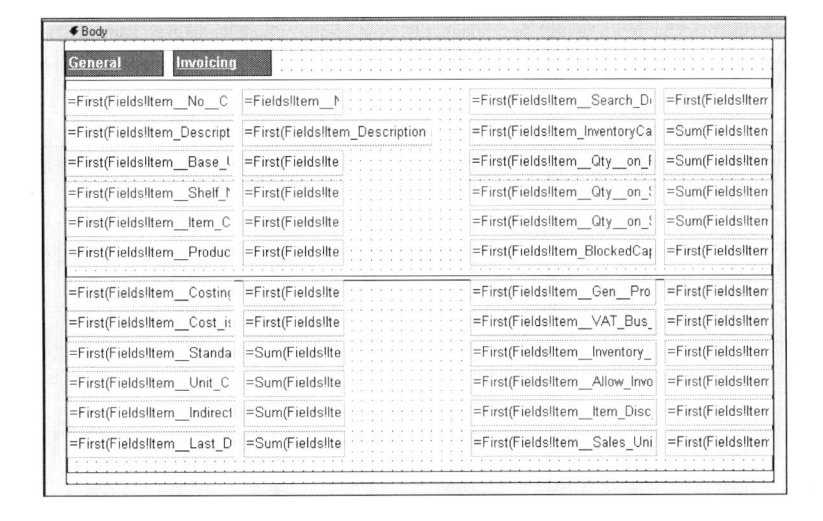

[Report design screenshot showing Body section with General and Invoicing tabs, containing multiple rows of =First(Fields!Item_...) and =Sum(Fields!Item...) expressions arranged in columns]

Now comes the magic trick:

1. Select the rectangle containing the general information and select the `Toggle Item` property. You can find it under the **Visibility** group in the property list. In the dropdown list of the `Toggle Item` properties look for the name of the general text box and select it.
2. Do the same for the other rectangle containing the invoicing information and the invoicing text box.
3. Save the report in Visual Studio.
4. Import the report in the Classic Client.
5. Save the report in the Classic Client.
6. Run the report.

Visualization Methods

This is what you should see:

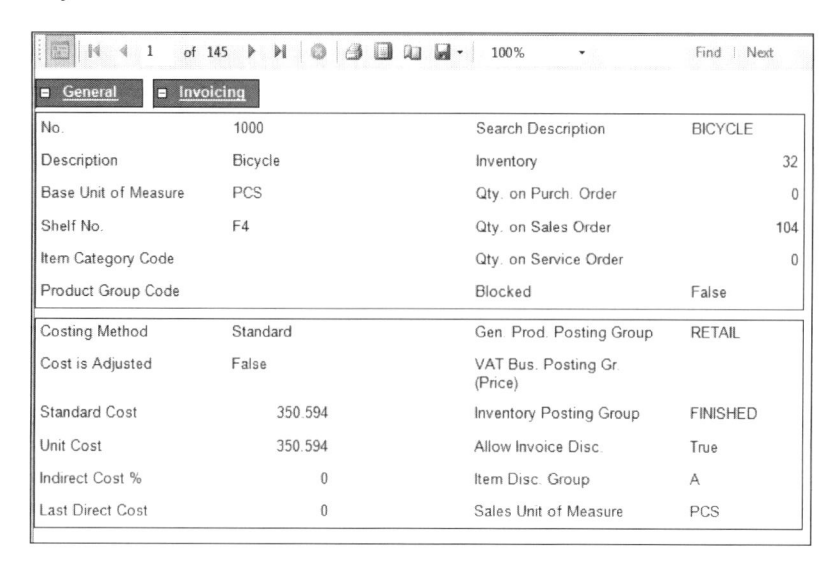

No.	1000	Search Description	BICYCLE
Description	Bicycle	Inventory	32
Base Unit of Measure	PCS	Qty. on Purch. Order	0
Shelf No.	F4	Qty. on Sales Order	104
Item Category Code		Qty. on Service Order	0
Product Group Code		Blocked	False
Costing Method	Standard	Gen. Prod. Posting Group	RETAIL
Cost is Adjusted	False	VAT Bus. Posting Gr. (Price)	
Standard Cost	350.594	Inventory Posting Group	FINISHED
Unit Cost	350.594	Allow Invoice Disc.	True
Indirect Cost %	0	Item Disc. Group	A
Last Direct Cost	0	Sales Unit of Measure	PCS

When you click on + or – before the **Invoicing** text box, then the **Invoicing** rectangle will disappear. When you click on it a second time, the rectangle will appear again, and so on. The same functionality is available for the **General** text box.

Using the `Toggle Item` and `Hidden` property, you can hide any report item, including groups, columns, or rows in a table or matrix. You can hide them from view when the report is rendered in HTML, cause a report item to toggle between visible and hidden when the user clicks on another report item, or hide them based on the contents of other report items.

The primary use of hidden items is to provide a report that shows summary data but also provides a way for the user to drill down into detail data. To create this drilldown effect, select the group, column, or row to hide, set its `Hidden` state to `True`, and then set the `Toggle item` to the name of a text box in a containing group. When the report is rendered, the user can click the text box to expand and collapse the detail data.

> **Note**
>
> Some rendering extensions display hidden items.
>
> Excel rendering extension displays and expands hidden matrix data regions. All rows and columns are visible.
>
> The show-and-hide toggle on report items is supported only by rendering extensions that support user interactivity, such as the HTML rendering extension.

If the value for the `Hidden` property is true, and the `Toggle Item` element is not set, then the report item is not rendered. If Toggle Item is set, the toggle image is displayed next to a toggle item.

You can use the `InitialToggleState` property of the text box selected as a `Toggle Item` to decide the initial visibility state of the toggle image.

When you use a list data region in a report and set a page break at the beginning or end of the group expression, then when you export the report to Excel at runtime, each group will become a separate sheet in Excel. As an example in this report, we grouped the list on **Item No** and set the `Page Break At End` of the group. When you run the report and export to Excel you will see the following:

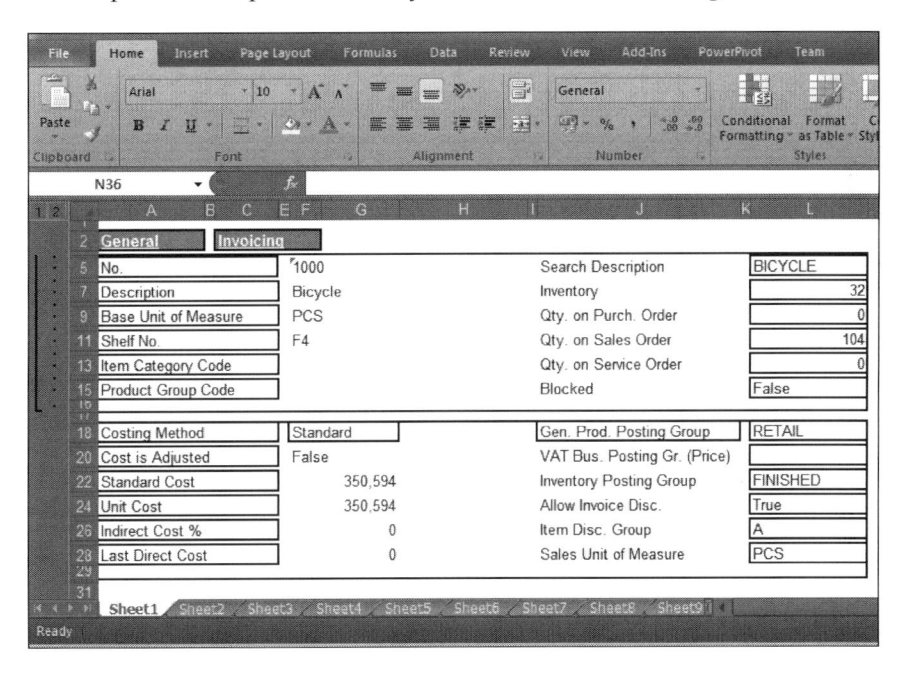

For every item a separate **Sheet** is created. At this moment there's no possibility to define the names of these sheets. In RDL 2008, a new property was introduced: `PageName`, which is available in all data region controls, but this is not yet available for Dynamics NAV enhanced reports.

Document Outline

When developing the list report containing the list, rectangle and text box controls, it's very easy to make mistakes and sometimes very difficult to debug those mistakes. A very useful tool inside Visual Studio can then come in to assist you, the **Document Outline**.

Visualization Methods

To open the **Document Outline**, select the **View** menu, then **Other Windows**, and then **Document Outline** as shown in this screenshot:

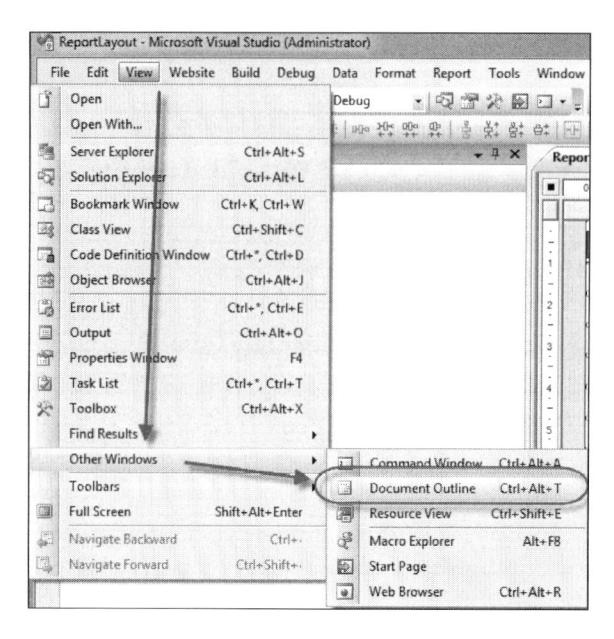

The **Document Outline** window will then appear in the report designer as shown for this report:

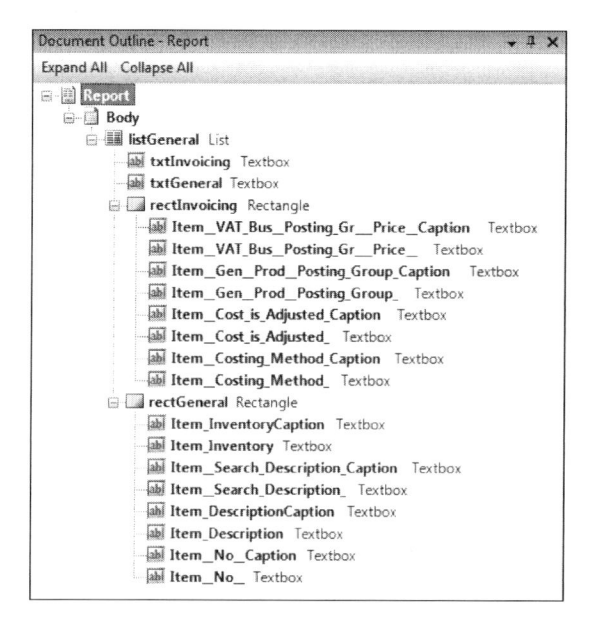

As you can see in the **Document Outline**, the report exists out of a **Body** and **List**. Inside the **List** are two **Rectangles** and inside the rectangles some text boxes.

Not only can you clearly see the **Outline** of the report, you can also access properties of report elements by right-clicking on them, as shown in the next screenshot:

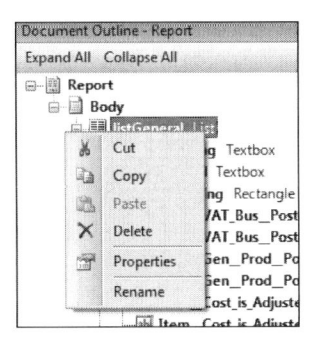

Furthermore, when you select a control in the **Document Outline**, it also gets selected in the report.

Another great use for the Document Outline window is when you nest controls and cannot find them anymore, or cannot select them anymore, or you don't know how it was done. It is also very handy when controls are hidden behind each other. Personally, I think this **Document Outline** is a great help when developing reports for the Role Tailored client.

What is the List control used for?

The list provides you with more flexibility than a table or a matrix. However, it might require more work to obtain the perfect layout using a list, because you don't have columns to help with alignment of data.

Because a list automatically provides a container, you can use a list to display grouped data with multiple views. To change the default list to specify a group, edit the details group, specify a new name, and specify a group expression. Actually, the choice between using a rectangle or a list as a container for other data regions or items comes down to the choice of the ability to have that extra grouping or not.

For example, you can embed a table and a chart that show different views of the same dataset. You can add a group to the list so that the nested report items will repeat once for every group value.

Visualization Methods

Dynamics NAV 2009 uses list containers to help simulate the CopyLoop/PageLoop construction. When a user runs a document report, he or she can select to print multiple copies of the document, via the **Number of Copies** option in the **Request Form/Page**. The body of the report will print x times, x corresponding with the value the user entered in the options tab + 1. To accomplish that in the Visual Studio Report Designer, a List control is used as a parent control for all other controls in the Body. Then, the List is grouped according to an output number variable in the dataset. The technical details on this kind of report development will be covered in the next chapter.

In some reports and in some localizations of Dynamics NAV instead of a list, a table is used. For example, in the standard Sales Invoice and Purchase Invoice reports in the US 2009 R2 localisation, there's no list in the body of the report. Everything in the body is contained in a table data region.

> **Remark**
> To delete a list, right-click any empty space in the list and click **Delete**. Be careful, deleting a list will also delete all objects contained in the list.

Undo/Redo

Whenever you make a mistake in Visual Studio, you have the choice to undo your actions.

In the toolbar, you can use the following buttons to **Undo/Redo**:

In Windows, you will probably alread be familiar with these options and their shortcuts:

- *CTRL + Z* (undo)
- *CTRL + Y* (redo)

Did you know that in Visual Studio, you don't have to keep pressing *CTRL + Z* to go back to one particular action? Using the **Undo/Redo** arrows in the toolbar allows you to **Undo/Redo** multiple actions at once, as shown in the next screenshot:

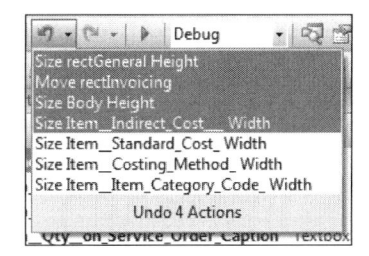

> **Note**
> Be careful when selecting many actions to **Undo**. It can take Visual Studio a long time to refresh the screen. There might even be enough time to have a coffee or two in the meantime.

Matrix boxes

When we already have the table data region that allows us to group the dataset on row level, what would the matrix data region give us as an added value? The answer is: **column groupings**.

Basically, a matrix is like a crosstab or pivot table in Excel. A matrix can have dynamic columns and rows and static columns and rows. A matrix data region in Reporting Services is very much like a matrix control on a form in the Dynamics NAV Classic Client. It's not completely the same. This is the definition of the Matrix control in the Classic Client:

> *A matrix box is a composite control that can show information from several tables at the same time. The first two tables are the vertical and the horizontal table of the matrix box control. In the matrix part of the control, each cell can be used to display information that is calculated on the basis of fields in these two tables, or information that is retrieved from other tables (with values from the first two tables being used to select records, for example by setting filters). Each cell in the matrix is the intersection of a record from the vertical and the horizontal table.*

In Dynamics NAV RDLC there's only one dataset that is generated. In a form combined with a matrix you can have several source tables and connect them in the matrixbox. Just because we only have one dataset, that doesn't mean the data can only come from one table. The data region in RDLC will be bound to this dataset. It is up to the developer to select the correct row and column groups to get the desired result.

Visualization Methods

It was said that when Dynamics NAV 2009 was first released, even before it was released, that on a page object there was no possibility to create matrix like pages. As a workaround it was suggested to create RDLC reports with the matrix data region. Since the release of Dynamics NAV 2009 SP1, a way of creating Matrix like pages was introduced and the workaround via reports was not really required anymore. This being said, I believe the matrix data region has several advantages over the matrix like pages in Dynamics NAV 2009. Let's first have a look at how you can use this matrix.

When you first create a matrix in Report Designer, the matrix displays four cells. The upper-left cell is the corner cell. You can use the corner cell to display a label for the matrix, or you can leave it empty. The upper-right cell is a column header, which can contain a field or expression by which to group the data. The lower-left cell is a row header, which can also contain a field or expression by which to group the data. The lower-right cell contains an aggregate expression for the detail data.

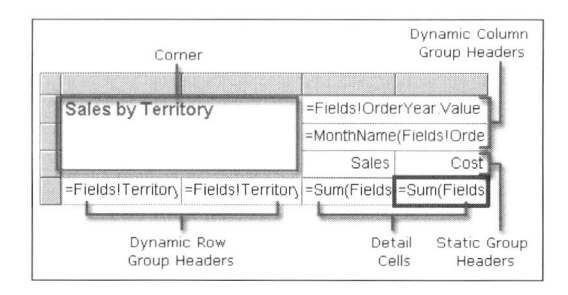

When the report runs, dynamic column headers expand right (or left, if the `Direction` property of the matrix is set to `RTL`) for as many columns as there are groups. Dynamic rows expand down the page. The data that appears in the detail cells are aggregates based on the intersections of columns and rows.

After you add a matrix, you can add fields to the matrix. Each cell in the matrix contains a text box by default. You can type any expression into any cell, or you can change the item within the cell to another item (for example, change a text box in a cell to an image).

As you can see in the following screenshot, to create a new dynamic column that contains an existing dynamic column, you would drag the field to the existing column header, position it so that a bar is displayed on the top border of the header cell, and then drop the field:

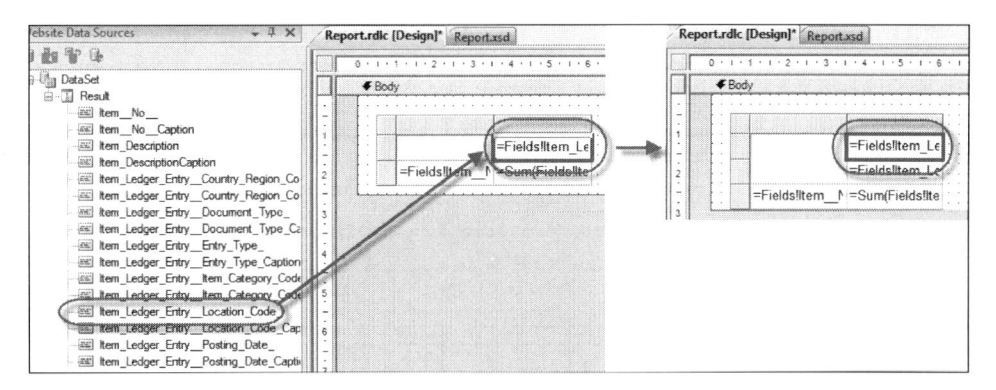

You can also add static rows and columns to display additional detail data. When you add a static column or row, Report Designer divides the header into two, but instead of arranging the headers so that one header resides within the other, each detail cell is displayed side-by-side with headers that contain a static label. For example, a static column or row can be a detail cell with a field for projected revenue, next to another detail cell with a field for the actual revenue:

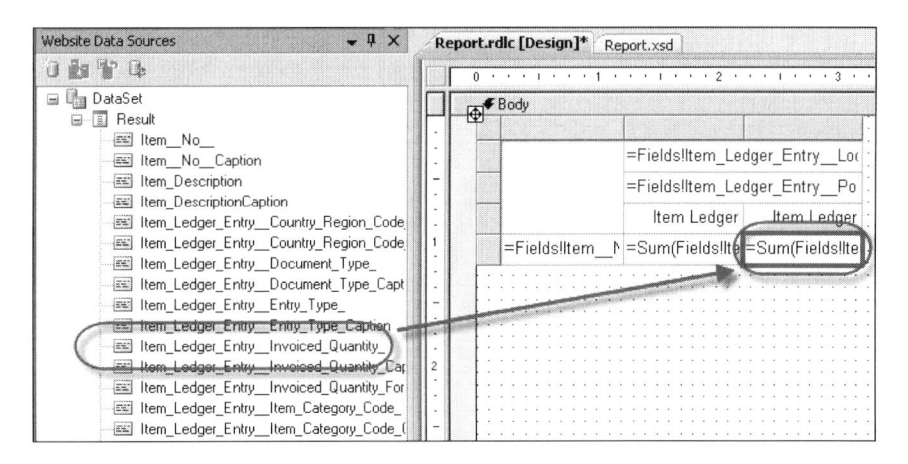

Visualization Methods

To add a subtotal to a matrix, add a subtotal to an individual group within the matrix. Groups do not have subtotals by default. To add a subtotal to a group, right-click the group column or row header and then click **Subtotal**. This will open a new header for the subtotal. Reporting Services will calculate the subtotal based on the aggregate in the data cell for the group.

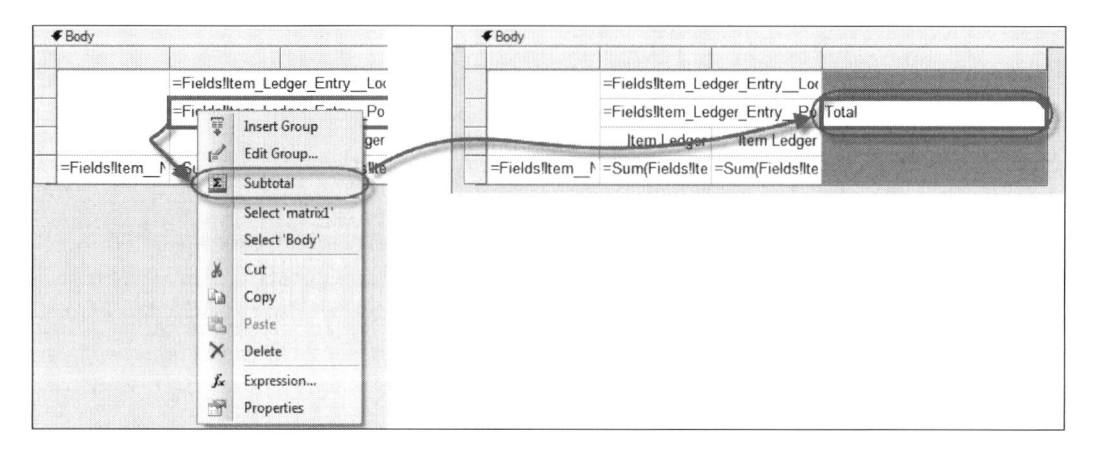

Using the matrix property: `GroupsBeforeRowHeaders`, you can move the row headers between columns, so that columns of data appear before the row headers. The value for this property is an integer; for example, a value of 2 will display two groups of matrix data before displaying the column containing the row headers.

A real world example of a situation when a matrix is the ideal data region might be a report showing item inventory by item and by location in the warehouse. Another example might be the availability of items (projected inventory) by location and over time (period). In the next section about advanced matrix techniques we will be building a matrix report showing the inventory by item and location.

> **Dragging a matrix**
> If you want to move a matrix that is on the body of your report, simply click on the top left corner of the matrix. You will then see an outline that you can click and drag to another location.

More advanced matrix techniques

When using matrix data regions it will sometimes require some workarounds to be able to implement the same kinds of feature that you use on table data regions, like different colors for totals and alternating row colors.

Using colors in a matrix

When you use a table to visualize data, you can see very clearly in the table data region whether the cell is part of the details, header, footer, group, and so on. This is because, for each of these, there are different lines in a table and the row handlers have a different icon for each different level of scope.

In a matrix, this is not the case. In the matrix, in the following screenshot, there's the item inventory, by item number, and location, with subtotals for the location and item groupings:

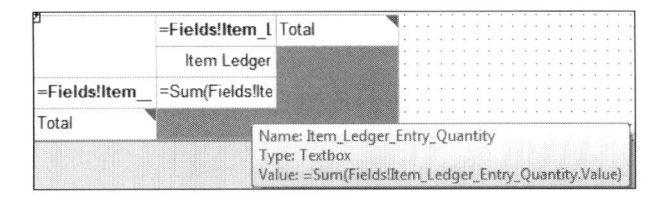

To create the matrix, follow these steps:

1. Create a new report and use the **Item Ledger Entry** table as the data item.
2. On the body of the report, in the section designer, add the fields: **Item No**, **Location Code**, **Quantity**.
3. Go to Visual Studio using **View | Layout** in the menu.
4. Select a matrix in the toolbox and add it onto the body of the report.
5. Select the **Quantity** field from the dataset and drag and drop it in the **Data** cell from the matrix control.
6. Select the **Item No** field from the dataset and drag and drop it in the **Rows** cell left to the **Data** cell.
7. Select the **Location Code** field from the dataset and drag and drop it in the **Columns** cell above the **Data** cell.

Your matrix should now look like the following screenshot:

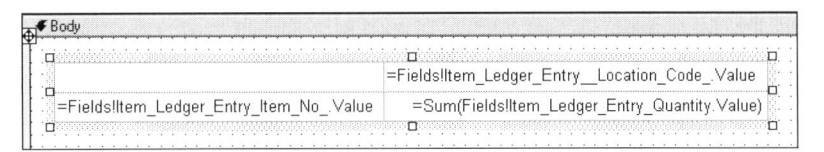

Visualization Methods

To show totals by item and by location, we will now add totals in the matrix. To do this, follow these steps:

1. Right click on the cell at the top right of the matrix. It's the cell with the group on **location code**. In the dropdown that appears, select the option subtotal, as shown in the next screenshot:

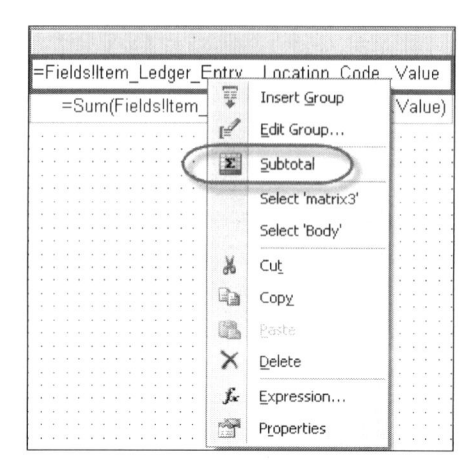

2. Repeat this step for the text box containing the **item no**.

As a result, the matrix will now calculate and show totals. The cells in which the totals will be shown are marked in grey, at design time, and they're disabled.

What do you do if you want the detail cells and group totals to get different background colors at runtime? You could put an expression behind the Backgroundcolor property of the cell, but how to differentiate between details and group levels?

To help you in this scenario you can use the InScope() function. The InScope() function checks to see whether the current item is in the specified scope. As you can see in the next screenshot, every part of a matrix can be given a different color using the following expressions:

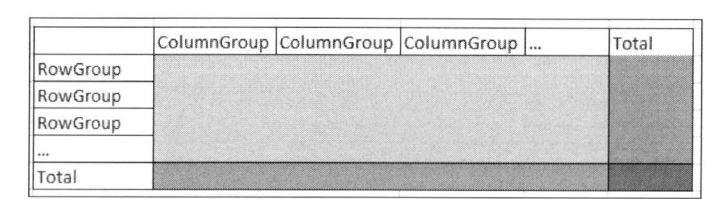

Expression example code:

```
=IIf(InScope("ColumnGroup"),
IIf(InScope("RowGroup"),"LightBlue", "Orange"),
IIf(InScope("RowGroup"),"DarkGreen", "DarkBlue")
)
```

When you try this, the result might be that every cell gets the blue `BackgroundColor`. If that's the case, then you have probably used the wrong group names. Group names are important and must match exactly. In my example, the expression is:

```
=IIf(InScope("matrix3_Item_Ledger_Entry__Location_Code_"),
IIf(InScope("matrix3_Item_Ledger_Entry_Item_No_"),"LightBlue",
"Orange"),IIf(InScope("matrix3_Item_Ledger_Entry_Item_No_
"),"DarkGreen", "DarkBlue"))
```

Because the names of the groups in the matrix are:

```
matrix3_Item_Ledger_Entry__Location_Code_ and matrix3_Item_Ledger_
Entry_Item_No_
```

To solve the problem you can either rename the groups of the matrix corresponding to the expression, or change the expression corresponding to the actual group names. To see the group names, open the properties of the matrix and in the window that opens select the group tab, as shown in the following screenshot:

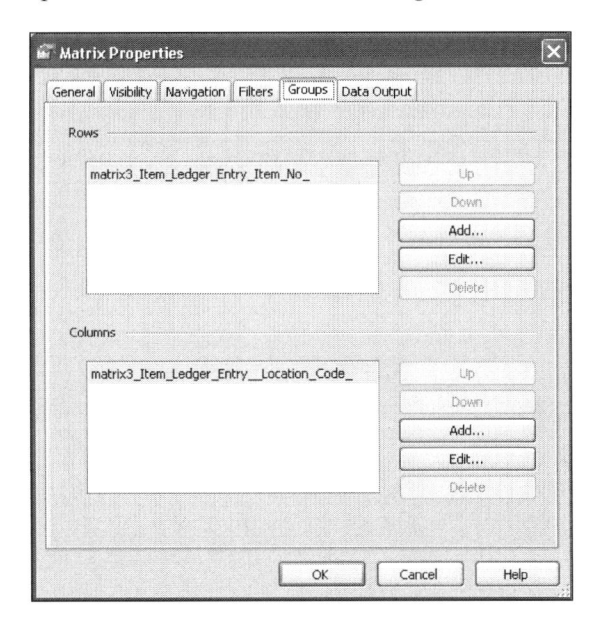

Visualization Methods

Remember:

- Totals for a row fall out of the scope of the column groups
- Totals for a column fall out of scope of the row groups
- The grand total falls out of scope for both row and column groups

Green bar matrix

When we used a table in the previous chapter, there was a very simple way to give a different color to even and uneven rows. We used this expression:

```
=Iif(RowNumber(Nothing) MOD 2,"Limegreen","White")
```

But when you do this in a matrix, for the data cell and then run the report, you will get the following error:

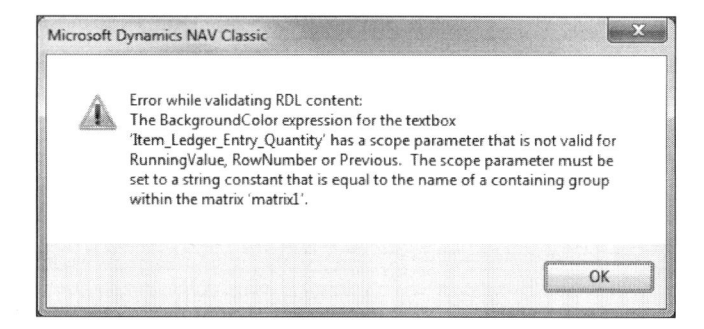

> Microsoft Dynamics NAV Classic
>
> Error while validating RDL content:
> The BackgroundColor expression for the textbox 'Item_Ledger_Entry_Quantity' has a scope parameter that is not valid for RunningValue, RowNumber or Previous. The scope parameter must be set to a string constant that is equal to the name of a containing group within the matrix 'matrix1'.

The error states that you cannot use `Nothing` as the scope for the `RowNumber` function in a matrix. Instead of `Nothing`, you should use the name of one of the groups. Apply this, as shown in the following screenshot:

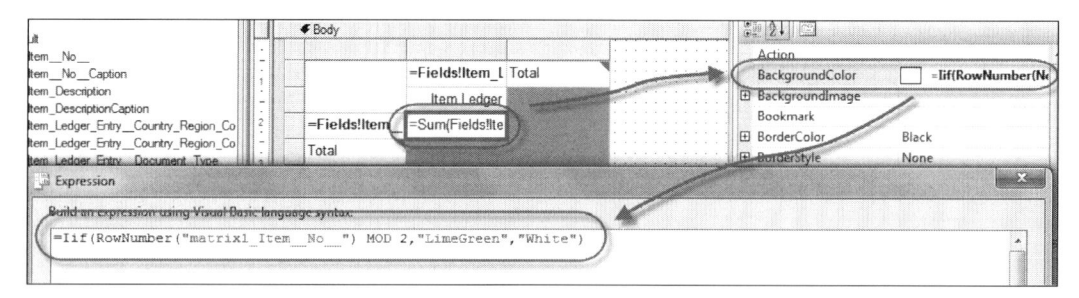

```
=Iif(RowNumber("matrix1_Item__No__") MOD 2,"LimeGreen","White")
```

When you now run the report again, you get this as a result:

	YELLOW	RED	GREEN	OUT. LOG.	BLUE	OWN LOG.	WHITE	Total
	Item Ledger Entry Quantity	Item Ledger Entry Quantity	Item Ledger Entry Quantity	Item Ledger Entry Quantity	Item Ledger Entry Quantity	Item Ledger Entry Quantity	Item Ledger Entry Quantity	Item Ledger Entry Quantity
1984-W	-10		4	3		3		0
1988-S		43		83		41		167
1988-W		13	5	8				26
1992-W			-1	5		6		10
1996-S		116	22	-1		44		181
2000-S			12	17		134		163
70000	2000					2202		4202
70001	2000	15			0	2310		4325
70002		3			0	2508		2511
70003		31			0	2094		2425
70010	25					2270		2295
70011			-1			2212		2211
70040						2221		2221
70041						2024		2024
70060			249			583		832
70100						3641		3641
70101						3718		3718
70102			-1			3231		3230

There is currently no `GroupNumber()` function on which to base a green-bar calculation in a matrix.

`GroupNumber` can be (mostly) simulated by using the `RunningValue` function to get a running distinct count of group expression values. However, the trickiest part of green-bar in a matrix is the fact that some matrix cells may contain no data at all. This makes the group number calculation incorrect for empty cells.

To work around this, you need to effectively calculate the group number in the row header and then use that value inside the data cells.

There are several ways to do this, for example by using a fake inner row grouping or by using a rectangle in the row group.

I will show you the workaround with the rectangle, because it is a good example of the usage of a rectangle in a report, so you might also be able to use this trick on other kinds of reports.

> **Note**
>
> There's a blog from Chris Hays that explains how to do this using a fake inner row which can be found here: http://blogs.msdn.com/b/chrishays/archive/2004/08/30/greenbarmatrix.aspx

Visualization Methods

This is what we need to do:

1. Drag and drop the rectangle from the toolbox onto the body of the report.
2. Drag and drop a text box from the toolbox, into the rectangle.
3. Drag and drop another text box from the toolbox into the rectangle.
4. Change the Name property of the second text box to Color.

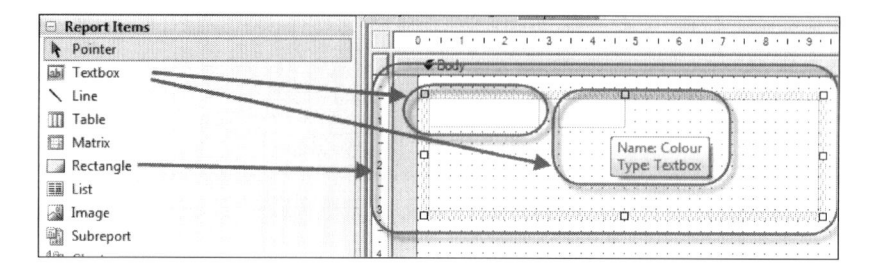

5. Rearrange and resize the two text boxes so that they are behind each other in the rectangle.
6. Then resize the rectangle's height and make it the same as the height of the text boxes.

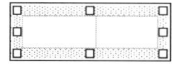

7. Cut and paste the rectangle onto the row group level in the matrix.
8. Drop the dataset field on which to group, into the text box inside the rectangle.

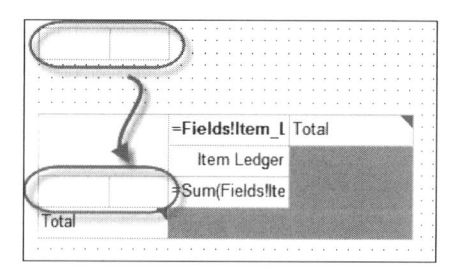

9. Select the text box named Color in the rectangle and change its Value expression to this:

    =Iif(RunningValue(Fields!Item__No__.Value,CountDistinct,Nothing) Mod 2,"Khaki","LemonChiffon")

10. Set the Hidden property as True for the Color text box.

11. Select the text box containing the data and put this expression in its `BackGoundColor` property:

    `=ReportItems!Color.Value`

12. Save/Import/Save & Run the Report:

	YELLOW	RED	GREEN	OUT. LOG.	BLUE	OWN LOG.	WHITE	Total
	Item Ledger Entry Quantity	Item Ledger Entry Quantity	Item Ledger Entry Quantity	Item Ledger Entry Quantity	Item Ledger Entry Quantity	Item Ledger Entry Quantity	Item Ledger Entry Quantity	Item Ledger Entry Quantity
1988-S		43		83		41		167
1988-W		13	5	8				26
1992-W			-1	5		6		10
1996-S		116	22	-1		44		181
2000-S			12	17		134		163
70000	2000					2202		4202
70001	2000	15			0	2310		4325
70002		3			0	2508		2511
70003	300	31			0	2094		2425
70010	25					2270		2295
70011		-1				2212		2211
70040						2221		2221
70041						2024		2024
70060		249				583		832

The technique of putting multiple text boxes in a rectangle and then cutting/pasting the rectangle into a matrix is frequently called the **cells-in-cells** technique.

> A good place to have a look for some advanced matrix reporting techniques would be this blog: `http://www.simple-talk.com/sql/reporting-services/advanced-matrix-reporting-techniques`. It contains some interesting workarounds for RDL reports that might be useful when developing Dynamics NAV enhanced reports.

Chart data regions

A chart is a data region, similar to a table and matrix, but the data is presented graphically. This makes it easier to spot trends and variances just by looking at the chart. It is the ideal control to visualize data in a report. You could for example use or embed a chart in another report item to format data to help the user visualize amounts in a report.

When you click on the chart, Report Designer displays three drop zones, one for each of these areas. You can drag fields from the fields list onto each of these drop zones.

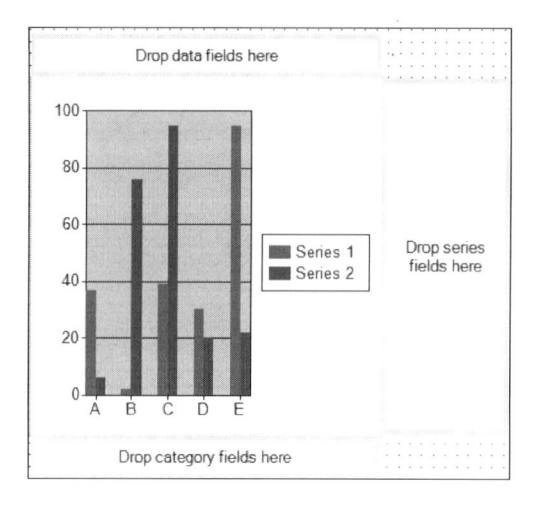

Chart areas are similar to groups in a matrix:

- A chart category group is equivalent to a matrix column group
- A chart series group is equivalent to a matrix row group
- A chart value is equivalent to a static matrix row group
- A chart data value or data point is equivalent to a matrix cell

When you add a chart to the report, it must contain at least one value. The data is shown as data points in the chart and colors, markers, formats, labels, and symbols; 3-d effects can be used. As like in the matrix, a chart has no detailed level of data.

Reporting Services supports the following chart types: column, bar, line, pie, scatter, bubble, area, doughnut, and stock. Once the chart region is placed on the report canvas, you can change the chart type by right-clicking on it and using the context menu or by selecting the **General** tab in the **Chart Properties** dialog box, as shown in the next screenshot:

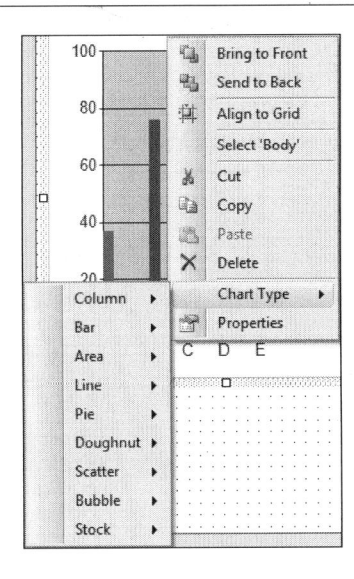

The following table describes the different chart types and subtypes:

Chart Type	SubType	Description
Column, Bar, Area	"Simple"::Plain, Stacked, "100% Stacked"::PercentStacked	Best suited for comparing groups of series such as territories.
Line	"Simple"::Plain, Smooth	Best suited for data where time is shown on the X-axis.
Pie, Dougnut	"Simple"::Plain, Exploded	Shows percentage of whole fractional relationships.
Scatter	"Simple"::Plain, Line, Smooth	For plotting points to show data distribution. Plots points by specifying both X and Y coordinates.
Bubble	Plain	To plot point by specifying both X and Y coordinates and size of the plotted point.
Stock	HighLowCloseOpen, HighLowClose, Candlestick	Best suited for stock charts showing highs, lows, and change in value over time.

In Chapter 5, *Developing Specific Reports*, I will provide some examples of how to use a chart inside a report and how it can be manipulated to visualize information in different ways.

Adding images to your report

When you use the Visual Studio Report Designer for creating reports for the RoleTailored client, you can add images such as your company logo to a report.

Basically, images are independent report items. Of course, an image can link to fields from the dataset, a URL, or a file. Different image types are supported such as: bmp, gif, jpg, png, and so on.

To add an image to a report, select the image control in the toolbox and drop it onto the report. An empty image will be shown, as you can see here:

Then, go to the property list of the image control.

> **Tip**
> For image controls, it's better to use the property list instead of the property popup. This is because the property popup doesn't contain all the properties that we need to set to be able to show an image.

There are three properties you need to set for the image:

- MIMEType
- Source
- Value

The `MIMEType` identifies the Multipurpose Internet Mail Extensions (MIME) type of the image. The following values are valid for the `MIMEType` element:

- image/bmp
- image/jpeg
- image/gif
- image/png
- image/x-png

`MIMEType` is required if the `Source` is `Database`. If the value of `Source` is not `Database`, `MIMEType` is ignored.

Source indicates the source of the image specified in the `Value` element and can contain one of the following values:

- External:
  The image is stored on a server and can be accessed via a relative path (URI).
- Embedded:
  The image is embedded in the report and is accessed via its name.
- Database:
  The image is coming out of the dataset, for example a BLOB field.

With an external image, the source file is stored outside of the report in a location that must be accessible from the Role Tailored client, such as on a file server or local computer. The image is referenced from the report and loads when the report opens. To use external images on a report, the `EnableExternalImages` property must be set to Yes.

> **The `EnableExternalImages` property**
>
> This is a report property in the classic designer that sets whether external images are allowed on a report.
>
> The `EnableExternalImages` property exposes the `LocalReport.EnableExternalImages` property of the `Microsoft.ReportViewer.WebForms.LocalReport` object, which is embedded in Microsoft Dynamics NAV 2009. This object is part of the **ReportViewer** control that is available in Visual Studio for adding reports to your application.

> **Note**
>
> When you use external images, you should be sure the image is safe. Because there's no control, it could potentially be a malicious image. To avoid that, by default the `EnableExternalImages` property is set to false. Also important to remember is that you have no control over what happens to an external image. If the URI is not available or the external machine/server cannot be accessed, then your image will not show up or might cause a runtime error to occur.

Let's make an example and add the company logo to the header of a report. The report contains a list of Items, the header will contain the company logo as an embedded image and the body will contain a table with the item information. We will also display the item picture in the table.

Visualization Methods

Let's start by embedding the company logo in the report. You can do this using the `Report, Embedded Images` menu. A window opens which allows you to import an image by clicking on the **New Image** button:

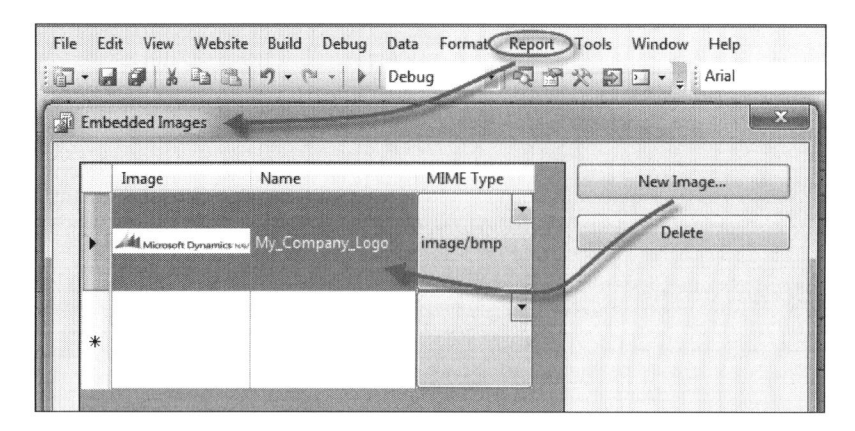

Now that the company logo is embedded in the report, you can add an image control to the header of the report, and set its data properties as in the following screenshot:

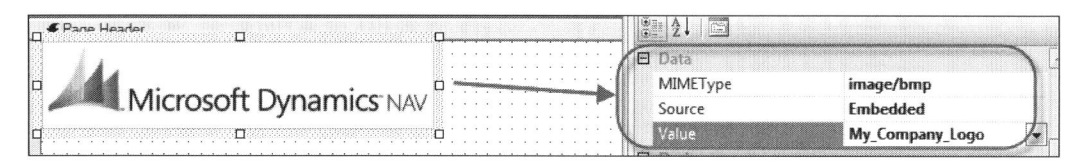

Notice that as soon as you select the `Value` for the embedded image that the image refreshes and the logo appears.

Now it's time to add the item picture in the table. Do this by selecting an image control in the toolbox and dropping it on the text box in the table. Next, set the properties of the image as displayed in the following screenshot:

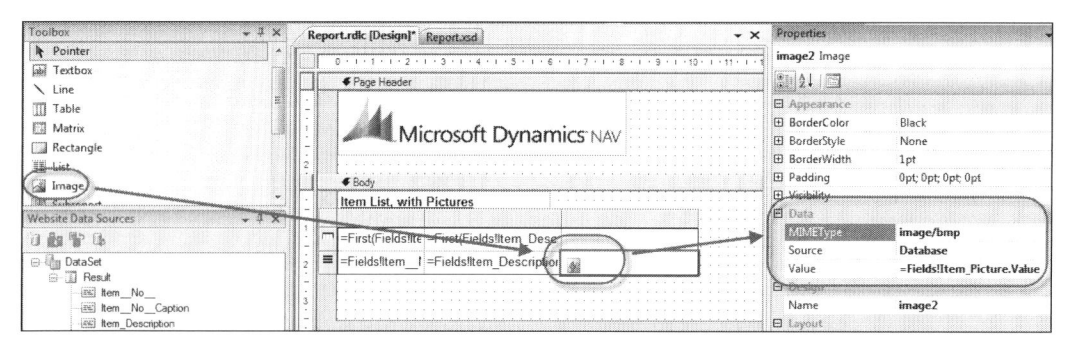

[166]

When you run the report, this is the result:

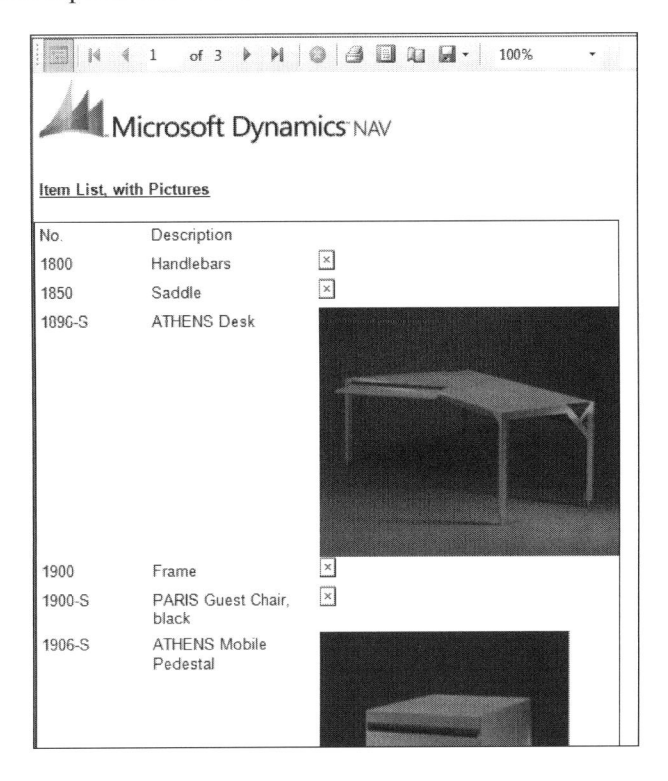

As you might notice, the items that do not have a picture are shown with a red x. It is better not to display these red crosses and instead hide the image when there's no value. You can do this by using the following expression in the `Hidden` property of the image:

```
=Iif(Len(Convert.ToBase64String(Fields!Item_Picture.Value)) > 0,
False,True)
```

Visualization Methods

The result will then be as follows:

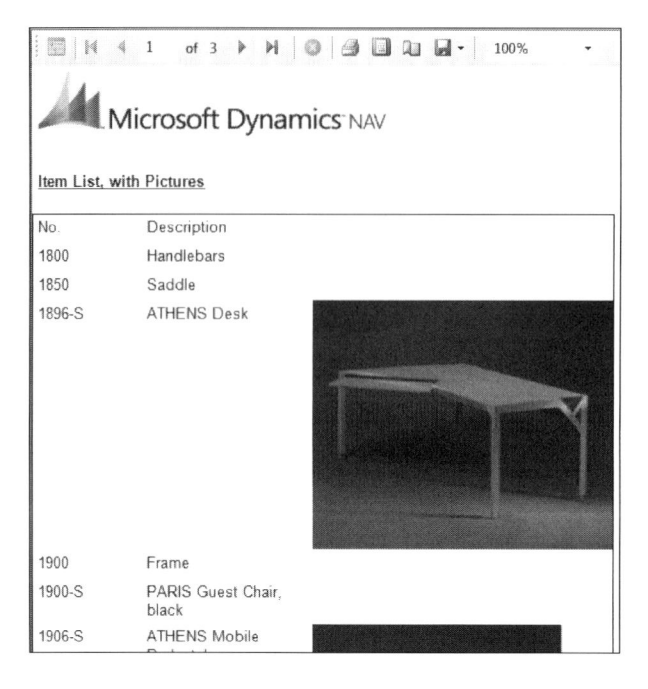

To further fine-tune the layout of the report, I suggest using the `Sizing` property of the image. The `Sizing` property of the image has the following possible values:

- `AutoSize`: Grows or shrinks borders of the image item to fit the image
- `Fit`: Resizes the image to match the height and width of the Image element
- `FitProportional`: Resizes the image to match the height and width of the image element, preserving the aspect ratio
- `Clip`: Clips the image to fit the height and width of the image element

You can use this property to determine the appearance of the image when it does not conform to the specified size.

Expanding/collapsing report sections

In RDLC reporting, you can control the visible (or should I say hidden) properties of any control in a report. This feature can help you create so called drill down reports.

A drill-down report is an interactive report that allows you to expand and collapse sections of the report to display information when desired.

By using dynamic visibility, you can create a report that enables the user to show or hide the detail it contains. You can hide any report item based on the contents of other report items including groups, columns, or rows in a table or matrix.

Hidden report items enable the user to toggle between summary and detail views ("drilling down"). When the report is rendered, the user can click the text box to expand and collapse the detail data.

Follow these steps in Report Designer to create this drill-down effect:

1. Select the group, column, or row to hide.
2. Set its hidden state to True.
3. Set the toggle item to the name of a text box in a containing group.

Depending on the rendering format chosen, hidden items may or may not be shown in the report. For example, when rendering reports in the Report Viewer, Hypertext Markup Language (HTML) will render show-and-hide toggles on report items and not render hidden items, whereas when you export the report to PDF, it will not render hidden report items.

> **Note**
> The value for toggle item must be the name of a text box that is either in the same group as the item that is being hidden or in another group or item in the same grouping hierarchy.

As an example, let's add a drill-down to the report we created in the chapter *Creating Role Tailored reports*. The report contained a customer data item and displayed the list of customers in a table, grouped by salesperson, as you can see in the following screenshot:

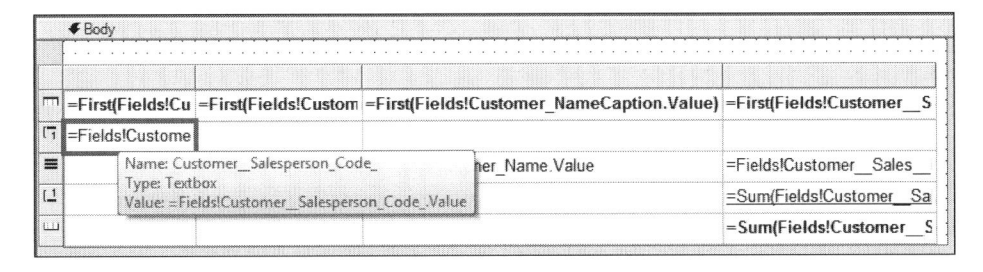

Follow these steps to add a drilldown to the report:

1. Right-click on the table handler to open the table properties window.
2. Click on the **Groups** tab.

Visualization Methods

3. Click on **Details Grouping.**
4. In the window that opens, click on the **Visibility** tab.
5. Select **Initial visibility | Hidden**.
6. Select the option: **Visibility can be toggled by another report item**.
7. In the dropdown, select the text box that contains the **Salesperson Code** field as the toggle item, as shown in the next screenshot:

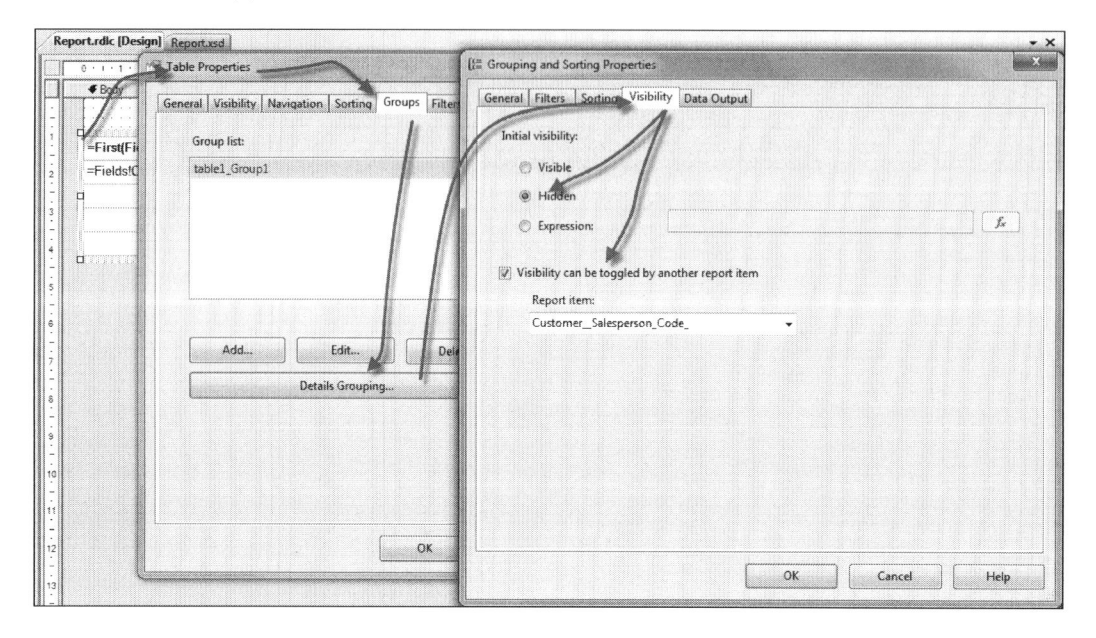

When you run the report, it will display a toggle icon in the **Salesperson Code** text box, which you can use to toggle the details, as shown in the next screenshot:

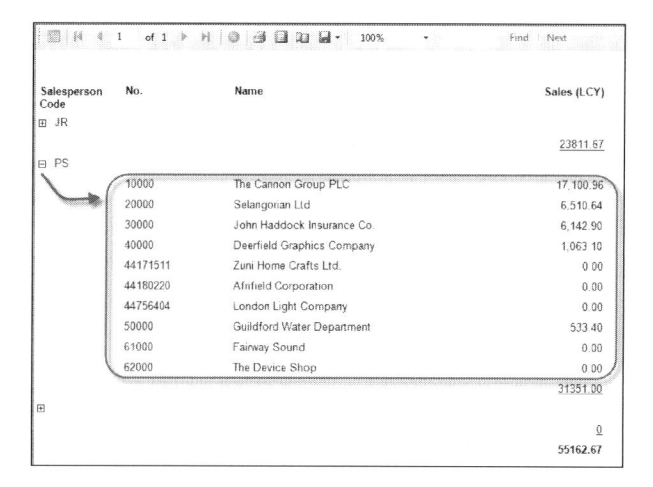

> **Exporting to Excel**
> When you export a report that has expand/collapse to Excel, then the expand/collapse will also work in Excel. The system will create groupings in Excel for every level of expand/collapse and you can expand/collapse them all at once or one by one.

Interactive sorting

You can give the user the possibility to change the sorting on reports at runtime. This is achieved via properties on column headings to provide interactive sorting in a report. You can specify sorting for multiple columns in the same table, list, or matrix, and for nested or grouped data.

To specify interactive sorting:

1. Right-click a column heading (for example, a column in a table header), and select **Properties** to open the Text box Properties dialog box.
2. Click on the **Interactive Sort** tab.
3. Select **Add an interactive sort action to this text box**.
4. To specify a sort expression, select the field that corresponds to the column for which you are defining a sort action (for example, for a column heading named "Title", choose =Fields!Title.Value). Specifying a sort expression is required.
5. Select the data region and scope for the sort. This step determines whether the sort action applies to all of the data regions in a report, is limited to the data region that contains the text box, or is scoped to some other set of data regions that you choose.
6. Click **OK**.

Visualization Methods

To verify the sort action, you can run the report. Columns that support interactive sorting have arrow icons to indicate sort order. To toggle the sort order between ascending and descending, click the column heading:

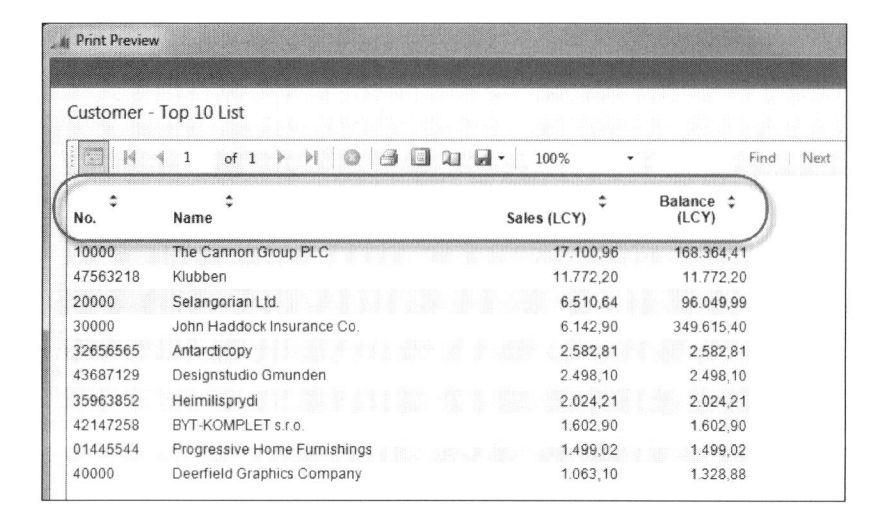

> **Tip**
> It seems that, in order to display the interactive sort button in reporting services, your table column must be at least `0.375`in wide. If it's any smaller, the button will not display.

Using the document map

Another way to provide user interaction in a report is by using a document map. A document map will present itself as a table of contents next to the report. Users can click on an entry in the document map, and the report will jump to that record in the report.

To create a document map, you have to associate a document map label to a text box in the report. To do this, right-click the text box and open its properties. Select the navigation tab. In there you will see a **Document map label** property:

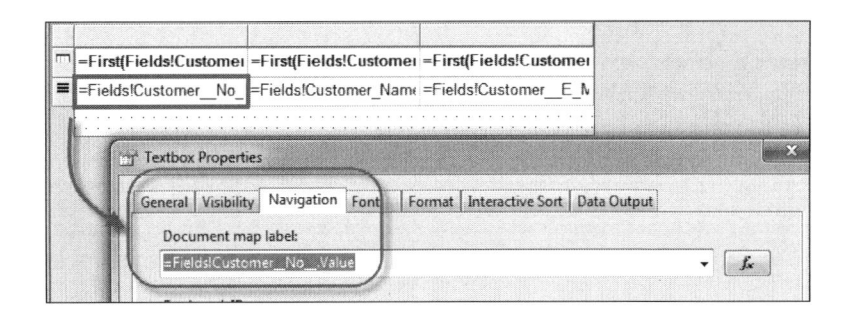

Use it to select a label, or an expression, to become the label. This value will then become a value in the document map:

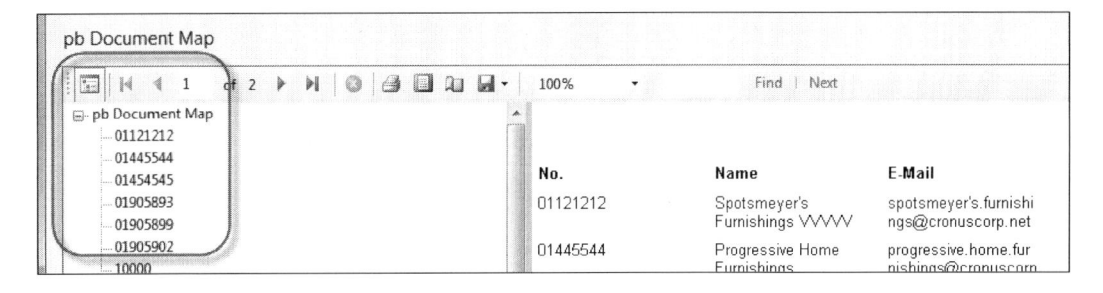

Let's make it a little bit more interesting and add a couple of groups to the table. Let's group by **Country**, **City**, and **Salesperson**. Wouldn't it be great to be able to also add these groups in the document map?

Well, if you simply apply the same technique to the text boxes that show the group headers, this will become the result:

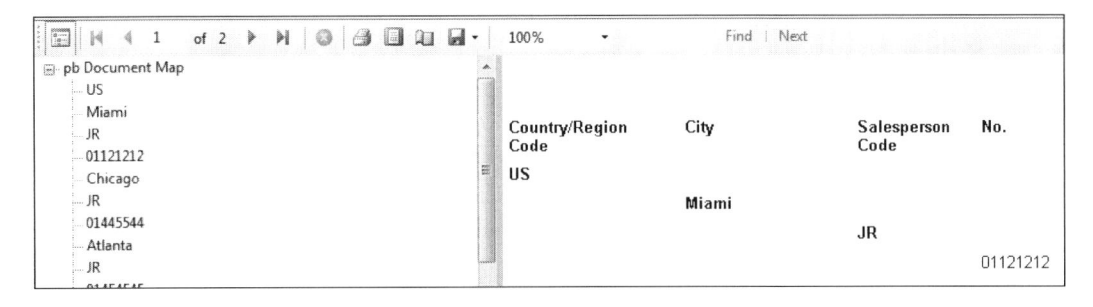

The group header fields **Country**, **City**, and **Salesperson Code** are now also shown in the document map, but it's not very user friendly to read.

Visualization Methods

Instead of applying the same technique to the text boxes of the **Country**, **City**, and **Salesperson Code**, remove the document map label and use the group property window instead. There you will see, in the property window of each group, the **Document map label** as is the next screenshot:

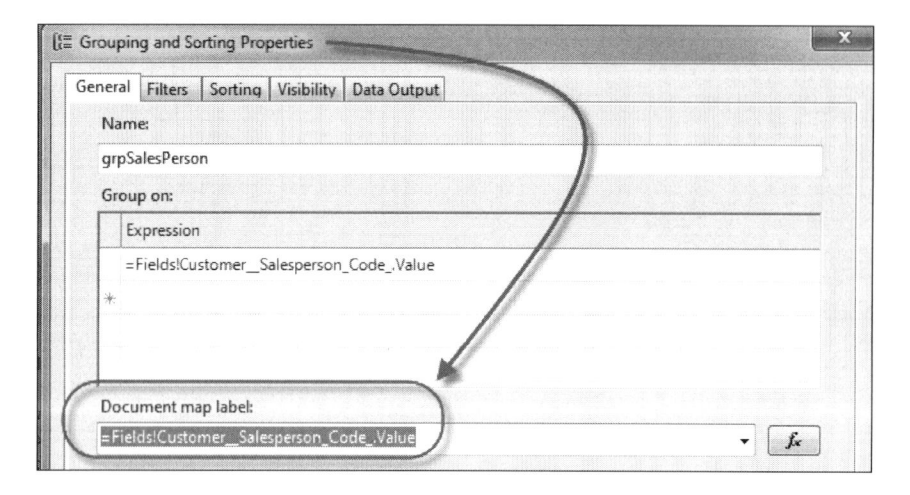

If you use that property in all three groups to generate the **Document map label**, then the report will look like this at runtime:

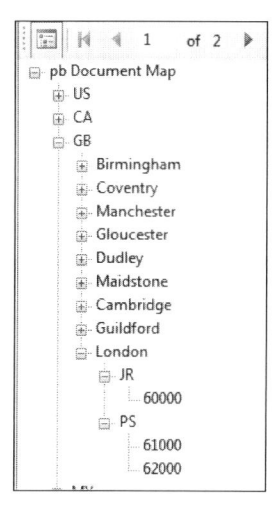

As you can see, the document map is now properly indented according to the groups and their corresponding levels, which is much more user friendly. Furthermore, when you run this report and export it to Excel, then in Excel you will get two sheets. The first one will contain the document map. Each item in the document map is a link to a record on the second worksheet, which contains the data of the report.

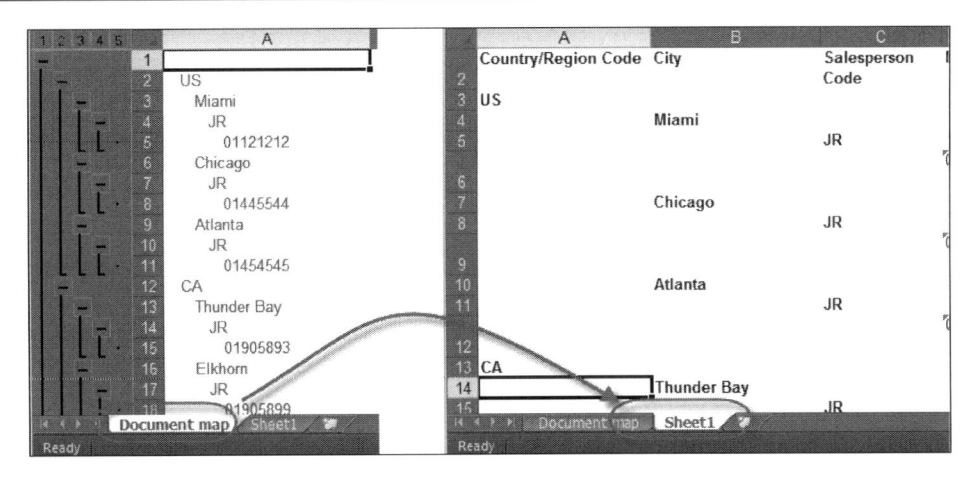

Of course, the document map will also be available in the PDF output format.

Linking reports

Linking a report to another report or to a page can provide a very big added value to a report. It allows for a deeper integration with the Role Tailored client and also other applications your customer might be using. Instead of them having to search for related information the report will be connected to all related information, independently where it is stored. Adding links in enhanced reports is very easy and is available on report items and in data regions. You could for example also make a link between the report and a SharePoint environment. This allows for the creation of connected dashboards.

When you add a link to a text box, image, or chart element, you can specify one of two types of links:

- A link to a URL provides a link to a web page, typically outside the report
- A bookmark link provides a link to a bookmark, or anchor, within the current report

Visualization Methods

You can see this when you open the property window of a text box and click on the **Navigation** tab, as shown in the following screenshot:

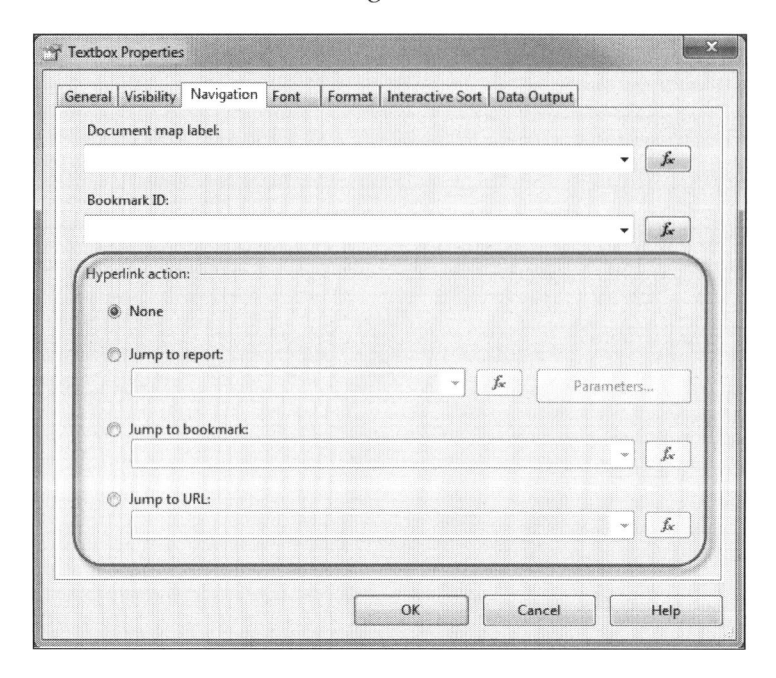

In Reporting Services, there's also a third kind of link, a drill through link that gives you the possibility to link to another report on the Report Server. In the screenshot above, it is the option: **Jump to report**.

Because Dynamics NAV RDLC works in another way, it is currently not possible to make use of this type of link. Maybe in a future release this might become an option. But, actually, we don't really need this, because you can make use of the URL link type to link towards another report or even a page object in Dynamics NAV. I will provide you with an example of this kind of link and how to construct it in a few moments. First, let's have a look at bookmark links.

Bookmark links

Bookmark links allow users to move to another area or page in a report by clicking on it. To create a bookmark, set a bookmark on the destination report item and add bookmark links on report items that users should click, such as a word or button, to jump to the bookmarked report item. You can set bookmarks on any report item, but you can only add bookmark links to text boxes and images.

The `Bookmark ID` can be any string, but it must be unique in the report. If the `Bookmark ID` is not unique, a link to the `Bookmark ID` will find the first matching bookmark.

For example, when you have a report containing data that will be spread out on many pages, you might want to use bookmark links to create navigation inside of the report.

In the following example, we have a report that contains a list of contacts. After the table that contains the contacts there are two charts. To make it easier for the user who runs the report to navigate directly to the charts in the report, two text boxes have been added. The first text box, **View Chart**, is positioned before the table and the second text box, **Back to Top**, is positioned after the table and before the charts. The idea is that when the user clicks on **View Chart(s)** he will be redirected to the charts. When he clicks on the text box **Back to Top** he will be redirected to the beginning of the report.

This is a screenshot of the report at runtime:

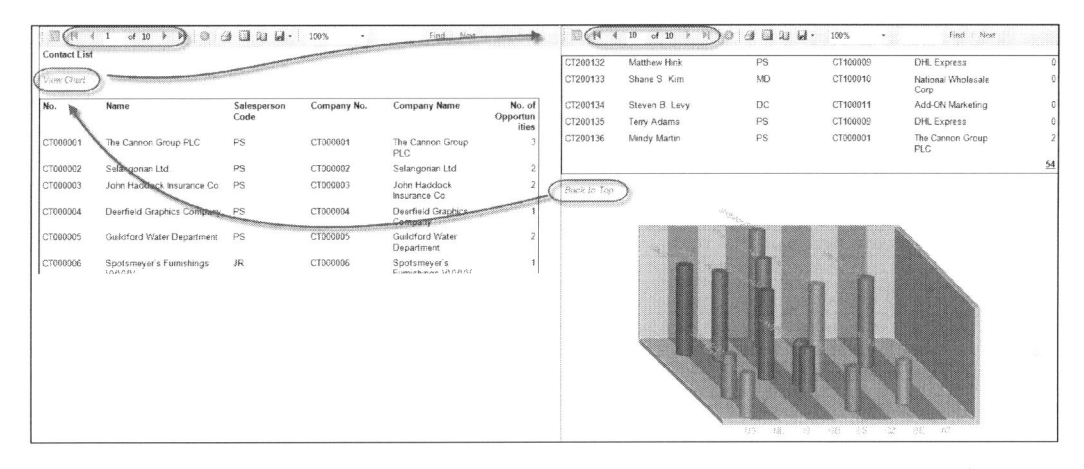

Visualization Methods

To do this, you need to put the following properties in the **Navigation** tab of the first text box.

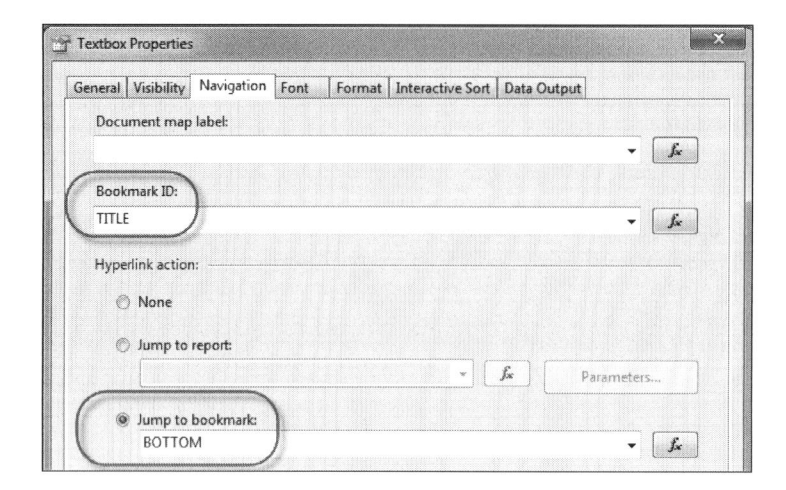

And then you put the following properties in the second text box:

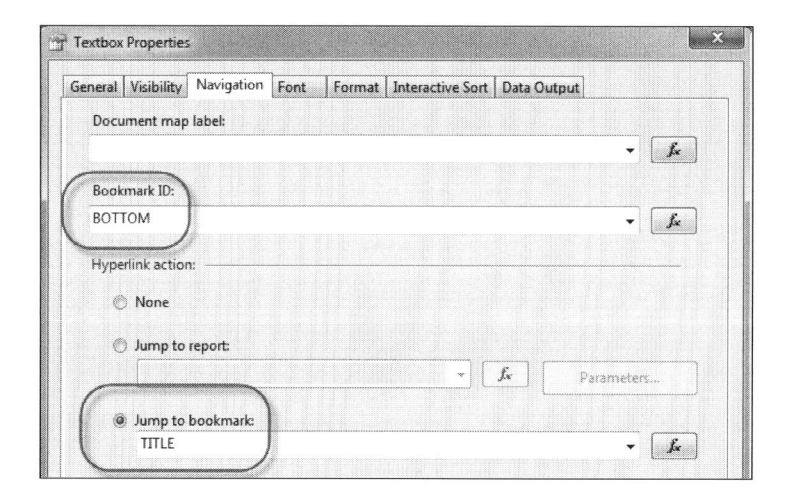

This example is very basic and easy to implement. You can use it when you are creating dashboard style reports and want to include an internal navigation inside the report.

Bookmark links do not have to be static as in the previous example, but they can be dynamic. By using the expression editor, you can make the `Bookmark ID` jump to bookmark values depending on an expression. For example, you might have the previous report extended with a list. In this list, you might show the details of a contact, much like a contact card page in Dynamics NAV, and include a page break after every contact. Then, you could create bookmarks from within the table to the list. So when the user clicks on a contact in the table, he will be redirected to the list that will contain the detail info of the clicked contact.

1. Create a list at the end of the report.
2. Put fields from the dataset into the list:

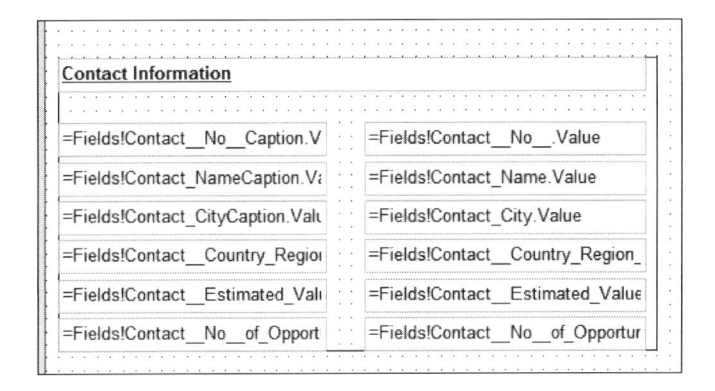

3. Group the list on the **Contact No**.
4. Use the grouping property **Pagebreak at Start**.
5. Use the list property **Insert a page break before this list**.

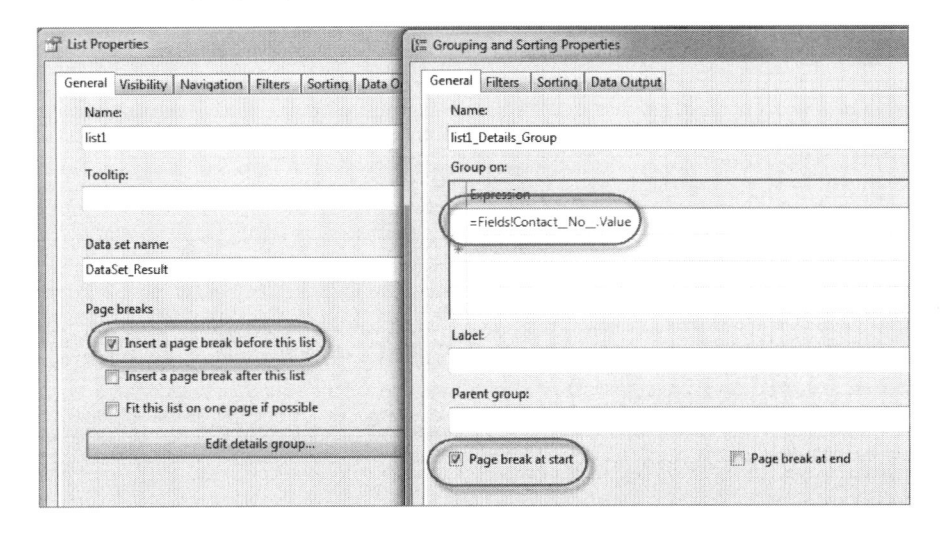

Visualization Methods

6. Select a text box in the list and give it a `Bookmark ID` containing the **Contact No**:

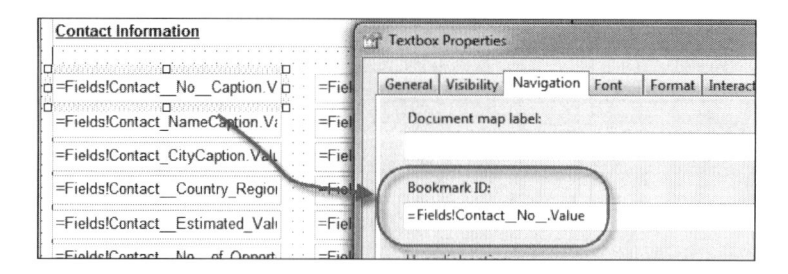

7. Select a text box in the table and give it a **Jump to bookmark** property containing the **Contact No**:

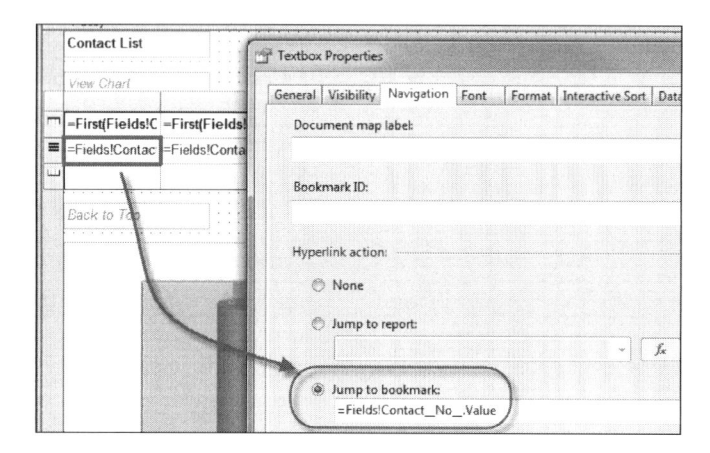

Now run the report and test the navigation. And you might notice that when you export the report to Excel, the navigation still works.

> This report is available as a `.txt` and `.fob` file. (R90007:pb_Bookmarks)

Hyperlinks

You can add a hyperlink to a report item so that a user can access a web page by clicking the item. A hyperlink can be a static URL or an expression that evaluates to a URL. If you have a field in a database that contains URLs, the expression can contain that field, resulting in a dynamic list of hyperlinks in the report.

But, the URL might also be a link to a Dynamics NAV 2009 report or page object.

You might remember that to run a report you can use the following construction:

```
DynamicsNAV:////runreport?report=XXX
```

And to run a page you can use the following construction:

```
DynamicsNAV:////runpage?page=xxx
```

Actually, you can do a lot more with these URLs.

Hyperlinks enable users to send or save quick links to specific pages in Dynamics NAV. For example, you could create a hyperlink to a specific list page. Hyperlinks can also be used to specify parameters, such as server name, server service, or company. The following table shows some examples of hyperlinks and provides information about how to specify parameters:

Parameters	Description	Syntax
Company name	Enables you to switch a company (case sensitive).	`DynamicsNAV:////<CompanyName>/RunPage?Page=<pageid>`
Navigate	Enables users to send or save quick links to specific pages.	`DynamicsNAV://///navigate?node=<service>`
RunPage	Enables you to run a specific page.	`DynamicsNAV:////runpage?page=<page id>`
RunReport	Enables you to run a specific report.	`DynamicsNAV:////runreport?report=<report id>`
Server name	Enables you to switch servers.	`DynamicsNAV://<ServerName>///RunPage?Page=<pageid>`
Optional port number	Enables you to specify an optional port number in the range 1-65535. The default port is 7046.	`DynamicsNAV://<ServerName><:Port>///RunPage?Page=<pageid>`
NST Service instance	Enables you to specify a Service instance. You can find this value in the `CustomSettings.config` file.	`DynamicsNAV:///<Service>//RunPage?Page=<pageid>`

> **Note**
> If you omit a parameter, such as `Server` or `Service`, do not remove the accompanying forward slash, as this will change the overall structure of the hyperlink.

Filtering a report

In addition, you can filter the data in the report by adding a filter string to the command. The filter string has the following format:

```
&filter=<table>.<field>:<value>
```

To specify the table, you use the `DataItemVarName` of the data item. To specify the field, use the field name. If the field name contains special characters, then you must enclose it in quotation marks by using the URI escape sequence `%22`. The colon operator separates the two parts of the filter string. To specify the value, you can either use a single value or a comparison operator and a value. The following are the valid comparison operators:

- > (greater than)
- >= (greater than or equal to)
- < (less than)
- <= (less than or equal to)
- <> (not equal to)

The wildcard character * is permitted in the value.

You can specify multiple filter strings by concatenating them. For example, the following command filters on cities that begin with M and names that begin with A:

```
DynamicsNAV://///runreport?report=104&filter=Customer.City:M*&filter=Customer.Name:A*
```

Filtering a page

You can also specify the following additional parameters in a page URL:

Parameter	Description
Personalization ID	Specifies the unique identification used in personalization to store settings in the User Metadata table. If a personalization ID is not found, the page is launched without personalization.
Bookmark	Positions the cursor on a single record in a table. Only automatically generated bookmarks should be used. If you enter an incorrect bookmark, you will get an error message.
Mode	Enables you to open a page in a specific mode. Other modes include: view, edit, create, select, and delete.

The question now is how to generate the bookmark. What is the bookmark of a record in a table? The answer is this:

```
FORMAT(RecRef.RECORDID,0,10)
```

You have to use the `RECORDID` function, from a `RecordRef` variable, to obtain the bookmark. This has to be done using C/AL code in the Classic designer.

For example, you have a report containing contact data and when the user clicks on a contact you want the corresponding contact card page to be displayed, positioned on the selected record.

To be able to have the bookmark as a separate field in your dataset in Visual Studio, you will need to put it in the `SourceExpr` property of a text box in the classic section designer. Before you can do that, you will have to obtain it via C/AL coding.

1. Create a `RecRef` variable.
2. In the `OnPreDataItem()` trigger of the **Contact** data item, place this code:
   `recrefContact.OPEN(5050);`
3. In the `OnAfterGetRecord()` trigger of the **Contact** data item, place this code:
   `recrefContact.SETPOSITION(Contact.GETPOSITION);`
4. Put a text box on the **Body** section of the report.
5. In the `SourceExpr` of this text box, place the following expression:
   `FORMAT(recrefContact.RECORDID,0,10)`
6. Give a proper name in the `DataSetFieldName` property: `ContactBookMark`.
7. Open the enhanced layout in Report Designer.
8. Open the property window of the text box you want to become the link.
9. In the **Navigation** tab, in the `Jump to URL` property use the following expression:
   `="DynamicsNAV:////runpage?page=5050&bookmark="`
   `&Fields!ContactBookMark.Value`

> **EnableHyperLinks**
>
> This report property in the classic report designer sets whether hyperlinks to URLs are allowed on reports. Microsoft Dynamics NAV 2009 cannot verify URLs and protect against malicious sites that may be harmful to your computer. You should set the `EnableHyperlinks` property to `Yes` only if you can ensure that hyperlinks on the report target trusted sites.

When you run the report, and click on the text box in the report, the page will open, as shown in the following screenshot:

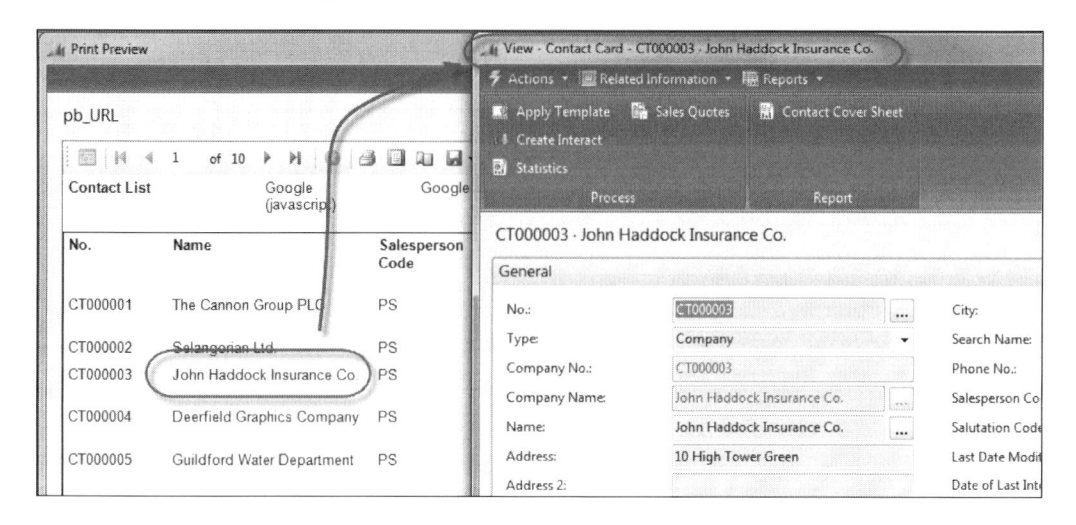

At this moment it is only possible to bookmark card and document pages. In future release(s), the possibility to bookmark other types of pages might be included.

> It is recommended to change the color properties and underline the text box that is used to click on for a hyperlink or bookmark. This will visualize to the user that he or she can click on the text box, similar to how it is done on a web page.

Multi-column reports

You can design a report that uses a multi-column layout, similar to a traditional newspaper column where data flows down multiple adjacent columns. A multi-column layout applies to the entire report. It is not possible to specify a multi-column layout on the top half of the report, and a tabular layout on the bottom half of the report. When you specify a multi-column layout, the report designer creates each column as a series of very narrow pages that are rendered in close sequence, giving the appearance of multiple columns. Properties that you set at the page level are applied to each column in the report. You can define as many columns as you want.

For best results, use data regions that provide repeating rows of data (for example, table or list box). A list box placed within a multi-column report will display data from the top left of the page to the bottom left of the page, and then continue the list in the adjacent column at the top of the page. If you want to use text boxes or images, put them in a list so that they repeat in each column.

To limit the amount of data that is contained within each column, define a group expression and then set a page break on the group. For example, you might add an expression that limits the number of rows per column.

The following is a screenshot of the **Report properties**, **Layout** tab:

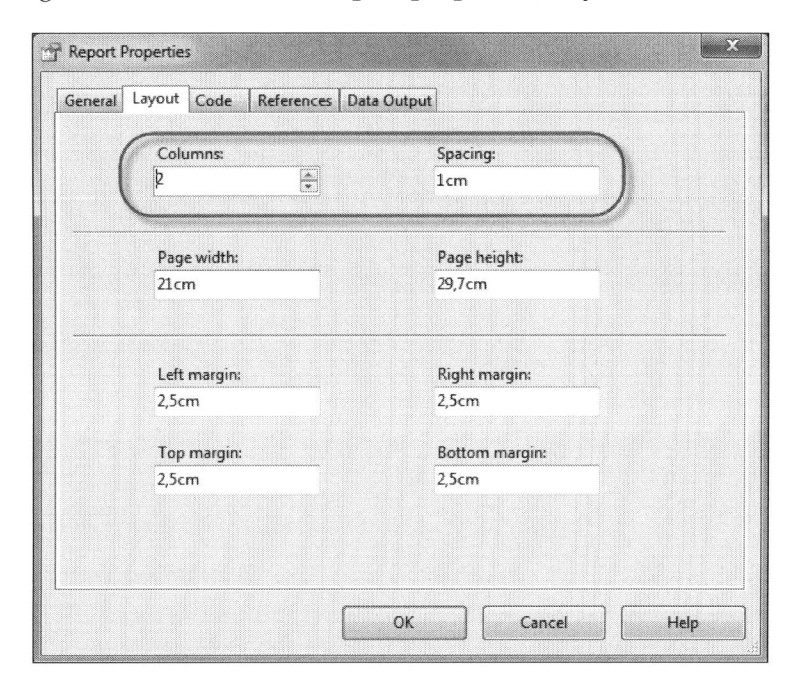

When you set the number of columns to higher value, the design surface of the report changes to represent the number of columns, as shown in the next screenshot. Only the first one can be edited. The other levels will be a copy of the first level.

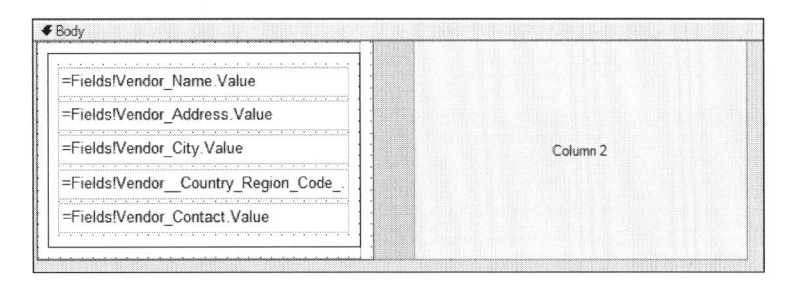

Visualization Methods

When you run the report in **Preview** mode, the multi column layout will not be shown; only when you switch to **Print Layout** mode will it become visible, as shown in this screenshot:

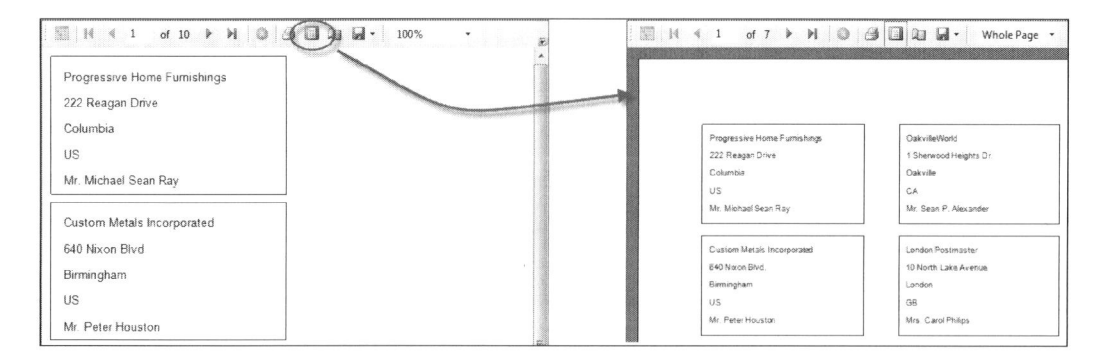

> **Print preview versus print layout**
>
> Multiple columns do not show in print preview mode, they only show up in print layout mode or when you actually print the report. This makes it more difficult to test a report. You should not trust the print preview and make it a habit to always test the print layout for a report. Unfortunately, there's no possibility to make the print layout the default option when running a report. You always have to manually click the print layout button. It might be a good suggestion for Microsoft to make it possible to change this behaviour or add an option to show the print layout by default.

Headers and footers

Page headers and footers provide you with an extra layer in reports. There are different types of headers and footers, depending on which level they are applied to:

- Report level
- Page level
- Data region: list, table, matrix
- Group level

A report level header/footer only appears on the first/last page of the report. These are usually text boxes that you place above/below data regions.

Page level headers and footers appear on all pages of the report, with the option to exclude the first and/or last page of the report, using the properties: `PrintOnFirstPage` and `PrintOnLastPage`.

To add/remove a page header/footer to a report you can use the **Report** menu, or right-click outside of the body of the report, as shown in the following screenshot:

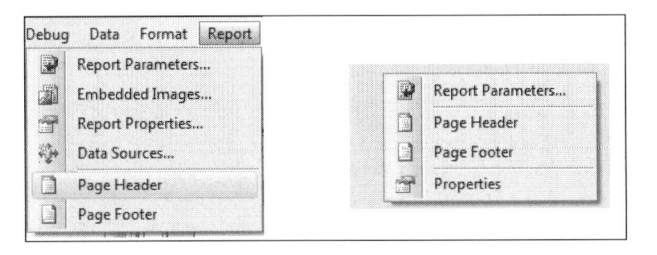

Page headers and footers can contain static text, images, lines, rectangles, borders, background color, and background images. You cannot add data bound fields or images directly to a header or footer. However, you can write an expression that indirectly references a data bound field or image that you want to use in a header or footer.

Remember that this is a consequence of the limitations of the RDLC 2005 specification. As soon as Dynamics NAV switches over to the RDLC 2008 specification, this will no longer be required and you will be able to put database fields directly on headers and footers.

Page headers and footers can contain static content, but they are more commonly used to display varying content like page numbers or information about the contents of a page.

To display variable data that is different on each page, you must write an expression. To put variable data in a header or footer, do the following:

1. Add a text box to the header or footer.
2. In the text box, write an expression that produces the variable data that you want to appear.
3. In the expression, include references to report items on the page (for example, you can reference a text box that contains data from a particular field). Do not include a direct reference to fields in a data set.

You cannot refer directly to a field from a text box in a page header or footer. (For example, you cannot use the expression `=Fields!LastName.Value`.)

Visualization Methods

To display field information in a page header or footer, place the field expression in a text box in the body of the report, and then refer to that text box in the page header or footer. The following expression displays the contents of the first instance of a text box named **TXT_LastName**:

```
=First(ReportItems!TXT_LastName.Value)
```

You cannot use aggregate functions on fields in the page header or footer.

Depending on the type of report you are creating and if the body contains other data regions, you might have to implement other workarounds to be able to have the information in the header displayed on every page of the report. In *Chapter 5, Developing specific reports* I will give you a detailed example on how this works.

Data region (list, table, matrix) headers/footers are available for example at the top and bottom of a table. Using data region headers/footers you can create reports that have the same headers/footers on every page and you also have control over them via properties (`RepeatOnNewPage`) and expressions. For example, you could create a table header and control via an expression when it should be hidden or not, similar to how it is done in the classic report designer with `currreport.SHOWOUTPUT(True/False)`.

Group level headers/footers are available in the beginning and ending of grouping levels in a table data region. You can repeat them on every page if desired.

Expressions

As you have probably noticed when we created reports in Visual Studio, report items use expressions to retrieve data from fields and perform calculations.

Some expressions are created for you automatically. For example, when you create a new report and drag fields from the dataset onto report items, the values of text boxes are automatically set to expressions that refer to the dataset fields by name.

For example:

```
=First(Fields!Customer__Sales__LCY__Caption.Value)
=Fields!Customer__Sales__LCY__.Value
=Sum(Fields!Customer__Sales__LCY__.Value)
```

> **Expressions are like formulas in Excel**
>
> Expressions can be compared with formulas in Excel. For example the value of a text box can be a constant or an expression, just like any cell inside an Excel worksheet.

The most common expression, as you can see in the examples above, refers to a field in the dataset. Besides dataset fields (`Fields!`) you can also reference other types of items, like for example:

- Text boxes on the report (`ReportItems!`)
- Global values: `PageNumber`, `TotalPages` (`Globals!`)
- User information: `UserID`, `Language` (`Users!`)
- Aggregate functions: `Sum`, `Min`, `Max`, `First`, `Last`, and so on.

Most properties of report items give you the possibility to use expressions to generate their value at runtime. The language you use to create these expressions is VB.NET (case sensitive).

You can create expressions in a report through the **Expression** dialog box or by typing expression syntax directly into a text box, a property window, or a group or sort expression field. The following screenshot shows the **Expression** dialog box:

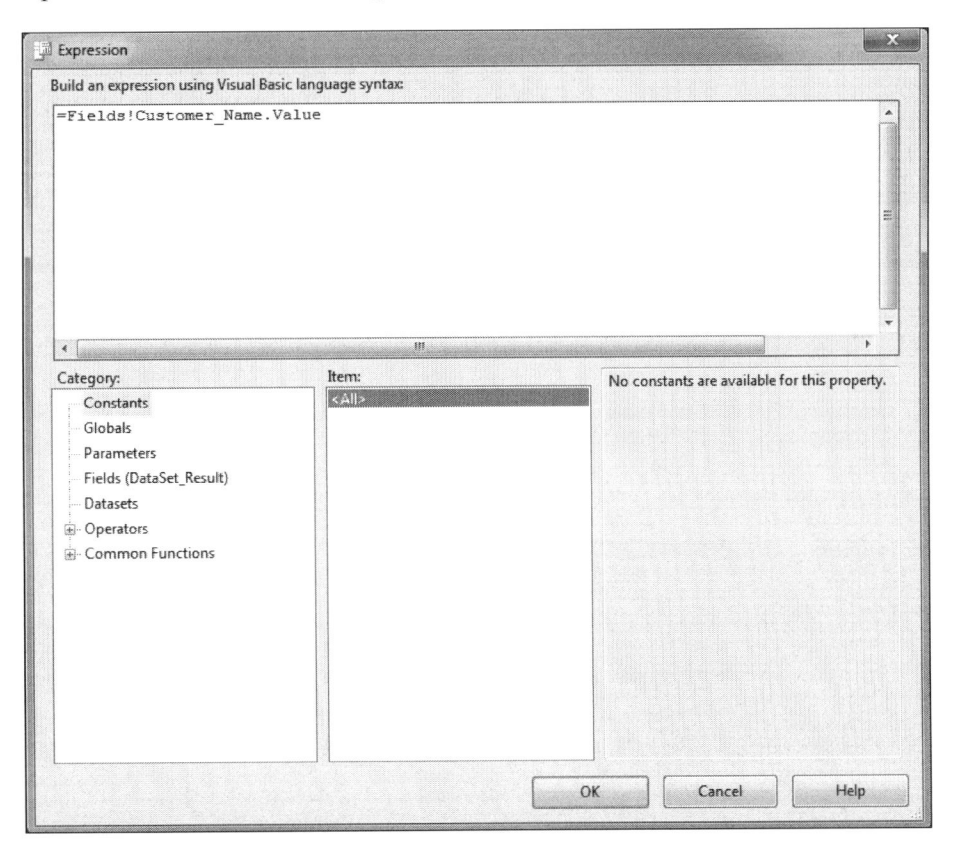

Visualization Methods

From many property text boxes or dialog box fields, you can select `<Expression>` from the drop-down list, as shown in the following screenshot:

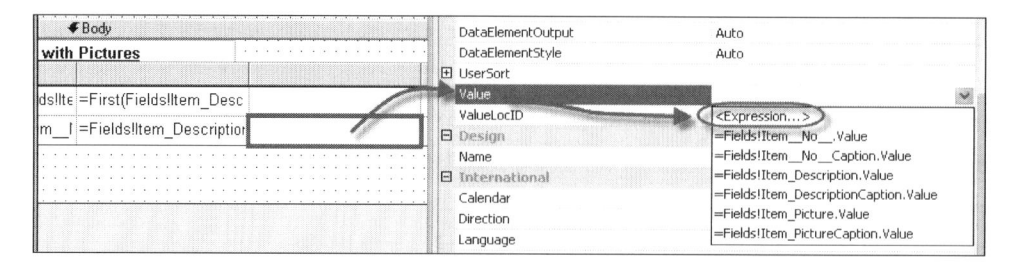

You can right-click text boxes and other report items to display a shortcut menu and then click **Expression**, as shown in the following screenshot:

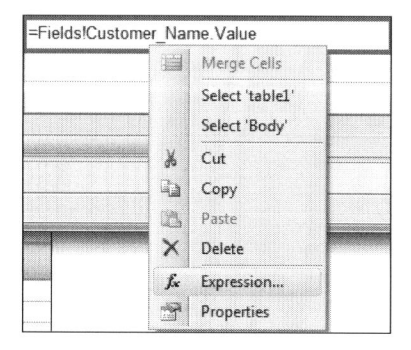

On some dialog boxes, the **fx** button is available for setting a property value:

You can write expressions that use functions from the Visual Basic Run-Time Library, and from the `System.Convert` and `System.Math` namespaces. You can add references to functions from other assemblies or custom code. You can also use classes from the Microsoft .NET Framework, including `System.Text.RegularExpressions`.

Reporting Services provides global collections that you can reference from expressions:

- DataSources
- DataSets
- Fields
- Globals

- Parameters
- ReportItems
- User

To refer to a collection from an expression, you can use standard Visual Basic syntax for an item in a collection.

> **Note**
> The way that Dynamics NAV 2009 uses RDLC 2005 has as a consequence that the Parameters collection cannot be used. Also, because currently, we can only have one dataset and datasource, there's no point in using the DataSets collection.

The **Expression Editor** is context-sensitive; the category items and descriptions change in response to the expression category you are working with. It supports intellisense, statement completions, and syntax coloring so that you can easily detect syntax errors. You can move and resize the **Expression Editor** if you want a larger work surface.

The expressions you create begin with an equal sign (=) and include constants, global values, fields, and other elements.

Before we go into detail about the different collections we can use in enhanced report design, we first need to understand better what exactly a collection is?

In general terms, a collection is an object used for grouping and managing related objects. For example, every report has a collection of controls. This collection is represented as an object in Visual Basic. This particular object in this example is the ReportItems collection and can thus be used to manipulate items on the report.

A collection usually allows you to retrieve a control, via code, in the collection by its index, and to loop through the elements of the collection using a For Each...Next statement.

Basically, collections contain items, which can be values or objects. A collection can also contain methods and properties.

The Fields collection

The Fields collection is typically used to display data in text boxes in a report, but it can also be used in other report items, properties, and functions.

When you drag a field from the dataset window onto a report item on the report layout, the content of the report item is set to the `Value` property of the field by default:

- For a data region, the value for each row in the dataset is set to `=Fields!FieldName.Value`
- The contents of a report item that is not a data region is set to a single value such as `=First(Fields!FieldName.Value)`

The Globals collection

The `Globals` collection contains the global variables for the report. The following table describes the members of the `Globals` collection:

Global	Description
ExecutionTime	The date and time that the report began to run.
PageNumber	The current page number. Can be used only in page header and footer.
TotalPages	The total number of pages in the report. Can be used only in the page header and footer.
ReportName	Currently not available in Dynamics NAV RDLC.
ReportServerURL	Currently not available in Dynamics NAV RDLC.
ReportFolder	Currently not available in Dynamics NAV RDLC.

For example, this expression, placed in a text box in the footer of a report, provides the page number and total pages in the report:

```
=Globals.PageNumber & " of " & Globals.TotalPages
```

The ReportItems collection

The `ReportItems` collection contains the text boxes within the report. The value for a `ReportItems` item can be used to display or calculate data from another field in the report.

- This expression, placed in a text box, displays the value of a `ReportItem` text box named **Text box1**:

  ```
  =ReportItems("Text box1").Value
  ```

- This expression, placed in a text box in the page header or page footer, displays the first value per page of the rendered report, for a text box named **LastName**:

    `=First(ReportItems("LastName").Value)`

The User collection

The User collection contains data about the user who is running the report. The following table describes the members of the User collection:

User	Description
Language	The language of the user running the report. For example, en-US.
UserID	The ID of the user running the report. The value is determined by the Dynamics NAV Role Tailored Client, which uses Windows authentication.

Functions

The following table describes the aggregate functions that are supported. You can use aggregate functions in expressions for any report item.

> **Data type for aggregate functions**
>
> All data used for an aggregate calculation must be the same data type. To convert data that has multiple numeric data types to the same data type, use conversion functions like `CInt`, `CDbl`, or `CDec`.

Function	Description
Avg	Returns the average of all non-null values from the specified expression
Count	Returns a count of the non-null values from the specified expression
CountDistinct	Returns a count of all non-null distinct values from the specified expression
CountRows	Returns a count of rows within the specified scope
First	Returns the first value from the specified expression
Last	Returns the last value from the specified expression
Max	Returns the maximum value from all non-null values of the specified expression

Visualization Methods

Function	Description
Min	Returns the minimum value from all non-null values of the specified expression
RowNumber	Returns a running count of all rows in the specified scope
RunningValue	Uses a specified function to return a running aggregate of the specified expression
StDev	Returns the standard deviation of all non-null values of the specified expression
StDevP	Returns the population standard deviation of all non-null values of the specified expression
Sum	Returns a sum of the values of the specified expression
Var	Returns the variance of all non-null values of the specified expression
VarP	Returns the population variance of all non-null values of the specified expression

All aggregate functions require you to specify an expression and a scope. The expression defines the field on which to apply the aggregate function. The expression is usually a numeric field from the dataset, or it could be another expression. The scope is usually the name of the dataset, group, or data region that contains report items to which to apply the function. In other words, the scope defines which detail rows from the dataset are accessed via the function.

To apply the AVG function, you would use the following syntax:

```
=AVG(Expression, Scope)
```

To return the average of all sales in the outermost data region, you would use the following expression:

```
=AVG(Fields!Sales.Value, Nothing)
```

The scope argument gives you different possibilities.

First, if you omit the scope, you get the current level, if the expression is at group header or footer level. If you use the expression on a detail row, you will get the lowest available grouping. When you use the keyword Nothing, you will get the entire dataset. This gives you the possibility to calculate a percent of total value.

When you use the name of the grouping level as the scope, you will get all the rows that have the same value for that grouping level. The grouping level name should be entered as a string, surrounded with quotes (`"string"`), from the current or higher level within the report. The string is case sensitive. This will allow you to calculate the percentage of group values.

Expressions give you the possibility to create calculated columns in a report, for example in a table, chart, or matrix data region. Examples of these kinds of calculation are explained in detail in the next chapter, in the section about top X reports.

Expressions can be used to enhance and enrich reports; they are what make reporting services such a rich reporting engine. Almost any property can be linked to an expression.

Instead of listing examples of expressions, I think it is more interesting to see how expressions are used in actual reports, so in the examples in this and the following chapters you will see how expressions can be used to achieve different goals.

> More information about expressions can be found in Microsoft Books Online here: `http://msdn.microsoft.com/en-us/library/ms159238(v=SQL.90).aspx`

Useful tips and techniques

There are a couple of things you should think about when developing reports for a customer. Applying these simple techniques will make sure your reports have a similar look and feel and so will become easier to use and more user friendly.

Many of the tips I present in this section are not applied to the example reports used in this book. This is because these reports are used as examples to explain certain aspects of report design. In real life, you should pay attention to and spend time on the look and feel of any report you develop. In the end, like a website, the perception of a report is made in the first few seconds when the user sees it for the first time. It is not difficult to improve the look and feel of a report, but it is often not a priority on the to-do list of most developers.

Use a title, page numbers, and show applied filters

If you want to improve the readability of your report then add a title to it. You can do this by clicking and dragging a text box from the toolbox onto the report just above your List/Table/Matrix control. Another possibility is to use the header of the report to contain the title. The title of the report can be the same as the name of the report and it should explain to the user what to expect.

The report should also contain information about the current page number and, if possible, the total number of pages.

When a user runs a report he or she has the possibility to specify and apply filters on the dataitem(s). It should be a best practise to mention that on the report. You can use the GETFILTERS C/AL function in C/Side to retrieve the applied filter. By doing this, you avoid the situation that a user filters a report, then prints it on paper and forwards it to technical support, because he/she believes there's an error in the report because information is missing. When you print the applied filters, this kind of misunderstanding can be avoided. In case the filter information takes up too much space on the report or page header, you could make it an option in the request page or you could put the filters inside a rectangle, which the user can show or hide (expand/collapse).

> **Dummy report**
>
> Ideally, you should create a standard report header (or page header) containing this information and apply it on all reports. That way you only have to define and design it once and you can reuse it on other reports. This standard report header/footer could become a dummy report in the object designer, which you could use as a template whenever you need to create a new report.

Another possibility is if you plan to use an existing dataset when creating a new report, rather than starting with a blank report, copy an existing report, and delete the data regions from it. This can help preserve the appearance of the other reports (especially if standard colors, layouts, and logos are used) and minimize the effort when starting a new report.

Using rectangles, lines, and images

You can use rectangles, lines, and images to create visual effects within a report.

Rectangles and lines are not associated with data. Images can either be static or based on data in a database.

Lines and rectangles can be used for visual effects. A rectangle can also be used as a container for other items. When you move the rectangle, the items that are contained within the rectangle move along with it.

Adding a report border

You can add a border to a report by adding borders to the headers, footers, and report body. In the header, add a left, top, and right border. In the body, add a left and right border. In the footer, add a left, bottom, and right border. If you do not use headers in your report, you can place borders around just the report body.

> **Borders on page headers/footers**
>
> If you add a report border that appears on the page header and footer, do not suppress the header and footer on the first and last pages of the report. If you do, the border may appear cut off at the top or bottom of the first and last pages of the report.

Tracking report usage

When you spend a lot of time (and budget) developing and customizing reports, it is usually very interesting to be able to determine, after some time has passed, if these reports are actually being used and so providing a return on investment. That's why it is very important to have the information at your disposal that can help you in this kind of analysis.

> **ExecutionLog**
>
> In server-side reporting services, this information is generated, monitored, and stored by SQL server in system tables in the report server database. You can consult it using a specially constructed view: **ExecutionLog** (1, 2, or 3 depending on the version). You could even build a ssrs report based on this view. (Examples of these kinds of reports can be downloaded from www.codeplex.com).

Visualization Methods

Unfortunately, in RDLC reporting there's no report server and the information is also not stored or available in the Dynamics NAV database. That's why I recommend one of the following.

You can creat a table, very much like the execution log view, with the following fields:

- ReportName
- UserName
- ExecutionDateTime
- Filter
- TimeStart
- TimeEnd

In the C/AL code of a report, you could then use a function that would update the information in this table every time a user executed the report. It will take some time to implement it in all your reports, but there are great advantages involved.

Another solution can be found on this blog from Microsoft: http://blogs.msdn.com/b/nav/archive/2011/06/23/how-to-log-report-usage.aspx

It is a hotfix that was released recently that you need to install and then, via some C/AL coding you can create a solution with a table inside the Dynamics NAV database which will log report usage. At this moment it only works for classic reports, not for enhanced (RDLC) reports.

For example, if you notice that a specific report is never executed, but it was a big requirement in the implementation, you can then investigate why no one is using the report. Maybe in the meantime the business has changed or there might be something wrong with the report. This kind of information can also be helpful when you face the task of having to do an upgrade. Reports that are not required, should not be upgraded or at least have a low priority. Usually, in real life, if you don't have this kind of information, your only source of report usage information is the customer (key user, responsible, etc.) If they don't know then they will say it is important rather than say that it's not required to upgrade.

Furthermore, having this information can be of assistance in performance tuning reports. When users complain about performance, for example slow reports, in many cases the only information they provide is: it's too slow. Knowing which reports are executed the most and when they are executed and how much time it takes to execute them can be of enormous help. Pinpointing the bottleneck in performance tuning an application is usually the first and most difficult step.

> **Using SQL monitoring tools**
>
> SQL Server has tools you can use to monitor what's going on in the database and instance level. Examples of these tools are SQL Profiler, Database Engine Tuning Advisor, and Dynamics Management Views. You can also use these tools to monitor the performance of NAV reports. This can help for example in determining whether the correct indexes are being used.

Checking on empty datasets

It can happen that when a user runs a report, for some reason, no data is returned and so the report layout is empty. Instead of letting the user wonder what went wrong it is better to catch this situation in C/AL code and display an appropriate message in the report. Another option is to use the `NoRows` property of a data region. This will return a message to the user if no data is returned when executing the report.

Using a report layout setup table

Using the same height for table rows in all reports gives a more professional and consistent impression. Especially when some reports are developed via the `View, Layout` option and others via the `Tools| Create Layout Suggestion` feature, row heights can vary.

In the same way, it could be advised to also use alternating row colors, with the same colors in all your reports. For these kinds of purposes, it could become interesting to create a report layout setup table in which you store this kind of information. That way you can also provide the user a way of changing values in this table via a page and so, all reports will take the new value(s) into account.

Blanking properties

It can make a report easier to read when you do not display 0 values on it, but instead hide them.

In the classic report designer, there are properties to achieve this goal, but in RDLC those properties have no effect. Instead, to do this you could use a format code: '#,#' or you could use custom function(s) like `BlankZero`, `BlankPosition`, and so on.

Pagination

Despite the paperless office, users will still actually print reports. Because many users will use the PDF export functionality, it's a best practise to plan the size and paper orientation of the report.

The report items you use will determine the size and orientation, but you can define page size to optimize report layouts. You can do this by using the `PageSize` property settings. For print preview (HTML) specify `InteractiveSize`. Also, remember to change the default margins in the report property window.

Use page breaks to hide overhead. When a report returns a large number of rows, you can use page break properties to hide much of the processing to the user. This will make sure that the user can already see the first page of the report, while the other pages are still being prepared.

Use rectangles

You can group report items inside rectangles so you have more controlled and consistent formatting and easier movement. You can use rectangles to hide multiple objects at once. You can put a report item inside a rectangle by dragging and dropping it. To verify, make sure its `Parent` property is set to the rectangle.

Give everything a proper name

Always name all objects and items within the report; this makes debugging easier. Naming objects as you create them will save a lot of time later in the testing process. It also helps when you need to use the `ReportItems` collection, or implement toggle item(s).

Test, test, and test

As I already explained in this chapter, print preview and print layout are not the same. You should always test the look and feel of your report via print layout. This becomes even more important when you are going to apply visualisation techniques, because not all of the things you see in print layout will actually become available in the Excel or PDF rendering extensions. For example when you nest a matrix inside a text box in a table data region, it might look fine in preview, but when you print it on paper or export to Excel it might not render at all.

Another example is when you use the `Hidden` property to hide a row that contains data that you need to display it in the header of a report. When you hide the individual text boxes there's no problem, but when you hide the complete column or row, then it will no longer be available in the `ReportItems` collection.

These kinds of issues will only come to light when you extensively test your reports.

Pagination, page widths, and fonts are all important to test in the different export formats: Excel and PDF, because they might not be rendered as expected or sometimes not rendered at all.

A dataset test is also a recommendation. If there's a problem, it will be either in the dataset or in the layout. Testing the dataset is therefore crucial.

In some instances, the actual printer hardware and settings that are used might produce different results between different printers. Make sure you always test on exactly the same printer hardware that is used in the live environment.

There are some very good testing and project management methodologies that you can implement. Microsoft SureStep would be my first choice. More information about Microsoft SureStep can be found here: `http://www.microsoft.com/dynamics/support/implementation/success.aspx`.

A very good book about this subject would be Microsoft Dynamics Sure Step 2010 from Packt publishing: `http://www.packtpub.com/microsoft-dynamics-sure-step-2010/book`.

Summary

In this chapter, I have introduced new data regions like the list, matrix, and chart. I have explained how they work, giving you an overview of the effort involved and possibilities these data regions can offer to you as a report designer.

Creating document reports like invoices and so on can be quite challenging because of the number of workarounds that can be implemented to simulate desired behaviour.

I will also give you a view on how to create and use key performance indicators and conditional formatting in reports, using more advanced expressions to manipulate the behaviour of controls in a report depending on the data coming out of the database.

Databars and sparklines are new controls added in SQL Server Reporting Services 2008 R2, and so not yet available in the Dynamics NAV report designer. But that does not mean there are no other ways to obtain implement these techniques.

The next chapter will build on the concepts of data regions and controls introduced in this chapter, but in the context of developing specific kinds of reports.

5
Developing Specific Reports

When you implement Dynamics NAV 2009 for a customer, the first kinds of reports you will probably have to work on are the document reports. These reports (for example, Invoice, Credit Memo Picking Slip, and so on) are used in communication between your customer and third parties and so they will need to be modified according to the look and feel used at the customer. To understand the amount of work involved and the types of workarounds that might need to be applied in these reports, this chapter will give you a good overview.

Migrating reports from the Classic client towards the Role Tailored client involves a lot of work and in the end your customer might not even see the difference at runtime between the old reports and the ones migrated with an enhanced layout. To create some added value, you might want to make use of more visualisations like for example conditional formatting, data bars, and spark lines. In this chapter, I will give you a view on how to develop these kinds of specific reports.

In this chapter, we will cover:

- Document reports
- TOP X reports
- Creating KPIs and conditional formatting dashboards
- Implementing conditional formatting

Document reports

The most difficult types of reports to port from the Classic client towards the Role Tailored client are document reports. The reason for this is the way in which the reports were developed in the Classic client. If it is your requirement to create an enhanced report with exactly the same appearance, layout, and functionality as available in the Classic client, then you will need to spend some time in applying workarounds in RDLC to overcome some of the limitations of enhanced reports.

What's so special in a document report compared to other reports?

The number of copies option

When running the Sales Invoice report for example, on the request page the user has an **Options** tab in which they can select the number of copies (**No. of copies**) required. Depending on the number entered by the user, the report will print x extra copies for every page. This implies that you need to develop the report so that it somehow takes into account the extra copies to be printed for the report. To make it a little easier, you only need to find a solution for the body of the report, because the header (and footer) sections in Visual Studio report designer will follow the body.

How can you make the body of a report print multiple times? There's no property that can help us here. The properties that you can set for the body of a report are only associated with formatting and layout, but not behaviour.

Let's think back to the beginning of this book, when we developed our first enhanced report. We created a customer list report, but it only printed the first record the first time we ran it. To make it print for every record we used a **data region** control (list, table, matrix, and so on). Maybe there's a data region control that could allow us to print the information multiple times?

When you examine the properties of the data region controls (list, table, matrix, chart) you will not find any property that will implement a number of copies behaviour. In server-side reporting services, you could develop a custom control and implement such a property, but at this time, custom controls are not supported by Dynamics NAV reports.

So, if there's no property and/or data region available in the Visual Studio report designer that can help us, let's have a look at how it is implemented in the Classic client. In classic document reports, the number of copies option is implemented by making use of virtual tables, to be more specific, the Integer virtual table. Via C/AL code the Integer table is filtered depending on the number of copies selected in the request page and then the data items containing the information that needs to be copied a number of times are indented with the integer table(s). By looping multiple times over the integer tables, the data items and their corresponding sections are printed multiple times.

Let's create an example. Start by creating a new report, using for example the Item table as a data item. On the **Section designer**, put some fields from the Item table. Then, create an enhanced layout for the report. In the Visual Studio report designer, use a table data region to display the fields from the Item table. If you were to run this report, it would be a simple list of items. Now, let's build in the option for the user to select a number of copies. In the Classic designer, create the following global variable: NoOfCopies.

> Some developers prefer the use of the `int` prefix in the variable name. It is considered a good practice to use prefixes that announce the data type of the variable. This will make your code easier to read. Now, because the Dynamics NAV developer environment always sorts globals and locals alphabetically, suffixes might produce a better sorting then prefixes. Still, I prefer the use of prefixes over suffixes. It should also be mentioned that the use of prefixes and suffixes is not Dynamics NAV standard. If you want to keep the code consistent with the Dynamics NAV code developed by Microsoft you should not use prefixes or suffixes. Personally, I prefer to use prefixes, but in order to keep the code consistent with standard Dynamics NAV code, I will not use them in this book.

Create a request page so the user can enter a value in the `NoOfCopies` variable. Put the `NoOfCopies` variable in a text box on a section, so that it becomes available as a field in the dataset in Visual Studio.

At this point, we are not any closer in making this report print its body multiple times. We need to embed the elements that are currently in the body in a container that will print itself multiple times. A list data region would be a good candidate to do the job.

So, to summarize:

1. Create a list data region in the body of the report.
2. Cut/paste the table data region inside the list data region.

To make sure that the content of the list (being the table) prints multiple times, you will need to create a grouping in the list. The question now is what to use to group on?

When I ask this question to students following my reporting course I usually get the answer: use the `NoOfCopies` variable to group on. Well, this would not help. The reason is that the `NoOfCopies` variable has the same value for every record in the dataset, so grouping on it makes no sense at all. We need a variable that has a different value, a looping variable that changes for every time a copy needs to be presented. To solve this problem, we will use a virtual table as a data item: the Integer table.

Developing Specific Reports

Go in the data item designer and add the Integer table below the Item table and indent it as shown in the following screenshot:

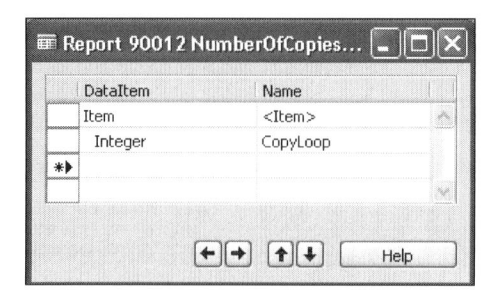

As you can see in the screenshot, the property `DataItemVarName` of the Integer data item has the value **CopyLoop**. This name can now be used to refer to a record from the data item. **CopyLoop** is used as the standard `DataItemVarName` in document reports.

Now, to avoid the report from going into a loop over all integer values, we will need to filter the integer table. The filter value will depend on what the user will enter as the **Number Of Copies** value. To be able to set this dynamic filter on the Integer table, we will use C/AL code in the triggers of the Integer table.

First define the following global variables, as shown in the next screenshot:

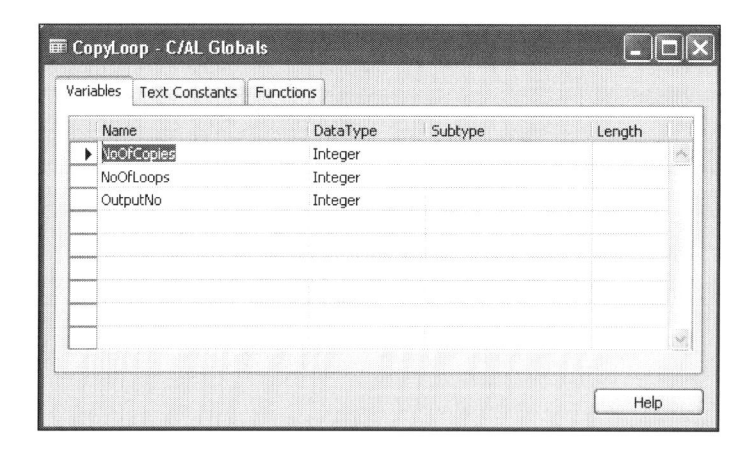

To define a Global variable, use the menu: **View | C.AL Globals** to open the window and enter the `Name` and `DataType` of the variables.

Next, select the Integer data item in the data item window and go to the C/AL code using the **C/AL Code** button in the menu or the shortcut *F9*. This will open the **C/AL Editor** window and the trigger of the Integer (**CopyLoop**) data item.

Put the following code in the `OnPreDataItem()` of the Integer data item:

```
NoOfLoops := ABS(NoOfCopies) + 1;
SETRANGE(Number,1,NoOfLoops);
OutputNo := 1;
```

The `OnPreDataItem` trigger will execute before the Integer data item is processed and is used to initialize variables and filter the Integer data item, depending on what the user enters in the request page. We will increment the value entered by the user with one and use that to filter the integer table. The reason for this is that we need to know the exact number of times the body needs to be printed and this is: one plus the number of copies. The `ABS` function takes the absolute value of the number entered by the user. In case the user enters a negative value, the result of the `ABS` function will be positive. Then, we will initialise a counter variable: `OutPutNo`.

Put the following code in the `OnAfterGetRecord()` trigger of the Integer table:

```
IF Number > 1 THEN
  OutputNo += 1;
```

This means that when we loop over the Integer table, your counter will be incremented.

Create a text box on the body section of the Integer data item. Use the `OutPutNo` variables as the `SourceExpression` in this text box. This will make the variable become available in the dataset in Visual Studio.

In the RDLC layout of the report, use the `OutPutNo` variable as a grouping expression in the list data region, as shown in the following screenshot:

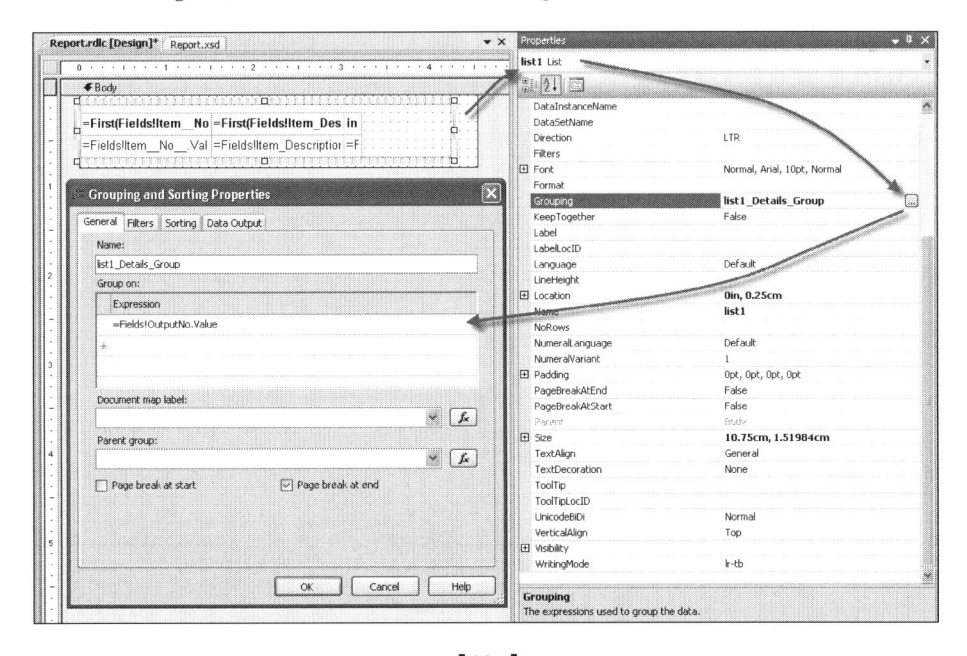

Developing Specific Reports

1. Select the list on the **Body** of the report.
2. Open the **Properties** of the list data region.
3. In the **Grouping** property, click on the button containing the three dots.
4. In the **Grouping and Sorting Properties** window that opens, use `=Fields!OutputNo.Value` as the **Group On expression**.
5. Click on the **Ok** button to close the popup.
6. Make sure you enable the property: `PagebreakatEnd` in the list grouping.
7. Save and run the report and you will notice that you have implemented the number of copies feature.

The property **Page break at end** will generate page break at the end of each instance of the group on `OutputNo`. This makes sure that every copy starts with a new page.

The result will look like the following screenshot:

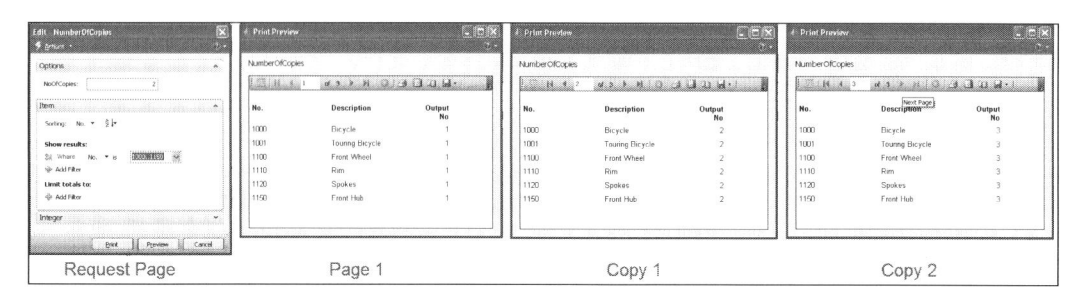

| Request Page | Page 1 | Copy 1 | Copy 2 |

In this screenshot, I have filtered the report, in the **Request Page**, to only show items with a number between **1000** and **1150**. As a result the report only shows six items, and fits on one page. The **NoOfCopies** text box contains a value of **2**, so the report creates two copies, as shown in the above screenshot.

This report only displays the **Item No**, **Item Description**, and **OutputNo**, because it is used as a proof of concept. You can further fine-tune the report to show more relevant information and include more data items. As an example you could use report `206` **Sales – Invoice**.

Displaying data-bound information in the header

One of the features of most document reports is customization by the end user. For example, when implementing Dynamics NAV in the **Sales and Receivables** setup, the user has the possibility to select where the company logo should be positioned in document reports: left, right, centre, or not at all. And this company picture is stored in the database and will be shown in the header of the report, so it is visible on every page. Besides the company logo, other data-bound information will also be visible on the header of the report, like for example the company information and address.

In the previous chapter, *Visualization Methods*, we have seen how to add a header and footer to a report, for example to show page numbers or an embedded image. In a typical document report, the company logo will not be an embedded image, but an image stored in the database. In this case, the user only has to change the logo in the company information table and it will be used on all relevant reports. The same is true for the company address.

Let's look at an example of how to show a database field on the header of a report. We'll create a new report, using the Sales Header table and the Company Information table. The Sales Header table will become a data item; the Company Information table will become a global variable.

> **DataItem or variable?**
>
> How do you decide whether a table should become a data item or if it is better to access its data via a variable (Global/Local)? There are several reasons to base your decision on, and maybe one of the most important is performance. A very important factor in Role Tailored report performance is the size of the dataset: the smaller the better. The size of a dataset is determined by the number of columns and the number of rows. The number of columns is something you usually cannot diminish. If you only put the fields on the sections that you will actually need in the dataset, then that's about all you can do. But the number of rows will depend on the number of data items, the way the data items are indented, and how they are filtered. Secondly, the size of the dataset can also depend on which section you add the fields to.

In the case of the Company Information table, it is a setup table so it will contain only one record; the overhead is not so big. But, we will use the company logo, and that is stored in a BLOB data format. Because a BLOB field could potentially contain 2 gigabytes of information, it is advised not to multiply this by the number of records in the dataset.

Developing Specific Reports

A possible solution would be to set the Company Information table as a separate data item. Then, because it only contains one record, it would only be one row added to the dataset. Personally, I prefer to use an integer data item, filtered on one record, and put the fields that are required only once on the section of this data item. Then, if you require information from other tables, you can reuse the integer data item and its section(s).

These are the steps required so far:

1. Create a new report.
2. Create two data items, below each other, starting with the Integer table and then the Sales Header table.
3. Create a **Header** section for the Sales Header table.
4. Add some fields from the Sales Header table to the **Body** section of the data item; for example use the following fields: **Document Type, Sell-to Customer No., Bill-to Customer No., Bill-to Name.**
5. Move the labels from the fields you just added to the **Header** section of the data item.
6. Create a global variable with the name `CompanyInformation`, **DataType** `Record`, and **Subtype** `Company Information`.
7. Select the first empty line in the data item designer and click on the **C/AL code** button or use the *F9* shortcut.
8. Type the following code in the `OnPreReport()` trigger:

   ```
   CompanyInfo.GET;
   CompanyInfo.CALCFIELDS(Picture);
   ```
9. Show the **Toolbox** using the menu **View** | **Toolbox** or the **Toolbox** button.
10. Add two text boxes from the toolbox to the **Body** section of the Integer data item.
11. Set the `SourceExpr` property of the first text box to `CompanyInfo.Name`.
12. Set the `SourceExpr` property of the second text box to `CompanyInfo.Picture`.

In the following screenshot you can see an example of the use of Integer data item in combination with the Company Information table:

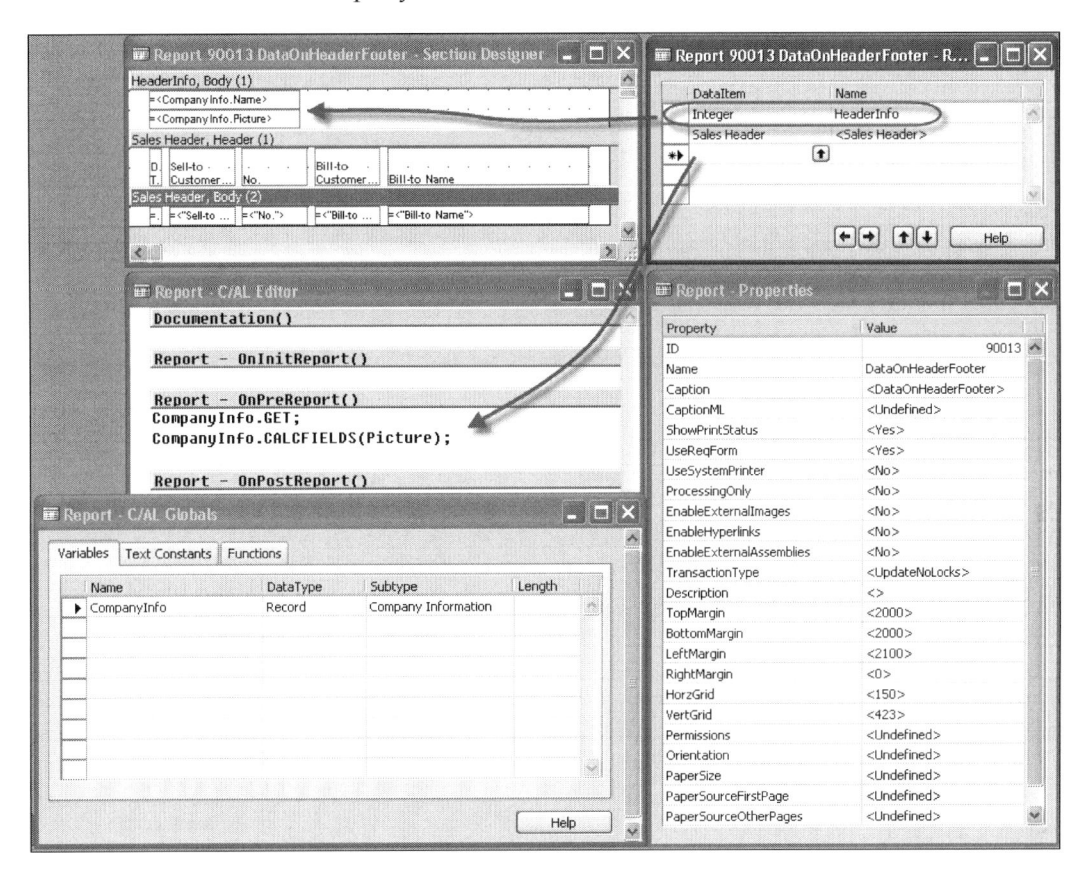

When you run the report (after saving it of course), you can visualize the dataset using the **About this report** feature in the Report Viewer. You can open it using the following steps:

1. Run the report.
2. In the request page click on **Preview**.
3. In the **Print Preview** window that opens, the layout of the report is empty, because we did not yet create an enhanced layout.
4. Click on the button with the question mark in it, at the right top of the screen, and select the option **About This Report** in the dropdown box that opens, or use the shortcut *Ctrl+Alt+F1*.
5. A message appears explaining that the next time you run the report the dataset will be available via the option **About This Report**.

Developing Specific Reports

6. Close the report.
7. Repeat steps 1 to 4 to see the dataset, as shown in the next screenshot.

Notice the difference between the first line and the rest.

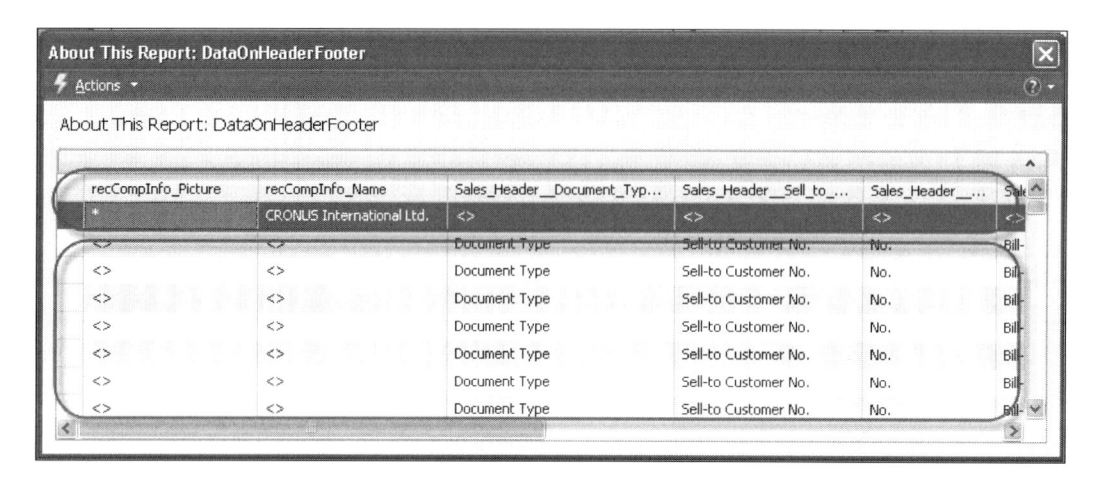

recCompInfo_Picture	recCompInfo_Name	Sales_Header__Document_Typ...	Sales_Header__Sell_to_...	Sales_Header__...	Sel
*	CRONUS International Ltd.	<>	<>	<>	<>
<>	<>	Document Type	Sell-to Customer No.	No.	Bill-
<>	<>	Document Type	Sell-to Customer No.	No.	Bill-
<>	<>	Document Type	Sell-to Customer No.	No.	Bill-
<>	<>	Document Type	Sell-to Customer No.	No.	Bill-
<>	<>	Document Type	Sell-to Customer No.	No.	Bill-
<>	<>	Document Type	Sell-to Customer No.	No.	Bill-

If you don't use a separate data item but add the Company Information fields to the section of the Sales Header data item, then this would be the generated dataset:

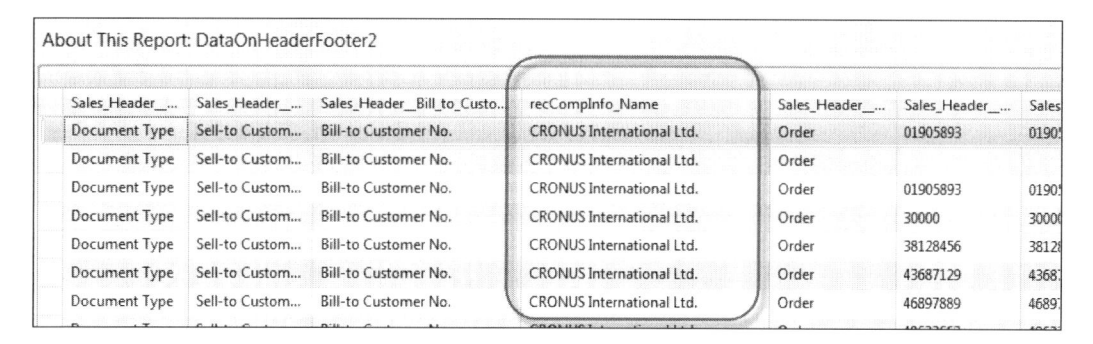

Sales_Header_...	Sales_Header_...	Sales_Header__Bill_to_Custo...	recCompInfo_Name	Sales_Header_...	Sales_Header_...	Sales
Document Type	Sell-to Custom...	Bill-to Customer No.	CRONUS International Ltd.	Order	01905893	0190
Document Type	Sell-to Custom...	Bill-to Customer No.	CRONUS International Ltd.	Order		
Document Type	Sell-to Custom...	Bill-to Customer No.	CRONUS International Ltd.	Order	01905893	0190
Document Type	Sell-to Custom...	Bill-to Customer No.	CRONUS International Ltd.	Order	30000	3000
Document Type	Sell-to Custom...	Bill-to Customer No.	CRONUS International Ltd.	Order	38128456	3812
Document Type	Sell-to Custom...	Bill-to Customer No.	CRONUS International Ltd.	Order	43687129	4368
Document Type	Sell-to Custom...	Bill-to Customer No.	CRONUS International Ltd.	Order	46897889	4689

As you can see, the Company Information fields are added to every row and as you can imagine, not really improving the performance of the report.

If you want to take this to the next level, you could implement a similar solution for the `Caption` fields. The `Caption` of a field is the same for every record, so why put it on every record of the dataset? As shown in the next screenshot, you could also move the `Caption` fields to the integer section:

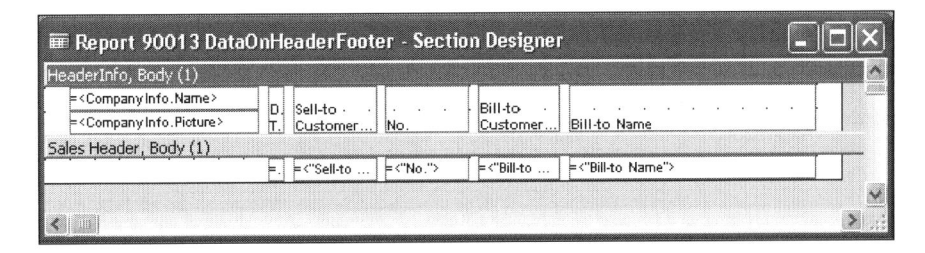

And then, this will generate the following dataset:

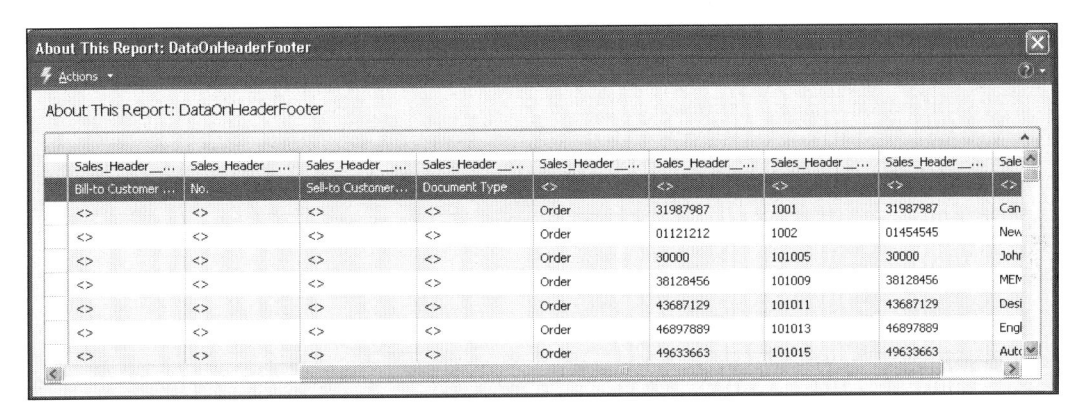

The `Caption` fields, like the other fields on the integer section, are available in the first record of the dataset and are not repeated on all of the other lines and so reducing the dataset overhead.

Now that we have our Company Information fields in the dataset, it's time to put them on the header of the report.

So, follow these steps:

1. Use the **View** | **Layout** option in the menu of the Classic report to open Visual Studio and generate an empty RDLC layout.
2. Add a header, via the menu: **Report** | **Page Header**.
3. Put the Company Name in a text box on the header, by dragging it from the **DataSet** onto the **Page Header**.
4. Save the report in Visual Studio.
5. Import the RDLC back into the Classic designer.
6. Save the classic report.

Developing Specific Reports

You will notice that the following error message will appear:

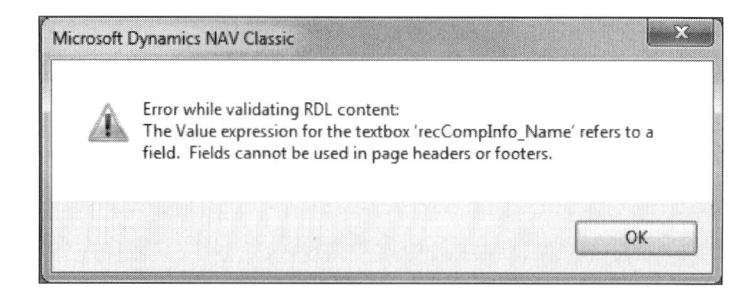

> **Microsoft Dynamics NAV Classic**
>
> ⚠ Error while validating RDL content:
> The Value expression for the textbox 'recCompInfo_Name' refers to a field. Fields cannot be used in page headers or footers.
>
> OK

It seems that fields cannot be used in page headers or footers.

> **Note**
>
> This is a restriction in Reporting Services RDL(C) 2005. Actually, in the RDL(C) 2008 specification it is possible to refer to fields from within a page header or footer. Dynamics NAV 7 will probably support the 2008 RDL(C) specification, so you will probably not need to apply this workaround in the future, but if you are using Dynamics NAV 2009, you will have to. And even if you don't have to use this specific workaround anymore in the future, the ideas behind it are still important to grasp to help you understand the reporting services engine.

So, if we can't put the **Company Name** field on the header of the report, let's put it where it is allowed; let's put it on the **Body**. Furthermore, after putting it on the body, let's hide it because we don't want to see it on the body of the report.

To hide a text box, follow these steps:

1. Select the text box and click on **View | Properties Window** or use the shortcut *F4* to open the property list if it's not already open.
2. Look for the **Visibilty** category in the property list window and open it by clicking on the little + button before it.
3. Select the `Hidden` property and set it to `True`.

Now, we need to find a way to be able to access the information stored on the report **Body**, from within the **Header**. This can be done using the `ReportItems` collection. More information about collections is available in the previous chapter, *Data Visualizations*. The `ReportItems` collection gives you access to all the text boxes on the body of the report. The syntax is:

`=ReportItems!NameOfTextbox.Value`

So, let's put this expression to work.

Follow these steps to add a text box to the **PageHeader**:

1. Add a text box to the **Page Header** in Visual Studio.
2. Right click on the text box and select **Expression** from the dropdown menu that appears.
3. In the **Expression Editor** window that opens type the following expression:
   `=ReportItems!CompanyInfo_Name.Value`
4. Click **Ok**.

Follow these steps to add an image to the **Page Header**:

1. Add an image to the **Page Header** in Visual Studio.
2. Select the image and open the **Properties** window.
3. In the **Properties**, look for the group called **Data** and open it with the little + button before it.
4. Apply the following value `image/bmp` to the property `MIMEType`.
5. Apply the following value `Database` to the property `Source`.
6. Type the following expression: `=ReportItems!CompanyInfo_Picture.Value` in the property `Value`.
7. Resize the image to make it a little bigger.

For testing purposes we will add two extra text boxes, to see at runtime where the **Page Header** ends and the **Body** begins:

1. Add a text box to the end of the **Page Header** with the `Value: This is the end of the Page Header`.
2. Add a text box to the end of the **Page Header** with the `Value: This is the end of the Page Body`.

Developing Specific Reports

If all goes well, you should now see the Company Name on the header of your report, but the Company Picture is empty, like in the following screenshot:

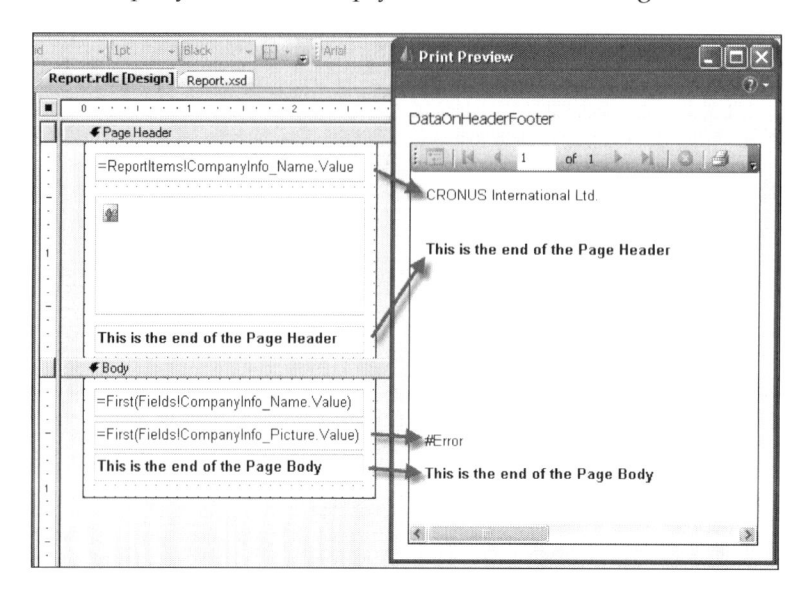

As you can see, the Company Name is displayed on the Page Header and the Company Picture is not.

> **Text box naming**
> When you create a textbox on a report, its name will be automatically filled in. It will depend on its contents, but in many cases the report engine will give a name like `TextboxX`. If at a later stage you wish to reference this text box via the `ReportItems` collection it will be easier if you had named the textbox with a self-explaining name so that when using `Reportitems` you know which textbox you are referencing and don't have to guess. The same tip is valid for group names.

Why is it not displaying the Company Picture?

There are multiple answers to this question. First of all, check and see that there's a picture available in the Company Information table. Second of all, check if you have added the appropriate code, in the `OnPreReport()` trigger, in your report to calculate the BLOB field, as follows:

```
recCompInfo.GET;
recCompInfo.CALCFIELDS(Picture);
```

> **No PictureBox control**
> Make sure you put the **CompanyInfo.Picture** field on a section, using a textbox. If you use a **Picturebox** control, it will not become a field in the dataset in Visual Studio.

If all of these conditions are met, you will still not see the picture in the header. An error is occurring, but no error is displayed. If you would unhide the textbox in the body of the report, containing the Company Picture, it would contain the text: `#Error` at runtime, as shown in the previous screenshot. This means that the report engine is not capable of transforming the BLOB field in the dataset to a text format in the textbox in the **Body**.

> **Don't use an Image control as a container in the body either**
> The textbox is not capable of containing the image data, because it tries to store it in a text format but is not capable of converting BLOB to text. You might want to use an **Image** control instead, hide it and try to reference it from within the header. The problem is that the `ReportItems` collection can only reference textboxe, not image controls. So this is not a solution.

We will need to assist the textbox so it will be capable to convert the BLOB datatype into text. To do this, we will use a .NET function from the `Convert` library:

```
Convert.ToBase64String()
```

> This function comes out of the .NET framework and more documentation can be found on the Microsoft site: `http://msdn.microsoft.com/en-us/library/system.convert.tobase64string.aspx`

It converts an array of 8-bit unsigned integers to its equivalent string representation that is encoded with base-64 digits. To translate this into human words, the function will convert our image to text.

Then, the text can be referenced via the `ReportItems` collection, but to be able to use this in an image control, it will need to be converted back again into an image. To do that, you can use the following function:

```
Convert.FromBase64String()
```

Developing Specific Reports

Follow these steps:

1. Change the expression in the textbox in the body that contains the Company Picture from =First(Fields!CompanyInfo_Picture.Value) into =Convert.ToBase64String(First(Fields!CompanyInfo_Picture. Value)).
2. Change the expression for the Value of the Image in the Page Header from =ReportItems!CompanyInfo_Picture.Value to =Convert.FromBase64String(ReportItems!CompanyInfo_Picture.Value)
3. Hide the text box in the body that contains the Company Picture.

The following screenshot shows how to implement the functions in the report:

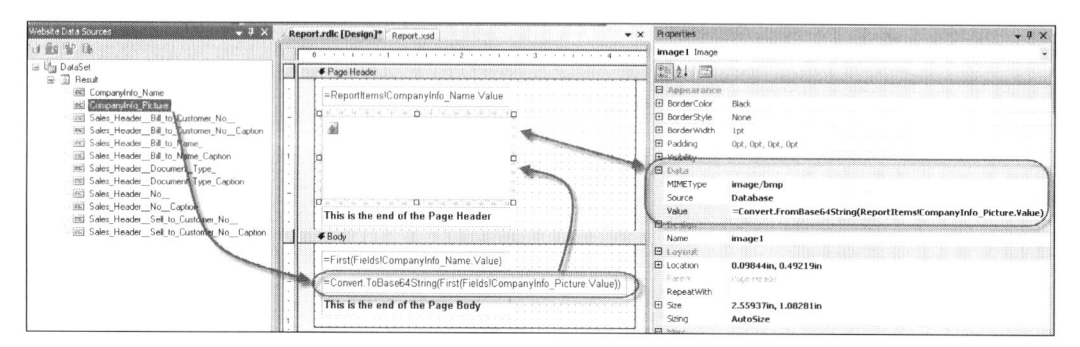

To summarize, these are the steps to add an image to a Page Header in Visual Studio report designer:

1. Add the **Picture** field from the dataset to a text box in the **Body** of the report.
2. Hide the text box you just added via its Hidden property.
3. Change the expression in the text box to: =Convert.ToBase64String(First (Fields! Picture.Value)).
4. Add an **Image** to the **Page Header** of the report.
5. Set the **Image** to be MIMEType of image/bmp, Source: Database, and Value: =Convert.FromBase64String(ReportItems!Picture.Value).

> **Hide text box containing image data**
>
> Remember to hide the text box on the body that contains the BLOB field. The BLOB is converted into a text string, and if you do not hide the text box containing it, you will see the textual representation of the image in the text box, and with the default auto grow properties of the text box it will occupy a lot of space and meaningless text on the body.

[218]

When you run the report, you should now see the company logo on the header of the report. But what happens when you go to the next page in the report? The logo disappears and is replaced with the following image:

Why is the company logo only available on the first page?

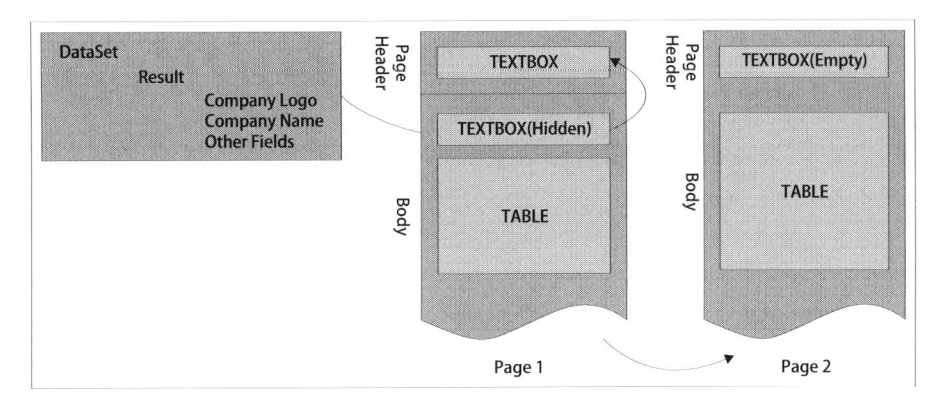

Basically, because the table data region has to display more rows than it can put on one page, it will continue on the second page, and so on. On the second page, there's no text box anymore in the **Body** that contains the Company Picture, only the table data region. That's why the **Page Header** is not capable of referencing the text box, simply because the text box is no longer on the **Body** as from page two.

How do we solve this issue? Basically, there are two solutions for this problem. The first is to make use of text box properties, as shown in the following screenshot:

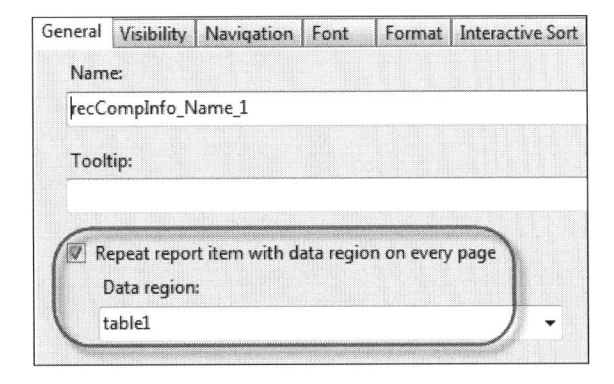

Developing Specific Reports

The property `Repeat report item with data region on every page` will make sure the text box remains available on every page where the table data region is displayed, and so solves our problem. This solution only involves enabling the properties on the text boxes in the body that contain the information that needs to be displayed on the header.

The other solution would be to move the text boxes from above the table data region to inside the table data region. When the text box is inside the table, for example as a hidden row or column, then it is of course available on every page where the table data region is. This solution is applied on almost all of the standard RDLC reports created by Microsoft.

What happens when your report contains multiple data regions?

As you can imagine, the same problem would occur again if you would have multiple data regions in the body of your report. For example below the first table data region you put another table data region (or matrix or chart or list). As soon as the report body does not contain the first table data region anymore, the Page Header fields that reference information in that first table data region will become empty again. Let me explain again using a drawing:

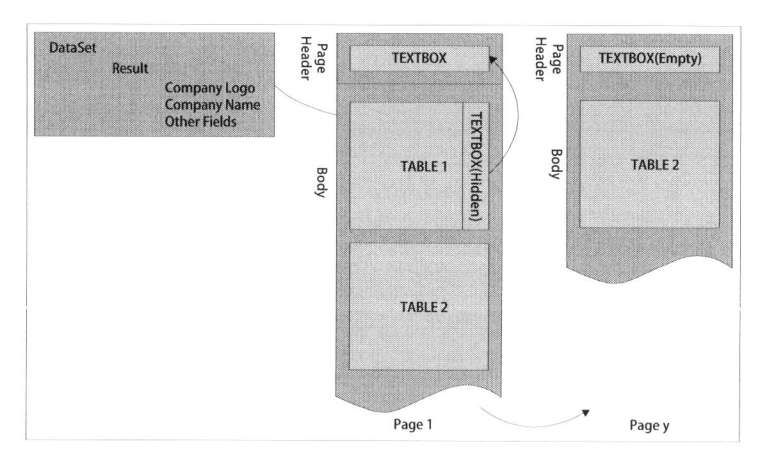

On page Y, when the only data region in the body is the second table data region, the **Page Header** would be blank again. Either of the previous solutions would not solve this issue. The solution is again to be found using either of the following workarounds.

What I prefer to do in this case is use a list data region. Use a list data region in the body as a container for all other data regions. So, in our example, put the two tables inside a list in the body of the report. Then you can connect the text boxes to the list data region via the same property: `Repeat report item with data region on every page`.

The problem left to solve in this workaround is how to connect the list to the dataset and what to group upon in the list so you don't change the way the data is presented. For this we can apply a little trick. In the list properties, use the `Data set name` property to connect it to the `DataSet_Result` dataset. Next, open the grouping details of the list and use the string "ALL" to group upon, as shown in the next screenshot:

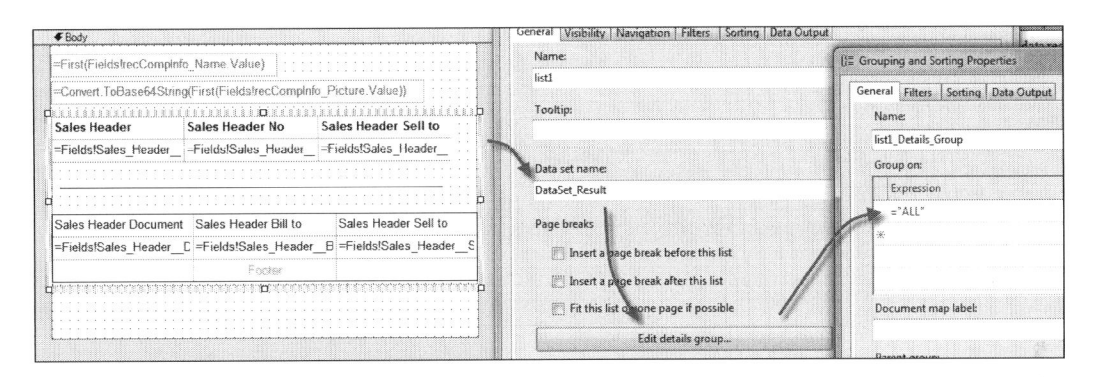

The other solution is to use global variables to store the data that needs to be shown in the header (or footer) of the report. This solution is also the one that Microsoft preferred to use, although it involves more work to be able to implement it.

The question now becomes: How do you create a global variable in Visual Studio report designer? How can you store a value in such a variable and how can you read a value from such a variable?

Well, to solve this problem we are going to use some custom coding in Visual Basic inside the report, and the place we can put this code is in the report properties. To open the report properties window, use the menu `Report | Report Properties`. In the window that opens, select the **Code** tab. The **Code** tab of a report is the place where you can define custom functions, variables, constants, and so on. So, in here we are going to define our global variables and functions, to be able to set and get values from these global variables.

We will start by creating a global variable. You can do this using the following code:

```
Shared MyVarXAsString
```

Then, we will need a function to store a value in the variable `MyVarX`:

```
Public Function SetMyVar(ByVal lvar as String)
  if lvar > "" then
    MyVarX = lvar
  end if
End Function
```

Developing Specific Reports

This function has a parameter `lvar` of type `String`. The value entered in this parameter will be passed along to the global variable `MyVarX`, but only if it's not empty.

And also a function to retrieve the value stored in `MyVarX`:

```
Public Function GetMyVar as String
    Return MyVarX
End Function
```

This function does not have any parameters; it simply returns what is inside the global variable `MyVarX`.

> **Comments &MsgBox()**
>
> `'` is the comment sign. If a line begins with `'` it will not be executed. Comments can be useful when documenting your custom code. It can also be interesting to use for debugging purposes. In this example, you could use a `MsgBox()` statement. Using this function you can show a message, like the C/AL function `Message()`, at runtime.
>
> Although it is very easy to show a message in a report at runtime, it is not recommended. It is recommended to use only for debugging purposes. A user usually perceives a message as an annoying feature in a report.

The following screenshot shows how to implement this in Visual Studio. Note that the text boxes in Red are marked as `Hidden`:

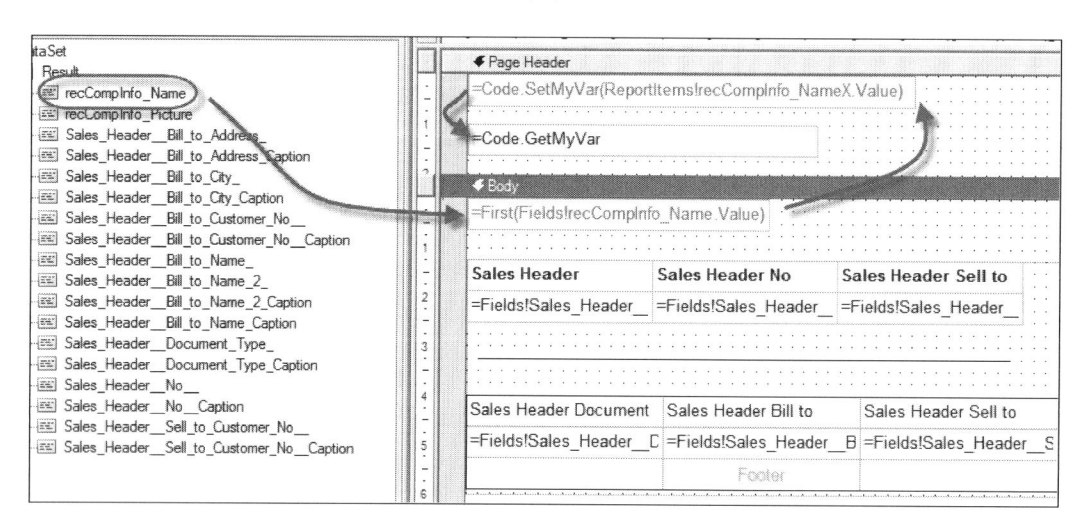

[222]

> **Important**
>
> The text box that contains the Set function should always be positioned above the text box that contains the Get function. The reason is that the report will execute code from top to bottom, and you first need to Set a variable before you can Get it.
>
> **Why** lvar> "" **?**
>
> Every time the body is printed by the report, the corresponding header (and footer) will also be printed (and executed). This implies that for every page in your report, the Set function will be executed. Because the value you provide to the Set function comes from a text box in the body and that text box does not always contains a value, depending on the page, you have to make sure that when there's no value, it is not stored in the global variable. To do this, the Set function will check to see if lvar> "" and only if it is, then store it.

We have now implemented the method of using a global (shared) variable and corresponding functions to Get and Set its value. As you can imagine, in a report there's usually more than one field you want to put on the header and that comes out of the database. Instead of having to create a separate variable and separate Get and Set functions, you could just use one Get function and one Set function and then extend them so they are capable of working with multiple global variables. An example of such a function is this:

```
Shared Data1 as Object
Shared Data2 as Object
Shared Data3 as Object
Shared Data4 as Object

Public Function GetData(Group as integer) as Object
If Group = 1 then
 Return Data1
End If

If Group = 2 then
 Return Data2
End If

If Group = 3 then
 Return Data3
End If

If Group = 4 then
 Return Data4
```

Developing Specific Reports

```
   End If
End Function

Public Function SetData(NewData as Object,Group as integer)
   If Group = 1 and NewData> "" Then
       Data1 = NewData
   End If

   If Group = 2 and NewData> "" Then
       Data2 = NewData
   End If

   If Group = 3 and NewData> "" Then
       Data3 = NewData
   End If

   If Group = 4 and NewData> "" Then
       Data4 = NewData
   End If
End Function
```

In this example, you can use the Group parameter to determine in which variable you want to Get or Set something. This function was created by Microsoft and is used in many document reports. You might consider changing the function to make it easier to understand for a novice developer or document the code.

Working with addresses in reports

In document reports, there are usually different addresses that need to be displayed, and sometimes also on the header of a report. In Classic reports, these addresses are passed into array variables and into a formatting **Codeunit** (Format Address), to make sure the address fields that come out of the database are passed along into the array variables (CustAddr, ShipToAddr, CompanyAddr) in the correct element of the array. Usually, these arrays are one dimensional arrays with eight elements. In the sections of the Classic report, you can directly reference the elements in the text boxes where they need to be displayed. In the RDLC layout of these reports, the elements of the arrays are all in the dataset. Usually, there are three or more of these arrays, each containing eight address fields. This would mean, to be able to show them on a header of the report, you would need to be using 24 text boxes on the body to store the info, to be able to pass it along to the Set function that will store it into 24 global variables.

Well, to save on text boxes and global variables in most document reports a workaround has been implemented for this.

The workaround will store the eight values in one variable. To do that, it will concatenate the eight values using a separator. In the case of the standard document reports in Dynamics NAV 2009, the separator is: Chr(177). As you can see in the next screenshot, the values from the dataset are all put inside one text box inside a mini table on the top of the body:

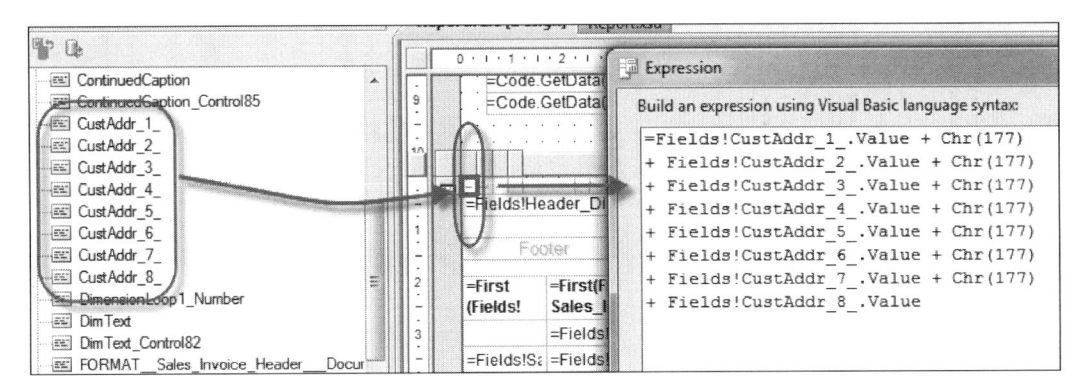

For the Set function this does not matter, but the Get function now needs to be extended to be able to select which of the eight values need to be retrieved from the variable. This is then the function used in for example **Report 206 Sales Invoice**:

```
Public Function GetData(Num as Integer, Group as integer) as Object
If Group = 1 then
  Return Cstr(Choose(Num, Split(Cstr(Data1),Chr(177))))
End If

If Group = 2 then
  Return Cstr(Choose(Num, Split(Cstr(Data2),Chr(177))))
End If

If Group = 3 then
  Return Cstr(Choose(Num, Split(Cstr(Data3),Chr(177))))
End If

If Group = 4 then
  Return Cstr(Choose(Num, Split(Cstr(Data4),Chr(177))))
End If
End Function
```

> Chr(177) corresponds to the +/- sign. But you could also use another code if you want to. The only requirement is that the separator you use is not present in your variable. For example if you used the – sign as a separator and the address contained a – sign, then it would be wrongly split by the Get function. So, choose your separator wisely.

Displaying the current page and copy number

To implement the number of copies feature, all of the controls and data regions of the body should be put into a single list container. This list is grouped with the `Document Header No` and on a field: `OutputNo` with the property `Page break at end` enabled.

If you put a text box on the header of the report containing the following expression:

```
="Page "& Globals!PageNumber &" of "& Globals!TotalPages
```

Then every page will get a different number. This is a problem because a copy of a page should have the same page number as the original. To calculate the correct page number, depending on the groupings in the list and the number of copies value you can use the following code:

```
REM Reset Page Number:

Shared offset as Integer
Shared newPage as Object
Shared currentgroup1 as Object
Shared currentgroup2 as Object
Shared currentgroup3 as Object

Public Function GetGroupPageNumber(NewPage as Boolean, pagenumber as
Integer) as Object
  If NewPage
offset = pagenumber - 1
  End If
  Return pagenumber - offset
End Function


Public Function IsNewPage(group1 as Object, group2 as Object, group3
as Object) As Boolean
newPage = FALSE
If Not (group1 = currentgroup1)
```

```
            newPage = TRUE
                currentgroup1 = group1
                currentgroup2 = group2
                currentgroup3 = group3
              ELSE
                If Not (group2 = currentgroup2)
            newPage = TRUE
                    currentgroup2 = group2
                    currentgroup3 = group3
                  ELSE
                    If Not (group3 = currentgroup3)
            newPage = TRUE
                        currentgroup3 = group3
                      End If
                  End If
              End If
            Return newPage
            End Function
```

The text box in your header that should display the page number can now use the following expression instead:

`=Code.GetGroupPageNumber(ReportItems!NewPage.Value,Globals!PageNumber)`

To make sure the page number is calculated correctly, you now also have to put a text box on the body of the report that contains the following code:

`=Code.IsNewPage(0,Fields!Document_Header_No_.Value,Fields!OutputNo.Value)`

> **The REM function**
>
> The REM function is an alternative for the `'` sign, to indicate comments. It is an old function that is almost never used anymore, but in some of the standard document reports, developed by Microsoft; it still seems to be used.

TOP X reports

A specific type of report you are sometimes asked to produce is the TOP X report. For example, a report containing sales revenue by salesperson where the data is not just a list of numbers sorted alphabetically but by sales revenue from highest to lowest, to see who is really performing in a certain period.

To be able to achieve this goal, you will need to sort and filter the data in your report.

Sorting is organizing report data in a certain order and filtering is about eliminating unwanted information within a report. The sort order you define in the Visual Studio Report Designer will take precedence over the order in which the dataset is generated/sorted.

> **Sorting and performance**
>
> Sometimes, students believe that because the sorting in Visual Studio overrides the sorting of the data items, that the data item should not be sorted at all because that would consume unnecessary resources. In fact, this is not true. It might very well be that you select a key for a data item (via its properties or via the SETCURRENTKEY function in C/AL code) and in Visual Studio apply a sorting according to another criterion, and achieve better performance when executing the report.
>
> SETCURRENTKEY determines the ORDER BY clause, and the way that NAV communicates with SQL Server. This will result in SQL Server always wanting to use an index that uses those fields, or else revert back to a clustered index scan, which is terrible for performance.
>
> Especially for large amounts of data, it is essential for reports to use an existing key that exists as an index on SQL Server. When using SETCURRENTKEY, it is further essential to specify the full key, not just a couple of the fields.
>
> The fact that the report is capable of resorting the data at runtime is a nice bonus, but you can't dismiss SETCURRENTKEY in the Dynamics NAV object. Selecting the right sorting order and making sure that the index exists has a big influence on performance.

Sorting can be achieved in all data region controls in Visual Studio (list, table, matrix, and chart) by opening the property view of the data region. For the list and table there's a **Sort** tab; for the matrix and chart you have to apply sorting at the group level. In all cases, a window will open as presented in the next screenshot to enter the sort criteria:

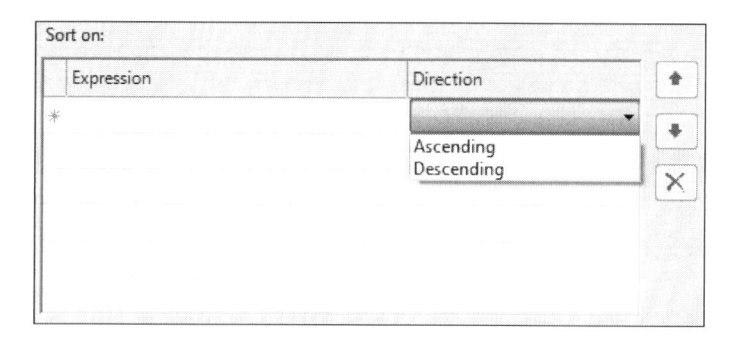

Follow these steps to open the **Sort on** window:

1. Right click on the list, table, or matrix and select properties in the dropdown box that appears.
2. Click on the **Sort** tab to apply sorting.

You can select any field or combination of fields from the dataset. There's even the possibility to sort on an expression. The expression might use a field presented on the request page or anything you would like it to be. Using an expression for sorting can make the sorting dynamic. Although interactive sorting is used a lot as an alternative for this, but interactive sorting was already explained in the previous chapter, *Data Visualizations*.

Sorting is one thing, but in TOP X reports filtering is more important. The idea is to filter the amount of information presented in the report to X number of records, X being a value selected by the user at runtime. But of course, if you want to select the top 10 customers according to the **Sales Amount**, you will need to sort the records according to **Sales Amount**, and then select the first 10 distinct customers. As you see, sorting can also be important in these kinds of reports.

Basically, there are two ways to create a top X report. You can do the filtering in C/Side or in Visual Studio. Although filtering in C/Side might have advantages for performance, it will require some programming. A good example of this can be found in **report 111 Customer Top 10** (or in **report 10062 Top __ Customer List** if you use the US version). The report will loop over the customer table and copy information into a temporary table, so filtering out the TOP 10 according to **Sales (LCY)** or **Balance (LCY)**. It then shows the results in a table and chart data region. The user also has the possibility to select the chart type in the request page.

An advantage of filtering in C/Side might be performance; another advantage is that the report will also work in the Classic client. While performance is not to be disregarded, I'm going to show you how to create a similar report with the filters applied in Visual Studio instead. Furthermore, Visual Studio allows for dynamic filtering using an expression. Since in version 6SP1 a performance improvement was implemented to make sure the report only fetches the data required to be able to render the current page and no longer all pages, the performance impact of dynamic filtering should be much better.

Creating a TOP X table

So, to start creating the report we will use the Customer table, as it contains all the fields we require: **Customer No**, **Customer Name**, **Sales (LCY)**, **Profit (LCY)**, and **Balance (LCY)**.

Developing Specific Reports

This report can be easily extended to include other chart types and other fields for filtering.

Start by creating global variables and a request page, so the user can select the top X value, the chart type, and the field on which to apply the filter.

Name	Data Type	Option String
intTopX	Integer	
intChartType	Option	Bar, Pie
txtTopXType	Option	Sales, Profit, Balance

These variables will become available on the request page, as shown in the next screenshot:

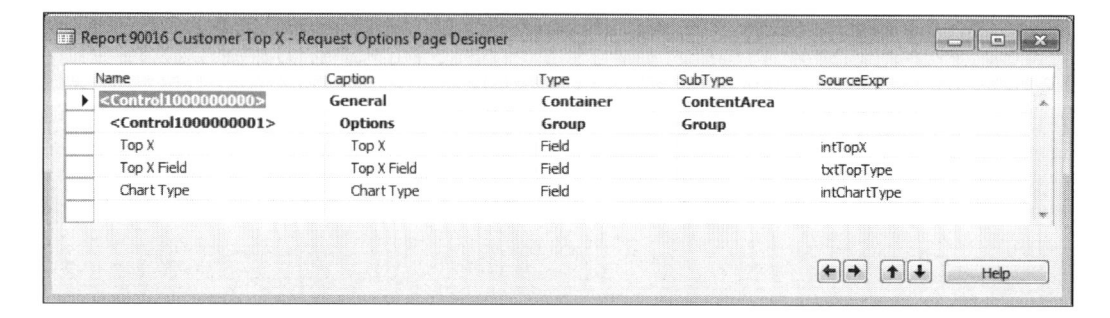

Name	Caption	Type	SubType	SourceExpr
<Control1000000000>	General	Container	ContentArea	
<Control1000000001>	Options	Group	Group	
Top X	Top X	Field		intTopX
Top X Field	Top X Field	Field		txtTopType
Chart Type	Chart Type	Field		intChartType

Remember to put these fields on a section for them to become available in the dataset.

Next, go to Visual Studio and create a table data region in the body of the report.

Give the report a similar layout then the standard **report 111 Customer Top 10** (or **report 10062 Top __ Customer List** if you use the US version).

The report contains a table data region that will show the top X customers, so put the **Customer No**, **Name**, **Sales (LCY)**, **Profit (LCY)**, and **Balance (LCY)** on the detail level, with a corresponding caption in the header level. For the numerical fields, you will also create a footer level to display the sums.

Below that we will show some extra totals. For example, if the user asks to view the top ten customers according to **Balance (LCY)**, below the table they will also see the total of the **Balance (LCY)** of the 10 customers compared with the grand total for all customers and also the two values expressed as a percentage. For this we will need to do some calculations.

The first question is how to filter to only see the top X records in a table. Actually, that's very simple. In the table properties, there's a **Filter** tab not very far from the **Sort** tab. In this **Filter** tab, you can of course define filter(s). You can select the field that needs to be filtered, the type of filter (**Operator**) and the **Value** used for filtering. In our case, the value used for filtering will come from the dataset, **Top X**. The operator will be **TOP N** and the field that we will filter upon will also depend on what the user has selected in the request page as **Top X Field**. You can see how to create the filter in the following screenshot:

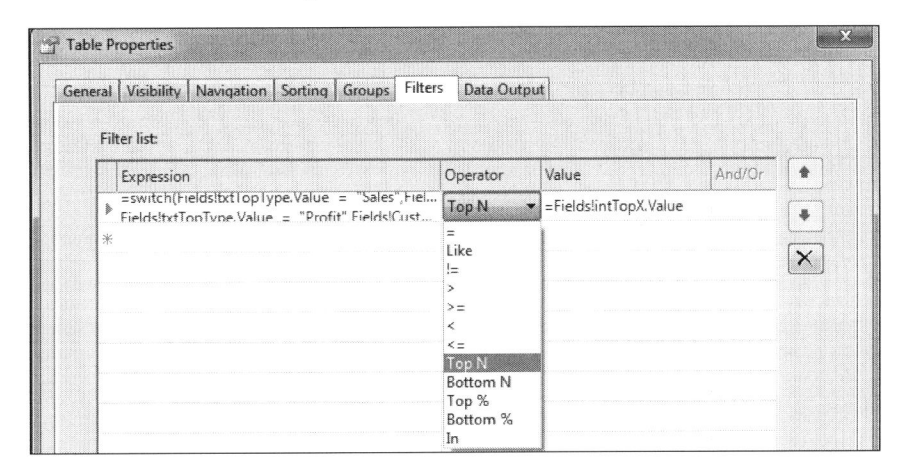

The expression used for the first field is:

```
=switch(Fields!txtTopType.Value = "Sales",Fields!Customer__Sales__LCY_
_.Value,
Fields!txtTopType.Value = "Profit",Fields!Customer__Profit__LCY__
.Value,
Fields!txtTopType.Value = "Balance",Fields!Customer__Balance__LCY__
.Value)
```

The `Switch()` function works like the CASE statement in C/AL code. It is a compound statement that will check multiple conditions and return corresponding results. In this case, if in the request page the user selected **Sales**, then the report will filter the top X **Sales (LCY)** values, if the user selected **Profit** then the report will filter on **Profit (LCY)**, and so on. This function can very easily be extended with extra values.

> **Expression readability**
> To make a complex expression easier to read and understand you can split it over multiple lines, just as you can in C/AL code.

Developing Specific Reports

This will take care of the filtering; now we need to find a way to calculate and show the totals. Because the table is always filtered using a **TOP N**, we cannot use the table to calculate the grand total. The grand total will need to be calculated outside and before the table and filter is applied.

To solve this problem, you can use a rectangle and in the rectangle you can put three text boxes that will hold the totals or sums, as you can see in this screenshot:

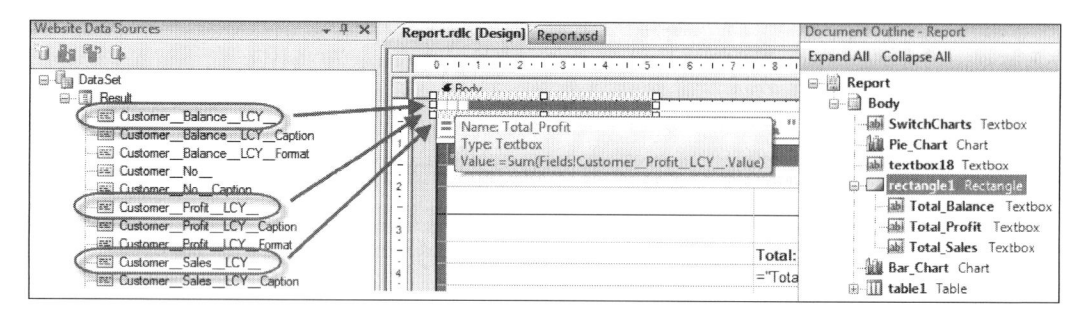

The reason to use a rectangle to hold the text boxes is so that when you need to move them, you only need to select and move the rectangle. Another reason is that you can hide the rectangle and everything contained in the rectangle is also hidden. This way the `Hidden` property of each item contained in the rectangle does not have to be modified. You can give it a red background color to show to the developer that it is hidden.

Now that we have the sums on the body, we just need to reference them in the table using the `ReportItems` collection.

There are three rows containing totals. Row one contains the top X total, row two contains the grand total, and the last row contains the percentage. The following are the expressions used in the rows:

Total row one:

```
=Sum(Fields!Customer__Sales__LCY__.Value)
```

Total row two:

```
=ReportItems!Total_Sales.Value
```

Total row three:

```
=ReportItems!Total_TopXSales.Value / ReportItems!Total_Sales.Value * 100
```

> **Divide by zero error**
>
> When you create an expression and divide two values it is best to check and see that you do not divide by zero or you will get an error at runtime. In this case, you could for example create a custom function and use that instead to do the division. An example of such a function to calculate a percentage is as follows:
>
> ```
> Shared Pct as Decimal
> Public Function CalcPct(Amount1 as Decimal, Amount2 as
> Decimal) as Decimal
>   If Amount2 <> 0 then
>     Pct = Amount1 / Amount2 * 100
>   else
>     Pct = 0
>   end if
>   REM Rounding precision = 0.1
>   Return ROUND(10*Pct)/10
> End Function
> ```

The total calculations for the other columns are similar, but instead of using **the Sales (LCY)** field you use the **Profit (LCY)** and **Balance (LCY)** fields.

The total fields are shown in column two to be able to align them a little more to the right then the detail rows of the table. To make sure this extra column does not show up in the detail rows, the first two columns of the detail rows have been merged.

> **Merging cells**
>
> Adding extra columns and/or rows in a data region and merging cells is a technique often applied in Reporting Services, as in Excel, to create certain layouts.

The text box between the table and the rectangle serves as a report title. The expression for this text box is:

```
="Top "& Fields!intTopX.Value &" customers, according to "&
Fields!txtTopType.Value
```

The expression makes sure the title is dynamically updated depending on what the user has selected in the request page.

Developing Specific Reports

> **Showing applied filters and options**
>
> It is a best practice to always foresee to be able to show the selected filters and options applied by the user in the request page. Doing this will help you whenever there's a discussion about the report between the end user and the developer. This can be done by using the GETFILTER() or GETFILTERS() function(s) on the data item(s) in C/AL code, and putting the results of the functions in a text box in the result set so you can put it in a header or footer of the report.
>
> If you filtered the report in Visual Studio, those values are not returned by C/AL code. If that's the case, you have to make sure to also display the applied filters in Visual Studio. If you used fields from the dataset as filter values, you could reference them in a text box on the header.

> As a reference you can import report 90016 Customer Top X.

Creating a TOP X chart

Our **TOP-X** table is ready, now it's time to focus on the chart(s). The first chart is a bar chart. Just add a chart data region from the toolbox and drop it below the table. The grouping will be on customer number; the value will be an expression, because it depends again on what the user selected in the request page.

To create the chart, follow these steps:

1. Add a chart data region from the toolbox onto the **Body** of the report.
2. Drag the **Sales (LCY)** field onto the **Data** zone of the chart.
3. Drag the **Customer No** field onto the **Categoryfields** zone of the chart.
4. Right-click on the **Sales (LCY)** field in the chart and select **Properties.**
5. Enter the following expression in the **Value** property of the **Values** tab in the popup window:

   ```
   =switch(Fields!txtTopType.Value = "Sales",Sum(Fields!Customer__Sales__LCY__.Value),
   Fields!txtTopType.Value = "Profit",Sum(Fields!Customer__Profit__LCY__.Value),
   Fields!txtTopType.Value = "Balance",Sum(Fields!Customer__Balance__LCY__.Value))
   ```

The popup window that was opened is presented in the following screenshot:

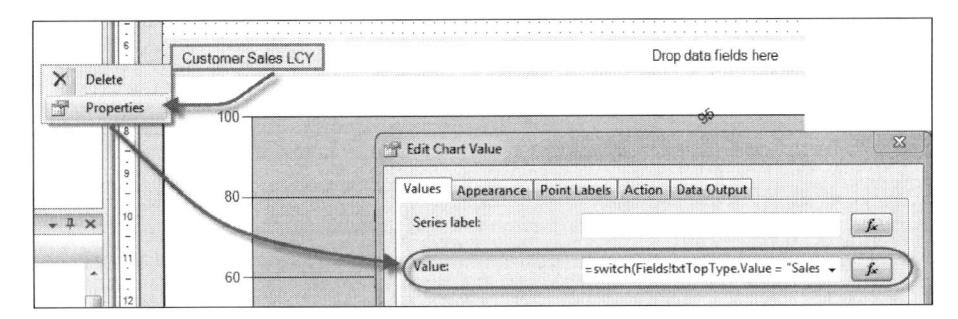

In the same properties window, you can also determine if and how point labels should be shown. As a data label, you can use the same expression.

The next thing to do is add another chart, but this time a pie chart. Instead of creating a new chart using the toolbox, you can just copy the existing chart and paste it as a new chart. After that you only need to modify the chart type of the pasted chart. The advantage of this method is that the expressions and properties you set for the original chart are also copied over to the new chart.

Use the same expressions for the pie chart, except for the point labels use the following expression:

```
=switch(Fields!txtTopType.Value = "Sales",Sum(Fields!Customer__Sales__
LCY__.Value) &"("& Fields!Customer_Name.Value &")",
Fields!txtTopType.Value = "Profit",Sum(Fields!Customer__Profit__LCY__
.Value) &"("& Fields!Customer_Name.Value &")",
Fields!txtTopType.Value = "Balance",Sum(Fields!Customer__Balance__LCY_
_.Value) &"("& Fields!Customer_Name.Value &")")
```

The **Datalabel** expression can be found in the **Point Labels** tab as shown in the following screenshot:

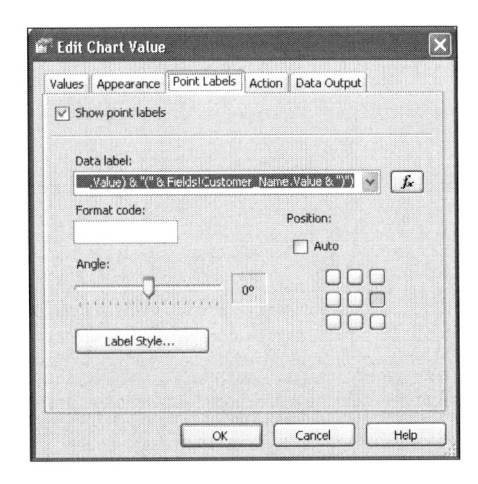

The idea was to also include the customer number inside the slices of pie, per slice. This makes it easier to read the chart. It could even make the chart legend obsolete.

The chart that needs to be shown in the report depends on what the user selects in the request page; to use the following expression in the hidden property of the charts:

Bar chart:

```
=Iif(Fields!intChartType.Value = "Bar",false,false)
```

Pie chart:

```
=Iif(Fields!intChartType.Value = "Bar",true,false)
```

To enable the user to change the chart type at runtime without having to rerun the complete report, also add a text box at the bottom of the report and assign it as the `ToggleItem` for both charts.

> The `Iif()` function has the following syntax:
> ```
> Public Function Iif(
>     ByVal Expression As Boolean,
>     ByVal TruePart As Object,
>     ByVal FalsePart As Object
> ) As Object
> ```
> It contains the following parameters:
>
> `Expression`
> Required. Boolean. The expression you want to evaluate.
>
> `TruePart`
> Required. Object. Returned if Expression evaluates to True.
>
> `FalsePart`
> Required. Object. Returned if Expression evaluates to False.
>
> Basically, you can use it like you use the `IF Expression THEN TruePart ELSE FalsePart;` statement in C/AL code.

The runtime version of the report should then look like the following screenshot:

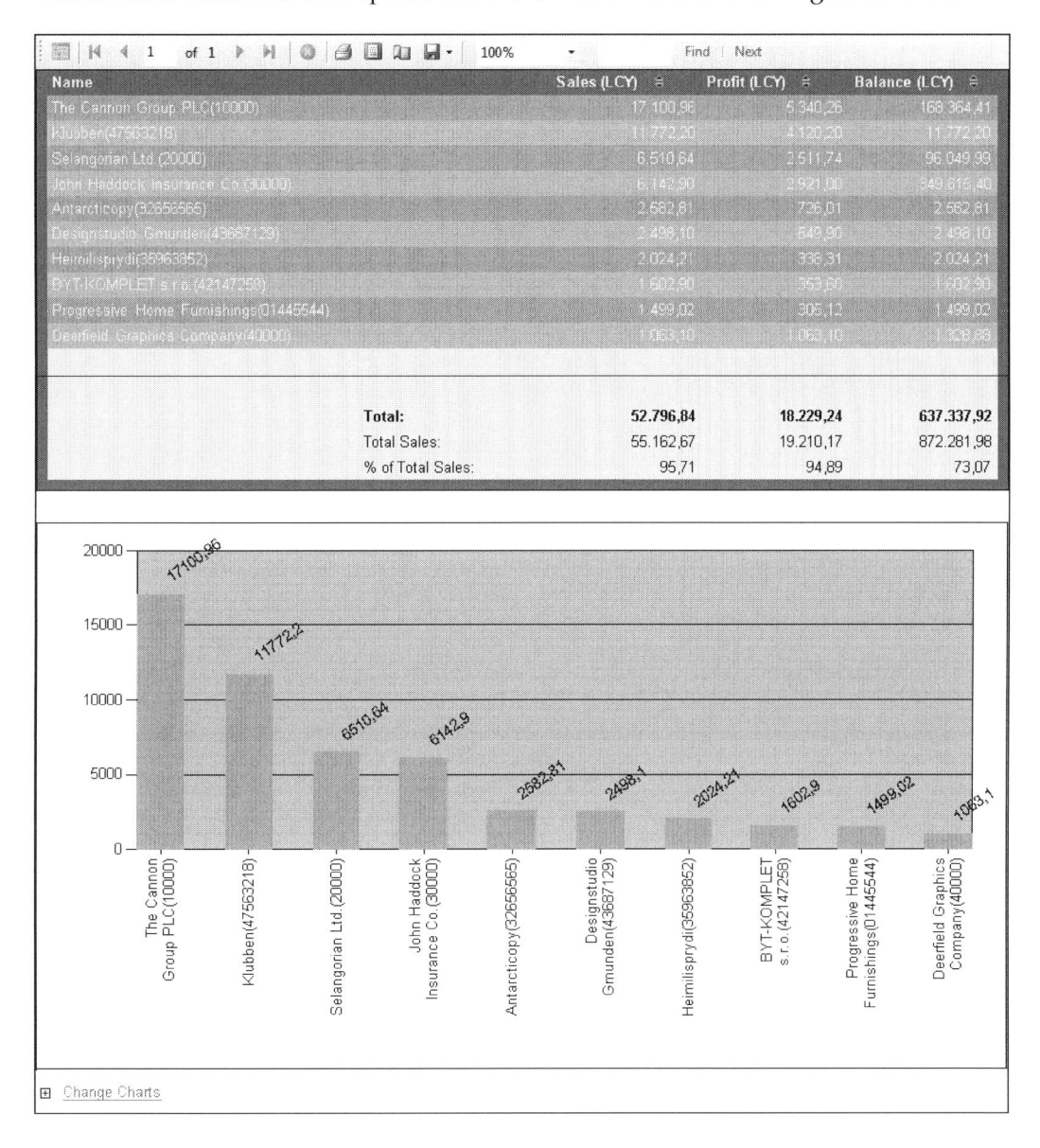

> As a reference, you can import report 90016 Customer Top X.

Developing Specific Reports

Using the wizard

There's no wizard available that can create an enhanced layout for your report, or is there? Actually, sometimes you can get quite far and save time by using the old existing wizard for Classic reports. For example, create a new report using the wizard, select the Customer as the table, and use **Tabular-Type Report Wizard**, as in the next screenshot:

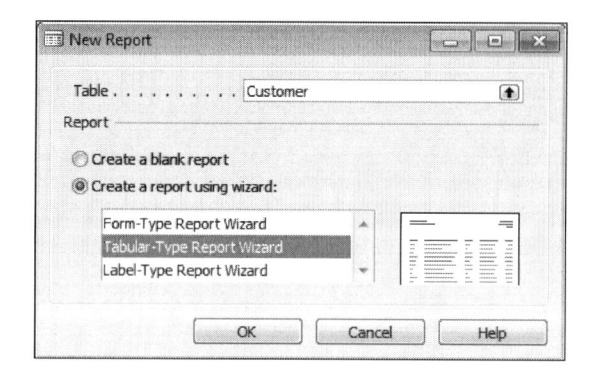

In the next pages of the wizard, you can select the fields you want to show in the report, the sorting and grouping fields, and the total to be calculated. Sections will be created according to the options selected during the wizard. You will get a result as shown in the following screenshot:

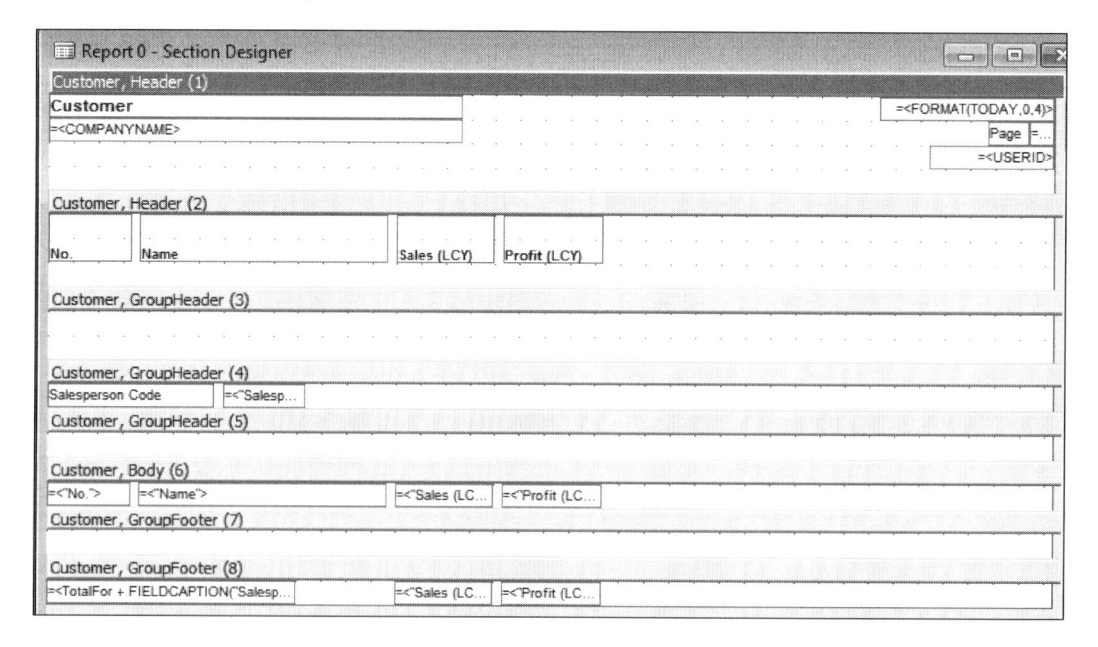

Next, go to the menu and select **Tools | Create Layout Suggestion**. Visual Studio will be opened and an enhanced layout will be generated as shown in the next screenshot:

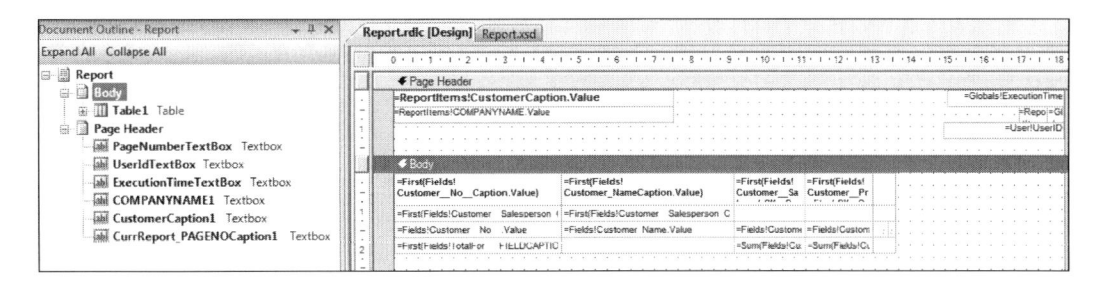

As you can see, there's also a header containing the **Company Name**, **PageNumber**, **UserId**, **ExecutionTime**… Using the Classic wizard combined with **Create Layout Suggestion**, you can create a basic report with just a few mouse clicks.

When you have to create an enhanced layout for lots of reports and you have a limited amount of time (budget), this might be a solution to speed up the report creation process.

> **Template report**
>
> A more interesting approach might be to manually create a template report containing the basic information you want to be available on all your reports. (header, footer, layout, colors, images…). You can even already include custom functions in that template report. Then, for every new report you have to create, you can start with the template and save time.
>
> It could even be interesting, and more timesaving, to give this report template a specific look and feel that has to be applied in all reports for that specific project.

Adding KPIs and conditional formatting

KPIs or Key Performance Indicators visualize the status of certain activities. It is now possible to achieve this in Dynamics NAV 2009 enhanced reports using conditional formatting and image controls.

I'm not referring to the same kind of KPIs available in most business intelligence systems, multidimensional databases (or cubes). In those scenarios, KPIs are used to evaluate the success of a certain activity or to measure the achievement of specific goals defined by the management. There are quantitative indicators that can be expressed as a numerical value, directional indicators specifying whether an organization is improving or not, financial indicators used in performance management, and so on. These kinds of indicators require a lot of analysis to define, measure, implement, and evaluate. It is a process or on-going project that can take many weeks or even months to implement.

Cubes or multidimensional databases are based upon the OLAP data model. OLAP stands for Online Analytical Processing and is basically a data model that allows for fast querying, reporting, and analysis. Since Dynamics NAV is not an OLAP system but an OLTP system, its data is too normalized to implement real KPIs.

> More information about OLAP can be found here: `http://en.wikipedia.org/wiki/OLAP_cube`

In this section, I will give an overview of the possibilities available at this point on how you can leverage RDLC reporting to provide an executive view of business performance indication.

Let's start with a very simple KPI. You want to present sales information with a salesperson. For this purpose, we have an existing report: "**114 Salesperson - Sales Statistics**". The information in this report is presented using a flat colorless text.

> Report **114 Salesperson – Sales Statistics** is available in the W1 version of Dynamics NAV. If you don't have this version, you can import the report (delivered with the book).

This is what the default report looks like:

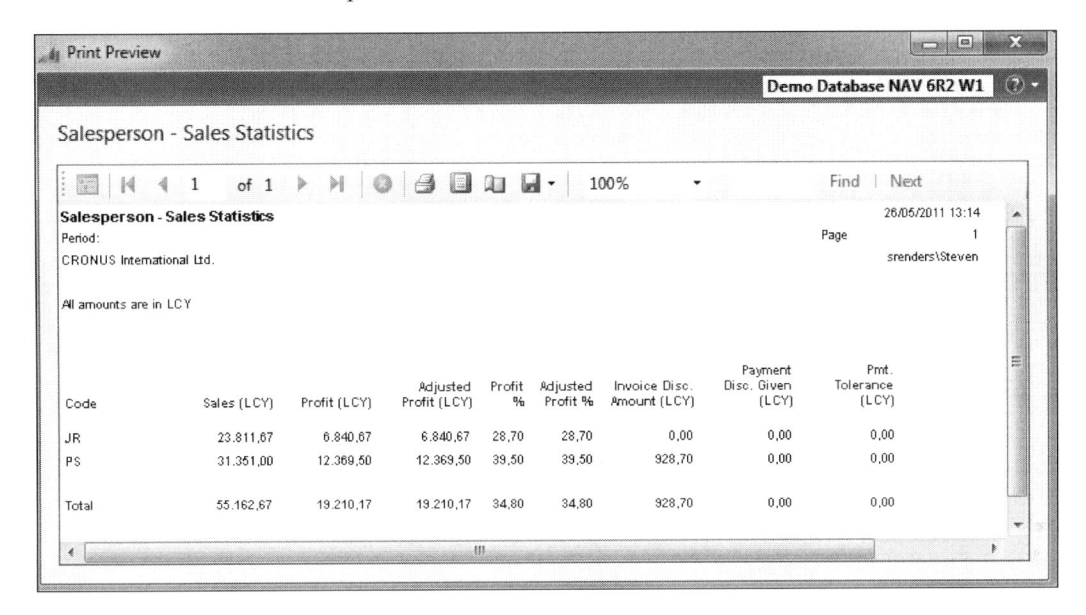

And this is how the report implementing simple KPIs could look:

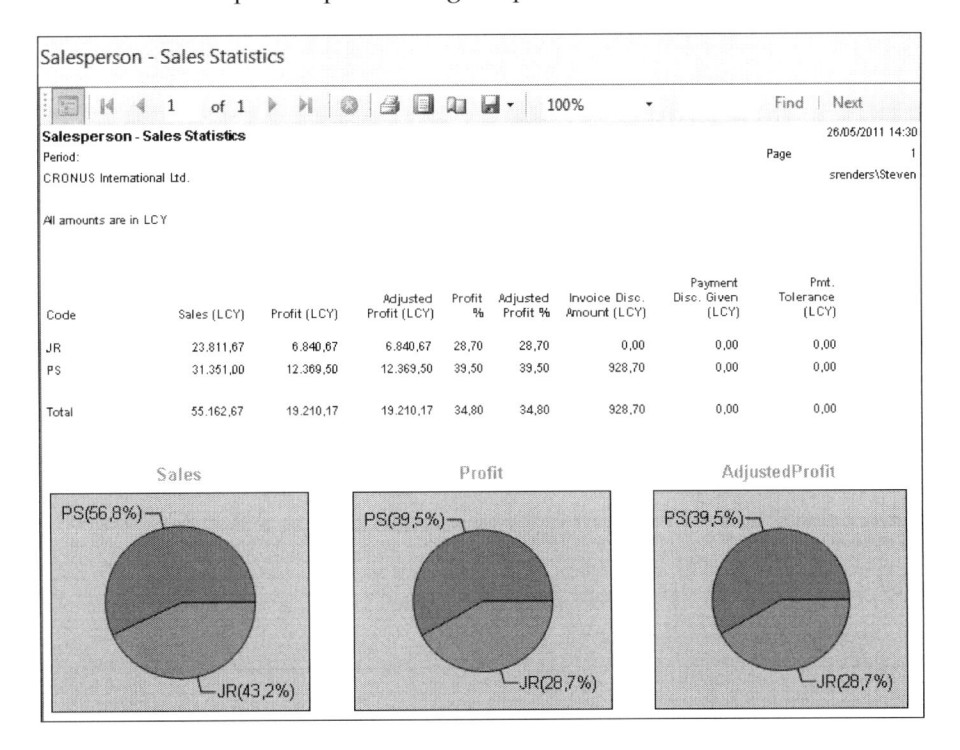

In this case, the report was enhanced using three chart controls, showing the same information that is available in the table above, but making the data easier to read and understand.

Enhancing the layout of a report doesn't always involve hours of work.

To create the charts follow these steps:

1. Open the enhanced layout of the report in Visual Studio.
2. Expand the size of the body, to make room for the charts below the table.
3. Add three charts below the table.
4. Use the **Cust_Ledger_Entry_Sales_LCY_field** as the **Data** field for the chart.
5. Use the **Cust__Ledger_Entry_Salesperson_Code** field as the **Category** for the chart.
6. Set the chart property `Palette` to `EarthTones`.
7. Repeat these steps for the two other charts, but pay attention to the following steps:
8. Use the field **Cust_Ledger_Entry_Profit_LCY** as the **Data** field for the second chart.
9. Change the expression for the **Value** to: `=Code.CalcPct(Sum(Fields!Cust__Ledger_Entry___Sales__LCY__.Value), Sum(Fields!Cust__Ledger_Entry___Profit__LCY__.Value))` for the second chart.
10. Actually, you can copy the expression from the Value field of **text box3** in the table data region.
11. Use the field **AdjProfit** as the **Data** field for the third chart.
12. Change the expression for the **Value** to: `=Code.CalcPct(Sum(Fields!Cust__Ledger_Entry___Sales__LCY__.Value), Sum(Fields!AdjProfit.Value))` for the third chart.
13. Actually, you can copy the expression from the Value field of **text box4** in the table data region.

To be able to show the percentages inside the charts and to combine them with the salesperson names, use the following expression in the **Chart Point Labels**:

First chart (Sales):

```
=Fields!Cust__Ledger_Entry_Salesperson_Code.Value &"("&Code.
CalcPct2(Sum(Fields!Cust__Ledger_Entry___Sales__LCY__.Value),
Sum(Fields!Cust__Ledger_Entry___Sales__LCY__.Value,"DataSet_Result"))
&"%)"
```

Second chart (Profit):

```
=Fields!Cust__Ledger_Entry_Salesperson_Code.Value &"("& Code.
CalcPct(Sum(Fields!Cust__Ledger_Entry___Sales__LCY__.Value),
Sum(Fields!Cust__Ledger_Entry___Profit__LCY__.Value)) &"%)"
```

Third chart (AdjustedProfit):

```
=Fields!Cust__Ledger_Entry_Salesperson_Code.Value &"("& Code.
CalcPct(Sum(Fields!Cust__Ledger_Entry___Sales__LCY__.Value),
Sum(Fields!AdjProfit.Value)) &"%)"
```

The functions used in the expressions in the chart are all defined in the report properties **Code** tab. All of these functions were already available in the standard report. The difference between the function `CalcPct` and `CalcPct2` is very minimal.

```
Shared Pct as Decimal
Public Function CalcPct(Amount as Decimal, Profit as Decimal) as
Decimal
    if Amount <> 0 then
        Pct = 100 * Profit / Amount
    else
        Pct = 0
    end if
    REM Rounding precision = 0.1
    Return ROUND(10*Pct)/10
End Function
```

The function `CalcPct` calculates a percentage based upon two parameters: `Amount` and `Profit`.

```
Shared Pct2 as Decimal
Public Function CalcPct2(Amount1 as Decimal, Amount2 as Decimal) as
Decimal
    if Amount2 <> 0 then
        Pct2 = Amount1 / Amount2 * 100
    else
        Pct2 = 0
    end if
    REM Rounding precision = 0.1
    Return ROUND(10*Pct2)/10
End Function
```

The function `CalcPct2` calculates a percentage based upon two parameters: `Amount1` and `Amount2`.

> The finished report containing the charts is delivered with the book and is report: SalesBySalesPerson (90018).

Simulating data bars

Data bar, **Sparkline**, **Gauge**, **Map**… are new controls added in SQL Server Reporting Services 2008 and beyond. You can find these controls in the toolbar in the Visual Studio report designer and integrate directly in your report like any other control. In the future release(s) of Dynamics NAV, they will probably become available, but in Dynamics NAV 2009 they're not available. But that doesn't mean that they cannot be used in reports. It means that we will need to find workarounds to simulate the same kind of behaviour. It might be a little more work, but in the end the user might not even notice the difference and by controlling everything manually using expressions instead of using ready-made controls we even might have a little more flexibility.

> In SQL Server Reporting Services, server side, it is possible to create custom controls and register and deploy them on a report server so they become available as new controls in the toolbox in Visual Studio. Although I haven't seen this technology used a lot at implementations, it opens an interesting possibility. It means that if you cannot do something with the existing available controls, you can extend the functionality of Reporting Services yourself to fulfil your requirements. I'm hoping that this might someday also become possible in RDLC and Dynamics NAV enhanced reports, like it already is at page level using control add ins or .NET interop. That would indicate that it might someday become possible to reuse controls developed for page objects, in report objects. I'm pretty certain that this will become a reality someday; the only question right now is when.

Simulating data bars is almost as easy as using the data bar control in RDLC 2008. As an example I will use report 712 **Inventory – Sales Statistics**. The report shows the list of items, grouped by **Inventory Posting Group**, as you can see in the next screenshot:

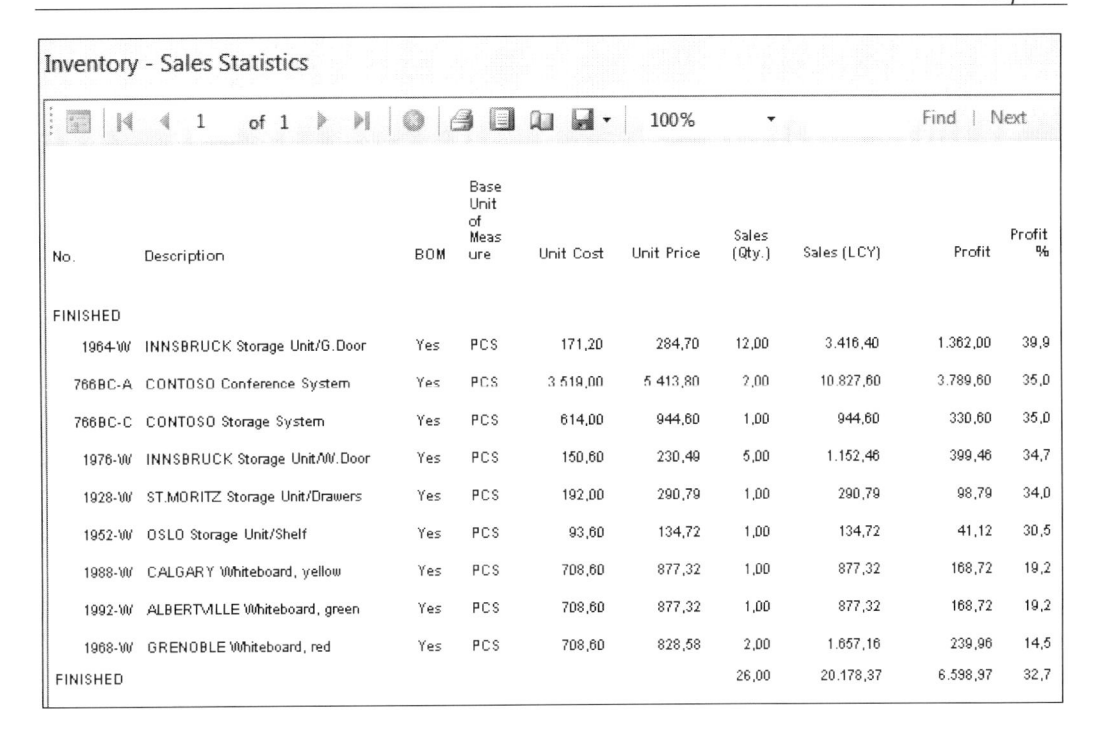

Inventory - Sales Statistics

No.	Description	BOM	Base Unit of Measure	Unit Cost	Unit Price	Sales (Qty.)	Sales (LCY)	Profit	Profit %
FINISHED									
1964-W	INNSBRUCK Storage Unit/G.Door	Yes	PCS	171,20	284,70	12,00	3.416,40	1.362,00	39,9
766BC-A	CONTOSO Conference System	Yes	PCS	3.519,00	5.413,80	2,00	10.827,60	3.789,60	35,0
766BC-C	CONTOSO Storage System	Yes	PCS	614,00	944,60	1,00	944,60	330,60	35,0
1976-W	INNSBRUCK Storage Unit/W.Door	Yes	PCS	150,60	230,49	5,00	1.152,46	399,46	34,7
1928-W	ST.MORITZ Storage Unit/Drawers	Yes	PCS	192,00	290,79	1,00	290,79	98,79	34,0
1952-W	OSLO Storage Unit/Shelf	Yes	PCS	93,60	134,72	1,00	134,72	41,12	30,5
1988-W	CALGARY Whiteboard, yellow	Yes	PCS	708,60	877,32	1,00	877,32	168,72	19,2
1992-W	ALBERTVILLE Whiteboard, green	Yes	PCS	708,60	877,32	1,00	877,32	168,72	19,2
1968-W	GRENOBLE Whiteboard, red	Yes	PCS	708,60	828,58	2,00	1.657,16	239,96	14,5
FINISHED						26,00	20.178,37	6.598,97	32,7

We will transform the report so it will show the **Profit%** in a more visual way, as in the next screenshot:

Item Inventory Posting Group	Item No	Item Description	Item Bill of Materials	Item Base Unit of Measure	Unit Cost	Unit Price	Sales Qty	Sales Amount	Item Profit	Item Profit Pct
RAW MAT										
	70011	Glass Door	No	PCS	36,90	70,49	6,00	422,95	201,55	47,7
RAW MAT							6	422,95	201,55	47,7
FINISHED										
	1964-W	INNSBRUCK Storage Unit/G.Door	Yes	PCS	171,20	284,70	12,00	3416,40	1362,00	39,9
	766BC-A	CONTOSO Conference System	Yes	PCS	3519,00	5413,80	2,00	10827,60	3789,60	35,0
	766BC-C	CONTOSO Storage System	Yes	PCS	614,00	944,60	1,00	944,60	330,60	35,0
	1976-W	INNSBRUCK Storage Unit/W.Door	Yes	PCS	150,60	230,49	5,00	1152,46	399,46	34,7
	1928-W	ST.MORITZ Storage Unit/Drawers	Yes	PCS	192,00	290,79	1,00	290,79	98,79	34,0
	1952-W	OSLO Storage Unit/Shelf	Yes	PCS	93,60	134,72	1,00	134,72	41,12	30,5
	1988-W	CALGARY Whiteboard, yellow	Yes	PCS	708,60	877,32	1,00	877,32	168,72	19,2
	1992-W	ALBERTVILLE Whiteboard, green	Yes	PCS	708,60	877,32	1,00	877,32	168,72	19,2
	1968-W	GRENOBLE Whiteboard, red	Yes	PCS	708,60	828,58	2,00	1657,16	239,96	14,5
FINISHED							26	20178,37	6598,97	32,7

How can you add data bars to a report? Well, the answer is: use a bar chart that contains only one line. So we are going to add a chart inside the existing table, in a new column. The idea is to show the bar besides the existing fields, in this case to the right of the **Profit %**.

When you add a new column, insert a chart in it; then your report will throw an error:

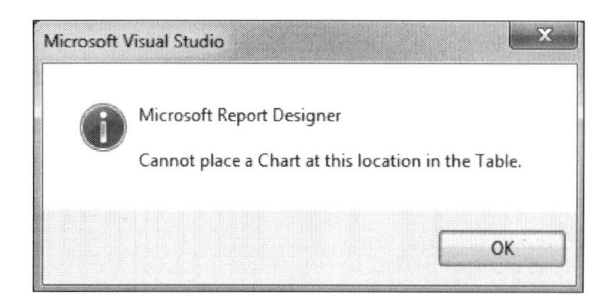

This is because a chart cannot be embedded in the detail level of a table data region. You have to put the chart inside a table header, table footer, group header, or group footer.

So, we will have to add a new group level in the existing table. At this time, the detail level is showing information about items, grouped by **Inventory Posting Group**. You could add a chart to the inventory posting group header, but at that location in the table there's no information about the detail level, the individual items. So, we will need to add an extra group, on **Item No**. After creating a new group on **Item No** you will have to move (cut and paste) all fields from the detail level onto **the Item No** group header level. Then, add an extra column and in there you can add the chart control.

This is how the RDLC looks before making any changes:

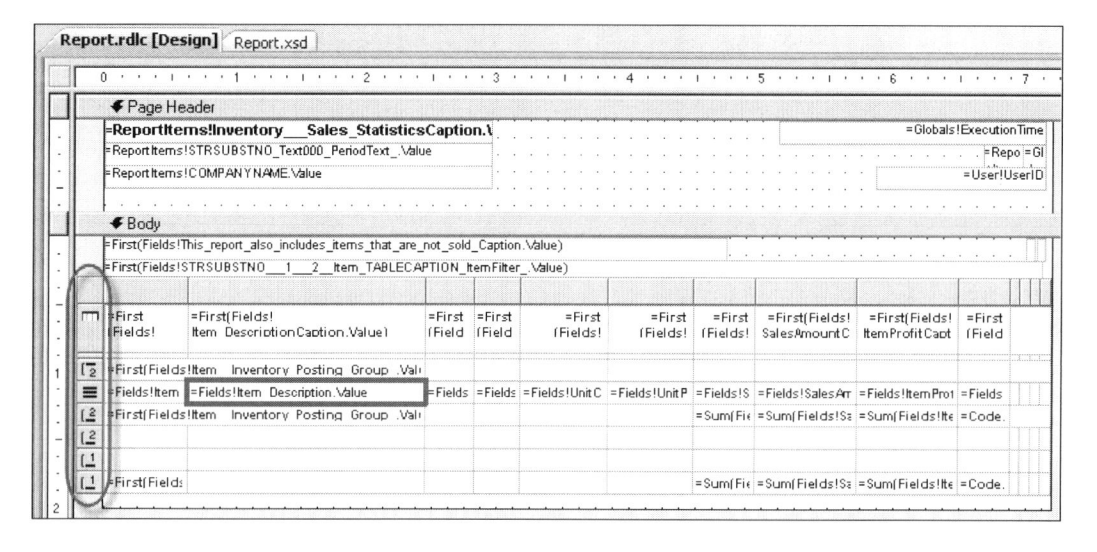

And this is how it looks after you change the table data region:

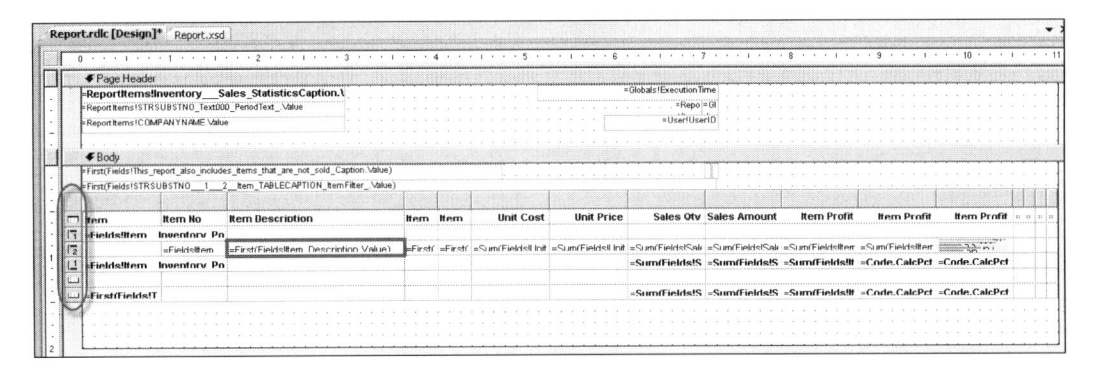

Right-click on the chart, and select the field **Profit Pct** as the `Data` field. To maximize the chart plot area for the bar, apply the following chart property settings:

1. Open **General Settings**.
2. Set to `Bar Chart` and turn off the legend.
3. Open **Data**.
4. Bind the chart to the same dataset as the table, `DataSet_Result`.
5. Add the **Profit Pct** field as the value to be visualized.
6. Turn off axis labels, gridlines, and tick marks on the X axis.
7. Turn off axis labels, tick marks, and set the maximum to 100.

This is a screenshot of the chart design:

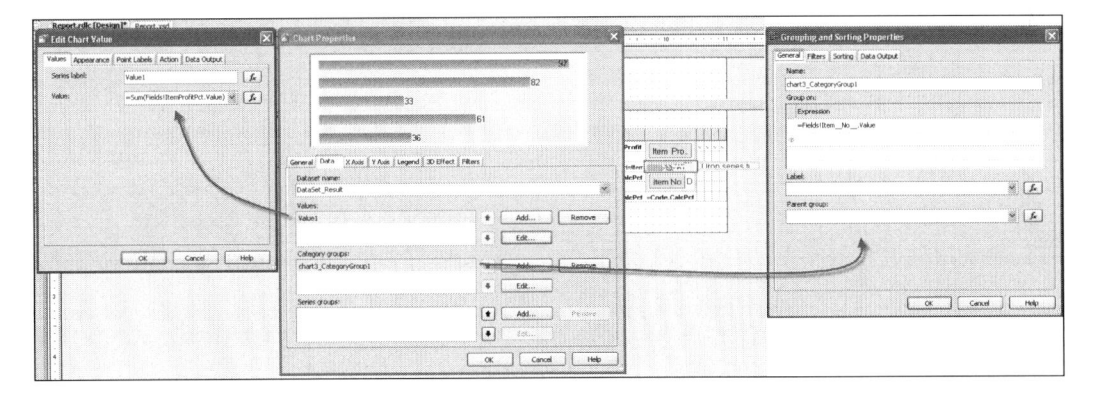

[247]

> **Don't forget the Y-axis max value!**
> When you simulate a data bar by nesting a chart inside a table then the max value in the Y-axis is very important to set. If you omit it then all the bars will get an incorrect size and sometimes even the same size. In this example, I used 100 as the max value for the Y-axis because I'm showing percentages and the maximum possible value is 100.

The way that the original report was created by Microsoft is using three groupings in the table. The first group was a fixed group, grouping on the value one. The idea behind it is to use the footer(s) from this group to display totals. Because, in my opinion, this extra group level is unnecessary and makes things too difficult, I recreated the table from scratch using only two groups, on **Inventory Posting Group** and on **Item No.** To be able to display the totals I'm using an extra footer for the first grouping. No extra group is required.

Because we will not be showing any information in the detail level of the table it's best to hide or even delete it, using its `Hidden` property.

Remember, when you recreate the table, don't forget to create four extra hidden columns to hold the information required for the header.

These are the steps required to recreate the table:

1. Add a table data region from the toolbox on the **Body** of the report.
2. Add columns to the table until there are 16 columns.
3. Right-click on the row handler or the detail level.
4. In the dropdown box that opens, deselect the **Table Details**. This removes the detail level from the table.
5. Open the properties popup window of the table and in the **General** tab, set **DataSet_Result** as the `Dataset` name for the table.
6. In the same popup window, click on the **Groups** tab to select it.
7. In the **Groups** tab, use the **Add** button to add a group.
8. In the **Grouping and Sorting Properties** window that opens, enter (or select) `=Fields!Item__No__.Value` as the **Expression** to group on.
9. Deselect the option **Include group footer** for this group.
10. Rename the group to **Grp_ItemNumber.**
11. In the **Groups** tab, use the **Add** button to add another group.

12. In the **Grouping and Sorting Properties** window that opens, enter (or select) `=Fields!Item__Inventory_Posting_Group_.Value` as the **Expression** to group on.
13. Rename the group to **Grp_ItemPostingGroup.**
14. Now you should have two groups; the first group is **Grp_ItemPostingGroup** and the second group is **Grp_ItemNumber.**
    If the two groups are in the wrong order, then use the Up/Down arrows in the Groups tab to change the group order.
15. Right-click the row handler of the table footer and select **Insert Row Below** to add an extra table footer.
16. Starting from the second column add the following expressions to the group header row of group two (every expression belongs in a different column):

    ```
    =Fields!Item__No__.Value
    =First(Fields!Item_Description.Value)
    =First(Fields!Item__Bill_of_Materials_.Value)
    =First(Fields!Item__Base_Unit_of_Measure_.Value)
    =Sum(Fields!UnitCost.Value)
    =Sum(Fields!UnitPrice.Value)
    =Sum(Fields!SalesQty.Value)
    =Sum(Fields!SalesAmount.Value)
    =Sum(Fields!ItemProfit.Value)
    =Sum(Fields!ItemProfitPct.Value)
    ```

17. Add static text in the table header row, corresponding to the labels of each column.
18. Now, you still have five empty columns at the right end of the table data region. One will be used for the chart and the other four columns will be used to store hidden information.
19. In the first column, add the expression `=Fields!Item__Inventory_Posting_Group_.Value` to the text boxes in the group header and group footer row of group one.
20. Merge this cell with the one directly to the right of it.
21. In the first column, in the cell in the second table footer add the following expression: `=First(Fields!TotalCaption.Value)`

Developing Specific Reports

22. In the group footer row of group one, add the following expressions, starting in column eight:

    ```
    =Sum(Fields!SalesQty.Value)
    =Sum(Fields!SalesAmount.Value)
    =Sum(Fields!ItemProfit.Value)
    =Code.CalcPct(Sum(Fields!ItemProfit.Value),
      Sum(Fields!SalesAmount.Value))
    =Code.CalcPct(Sum(Fields!ItemProfit.Value),
      Sum(Fields!SalesAmount.Value))
    ```

23. In the last four columns of the first row in the table, set the following expressions:

    ```
    =First(Fields!STRSUBSTNO_Text000_PeriodText_.Value)
    =First(Fields!COMPANYNAME.Value)
    =First(Fields!Inventory___Sales_StatisticsCaption.Value)
    =Sum(Fields!CurrReport_PAGENO.Value)
    ```

24. Next, set the `Hidden` property of these four columns to `True` and change the `ForeGroundColor` to `Red`. This will indicate to a developer that these text boxes are hidden.

25. Now, delete the original table and move the new table to the position where the old (deleted) table was placed.

You have now recreated the table. What is left to do is add a chart data region to the text box in the header of the second group, in column 12, and configure the chart as described earlier in this section.

In the end, the resulting table definition will look like the following screenshot:

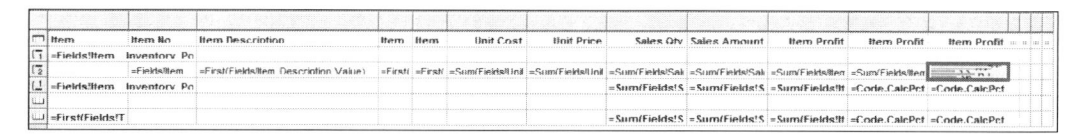

Another possibility to simulate data bar behaviour would be to use an embedded image. For example, you could create a simple bar image using Microsoft Paint, like this one:

This image could then be added inside the table as a new column. To resize it you could use an expression in the left or right padding properties. The padding determines the amount of free space to foresee. Increasing it would mean decreasing the image and so it would simulate data bar behaviour. Although it is possible to do this I would not advise it.

Simulating spark lines

The spark line control, just like the data bar control, was added in RDL version 2008 r2 and so is currently not available in Dynamics NAV 2009, but it can be simulated using a chart control. Again, as in the previous example(s) with the data bars, we are going to nest a chart data region inside a table or matrix data region.

Imagine you would like to create a report showing the amount of transactions or an item, by location in the warehouse and by year. The information for this report is stored in the Item Ledger Entry table. That's the table in which item transactions are posted. Of course, there might also be other interesting tables to look at such as the Value Entry table, but in this example I'm using the Item Ledger Entry table, because then you can imagine how to port this technique to other kinds of ledger entry tables.

The idea is to visualize the activity on a time scale. We could use the posting date for the X-axis, but the problem is that there might not be postings on all dates. So we would end up with gaps in the chart or the chart might become cropped. To avoid this problem, I'm going to include a virtual table, the Date table. It can be used as a calendar, and I'm going to connect it to the Ledger Entry table via the posting date, but allowing gaps.

To limit the amount of information I'm also going to filter the date table. If we do not filter the date table, we will end up with a never ending report showing information till the end of time. To filter the Date table, I will use some C/AL code to calculate the first and last date.

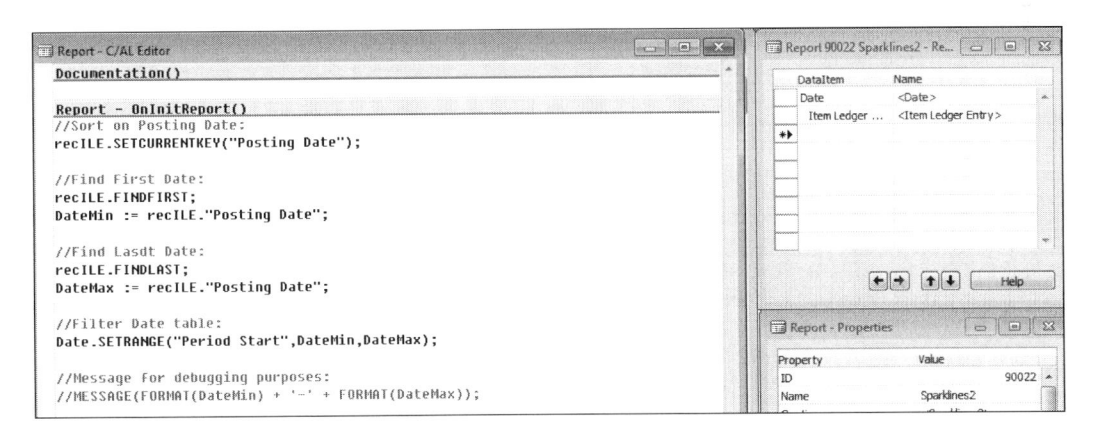

```
Documentation()

Report - OnInitReport()
//Sort on Posting Date:
recILE.SETCURRENTKEY("Posting Date");

//Find First Date:
recILE.FINDFIRST;
DateMin := recILE."Posting Date";

//Find Lasdt Date:
recILE.FINDLAST;
DateMax := recILE."Posting Date";

//Filter Date table:
Date.SETRANGE("Period Start",DateMin,DateMax);

//Message for debugging purposes:
//MESSAGE(FORMAT(DateMin) + '-' + FORMAT(DateMax));
```

Then, on the section(s) put the fields you require to be available in the dataset in Visual Studio. I'm using the following fields, because then I can also use them for grouping.

- **Period Start**
- **Item No**
- **Location Code**
- **Posting Date**
- **Quantity**

Next, I will create an enhanced layout in Visual Studio. I will use a table to hold the information.

First, I start by adding groups in the table. A group on **Item No**, a group on **Year**, and a group on **Location**. To group on **Year**, you can use the following expression:

```
=Year(Fields!Item_Ledger_Entry__Posting_Date_.Value)
```

Every group gets a group header and no footer. Then, after creating the groups, remove the details, footer and header, so that only the three group header rows are left. You did something similar in the previous section about data bars.

Now, we have a table with three groups, three columns, and three rows. Add an extra column to the right. This extra column will hold the chart(s).

The layout of the report should now look like the following screenshot:

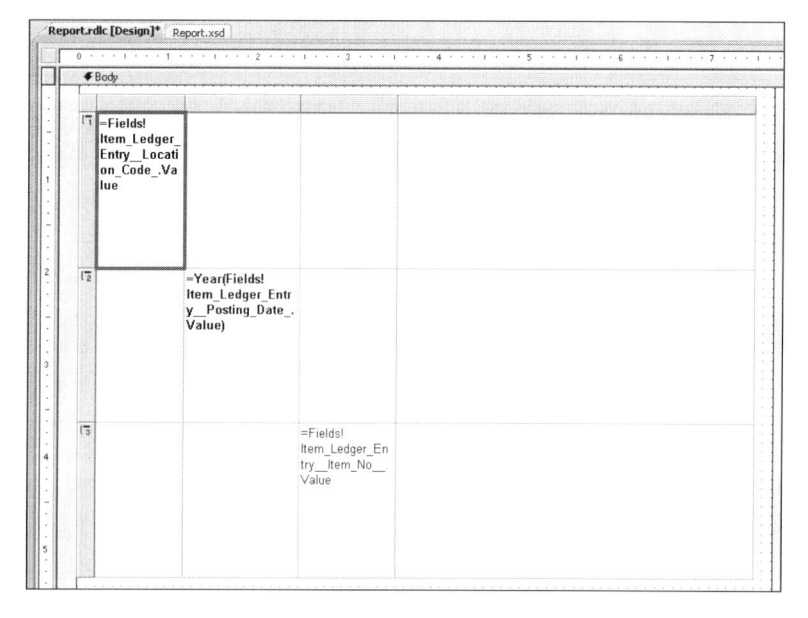

Chapter 5

On the **Item No** level (row three, column four), add a chart in the last column displaying the **Quantity** as the **Data**, use the **Period Start** as the **Category** group and use the **Item No** as the **Series** group. In the chart properties list, set `TypetoLine`, and set `SubTypetoPlain`.

Next, use the chart properties so you don't display the legend and no markers on the X and Y axis, as shown in the next screenshot:

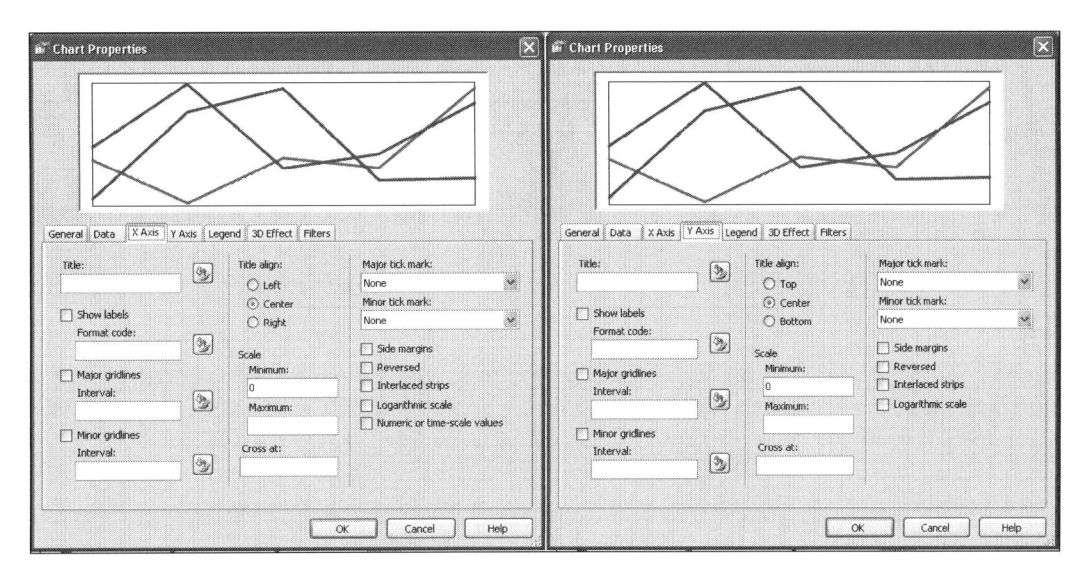

You can also change the colors and background colors, to display a little information as possible. You will end up with a chart as shown in the next screenshot:

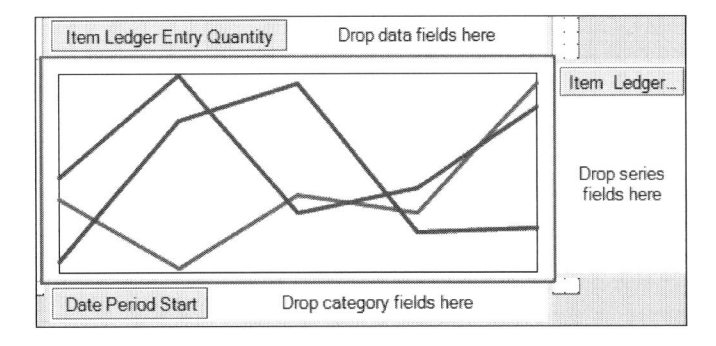

Developing Specific Reports

Next, do the same; add a chart that is, for the other two groups. But, in those charts, do not add a **Series** group on **Item No.** Instead only display the **Quantity** as data and group on **Period Start** as a **Category**.

Now, you can use the visibility (`ToggleItem` and `Hidden`) properties of the groups to create an expand/collapse group effect for each group. When you run the report it will look like this:

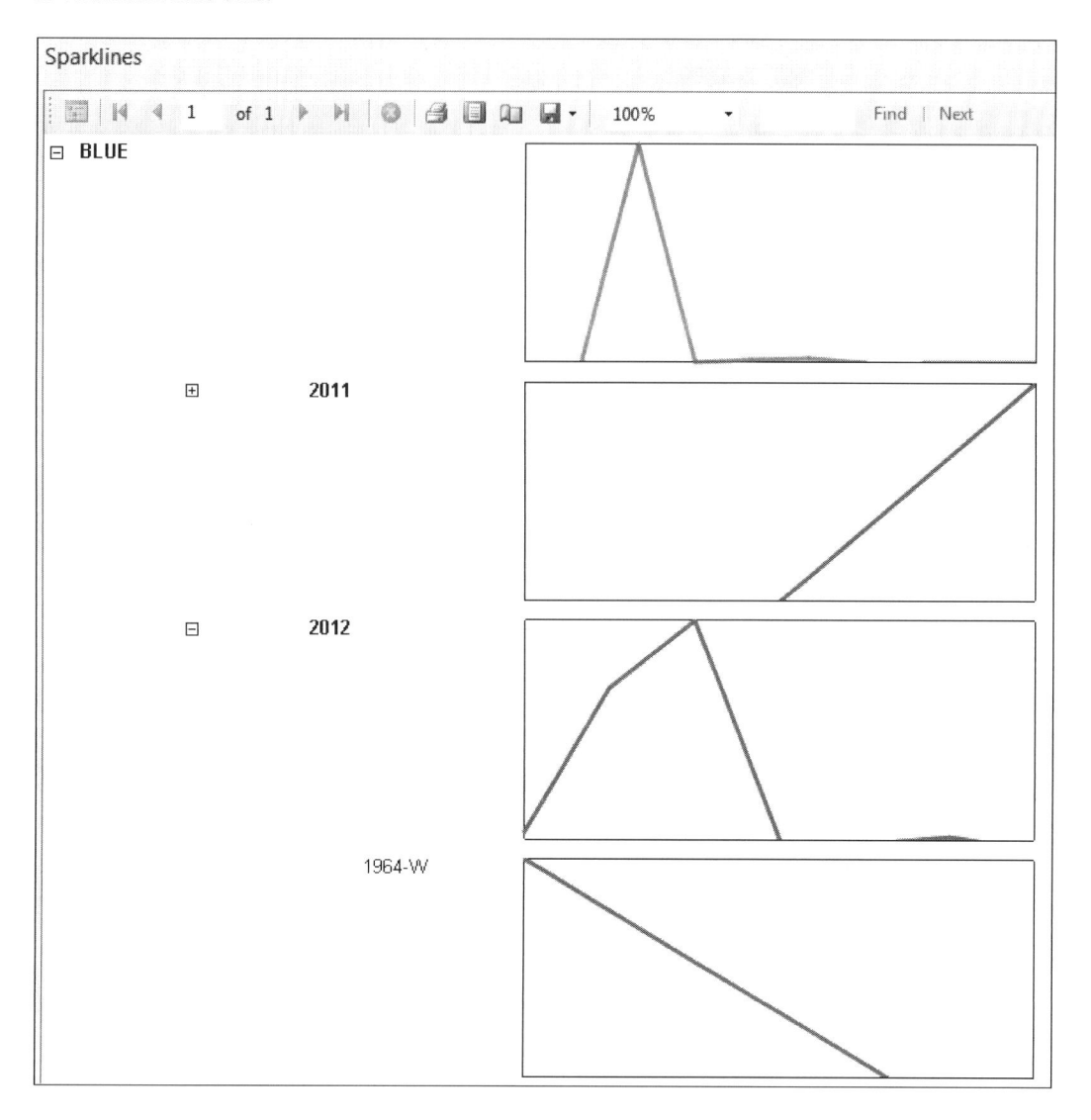

As an alternative, you could use a matrix instead of a table. For example, if you would create the matrix only using one chart, but with the same grouping and visibility properties like in this screenshot:

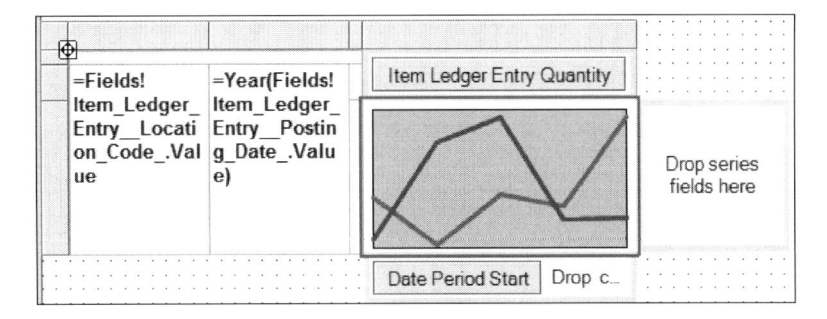

Then the result will look like the next screenshot:

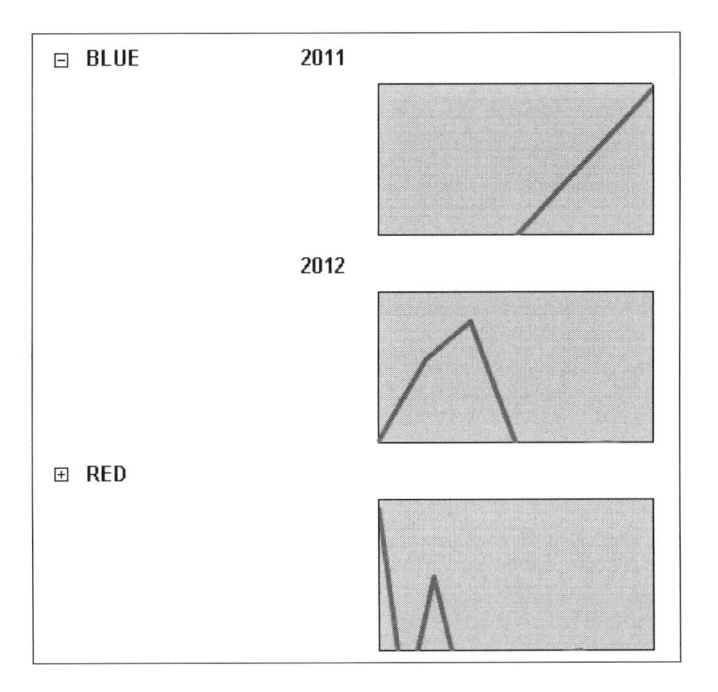

This report could very easily be changed to show the sales per **SalesPerson**. All you would need to do is change the Item Ledger Entry data item to a Customer Ledger Entry dataitem. Replace the group by fields on the sections. Then, open the enhanced layout and make the same replacements in the enhanced layout. The next example is a report with these changes implemented and also giving the user the possibility to toggle the matrix with a table and vice versa.

Developing Specific Reports

To implement the **Toggle Table/Matrix**, you have to create a report containing both the table and matrix in the body. Next, add a text box to the top of the body and use that text box as a `ToggleItem` for both table and matrix. This is very similar with what we did with the **Customer top X** report in the chapter *Data Visualizations*, to toggle between a pie chart and a bar chart.

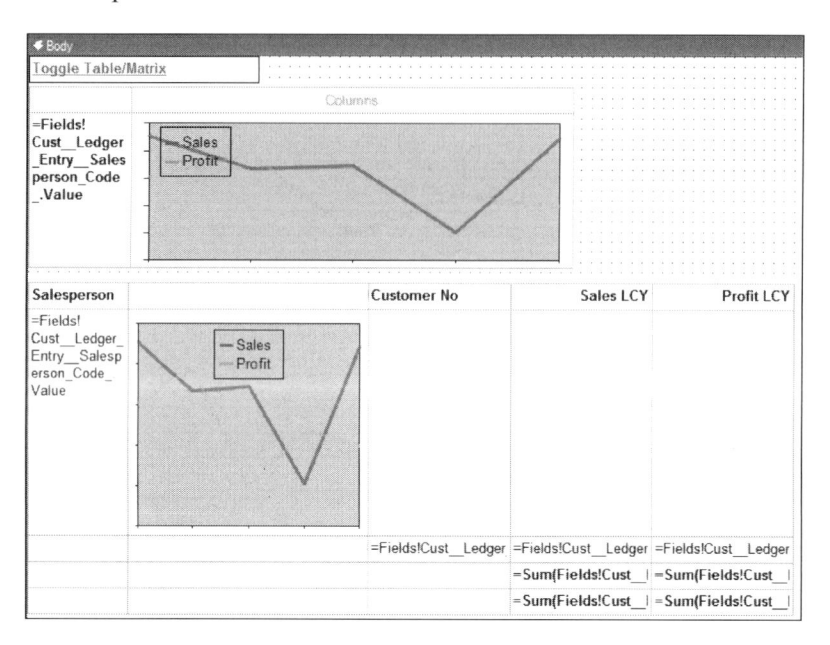

Resulting in the following report at runtime:

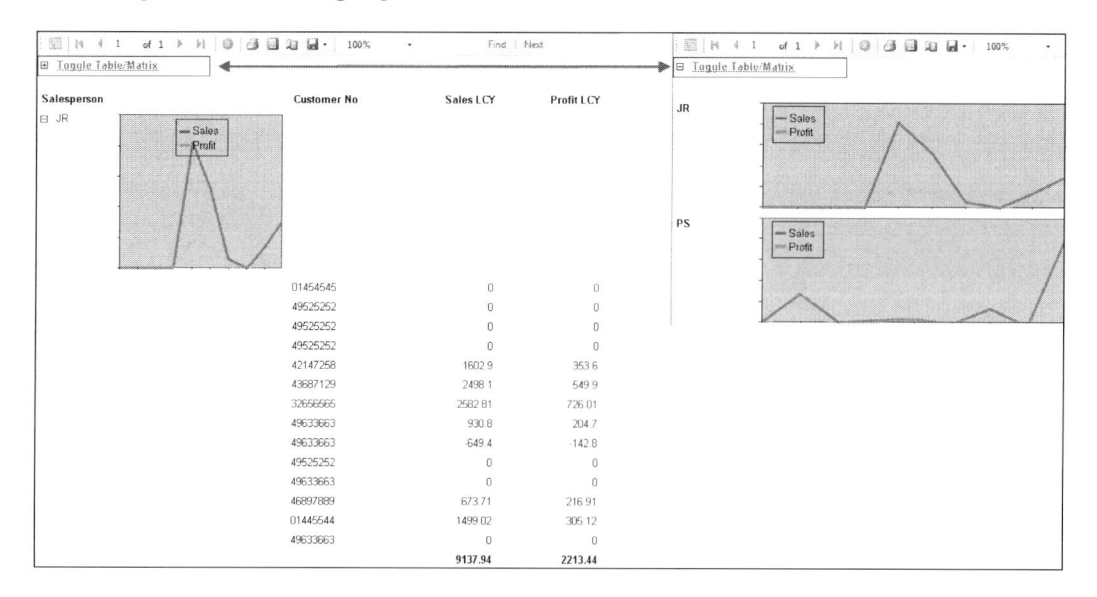

> As a reference, you can import three reports: 90021 Sparklines, 90022Sparklines2, and 90023Sparklines3.

Implementing conditional formatting

Conditional formatting is using a condition to determine the formatting of information displayed on your report. It means that, by using expression(s) you can change the way that information will be rendered on your report, making it easier to read and understand the report.

> **When to use conditional formatting**
>
> Although conditional formatting can increase the readability of a report it is important not to overdo it. Like in the early days of the World Wide Web when we developed our first web pages it was very tempting to include a lot of colors, pictures, moving and animated texts, and so on. But that doesn't necessarily improve the usefulness of a report, more the contrary. So, I would like to stress that conditional formatting should be used with a purpose, not just because it's possible.

Conditional formatting can be implemented using different methods. A very simple example is using the following expression:

```
=Iif(Me.Value > 0,"Green","Red")
```

This expression returns a name of a color, so it should be placed in the `Color` or `BackGroundColor` property of a text box.

A more complex variation of this expression could be:

```
=Switch(
    Me.Value > 10000,"DarkOliveGreen",
    Me.Value > 1000,"OliveDrab",
    Me.Value > 100,"ForestGreen",
    Me.Value > 10,"LimeGreen",
    Me.Value > 0,"GreenYellow",
    Me.Value = 0,"Yellow",
    Me.Value < 0,"Goldenrod",
    Me.Value < -10,"DarkGoldenrod",
    Me.Value < -100,"Orange",
    Me.Value < -1000,"DarkOrange",
    Me.Value < -10000,"Red")
```

Developing Specific Reports

In the previous chapter(s), we have already used the following example:

```
=iif(RowNumber(Nothing) Mod 2, "LimeGreen", "White")
```

You can use this one in the `BackGroundColor` property of a row to create the green bar effect, but this time using other colors.

As you can see, the `Color` properties of text boxes, rows, columns ... are ideal candidates for these kinds of expressions.

> **Report code**
>
> When you are planning to use more complex expressions, or even simple ones, for conditional formatting I would advise not to create and store the expressions in the individual properties, but to create custom functions. That way you can still call the custom function from wherever you want to inside the report, and you only have to maintain the function in one location.

Here's another example of an expression for the `BackGroundColor` property:

```
=Iif(RunningValue(Fields!Item__Inventory_Posting_Group_.Value,
CountDistinct, Nothing) MOD 2 = 1,"LimeGreen", "White")
```

This expression is most useful when you have a grouping in your report, for example the field **InventoryPostingGroup**. Placing the expression in the `BackGroundColor` property will create an effect so that when a new group starts it will get a different background color, instead of every line.

Essentially, this expression can be translated to read "If the distinct count of unique **InventoryPostingGroup** field values is 1 (and is therefore an odd number), return the color `LimeGreen`; otherwise return the color 'White'.

Remember to set this expression for the detail row and also the group header and/or footer row(s).

Conditional formatting can also be used to simulate KPIs. For example when a value is above or below a threshold a green, orange, or red bullet could be shown, as is the case in many business intelligence reports using traffic light indicators. This could easily be achieved using embedded images and an expression. All you would need to do is embed three images in a report and display them at the correct moment.

For example, when creating a report about items and inventory, it could be interesting to visualize when a specific item has to be reordered or is close to its maximum inventory level.

Start by embedding the required images into the report.

> **Naming**
> When you embed an image, the image will get a name that is usually the same as the filename. It's a best practise to change the name of the image to something self-explaining, as is also the case with naming of variables and functions.

Next, add an extra column into the table to hold the image and drag/drop an image from the toolbox onto this column. The type of image is embedded and the value will be an expression.

This could then be the expression used:

```
=Switch(Fields!Item_Inventory.Value = Fields!Item__Reorder_Point_
.Value,"yellowcircle",
Fields!Item_Inventory.Value < Fields!Item__Reorder_Point_
.Value,"greencircle",
Fields!Item_Inventory.Value > Fields!Item__Reorder_Point_
.Value,"redcircle")
```

Now, at runtime, the row height might change depending on the values of the other text boxes in the row. To avoid the image resizing at runtime, you can use the image sizing property. The image would then resize according to the row, but in a proportional way, which is not what you want it to-do. Usually, to avoid these kinds of layout issues with embedded images I would put the image inside a rectangle and define the height and width of the rectangle to fixed values. The image inside of the rectangle should then never grow bigger than the size of the rectangle in which it has been contained.

The next screenshot shows an example of an image in a rectangle and an image not in a rectangle:

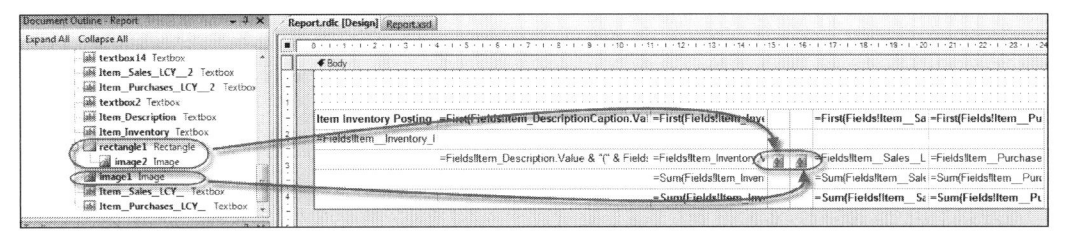

The next screenshot shows the difference in behaviour at runtime for the two images:

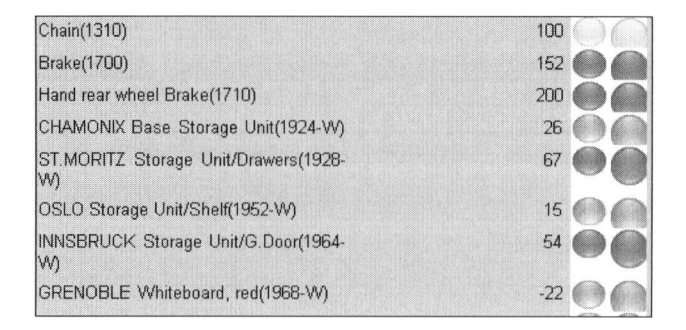

Chain(1310)	100
Brake(1700)	152
Hand rear wheel Brake(1710)	200
CHAMONIX Base Storage Unit(1924-W)	26
ST.MORITZ Storage Unit/Drawers(1928-W)	67
OSLO Storage Unit/Shelf(1952-W)	15
INNSBRUCK Storage Unit/G.Door(1964-W)	54
GRENOBLE Whiteboard, red(1968-W)	-22

Choosing the right colors

When implementing conditional formatting using colors and/or embedded images and/or charts be careful about the colors that you use, because not everyone might be able to distinguish between them. There are a couple of guidelines you can follow to avoid these kinds of issues:

- Indicators (KPIs, images…) should not only have a different color, but also a different shape. In the case of the example above, don't use circle shapes for all colors.
- When using charts you could use different types of markers per series.
- Instead of using different colors you could use different shades of grey and grey scales.

> **Report test**
> A simple way to test your report is to print it on paper without using colors of the printer. Print in black and white for example. If you can read the printed report then it is ok.

Summary

In this chapter we have seen how the enhanced layout for document reports is full of workarounds. We went into detail on the most important workarounds, understood how and why they are required and explored alternative solutions. An important point to remember about this part is that it can take a lot of time and effort to implement these workarounds and the only added value is so a report behaves the same in the Role Tailored client as in the Classic client. Right now, a Classic report also runs in the Role Tailored client, so reports do not have to be converted into RDLC. But in the next release of Dynamics NAV, the Classic client and Classic report layout (sections) will disappear, and so you will have to create an enhanced layout.

Top X reports are a classic request in BI and we have seen how to create and implement those kinds of requirements in Dynamics NAV. An important aspect to keep in mind here would be performance.

This chapter also demonstrates how to use the report wizard in combination with the create layout suggestion to generate an enhanced report with just a few mouse clicks, but as with the sections, the wizard will probably also disappear. Maybe it will be replaced with a new wizard, like one is available in server side reporting services and the report builder.

Last but not least, we have seen some techniques to create KPIs and simulate data bars in a report.

This chapter explained a couple of simple techniques that can make a big difference with little effort. The correct use of fonts, character size and weight, borders, and colors are important design considerations not only to make reports simply look better but to make them more useful, people-friendly, and to promote an image of professionalism and uniformity across your company.

6
Other Reporting and Business Intelligence Tools

By now, you should have a good understanding of what kind of reports are available in NAV 2009 and what kind of reports can be created using the standard NAV Report Designer tools. This chapter will give an overview of what is available outside NAV as reporting tools. In other words, what other tools are out there and how do you integrate them with Dynamics NAV.

Having said that, actually, it is almost impossible to give you a complete overview on what's available regarding Dynamics NAV and reporting tools. The main reason is that, when you use SQL Server as a database, it allows for many types of integrations with other systems. As a consequence, the list of external applications being able to connect to Dynamics NAV just keeps on growing and growing. That's why I will place more focus on the types of reporting tools and functionality, instead of just creating a list or ranking of reporting tools. Furthermore, in this chapter, I will focus mainly on the Microsoft tool stack. Even with these restrictions in place, it will be almost impossible to provide a complete overview; that's why I will focus on the technologies that are most compatible with Dynamics NAV.

In this chapter, we will cover:

- Reporting Services
- RDL and RDLC Comparison
- Microsoft Office Excel
- Business intelligence and NAV

Knowing your data and database

Before you try to connect an external tool to the Dynamics NAV application, some knowledge about the database can get in your way in understanding what's available in SQL Server and how to use it to your advantage.

First, we will investigate the structure of the internal NAV database. It is important to understand the database and tables and how they are related to be able to use them with reporting tools that will directly access the tables in the database.

Then, let's focus on the SQL database, because although you can access the native database via the NODBC driver, it is not recommended.

> **The NODBC driver**
>
> A common use of NODBC is for example to allow UPS or FedEx software to access and read the shipping address information in the Sales Header or the Sales Shipment Header table.
>
> But, the NODBC database driver is not optimized for performance. If you use it to transport a lot of data, it can slow down the Dynamics NAV application. Also, the NODBC driver does not allow all kinds of SQL statements. For example, it has difficulties executing certain JOIN statements. In my opinion and from my experience, I would not recommend using the ODBC driver for reporting purposes.

An advantage of using the NODBC driver would be that you can access flow fields and multi-language translation of tables and table names.

Dynamics NAV database design

The Dynamics NAV database, like many other databases, consists of tables. But there's one very important difference and that is the company. Any Dynamics NAV database consists of one or more companies and then each company contains the specific tables. Each table consists of records and each record consists of fields.

The following schema displays a typical Dynamics NAV database structure:

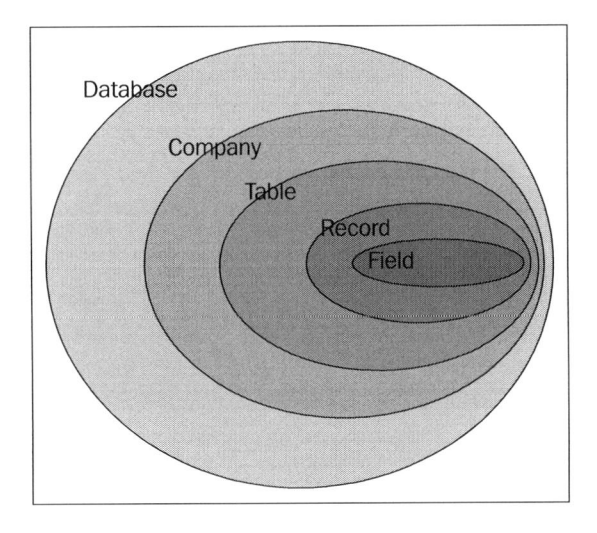

A Dynamics NAV database always contains at least one company. You can create multiple companies in a database and in every company, inside the same database, the same tables will be available. You can say that the company structure separates the data between companies inside a common database. Within a database, each company has exactly the same table names and table definitions. When you add a company to a database, the new company will contain the same list of tables that is available for the other companies. It is the data that is separated per company.

The Dynamics NAV database design can be managed with the **Object Designer**. The Object Designer can be opened via the menu bar using `Tools | Object Designer` or via the shortcut *Shift+F12*. On the left side, in the **Object Designer**, you can filter an object type by clicking on the corresponding buttons, as you can see in the next screenshot:

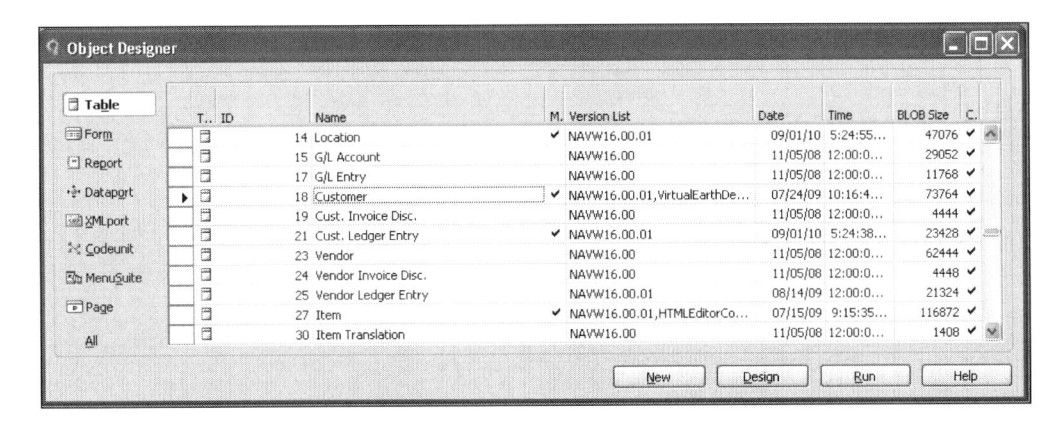

Other Reporting and Business Intelligence Tools

In this section, we are not going to explore every detail and designer available in the **Object Designer**. That would be content for a book about Dynamics NAV development, and there are already some very good books available about this subject. Instead we are going to have a look at a topic that is of interest to us when designing reports, that is table relations. Understanding how tables are related is crucial in report design, especially when you are using external tools to connect to a Dynamics NAV database.

> **Object Designer**
>
> We are going to use the **Object Designer** to reverse engineer tables or analyse table design for the purpose of designing reports. It is important to mention that the **Object Designer** can also be used to change objects. Actually, that is the main purpose of the **Object Designer**. Because of that, if you are not a developer or not familiar with the consequences of making changes, then you should never use the **Object Designer** to change objects and never save any changes when asked to by the **Object Designer**. If available, use a development or a test database for these purposes. In that case, if you should accidently change the design of an object, your production environment is not changed. If you are having any doubts, I strongly advice to consult your database administrator or partner before you try anything.

In the **Object Designer**, you can select a table in the list of tables and then click on the **Design** button. This will open the **Table Designer**, as shown in the next screenshot for the **Customer** table:

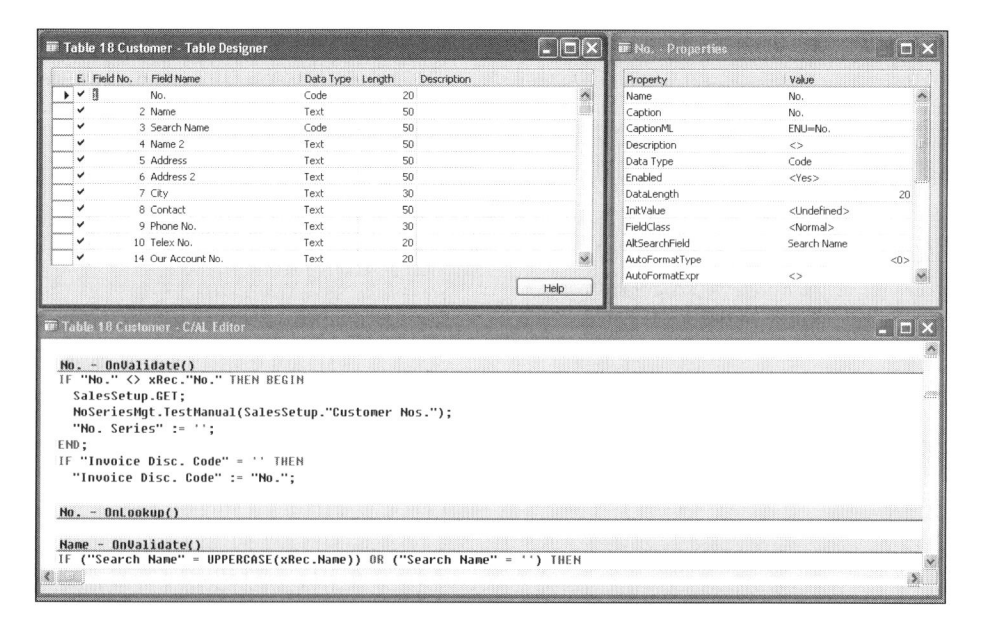

In the above screenshot, you can also see the **Properties** window and the **C/AL Editor** window. The **Properties** window can be opened using the menu **View | Properties** or the shortcut *Shift+F4*. The **C/AL Editor** window can be opened using the menu **View | C/AL Code** or the shortcut *F9*. Both of them are not visible by default.

When you select a field in the **Table Designer**, its corresponding properties are shown in the **Properties** window and the code in the field triggers is shown in the **C/AL Editor** window.

The **Table Designer** shows us by default the **Field No.**, **Field Name**, **Data Type**, and **Description** of every field in the table. It is also possible to show extra columns, such as **Caption**, **Field Class**, and **Option String.** All of these columns are also available as properties in the **Properties** window.

Selecting the first empty line in the **Table Designer** window displays the table properties and table triggers in the **Properties** window and **C/AL Editor**.

This is important to know, if you need to find out whether the table contains company-specific or database-wide information. As we have already discussed, every Dynamics NAV database has at least one company and every table resides in every company. Well, there are tables for which data is not split up per company. To create such a table you can use the table property `DataPerCompany`. If set to `Yes`, which is the default, then the table data is split up per company. If this property is set to `No`, then the table data is common in all companies of this database. This can be important to know when using a table in a report when exporting its data into a reporting or analysis tool such as Excel.

> `DataPerCompany`
>
> I strongly advise you never to make any 'quick' changes to the `DataPerCompany` table property, because it could have disastrous consequences. This property should only be changed if you understand, and have analyzed and thoroughly tested the consequences. It is possible to change this property and sometimes even interesting to do so, but never before having a functional and technical analysis done by an experienced consultant.

In Dynamics NAV, tables are related to other tables. The idea is to use different tables to store different types of information and not to store redundant information in the database. If data is used in multiple tables you can store it in one table and reference it using a table relation. A document, like for example a sales order, in Dynamics NAV stores its common information in the **Document Header** table, and the specific information is stored in the **Document Line** table. Examples of these types of document tables are: **Sales Header** and **Sales Line**, **Purchase Header** and **Purchase Line**, and so on. The **Document Header** table is then connected to the **Document Line** table using a table relation. In the case of all document tables in Dynamics NAV it is the field **No.** from the **Document Header** table that is linked to the field **Document No.** of the **Document Line** table. In some cases, an extra field, **Document Type** is used as a filter, which is usually of **DataType** `Option String`, in the same table relation; not all document tables contain a **Document Type** field.

Instead of storing document information in two tables, you could also store it in just one table. In that case, if your document contains multiple lines, you would have to copy and store the common information on every line and so create redundant data. Doing that would increase the size of the database and most likely decrease performance.

As an example let's have a look at the **Sales Header** and **Sales Line** tables. On the **Sales Line** table, there's a field **Document No.**. This field has the following `TableRelation` property: `"Sales Header".No. WHERE (Document Type=FIELD(Document Type))`.

This means that the **Sales Line** table is related to the **Sales Header** table from the field **Document No.** of the **Sales Line** table to the field **No.** of the **Sales Header** table. The field **Document Type** is used to filter the data, meaning that fields are related only if they have the same **Document Type**.

The **Document Type** field is used to store different types of documents inside one table. In this example the **Sales Header** (and **Sales Line**) table contains: Quotes, Orders, Invoices, Credit Memos, Blanket Orders, and Return Orders.

To summarize, tables can be connected via table relations and table relations can be filtered. Table relations can also be conditional. For example, the field **No.** from the **Sales Line** table has the following `TableRelation` property:

```
IF (Type=CONST(" ")) "Standard Text" ELSE IF (Type=CONST(G/L
Account)) "G/L Account" ELSE IF (Type=CONST(Item)) Item ELSE IF
(Type=CONST(Resource)) Resource ELSE IF (Type=CONST(Fixed Asset))
"Fixed Asset" ELSE IF (Type=CONST("Charge (Item)")) "Item Charge"
```

This means that the **No.** field of the **Sales Line** table is related to a field from another table, depending of the value of the field **Type**. If **Type** is empty, then the field is related to the table **Standard Text**, if **Type** is **G/L Account**, then the field is related to the table **G/L Account**, and so on.

A table relation can of course be very simple. For example, the **Sales Header** table is related to the **Customer** table via the field **Sell To Customer No.** on the **Sales Header** table, which is related to the **Customer** table.

Understanding table relations is crucial when designing reports on top of a Dynamics NAV database. Using the **Table Designer** and table properties you can find out exactly how tables are related.

There are many, many table relations between Dynamics NAV tables and it would be almost impossible to list them all.

> More information and documentation about table design and properties can be found on the Microsoft website here: http://msdn.microsoft.com/en-us/dynamics/nav/default.aspx

How is the Dynamics NAV database created in SQL Server?

The tables you see and manipulate in the **Object Designer** are maintained and synchronised on SQL Server by the database driver. This database driver is actually a .dll file, which can be found in the installation folder of the classic client. We have no access to its source code, but there are a couple of rules it follows that can be explained.

You might ask yourself the question: "Why is this important for me to know?" The answer is that when you are using Dynamics NAV 2009 on SQL Server, you might be interested to use Microsoft Excel (or other tools) to connect to the SQL database for reporting purposes. In that case, it is important to know what you can see in SQL Server and how to interpret what you see in SQL Server about the Dynamics NAV database. As another example, you might be an advanced SQL Server expert and expect to see specific behaviour like you are used to in other databases. Then, it is important to understand that the way that Dynamics NAV implements table relations and other features is not by using the corresponding SQL Server features. But that does not mean that there are no table relations or that these features are not implemented.

The first thing you need to understand is that the native database and SQL Server are completely different in many ways.

Other Reporting and Business Intelligence Tools

To manage a SQL Server database we are going to use the **SQL Server Management Studio**. You can find this in your **Start** menu, under **All Programs | Microsoft SQL Server**.

If you do not have the SQL Server Management Studio, it can be obtained and installed from the SQL Server product DVD or you could download and install the express version.

> More information about SQL Server Management Studio Express and where to download it is available at this Microsoft website: `http://msdn.microsoft.com/en-us/library/ms365247.aspx`

When you start SQL Server Management Studio (SSMS), you first have to connect to the SQL Server instance. Next, you can see what is contained in the selected instance. When you click on the **Databases** folder, you can see the available databases, as presented in the following screenshot:

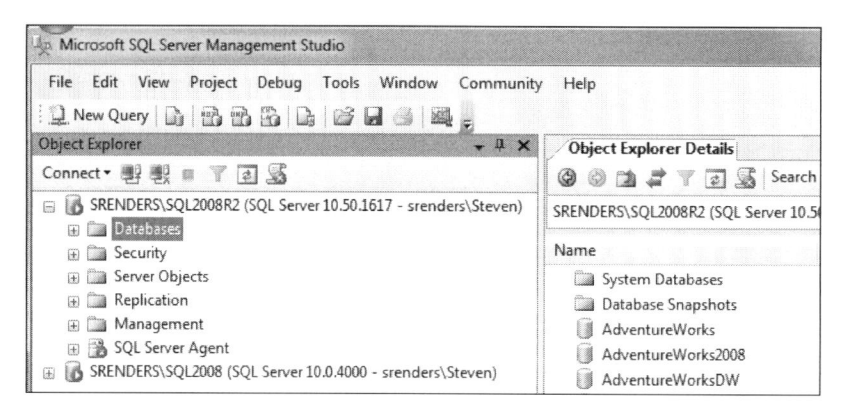

In the databases folder, you can then select your Dynamics NAV database, open it, and then browse the available tables in the database, as presented in the next screenshot:

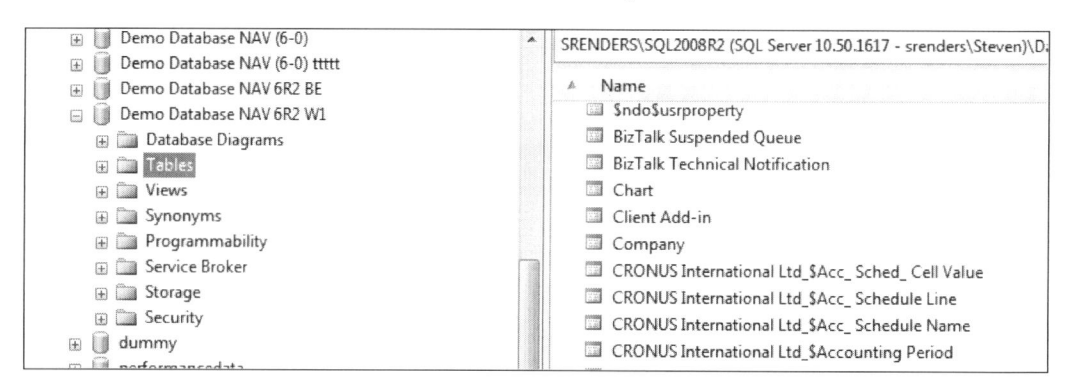

[270]

As you can see in the above screenshot, the tables usually begin with the name of the company, in this case CRONUS, followed by a $ sign and then the name of the table, as shown in the Object Designer.

> **Underscore**
>
> When creating a table or a field in a table in the **Object Designer**, you are allowed to use special characters like spaces, points, and so on. As SQL Server is stricter then the **Object Designer** in the naming of tables and columns, the database driver will replace spaces and special characters with an underscore. You can influence this behaviour via the database settings window in the classic client. If you go to **File** | **Database** | **Alter**, then select the **Integration** tab, you will find a setting with the name: **Remove characters**. The character you enter in here will be removed or replaced with an underscore in SQL Server.

You will notice that this is not applied to all tables. Not all table names include the company name. Why? Well, some tables contain data that is common to all companies. In the table designer in the classic client this is represented via the property `DataPerCompany`. When this property is turned off in SQL Server, the company name is dropped.

When you open the table in the **Object Designer** and do the same in SQL Server Management Studio (SSMS), you might notice some other differences, besides the names of tables and fields. For example, if you count the number of columns, you will notice that many tables in SSMS have fewer columns than the same tables in the classic client.

The reason for this is that flowfields and flowfilters are not present in SQL Server. The database driver does not synchronise these types of fields.

Other Reporting and Business Intelligence Tools

An example of such a field would be the field **Sales (LCY)** in the **Customer** table. If you select the **Customer** table in the **Object Designer** and open its design, this is what you will see in the properties of the **Sales (LCY)** field:

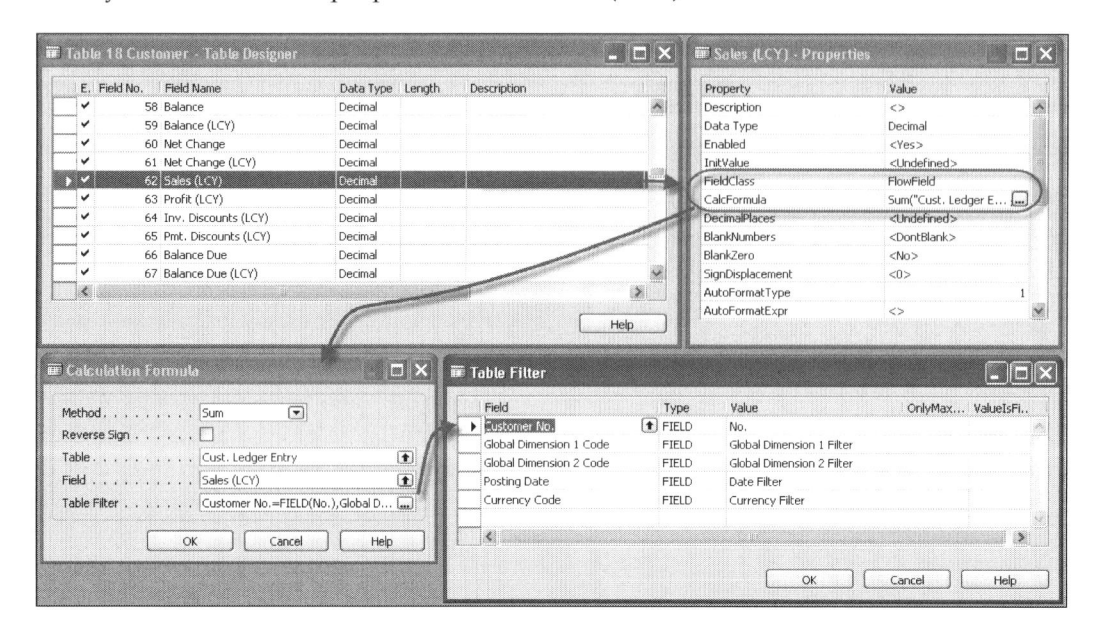

The field has a property `FieldClass` that is set to `FlowField`. And when you click on the assist edit button in the `CalcFormula` property, a popup window opens that displays the way that the field is calculated. Clicking on the assist edit button in the **Table Filter** field opens another popup window that shows the connection between the **Customer** table and the **Cust. Ledger Entry** table. To summarize, this means that the **Sales (LCY)** field is defined in the **Customer** table, but its value is calculated by taking the sum of the field **Sales (LCY)** in the **Cust. Ledger Entry** table for all corresponding records. The **Customer** table is a master table and the **Cust. Ledger Entry** table contains all the transactional information related to customers, including the **Sales (LCY)** value.

Flowfields are calculated fields. They are always calculated at runtime and as a consequence their values are not stored in the database and are not present in SQL server.

As you can see in the next screenshot, the **Sales (LCY)** field is not available in the **Customer** table in the SQL Server:

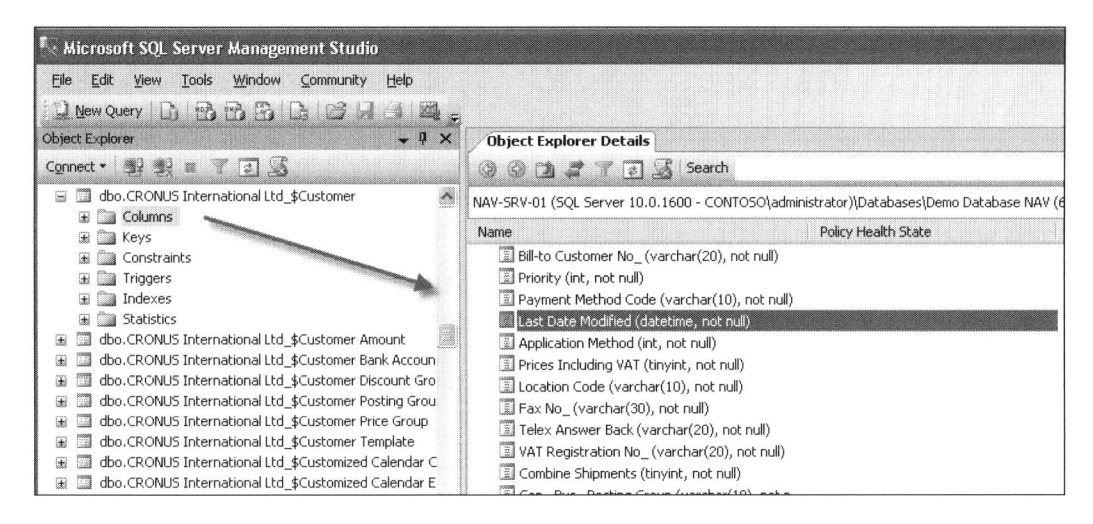

If you are creating a query to show **Customer** information and you want to include the **Sales (LCY)** field, then you could do that via a subquery or by using a `JOIN` statement to include the **Cust. Ledger Entry** table, as in this example.

Using a `JOIN` statement:

```
SELECT
    [CRONUS International Ltd_$Customer].No_,
    SUM([CRONUS International Ltd_$Cust_ Ledger Entry].[Sales (LCY)])
AS 'Sales (LCY)'
FROM
    [CRONUS International Ltd_$Customer] LEFT OUTER JOIN
     [CRONUS International Ltd_$Cust_ Ledger Entry] ON
        [CRONUS International Ltd_$Customer].No_ = [CRONUS International
Ltd_$Cust_ Ledger Entry].[Customer No_]
GROUP BY
    [CRONUS International Ltd_$Customer].No_
```

Using a sub query:

```
SELECT
    [CRONUS International Ltd_$Customer].No_,
    (SELECT
        SUM([CRONUS International Ltd_$Cust_ Ledger Entry].[Sales
(LCY)]) AS 'Sales (LCY)'
      FROM
        [CRONUS International Ltd_$Cust_ Ledger Entry]
      WHERE
        [CRONUS International Ltd_$Customer].No_ = [CRONUS International
Ltd_$Cust_ Ledger Entry].[Customer No_])
FROM
    [CRONUS International Ltd_$Customer]
```

Relations and foreign keys

One of the most difficult things to figure out when querying a database you don't really know is how tables are connected. For example, you see in the database that there's a **Customer** table and a **Contact** table and you know there's a relation between the two tables, but what kind of relation is it and which fields do you need to use to join the two tables? To assist you in this kind of scenario, SQL server has information that can help you. You can visualize the foreign keys from a table.

> What is a foreign key?
>
> There are many definitions for foreign keys in relational database systems, but summarized, a foreign key is a field (or multiple fields) from another table that identifies the link or connection or relation between those tables. The columns in the referencing table must be the primary key or other candidate key in the referenced table.

When you have a look at any Dynamics NAV database on SQL Server and look for foreign keys, you will not find any. In Dynamics NAV, there are many relations between tables, but these relations are not manifested as foreign keys in the SQL Server database. As a consequence, they cannot be used, out of the box, to figure out the fields to use when you need to join multiple tables in a query.

There is however a possibility to have the foreign keys created. For this, you need to enable a property in Dynamics NAV. When you've opened the Classic client, then open **File | Database | Alter** and then the **Integration** tab. In there you will see the `Maintainrelationships` property. By default it is disabled, but when enabled foreign keys will be created on SQL Server, for all table relations defined in the Dynamics NAV tables in that database. These foreign keys are created, but are not active. They could be used by someone who is trying to make sense of table relations of the Dynamics NAV SQL database.

> Important to remember is that the property `Maintain relationships` should never be activated on a live database. It should only be used on a development or test environment. The reason for this is that enabling this property could increase the load on the server because relationships have to be maintained and that creates extra overhead. There's too much potential for disaster to enable this property on your production database.

If you understand Dynamics NAV table relations and can use the **Object Designer** then you can use that to figure out how tables are related. If you are a SQL Server expert and don't know much about Dynamics NAV, you could use the SQL Server foreign keys to figure out table relations, but before you make any conclusions it is best to seek the advice of a Dynamics NAV expert.

Using an Entity Relationship model

To get a good overview of the tables and table relations it is recommended to build an ER model of your database. An ER model, or Entity Relationship model, provides a visual representation of the table relations in your database and will make reporting on it easier. An example of an ER model for the Dynamics NAV database can be found here: http://dynamicsuser.net/blogs/kine/archive/2008/08/04/the-art-of-nav-big-picture-of-nav.aspx.

But as you can see, it can get confusing very quickly. I would recommend building an ER model per functional area or area of interest, instead of one model for the complete database.

SQL Server allows you to create and store ER models inside SQL Server. In SQL Server that's called a database diagram. You can do this in SSMS.

To create such a diagram, first open SSMS, and connect to your SQL Server Instance. Then, expand the database node. In there you will now see a database diagrams node. When you right click on it, you have the option to create a new diagram. After you add an existing table, you also have the possibility to add all related tables. SQL Server will use the foreign keys to find related tables. Depending on the level depth that you select, more or fewer tables will be added in your database diagram.

Remember that to be able to do this, the database property `Maintain relationships` needs to be turned on and it is not recommended to do this on a live/production database.

> **Too many levels**
>
> As soon as you go three levels or deeper, the system will continue to find related tables until your diagram contains most of the tables in the database. This can take some time (between minutes and hours) to generate and of course is very useless. Multiple companies can also add a lot of confusion, especially when you start out with a non-`DataPerCompany` table such as the **Company** table.

> **Warning**
>
> When you add a table to a diagram, you also have the possibility to make changes to that table. When you then save the diagram, SQL Server will also apply those changes to the table(s) in the database. This is a situation that you absolutely want to avoid. The purpose is to create and save the database diagram, not to change the data model. This could have disastrous consequences on Dynamics NAV.

After adding tables, you can let the SQL Server diagram manager arrange the tables automatically. For example, when you add the **Company** table and its related tables, the diagram will look like the next screenshot:

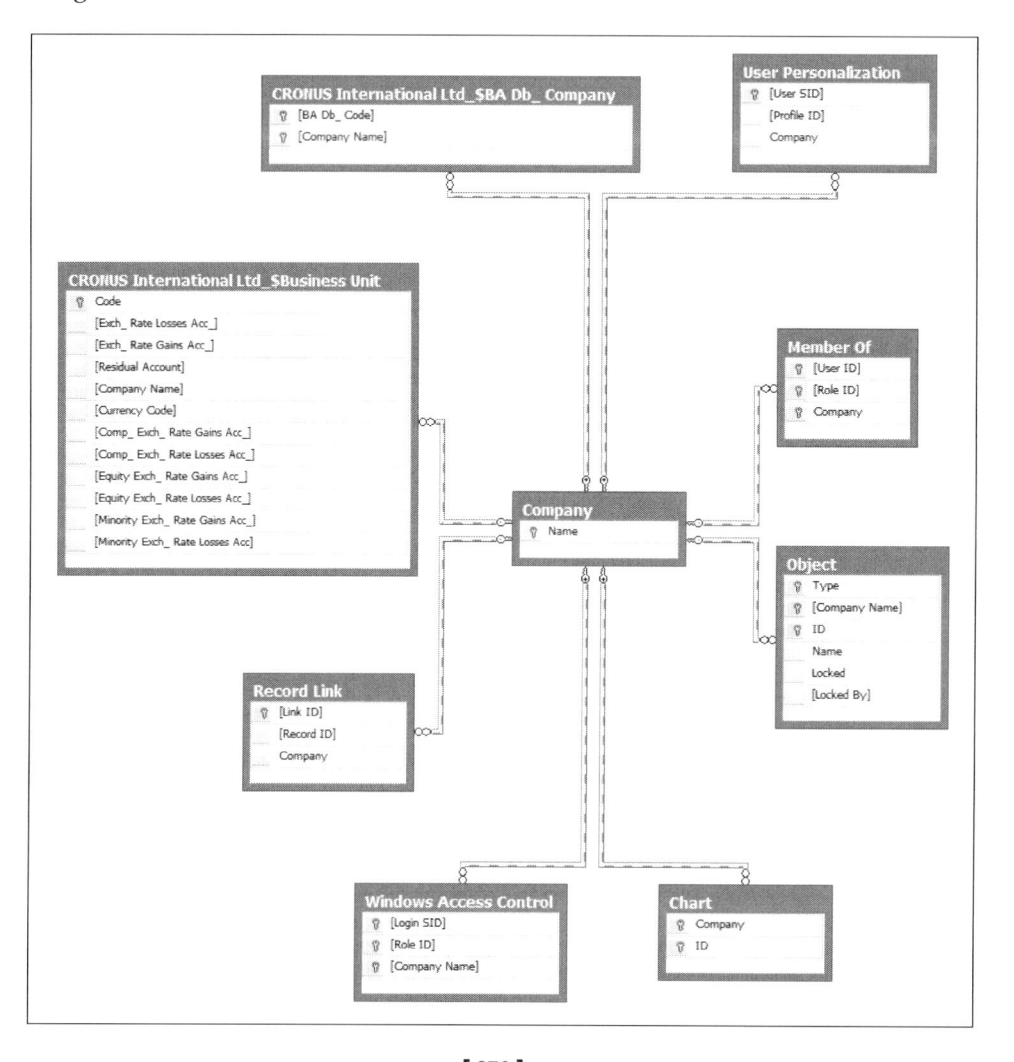

The diagram can be fine-tuned, for example by adding annotations. You can select to show only table names, all fields, only keys, and so on. The database diagram generator/editor in SQL Server is nice to have, but there are of course other tools that can do a better job, like for example Microsoft Visio.

> **Save time**
> Even if you are not planning to develop reports or a BI solution on top of Dynamics NAV, an ER model is a good tool to have. For example, novice developers usually find it difficult to learn how the Dynamics NAV database is structured. A good ER model could save them a lot of time.

The ER diagram above would be much more cluttered if there were more than one company. Most real life databases have multiple companies, and you should expect that to reflect in this diagram.

Reporting Services

The first technology you should check out, in my opinion, is SQL Server Reporting Services (SSRS). It is in fact the technology on which the RDLC reports are based, but RDL has much more to offer and has some interesting advantages.

Since you have invested your time to learn how to develop RDLC reports for the Role Tailored client, why not get a bigger return on investment on that? Is it possible to apply the knowledge gained to server side Reporting Services? I will try to answer that in this section.

SQL Server Reporting Services and in fact already is becoming an important reporting tool for Dynamics NAV. One reason is that it is available for free for anyone who is using the SQL Server database services. Another reason is that SSRS can connect to any Dynamics NAV database or version. It can even connect to a native NAV database, although I would not recommend that. Furthermore, with SSRS there are more possibilities for report design and visualisations. For example, the toolbox contains more controls, and reports can be generated automatically via schedules. Not to forget that to be able to run, consult, and export SSRS reports, all you require as a user is your browser. No installation is required, in contrast with the RDLC reports for which you need a Role Tailored client with a report viewer to run the reports.

Development of SSRS reports can be done with different tools. Basically, you have two options:

- Microsoft SQL Server Business Intelligence Development Studio (BIDS)
- Microsoft Report Builder

The main difference between the two tools is that with BIDS you can create a report solution and project that contains multiple reports. Report Builder can only work on one report at a time. Report Builder was meant to be used by the end user or non-technical report developer. But in fact, Report Builder can also be used by a 'real' developer because it has the same possibilities for report development as Visual Studio. I will give you an overview and compare both Report Designers in a later section in this chapter.

Reporting services reports are built in Report Design Language (RDL). That's why `.rdl` is used as the extension for SSRS reports. RDL is an open specification and actually nothing more than a special kind of XML file that contains tags, properties that can be understood and executed by the SSRS service. I already explained the origin of RDL and RDLC in *Chapter 2*, so I will not go deeper into it here. Where it comes from is less important than how you can benefit from it.

Let's have a look at how you can create a report. I'm first going to use the report builder and after that I will explain the added value of BIDS.

Using Report Builder

Report Builder can be downloaded from the Microsoft website and is completely free.

> You can download report builder from this location:
> `http://www.microsoft.com/downloads/details.aspx?FamilyID=d3173a87-7c0d-40cc-a408-3d1a43ae4e33`
>
> Then you can run the installation wizard to install it. During installation, it will ask you for the URL of your report server, but if you don't have a SSRS report server you can skip that and update the setting later. To determine whether you have a report server available, you could check the services on the server on which SQL Server is installed.
>
> If you see a service called **SQL Server Reporting Services (InstanceName)** and it is running, then you can ask the server administrator for the correct URL and login credentials.

There are three versions: 1, 2, and 3. Version 1 is the oldest and was not developed by Microsoft. In fact, because of the open nature of the RDL specification, you can use Notepad to create a report or you can create your own report development tool. The first version of report builder was developed by a third party and because of its success Microsoft took it; as from version 2 it introduced the ribbon interface and completely redeveloped the tool. Version 3 was released at the same time as SQL Server 2008 R2 and is also restricted to be used on SQL Server 2008 R2. So, if your Dynamics NAV database is not running on SQL Server 2008 R2 I would recommend using version 2 of Report Builder, unless you want to install an extra SQL server instance for reporting services.

> **Note**
> Report Builder 3 can connect to any SQL Server database as a data source, but it can only connect to a report server running on SQL Server 2008 R2 or later. So if you are running Dynamics NAV on an older SQL version and don't want to install an extra SQL Server instance for the report server, then I recommend using version 2 of Report Builder. Otherwise you should go for the latest version, because it contains the most possibilities and bells and whistles.

To create a new report using Report Builder, just launch it. The first thing it will do is try to make a connection to a report server. The idea is that, when connected to a report server you can open an existing report on it and change it or use it as a basis to create a new report. It also gives you a location to store a new report that you create with Report Builder, so you can store it directly on the server. In this demo I'm not going to store the report on a report server; I'm just going to create a report and run it, without using a report server.

The nice thing with Report Builder is the user friendliness. After you start it, it will automatically launch a wizard, as you can see in the following screenshot:

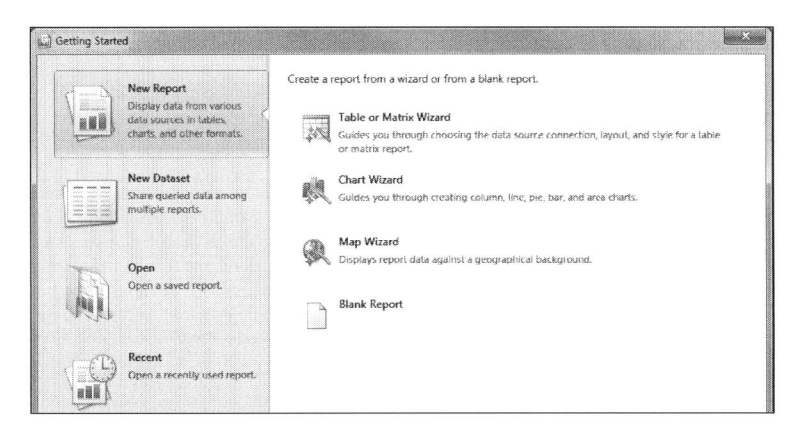

Other Reporting and Business Intelligence Tools

You can use this wizard to create different types of reports. Something you might notice in the screenshot is the **Chart** and **Map** wizard. In BIDS there is also a **Table** and **Matrix** wizard, but on top of that in Report Builder we have a **Chart** and **Map** wizard. These report wizards will let help and assist you in creating a report very quickly. In this example we will start the 'hard way', by creating a blank report.

A blank report looks like the following screenshot:

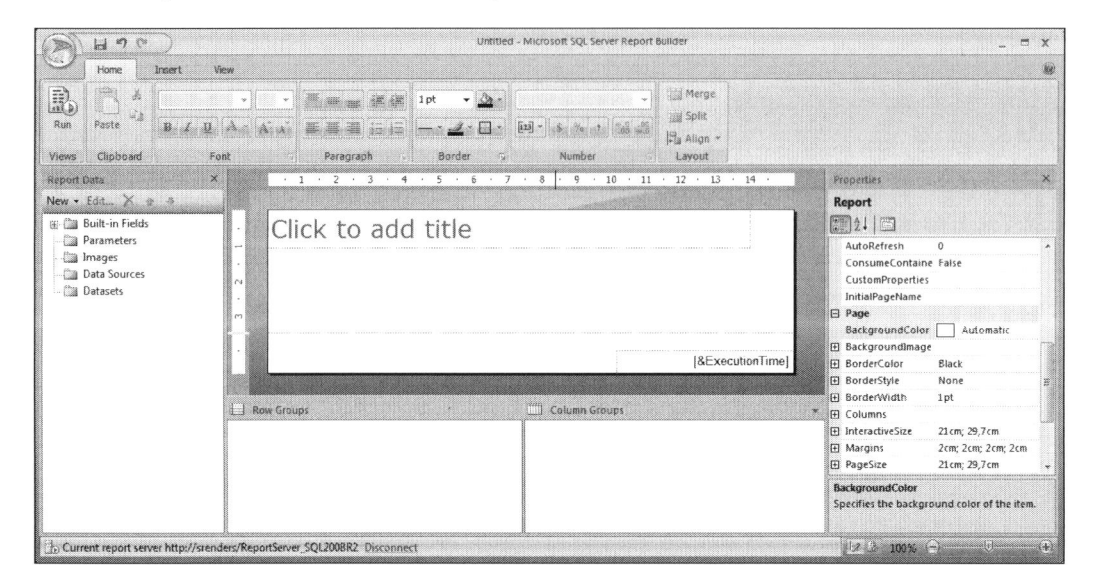

In this screenshot of Report Builder, all windows are visible, but they can be hidden if required. There are four areas that can be visualized/hidden:

- Report Data
- Grouping
- Properties
- Ruler

There are also three tabs:

- Home
- Insert
- View

At the bottom of the window, there's a status bar that displays the report server you are currently connected to. And at the bottom right you will find the zoom buttons, as you also see in Microsoft Office.

Creating Reporting Services reports always happens in three steps:

1. First, you create a connection to a data source and a query that fetches the required data from the data source.
2. Then, you create the layout for the report.
3. The third step is previewing the report and finally, when it is ready and tested, you can make it available to the end user by publishing it onto the report server.

The user can then use the browser to go to the report server website and run reports. Depending on the tool you use to create your report, those steps might be more complex or have more options.

The first step is now to create the connection to the Dynamics NAV database. All you require is the name of the server, the name of the SQL Server instance, and the name of the database. Of course, it would be recommended to also have a SQL Server database or Windows user/password available that has permissions to run queries on the database.

The Data Source is the object that will store the connection information. This Data Source can be stored inside the report, embedded that is. Or it can be stored on the report server, so it could be reused or shared by other reports. In this example, I will embed it in the report.

When you click on the **New** button in the **Report Data** pane, a dropdown window appears. In there, you can select the option **Data Source**. Now, a popup window opens. In there, you should give your data source a good name. Here, you have the option to reuse a previously created data source, browse for one on your report server, or create a new one. Click on the option **Use a connection embedded in my report**. You will see the **Data Source properties** window opening. When you click on the **Build** button, another popup window will open in which you can enter the SQL Server name and database name, as shown in the next screenshot:

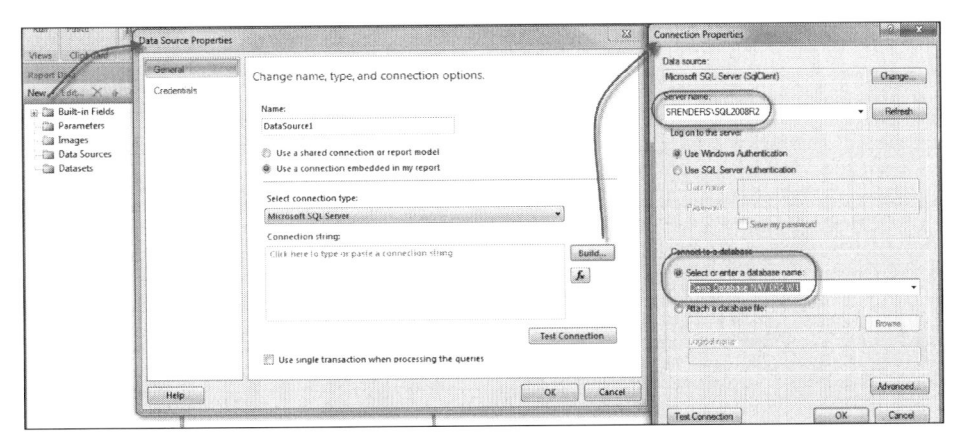

Other Reporting and Business Intelligence Tools

> **Localhost or .**
> When you do this on a laptop or on directly the server, you can enter a dot (.) as the server name. That's the same as entering `localhost`, which is also an option.

Now that we have a data source, we can create a query. The query, or result of the query, will become our **Dataset**. The **Dataset** will contain the fields that we can use in the report, just like the **Dataset** in an RDLC report for the RTC. The difference is that in SSRS you can have as many Datasets as you want, there's no restriction, unlike with the Dynamics NAV RDLC Report Designer.

To create a new Dataset, right click on the Datasets in the Report Data section of report builder. A popup window will open, to allow you to create the Dataset, as you can see in the next screenshot:

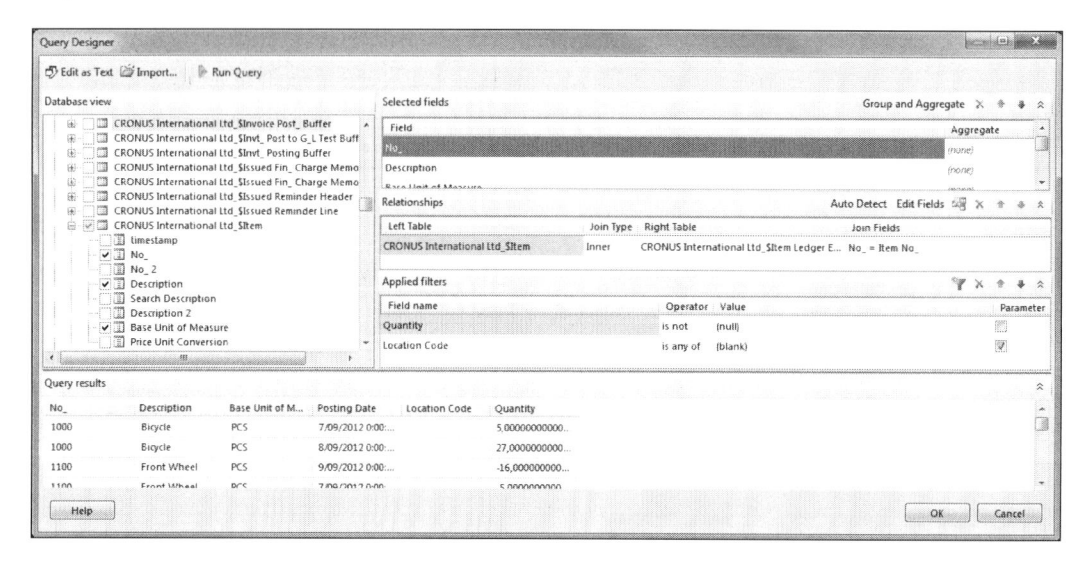

In this window, you can very easily select the table(s), view(s), and/or stored procedures you want to use in your report. When selecting multiple tables and corresponding fields you have to define the relationships between the tables in the pane at the right top of this window. You can let report builder auto detect the relationships, but of course that will only produce results if there are foreign keys in your database.

You can visually build your complete query, without having to write a single line of code of query language. Depending on the selections you make in this window, the underlying SQL statement is generated in the background. If you would like to edit this SQL statement, you can click on the **Edit as Text** button at the top left.

If you have a query that was already prepared you can import it via the **Import** button. Via this **Import** button, you can also reuse a query from another report.

Relationships between tables can be detected via foreign keys, but you can also define them yourself. To do that you can use the **Edit fields** button, to the right of the **Auto Detect** button. Another popup window will open, enabling you to define the exact join clause to connect the different tables.

You also have the option to calculate aggregates for fields from your dataset. For example, the Sum, Average, Minimum, and so on. In the applied filters section at the middle right of the window you can apply filters, very much as you would in the DataItemTableView property of a dataitem in the classic Report Designer. As you might remember, applying filters in the query will result in better performance compared to applying filter inside the report.

Very interesting here is the option to make filters become parameters. At the right of each filter line, you can select the option: **Parameter**. Doing this will make the filter a parameter, very much like you can have parameters in the request page of a report in Dynamics NAV.

On the top of the window there's a **Run Query** button. When you click it the query will be executed and the results are shown in the **Query Results** pane at the bottom of the window.

When you are pleased with your query, you can click on the **OK** button and it will be pasted in the following window:

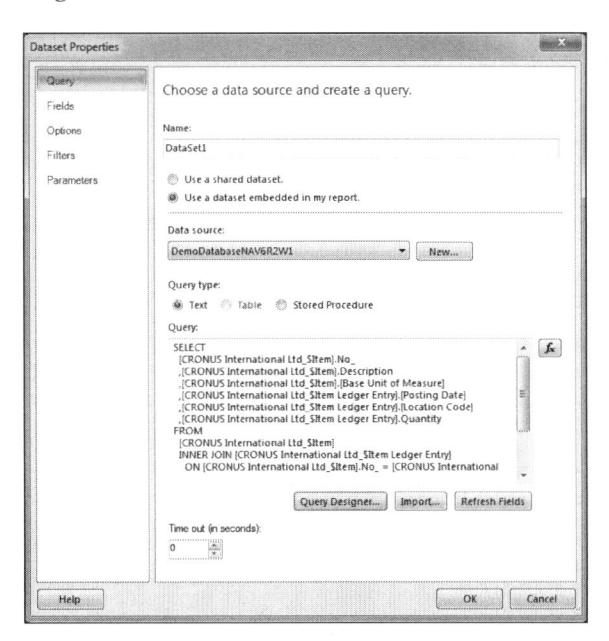

Other Reporting and Business Intelligence Tools

Actually, this is the window you start from when you click **Add Dataset**. When you click the **Query Designer** button in here, the window will open (see previous screenshot), where you can define the query. After defining the query, you get back to this window, in which you can tune the query execution properties. Click on the **OK** button to save and close the window. Next, your **Dataset** is created in your report. Right now, the **Dataset** is ready to be used on your report layout. It is always a good idea to give your **Dataset** a proper name, corresponding to the data it represents. This will make it easier when you will be using multiple **Datasets** and also when you want to publish this **Dataset** as a shared **Dataset**.

In SQL Server 2008 R2 Reporting Services, the possibility was added to publish a **Dataset** as a shared **Dataset**. This allows for reuse of the same **Dataset** by multiple reports, resulting in less overhead and maintenance of multiple **Datasets** in multiple reports. But it also provides an even better advantage. You now have the possibility to separate the work between **Dataset** developers and report developers. For example, you might be a non-technical person without knowledge of SQL statements (Dynamics NAV End User Company), but you know how to use Report Builder very well. You have a developer (Dynamics NAV Partner) prepare SQL statements containing the information you require in your report. The developer can then publish his or her **Dataset** to the report server and then you as a report builder can use and consume it. You don't have to be a SQL wizard anymore to be able to create a great report in SSRS!

If you used filters in your **Dataset** and one or more of those filters were marked as parameters, they will end up in the Parameters section of the **Report Data** pane. Above the **Parameters**, you will find the **Built-in** fields. Both sections are shown in the next screenshot:

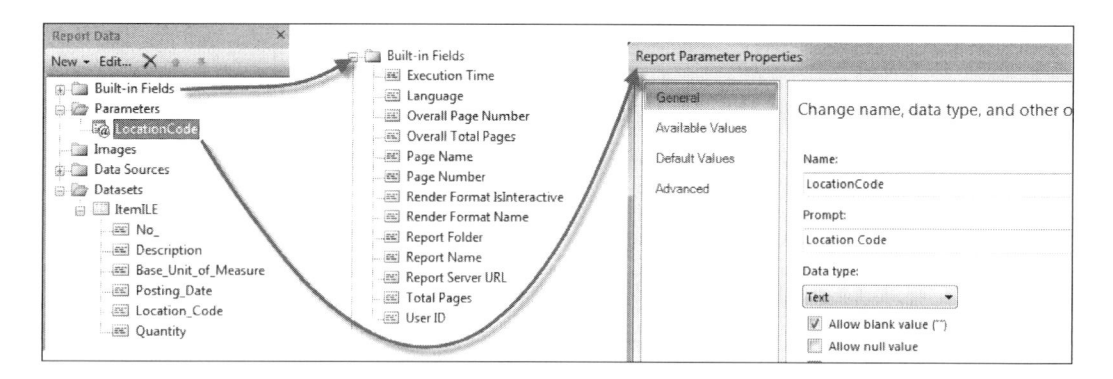

The built-in fields can be used (dragged and dropped) in your report, just like the fields from the **Dataset**. Usually, the built-in fields are used on a report header or footer. Some of these built-in fields we have already encountered before, in the Dynamics NAV Report Designer as **Globals**. In fact, they are the same but in SSRS R2 there are more of them. For example, besides the `PageNumer` and `TotalPages` there's also the `Overall Pagenumber` and `Overall Total Pages`. You can use these extra fields as page numbers depending on whether you are in a grouping or not.

Very interesting also are the `Render Format Name` and `Render Format IsInteractive` built-in fields. You can use them to determine at runtime whether the user who is running your report is exporting to Excel of PDF or any other format and so change the behaviour of the report depending on the render format selected by the user.

Now that we have our **Dataset**, it's time to create the layout for our first SSRS report. This is where you really notice the difference and added value of Report Builder compared to BIDS. To insert a report item or data region you can use the ribbon, as shown in the next screenshot:

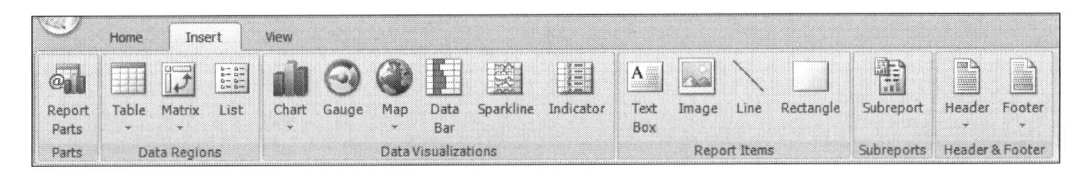

Or, you can just right click anywhere in the report and work with the following context menu:

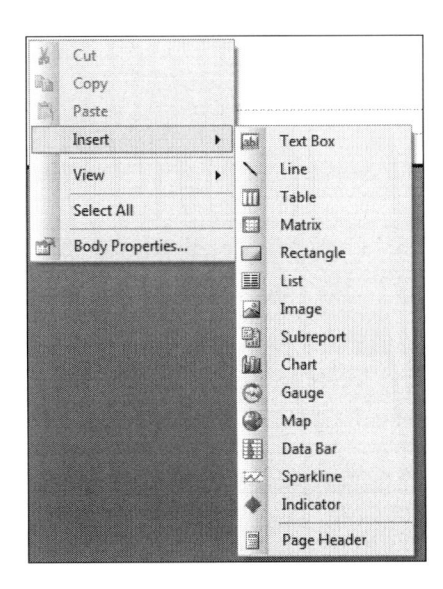

Other Reporting and Business Intelligence Tools

As you will notice, the toolbox contains more controls than in the Dynamics NAV Report Designer.

> **What is a Tablix data region?**
> The **List**, **Table**, and **Matrix** data regions we know from SQL Server 2005 and before have been merged into a new data region: the **Tablix** in SQL Server 2008. The **Tablix** can be tuned so it will look like a **List**, **Table**, or **Matrix**, but behind the scenes it is the same control.

The first button in the ribbon is called **Report Parts**. In fact in the R2 release on SQL Server 2008, functionality was added to Reporting Services so that you can also share and reuse parts of a report. You can publish a part of a report as a report part on the report server and then reuse it in another report. This allows you to create a report by using shared data sources, shared datasets, and report parts, built up of parts already available on the report server. You can, in theory, assemble your report so it consists completely of parts of other reports. This is a good example of taking reusability to the highest level.

As an example, create two datasets in the report using the following two SQL Queries. The first query is:

```
SELECT
   [CRONUS International Ltd_$Item].No_
,[CRONUS International Ltd_$Item].Description
,[CRONUS International Ltd_$Item].[Base Unit of Measure]
,[CRONUS International Ltd_$Item Ledger Entry].[Posting Date]
,[CRONUS International Ltd_$Item Ledger Entry].[Location Code]
,[CRONUS International Ltd_$Item Ledger Entry].Quantity
FROM
   [CRONUS International Ltd_$Item]
   INNER JOIN [CRONUS International Ltd_$Item Ledger Entry]
     ON [CRONUS International Ltd_$Item].No_ = [CRONUS International Ltd_$Item Ledger Entry].[Item No_]
WHERE
   [CRONUS International Ltd_$Item Ledger Entry].Quantity IS NOT NULL
   AND [CRONUS International Ltd_$Item Ledger Entry].[Location Code] IN (@LocationCode)
```

And the second query is:

```
SELECT
   [CRONUS International Ltd_$Location].Code
,[CRONUS International Ltd_$Location].Name
FROM
   [CRONUS International Ltd_$Location]
```

Now, add a matrix data region to the report, showing the **Quantity** as the data and a row group on **Item No** and column group on **Location**. As you see, data regions are very user friendly to implement. After inserting a matrix on your report, you can click on the individual cells to connect them to a field from a dataset. You can, but don't have to, drag and drop fields from your dataset onto the data region. You can see how this works in the next screenshot:

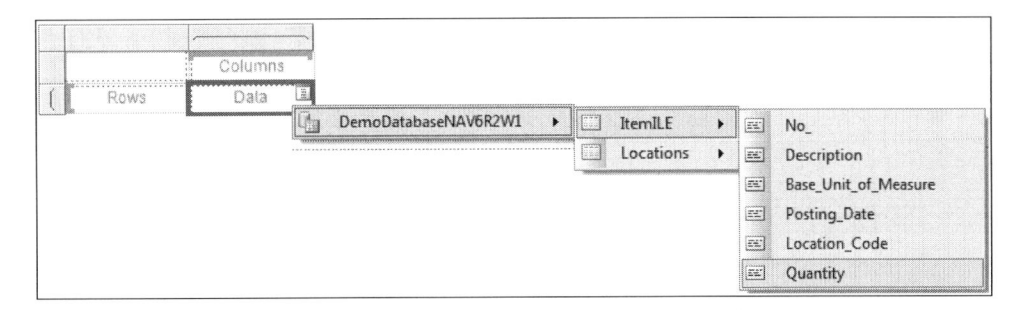

You can create groups by dragging and dropping fields in the **Rows** and **Columns** section in the matrix or by using the **Group** section at the bottom of the report builder as shown in the next screenshot:

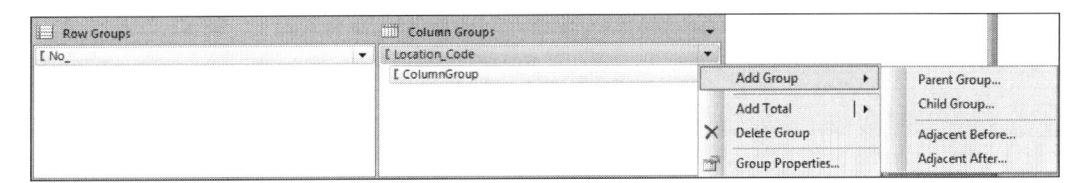

As you can see, it is now also possible to have adjacent groups in a matrix or table data region.

When you create the report, **Inventory by Location**, showing the **Item Ledger Entry Quantity** grouped by **Item No** and **Inventory** and run it you will notice a parameter bar automatically appears at the top of the report. This is because in the dataset we used a parameter.

> **Use the @ sign to create parameters**
> When you use a @ sign in a SQL query, the SSRS report engine will see it as a parameter and add it to the report parameters section in the report.

In the second query, for the locations, we used the following parameter: `@Location`. It is automatically detected as a parameter and when you run the report it shows up in the parameter bar and you can enter one or multiple values in the dropdown.

When you right click on a parameter in the **Report Data** section of your report, you can further fine-tune the parameter. You can define its data type and behaviour. You can determine whether to allow multiple values and you can decide what will be the default value(s) and available value(s). These available value(s) and default value(s) can be hardcoded or can come from another dataset. In our case, we will fill the @Location parameter with values coming out of the **Locations** dataset.

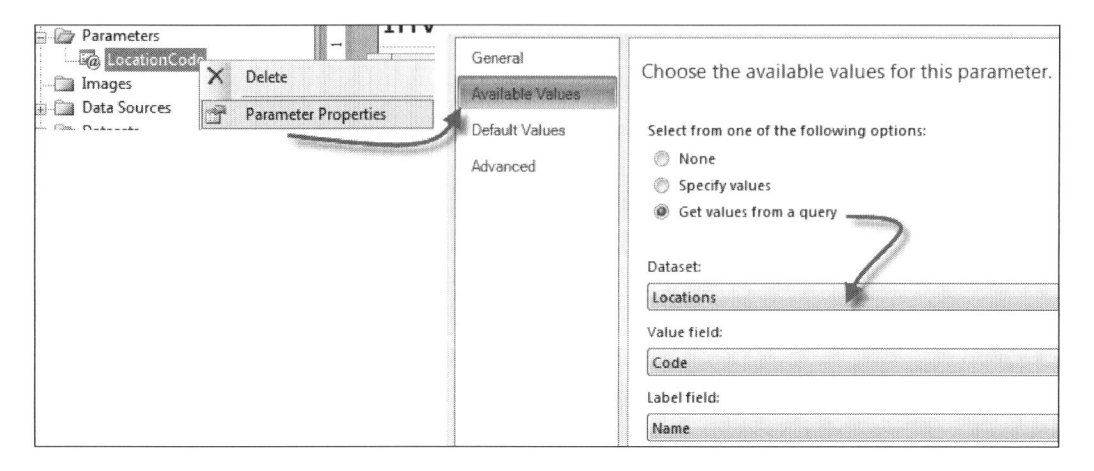

> **Parameters: Default and available values**
>
> When you use parameters in a report in SSRS, you should always provide default and available values for the user. Not only will it make your report easier to use, it is also safer. Allowing a user to manually enter text in a parameter possibly opens up your database for a SQL injection attack. Someone might enter a SQL statement in a parameter box. The information in a parameter is transferred to the SQL statement and executed on the data source. It has happened before, and is not as difficult as it would seem, to misuse this feature to 'hack' your database. It's better to prevent than to heal as we say in Belgium, so think about this when you design a report that might be exposed to the outside world.

Apply this in the report and then run it and this is what you will see:

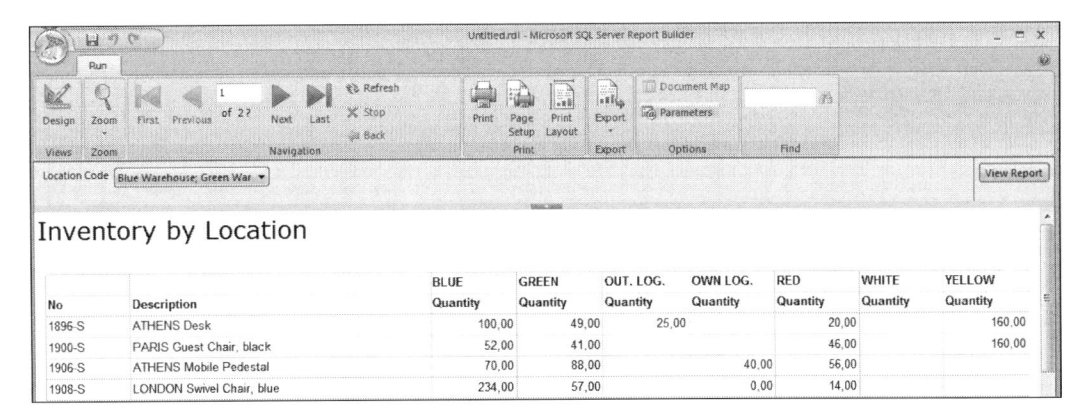

No	Description	BLUE Quantity	GREEN Quantity	OUT. LOG. Quantity	OWN LOG. Quantity	RED Quantity	WHITE Quantity	YELLOW Quantity
1896-S	ATHENS Desk	100,00	49,00	25,00		20,00		160,00
1900-S	PARIS Guest Chair, black	52,00	41,00			46,00		160,00
1906-S	ATHENS Mobile Pedestal	70,00	88,00		40,00	56,00		
1908-S	LONDON Swivel Chair, blue	234,00	57,00		0,00	14,00		

You have now created a report that shows **Inventory by Location** with the **Location Code** as a parameter. You did not have to write any code or SQL statement; everything was done via the user interface. You can further modify the report and add interactive and/or visualisation features, just as you would with a Dynamics NAV report. The difference in SSRS is that you have many more features at your disposal and they are very easy to integrate via the very user friendly Report Builder. There are also a couple of limitations, like for example having flowfields available.

> **Data source user: Read only**
>
> Another safety measure I would recommend is to use a user in the data source that only has read rights on the database. That way, if your report suffers from SQL injection, data can only be read, but not modified, deleted, or inserted.

Using BIDS

BIDS, or SQL Server Business Intelligence Development Studio, is a part of SQL Server that can be installed together. In fact, BIDS is the same as Visual Studio, but restricted to SQL Server project templates. You can find it in your **Start** menu, together with SQL Server:

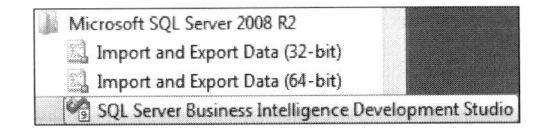

When you start it, you will see a user interface similar to the one you see when you open a Dynamics NAV report via **View | Layout**. In this case, you first have to create your project. This project can then contain as many reports, data sources as you want. To create a new project, click on **File | New**, and **Project**. A window opens in which you can select a project template. You can select **Report Server Project** or **Report Server Project Wizard**.

The wizard allows you to:

- Select a data source from which to retrieve data
- Design a query to execute against the data source
- Choose the type of report you want to create
- Specify the basic layout of the report
- Specify the formatting for the report

To get to know BIDS, I think it is more fun to start with an already prepared project. In our case, it can be very interesting to go to the following website: http://www.microsoft.com/download/en/details.aspx?displaylang=en&id=4236 and download a report pack that was developed for Dynamics NAV v4.

On this webpage, there are also other report packs available to download and use for free:

- Report Pack for Microsoft Dynamics Navision 4.0
- Report Pack for Microsoft Dynamics Axapta 3.0
- Report Pack for Microsoft Dynamics Great Plains 8.0
- Report Pack for Microsoft Dynamics Great Plains 9.0
- Report Pack for Financial Reporting
- Report Pack for Microsoft Internet Information Services (IIS)
- Integration Services Log Reports

The **Report Pack for Microsoft Dynamics Navision 4.0** contains 22 reports based upon a Dynamics NAV 4.0 world wide database. With some minor modifications to the data source and reports you can make it work on later versions as well. After downloading and installing the report pack, you can find it in the following directory:

```
C:\Program Files (x86)\Microsoft SQL Server Report Packs\Microsoft SQL Server Report Pack for Navision 4.0\Reports
```

To open it, you should double click on the `NavRptsEn.sln` file. When you do that, BIDS will open the project. Depending on your version of BIDS the project will be converted to the version that you use. This conversion is automatic and cannot be undone.

After opening the project, you will see the following list of reports:

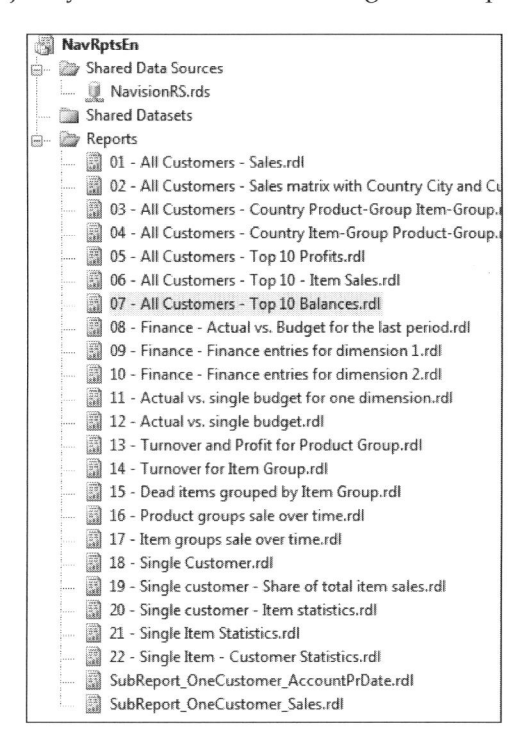

```
NavRptsEn
├── Shared Data Sources
│     └── NavisionRS.rds
├── Shared Datasets
└── Reports
      ├── 01 - All Customers - Sales.rdl
      ├── 02 - All Customers - Sales matrix with Country City and Cu
      ├── 03 - All Customers - Country Product-Group Item-Group.r
      ├── 04 - All Customers - Country Item-Group Product-Group.
      ├── 05 - All Customers - Top 10 Profits.rdl
      ├── 06 - All Customers - Top 10 - Item Sales.rdl
      ├── 07 - All Customers - Top 10 Balances.rdl
      ├── 08 - Finance - Actual vs. Budget for the last period.rdl
      ├── 09 - Finance - Finance entries for dimension 1.rdl
      ├── 10 - Finance - Finance entries for dimension 2.rdl
      ├── 11 - Actual vs. single budget for one dimension.rdl
      ├── 12 - Actual vs. single budget.rdl
      ├── 13 - Turnover and Profit for Product Group.rdl
      ├── 14 - Turnover for Item Group.rdl
      ├── 15 - Dead items grouped by Item Group.rdl
      ├── 16 - Product groups sale over time.rdl
      ├── 17 - Item groups sale over time.rdl
      ├── 18 - Single Customer.rdl
      ├── 19 - Single customer - Share of total item sales.rdl
      ├── 20 - Single customer - Item statistics.rdl
      ├── 21 - Single Item Statistics.rdl
      ├── 22 - Single Item - Customer Statistics.rdl
      ├── SubReport_OneCustomer_AccountPrDate.rdl
      └── SubReport_OneCustomer_Sales.rdl
```

And this shows us immediately the advantage of using BIDS; you can have multiple reports in one project. In Report Builder, you have the ribbon to add report items and data regions to a report; in BIDS you can use the toolbox instead. If you compare BIDS with Report Builder, BIDS is meant for developers and Report Builder is meant for end users, but in fact both tools contain the same building blocks and editors to create complete SSRS reports. In my opinion Report Builder is more developer friendly, and BIDS has a few more tricks up its sleeve when working on a report solution or project. There's for example the possibility to connect it to a version management tool like Visual Source Safe.

In my opinion, Report Builder would be a much better tool to incorporate into Dynamics NAV instead of BIDS as it is right now. Dynamics AX 4.0 uses Report Builder, but not the latest version. It still uses Report Builder version 1, which I absolutely would not recommend, since versions 2 and 3 add a lot of added value.

After you design multiple reports in BIDS, you can set the report properties to point to your report server and then with a single click you can deploy the complete project.

Comparing RDL and RDLC

In this section, I will compare RDL and RDLC. Both technologies have their advantages and disadvantages and it is important to remember how to get the maximum out of both of them.

SSRS	Dynamics NAV RTC Reports
RDL	RDLC
Runs on SQL Server	Runs on Workstation/Laptop (Client)
Define Query in SQL: • T-SQL • Views • Stored Procedures • Functions, DMV, DMF, …	Define data items in Classic Report Designer: • Data Item(s) • C/AL Code • Views via Linked Object(s)
Multiple Datasets	Always one DataSet
Multiple DataSources (OLAP, OLTP, Other, …)	Always one DataSource
Can query multiple companies	Always one Company
No Flowfields, FlowFilters available. Instead you can create a SQL subquery, view, function, stored procedure,…	Can use FlowFields and FlowFilters
No multilanguage functionality, possible via: Expressions, View, Translation Table…	Multilanguage functionality out of the box
Parameters in report	Parameters in Request Page
Toolbox contains more items and data regions	Toolbox restricted to version 2005
Report Designers: • BIDS • Report Builder	Report Designers: • BIDS version 2005 or 2008 combined with Classic Report Designer
End users can use Report Builder and reuse published and shared data sources and datasets and report parts	Too technical for end users

SSRS	Dynamics NAV RTC Reports
Export report as: • Pdf • Xls • Csv • Tiff • Word • Mhtml • Xml • Rss feed	Export report as: • Pdf • Xls
Runs as a Windows service and a web service.	Runs in Service Tier Can be exposed as a web service via a codeunit
Runs in Browser via Report Manager or SharePoint	Runs in Report Viewer called from RTC
Can be embedded in Visual Studio project	
Preview possible at design time in BIDS and in Report Builder	No preview possible at design time
Subscriptions (out of the box) available: • Email • Shared folder • Manual or Data Driven	Can setup JobSheduler in NAV: • Create Codeunit with SaveAsPDF or SaveAsXLS function • Email report
Many Report Packs available	Demo reports available via Team Blog and other blogs
Can access any DataSource via ODBC, OLE DB, .NET data provider, …	Only in NAV 2009 and SQL Server 2005 or 2008
Integration possible with NAV via: • Hyperlinks • Shortcuts in menu • Using buttons/actions and C/AL code • Can be customized via URL rendering parameters	• Create action(s) in RTC • Hyperlinks from report to a report or to a page
Very scalable. In SQL 2008, you can combine multiple servers to use one SSRS database.	Scalability depends on NST
Many caching options	No caching configurable

Other Reporting and Business Intelligence Tools

SSRS	Dynamics NAV RTC Reports
Monitoring via: • Report History • Log Files • Execution Log • TimeOut settings	No monitoring out of the box
Security: • Windows authentication in Browser (Report Manager and SharePoint) • Separate security setup in Report Manager then on SQL Server	Security: • Windows authentication in RTC

Using Microsoft Excel with Dynamics NAV

Microsoft Office Excel is still the preferred reporting tool for business analysts. In this section, I will explain how to use Excel in combination with Dynamics NAV. Power pivot is a new tool available in Office 2010, which can extend the possibilities of Excel reporting even further.

When you open Microsoft Office Excel, there should be a **Data** tab in the ribbon at the top. In previous versions of Office that do not have the ribbon interface, you can find a **Data Menu Item**. In there you have the possibility to fetch data from another data source, like for example a Dynamics NAV database.

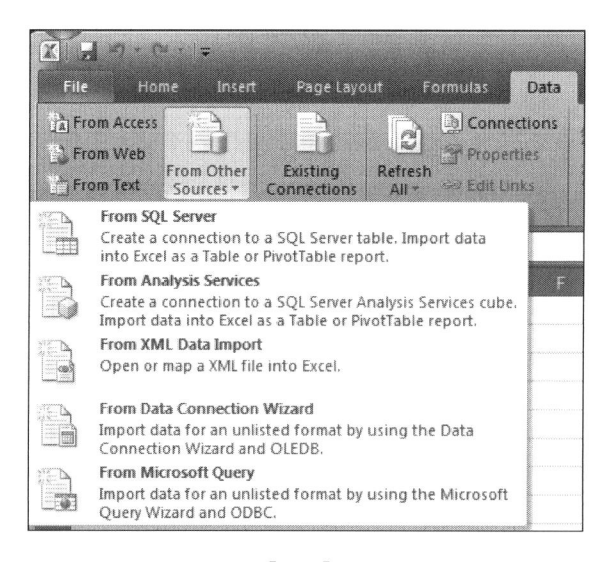

For example, you can select the **Data Connection Wizard** to connect to your Dynamics NAV database. In the first window, you will have to enter the connection information to your database, as in the next example:

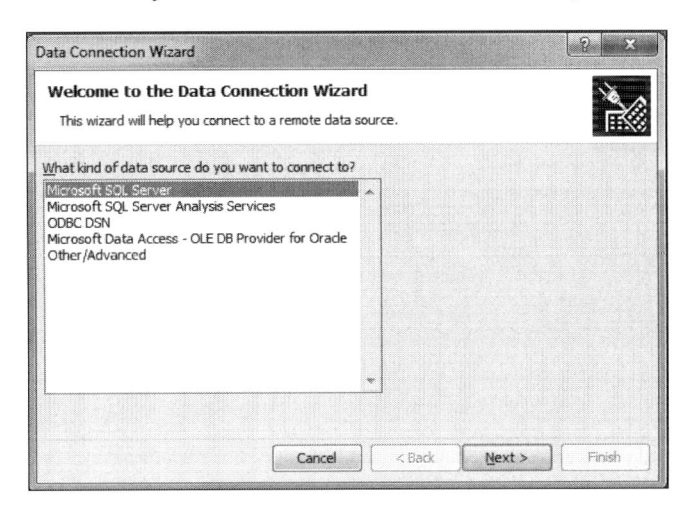

When you click **Next** the following window opens:

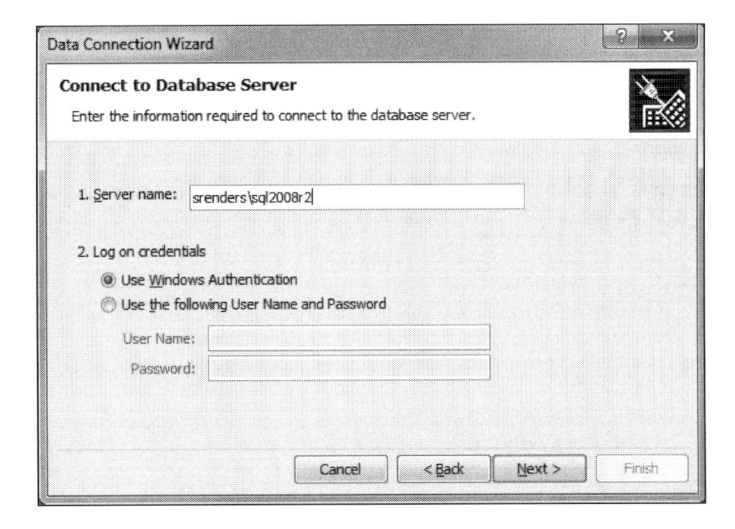

After you enter the connection information, click on **Next** and then you can select a database and a table to connect to. Remember that you can also choose to select a view instead of a table. You could for example have someone with a technical background prepare the query, save it as a view, and use it.

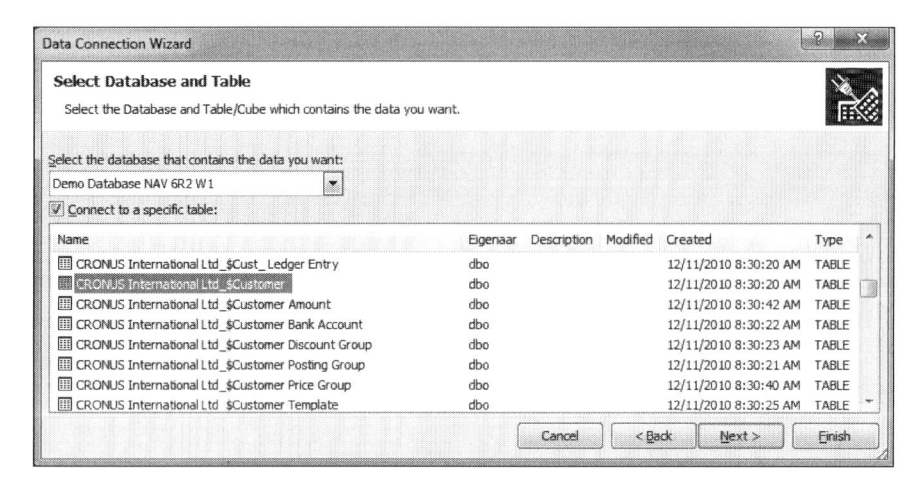

In the next window, you can save your connection settings in a .ODC file so you can reuse it later:

After clicking on the **Finish** button, you decide how the information needs to be available in Excel in the next popup window:

The data is fetched from the Dynamics database and copied over in Excel. Now, you can let loose your Excel skills on the data to create an Excel report or analysis. You can save the Excel file and there's a **Refresh** button in the ribbon that will update the data.

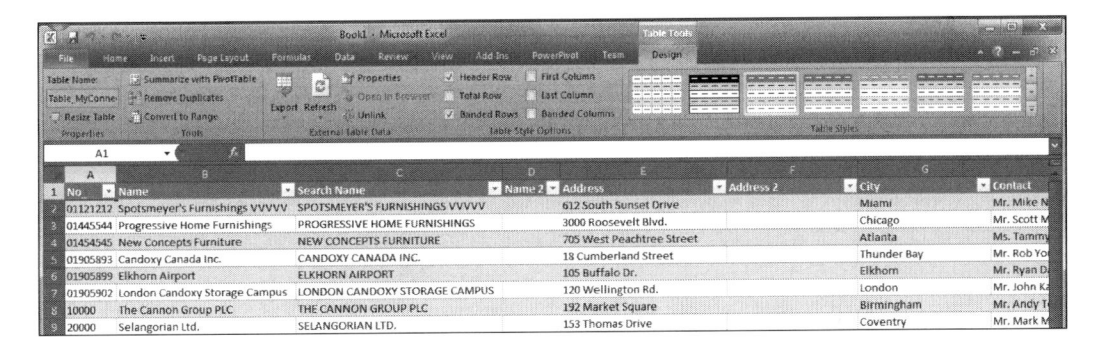

> **DSN**
>
> To make it easier for non-technical users, the administrator could create a DSN for the Dynamics NAV database. A DSN is a Data Source Name. It can be stored in a file or in the registry of the computer. When you use a DSN, you don't have to know and enter the connection string to the database.

Modifying Dynamics NAV data from Excel does not trigger the Dynamics NAV business logic and so must be avoided at all costs. The Dynamics NAV business logic resides in the Dynamics NAV objects, not in SQL Server. So if you access and make changes directly to the data in SQL Server, the business logic is not executed. Make sure that the data that is copied over to Excel, or any other tool you might have connected to the SQL database, and that changes are not allowed or not saved in the database. A simple solution would be to use a connection that only has read rights on SQL server, and so cannot make any modifications, inserts, or deletes.

Excel Data Mining Add In

Now that we have our Dynamics NAV data available in Excel, we can go a step further. Wouldn't it be great to be able to apply data mining to our ERP data? But, doesn't that require a complex setup and a data mining model in analysis services? Those kinds of projects take weeks or months to implement and are much too complex for us 'simple' users, or maybe not?

Well, Microsoft has created a free add in for Excel: **Microsoft Office Excel Data mining Add In**.

You can download it here: `http://www.microsoft.com/download/en/details.aspx?id=22187`

The add in requires an Analysis Services instance it can connect to, to create and store the data mining data. This can be a local Analysis Services instance or one on a server.

Once installed, you get an extra ribbon in Excel called **Data Mining**:

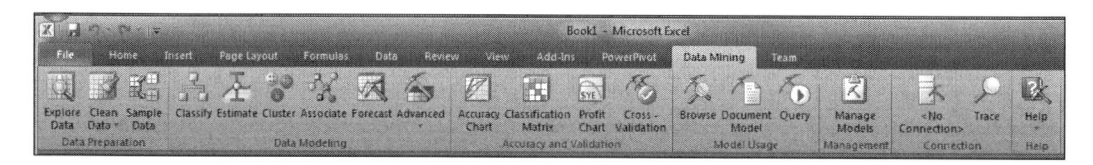

You can use this ribbon on the data you have in Excel, to discover key influencers, categories, exceptions, forecasting, associations, and so on. An example could be an export of customers to Excel with a lot of attributes for your customer like for example gender, degree, income level, marriage status, children, and also the amount of goods sold per customer. You can then have the system analyse the attributes and detect relationships.

Let's take the following example:

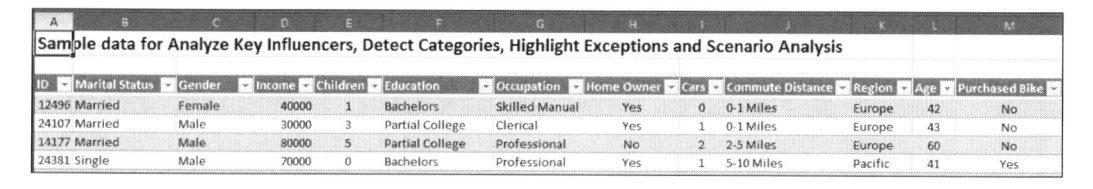

ID	Marital Status	Gender	Income	Children	Education	Occupation	Home Owner	Cars	Commute Distance	Region	Age	Purchased Bike
12496	Married	Female	40000	1	Bachelors	Skilled Manual	Yes	0	0-1 Miles	Europe	42	No
24107	Married	Male	30000	3	Partial College	Clerical	Yes	1	0-1 Miles	Europe	43	No
14177	Married	Male	80000	5	Partial College	Professional	No	2	2-5 Miles	Europe	60	No
24381	Single	Male	70000	0	Bachelors	Professional	Yes	1	5-10 Miles	Pacific	41	Yes

The screenshot above shows the attributes of our customers as columns. It also contains many rows of data. Actually, behind the scenes a lot of the algorithms involved are based upon mathematical statistical formulas. This means that they get more accurate when there's more data to analyse.

In this example, you can see a list of customers and the fact that they bought a bike or not. We can let the data mining algorithm investigate if there are any meaningful attributes that allow us to predict whether a specific customer is probably going to buy a bike or not.

This is just one of the many types of analysis that you can do with this add in.

After you click on the button **Classify**, you have to select a range as the data source. You can select the Excel worksheet containing your data. Then, in the next window you select one column that you want to be able to predict, for example **Purchased Bike**, and the other columns you think might have an influence on the bike buying behavior of your customers.

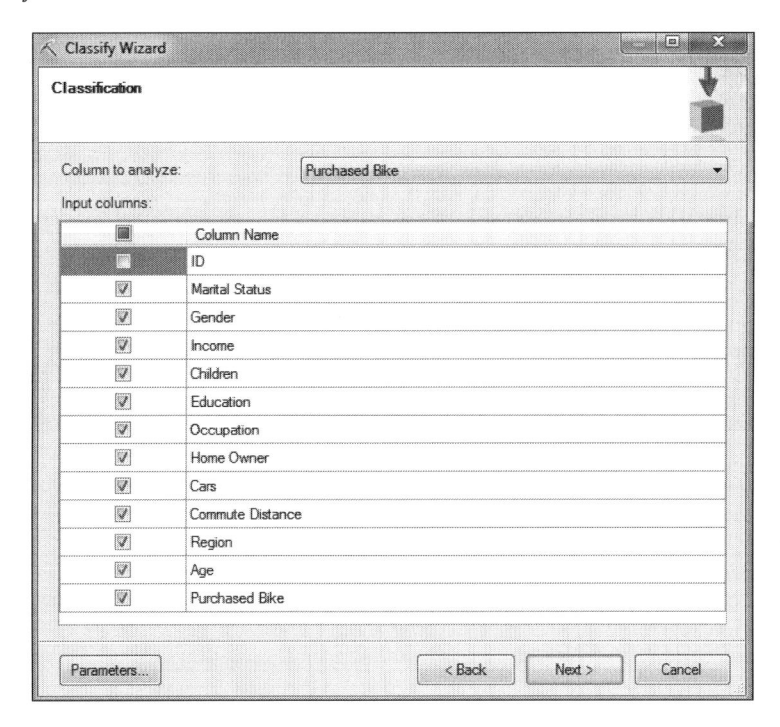

After analysing your data, the system will show the results, as presented in the next screenshot:

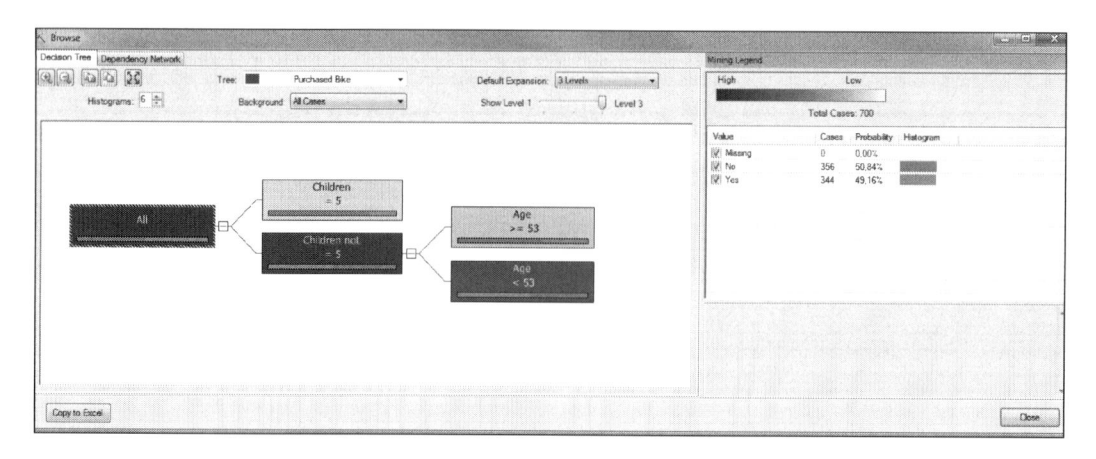

As you can see, the system classified your customers into separate groups with certain characteristics that could influence the probability of them buying a bike or not. In the next screenshot, you see that the system found, based upon the available data, that the two most important factors are **Age** and **Children**:

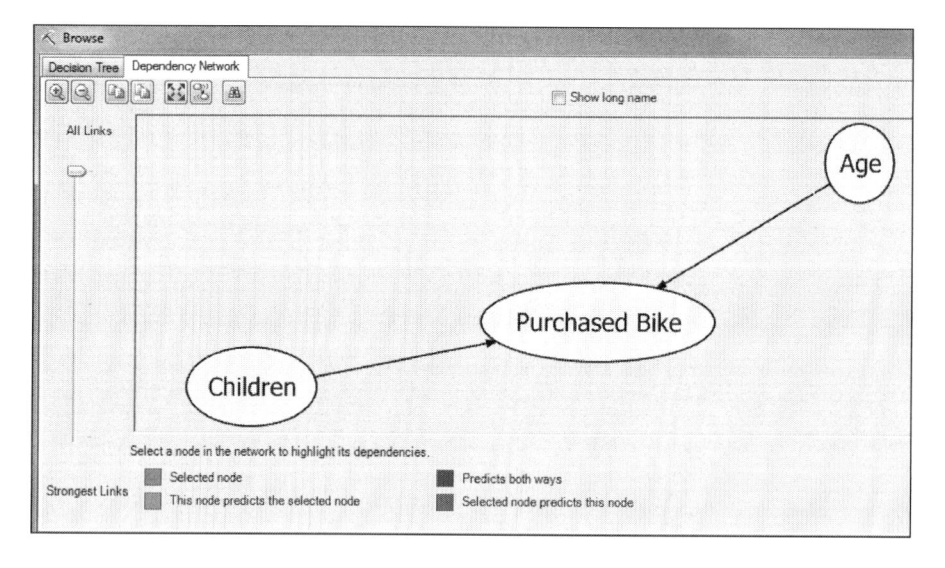

This seems very logical because when you have more children, you are more likely to buy more bikes and when you are older you are less likely to buy a bike. In many cases, the system will detect the obvious, but in many other cases the system can detect very interesting dependencies and correlations, which could change and improve the way you do business.

PowerPivot

Microsoft PowerPivot is an add in for Microsoft Office Excel 2010 and provides you with the power to create your self-service business intelligence Solution. It has a similar look and feel compared to Excel and because of which it is very easy to use and familiar if you are an experienced Excel user, which most of us are. PowerPivot is designed to be able to manage and analyse large sets of data. The data can come from many different types of sources, even the cloud. It also contains some easy to use data-sharing features, enabling you to share your results via SharePoint and the browser with your colleagues. PowerPivot contains built-in algorithms that can detect relationships. The IT department gets a central management dashboard they can use to monitor PowerPivot usage, ensure security, availability, and performance.

The advantages of PowerPivot over Excel are:

- You can import many millions of rows of data. The only limitation is the amount of memory of your local workstation or laptop
- You can merge data from many different types of data sources into one view or model, also named PowerPivot Application
- You can save your data and perform analysis in an environment you are familiar with, like Excel
- You can share your results online, where you can continue to slice and dice the data.

> More information, demos and tutorials about PowerPivot, including the download and installation instructions, can be found on the following website: http://www.powerpivot.com

Let's understand how to use PowerPivot with Dynamics NAV in the following example. I presume that you already have Microsoft Office 2010 and PowerPivot installed for this exercise:

1. Open Microsoft Office Excel 2010.
2. Select the **PowerPivot** tab in the ribbon at the top.
3. Click on the **PowerPivot Window** button in the ribbon at the top.
4. The PowerPivot window opens now.

Other Reporting and Business Intelligence Tools

At the top of this window, there are several buttons that allow you to select data from a variety of data sources, as you can see in the next screenshot:

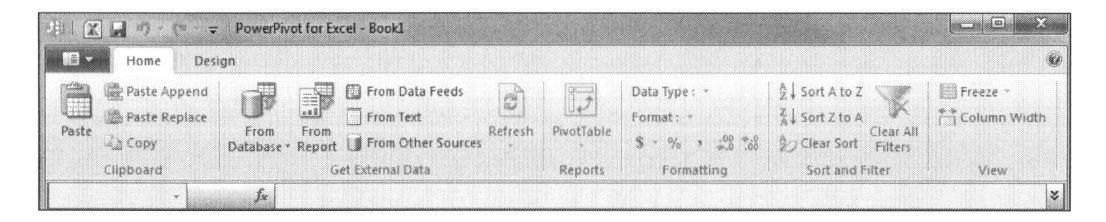

In this example, we are going to fetch the data directly from the Dynamics NAV database on SQL Server:

1. Click on the **From Database** button and select the option, **SQL Server**.
2. A window opens to allow you to connect to a SQL Server database.
3. Enter the name of the SQL Server and the authentication data (username & password).
4. Next, select the Dynamics NAV database in the dropdown list at the bottom of this window.
5. Click on the **Next** button.

> **Select tables or create a custom query?**
>
> In the next window, you can either write your custom query to retrieve data, or select your data based upon tables and views. Usually, when you use Excel or Reporting Services or many other kinds of reporting tools that connect to your database, it is advised to select the custom query option, because that allows you to define the table relations in your query. In PowerPivot that's not necessary. Even if you select the tables separately, you can still define the table relations afterwards. This is one of the advantages of PowerPivot over other 'similar' tools. You can even relate information coming from different data sources. No matter where the data comes from, you can get it into PowerPivot and create relations when required.

6. In the next window, you can select the tables you want to retrieve data from. In the column **Friendly name**, you can give each table a more user-friendly name.
7. By clicking on the **Preview & Filter** button at the bottom right of the window, a new window opens, allowing you to filter the data that will be retrieved from the database.

8. You can filter via a click on a column, on which a dropdown filter menu appears—a lot like the way you can filter in an Excel spreadsheet. Via a right click on a column you can remove a filter or create a table relation.

9. Click on the **Ok** button in the popup window and then click on **Finish** in the underlying window. In the last window, you can see how many rows were imported. When you close that window, you will see one or more worksheets opened in the PowerPivot window.

In the PowerPivot window, you can further manipulate the dataset. You can change the format and sorting of the data, add and remove filters, and create calculated columns.

Another reason why PowerPivot is so fast is because it's is running in memory. It is an in-memory, column-oriented database.

When you right click on a column you can create a table relation. If in the previous steps you selected multiple tables, like for example the **Customer** and **Customer Ledger Entry** table, you can relate them via the following window:

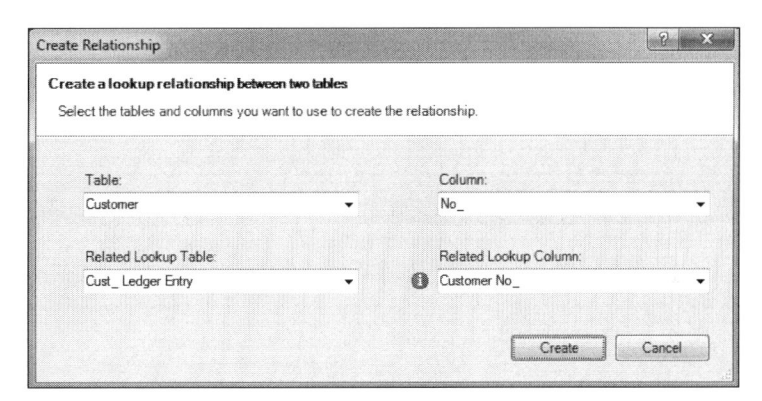

10. After you have created relations and/or calculated columns you are ready to create a report. To do this, click on the **PivotTable** button in the ribbon. The following menu will appear:

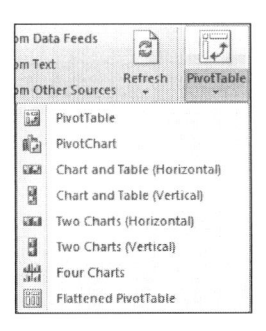

Other Reporting and Business Intelligence Tools

When you select an option, for example **Chart and Table Horizontal**, you can then determine whether you want it to be created in a new worksheet or in the existing one.

You are now redirected to Excel and can start creating your pivot table and chart, just as you would do in Excel. The difference is that here we have a couple of new options. You can add fields to **Slicers Horizontal** and/or **Slicers Vertical**.

When you do that, those fields are added on top or to the left of your pivot chart(s) and/or pivot tables. You can click in the Slicers to select or deselect dimensions and all of the pivot charts and pivot tables are updated automatically.

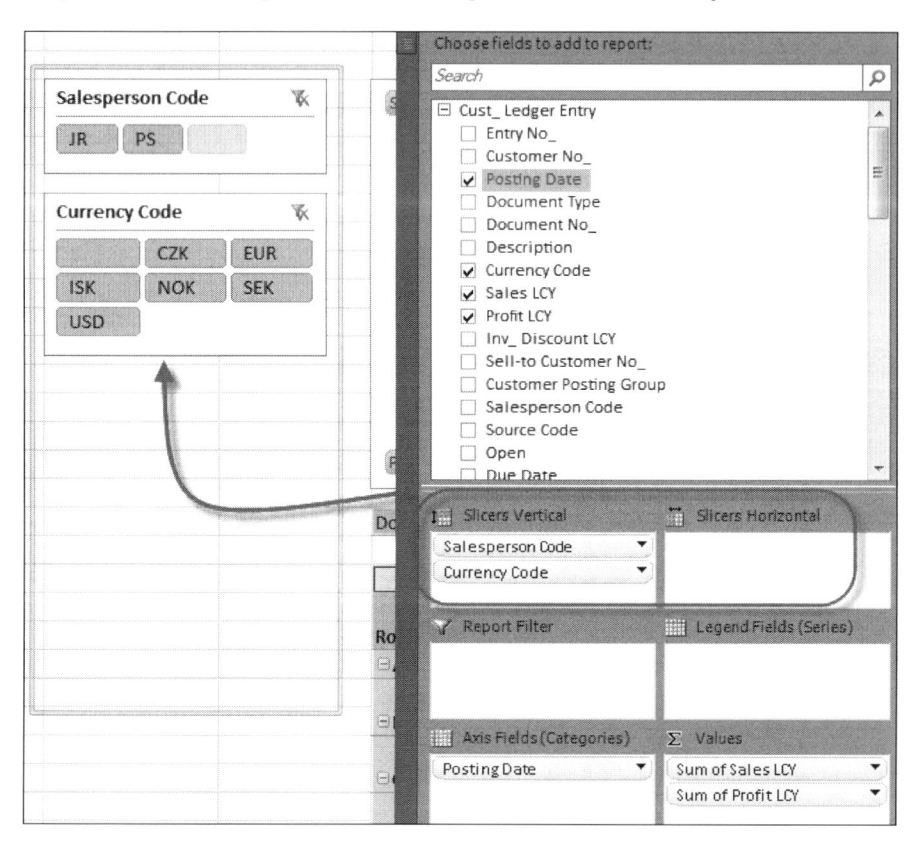

You are not limited to only four charts per report. Actually, when you create a new pivot table or chart, you are asked where you want it to be created. You can select an already existing worksheet.

Now that you have your first report created with PowerPivot in Excel, you can save it locally or in SharePoint. There's an update button that will refresh your report.

[304]

This was a very short demo on how to create a PowerPivot report based upon a Dynamics NAV database, but there are a lot of extra possibilities in this product. For example the expression language DAX really offers a lot of added value.

PowerPivot has been built with a completely new scripting language, called DAX. DAX stands for Data Analysis Expressions. DAX can be used to create simple or complex expressions. It comes with many functions that are similar to the one you are used to in formulas in Excel, but DAX has many more functionalities and is very fast.

> More information about the DAX expression language can be found on this Microsoft website: http://technet.microsoft.com/en-us/library/gg399181.aspx, including its official definition, as quoted below.

The Data Analysis Expressions (DAX) language is a formula language that allows users to define custom calculations in PowerPivot tables (calculated columns) and in Excel PivotTables (measures). DAX includes some of the functions that are used in Excel formulas, and additional functions that are designed to work with relational data and perform dynamic aggregation.

You have to keep in mind that the idea is that non-technical users will use PowerPivot, which is the main focus group. I believe that Microsoft has met this objective and that PowerPivot really has some growth potential.

There are already some Microsoft Dynamics partners who have developed or are developing PowerPivot-based BI solutions.

A nice feature of PowerPivot is of course that you can manipulate the dataset and even add data to it. In a lot of Business Intelligence reporting solutions that are available today, the end user does not have any, or has very few ways to change the data. The data comes out of the cube and cannot be changed. To make any changes would require changing the ETL process and that is time consuming.

PowerPivot can do just that. It can fetch its data from a cube, or multiple cubes, combined with data coming from other sources and when the data arrives in PowerPivot, you connect it and can make changes, calculate new columns, and even add new columns.

Business Intelligence and NAV

There are a lot of Business Intelligence tools out there and they can be used in combination with Dynamics NAV. Many of the BI tools out there are based upon the BI data model or the multi-dimensional data model.

In fact there is a big difference between the OLTP data model and the OLAP data model. Online transactional processing (OLTP) is typically what an ERP application like Dynamics NAV is all about. The OLTP data model is made so that the same data is not stored in multiple tables. The OLTP data model is a normalized data model. Some OLTP applications normalize more than others. Dynamics NAV is an example of an application that has a complex data model. For example the name of a customer or description of an item is stored in the Customer and Item table, but when you create an order (purchase, sale, production, return, and so on) the description is copied over to the document line table. When you post the document, the name or description is copied over to the posted tables, and so on. At the end, you will have the name and descriptions available in many tables and when you have to create a report the question very quickly arises, which one do you want to see on the report? The reason that Dynamics NAV stores the same information in multiple tables is a design decision for historical reasons. Doing that allows the user to change this data at multiple levels in the application and is usually a business requirement.

The OLAP data model was invented with two goals in mind:

- It should be very easy to read/understand.
- It should be very fast to query.

Basically, a cube is built around a single table. This table will contain the facts that we are interested in. It is called the fact table and it will contain the measures. These measures represent the numerical data of interest. For example, the following is a fact table called: **InternetSales** and it contains fields like **OrderQuantity**, **SalesAmount**, **UnitPrice**, and so on. Around this fact table we will put dimension tables. A dimension table contains attributes that we want to use to give meaning to the facts. For example a dimension could be product. A product could have a description, size, class, colour, and so on. Another dimension could be the customer. A typical customer has a name, city, gender, and so on. Another dimension could be time. A time has year, quarter, month, and so on as attributes. All these dimensions will help us to understand the data in the fact table. For example, the amount of goods sold for a specific product by a type of customer in a certain time period is a question you could answer using the above fact and dimension tables. The data model of a cube consists of fact tables surrounded by dimension tables, as you can see in the next screenshot:

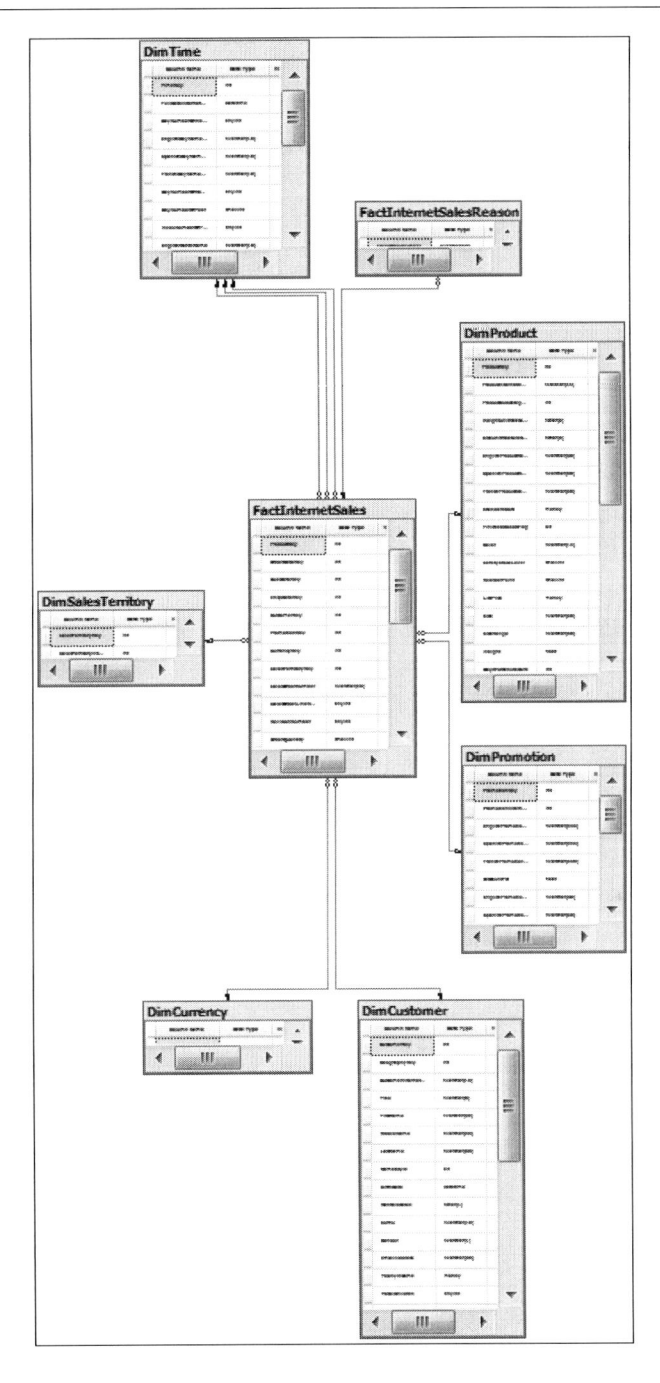

When you look at this model from a distance, you will notice that it resembles a star. The fact table in the middle surrounded by dimensions looks a lot like a star. That is why this database schema is called a **Star schema**.

Dimensions can become more complex. For example the product dimension might be extended with product categories and product sub categories, each with their own attributes. This way you will create table relations between dimension tables. When you apply this with more and more dimension tables, your database schema or ER model will start to resemble a snowflake. This kind of database schema is called a **Snowflake schema**.

For performance (and other) reasons, a **Star schema** is considered much better than a **Snowflake schema**, but which one you will use will be determined by your requirements.

The problem that arises now is how you can get the data from where it is to where it should go for reporting and analysis. Or in other words, how can you transfer the data from one (or more) OLTP data source(s) to an OLAP data model?

The answer Microsoft has for you on this question is SQL Server Integration Services (SSIS). SSIS is an ETL toolkit that allows the extraction of data from one or more data source(s). You can then transform the data that is required and load it into a target database. An SSIS ETL script could look like the following screenshot:

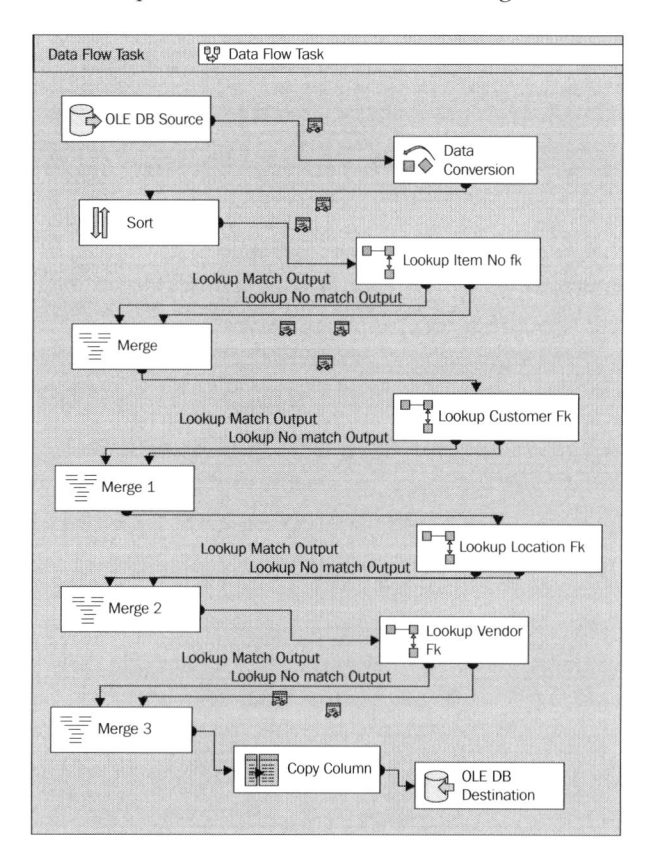

Once the data is in your multi-dimensional database, you can then use reporting tools to create BI reports. Microsoft Office Excel and SQL Server Reporting services are good examples of such tools. But there are in fact many, many third-party tools and applications out there capable of the same and even more.

Microsoft offers you all that you require to be able to build a BI solution. You have the SQL Server Database Engine for your OLTP database, which is Dynamics NAV. You can use SQL Server Analysis services to host your multidimensional database (or cubes), you can use SQL Server Integration Services to create an ETL solution, and you can use SQL Server Reporting services to create reports on the cube(s).

If you are an end user company and you are thinking about implementing a BI solution, remember that SQL Server has all that you require to be able to build such a solution. Of course, there are very good tools out there, probably with a corresponding price tag, that can do more or are easier to deploy.

In fact, because of these tools and the way that technology is evolving very rapidly, BI projects are no longer only affordable for big companies. Right now, there's a big boom in implementing BI solutions for smaller and medium-sized companies.

The most important thing not to forget when shopping for such a solution is to analyse and determine your requirements. Because there's no point in buying a big truck if you only require a small sedan.

In many cases, companies want a BI solution because everybody else has one or because it's the next logical step in your IT infrastructure. But before you begin analysing the market and available technologies, you should do an internal investigation. What kind of reports do you require? What should be the added value of the BI solution? What is the kind of information that you are currently missing or unable to analyse? Try to make an overview of the **AS IS** situation. Then, think about the **TO BE** situation. This is in many cases overlooked.

The TO BE situation could be where you will be or want to be in one to three years. If you don't select a solution that fits your needs for the coming years, then by the time you will have implemented your BI solution, it might be obsolete. That's why it is also important to select a solution or technology that allows for these kinds of changes and flexibility.

Business Analytics

Business Analytics (BA) is an add-on for Dynamics NAV from Microsoft that allows for the semi-automatic creation of a Dynamics NAV cube. Basically, you can define the fact tables (and corresponding measures) and dimensions you want to have available in the cube, from within the Dynamics NAV application. To do this, no knowledge is required about Analysis Services or Integration Services. In fact, the required ETL scripts will be automatically generated in Integration Services, as also the cube in Analysis Services.

You can find BA in the Administration menu of the Classic client, under Application **Setup** | **General** | **Business Analytics Setup**. When you select it, the following window opens:

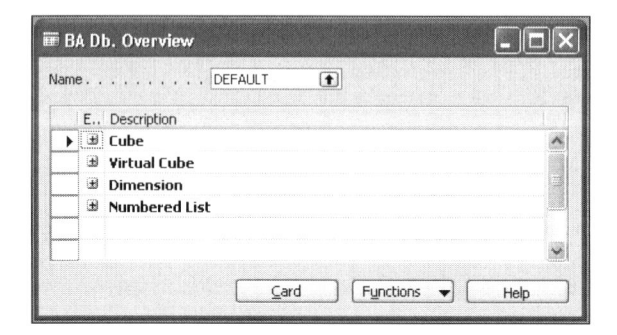

Using this window, you can define the structure of the cube and define measures, dimensions, and all other cube attributes and which tables to use in Dynamics NAV. For example, when you open the **Cube**, by clicking on the first plus sign in the above window, you can see the available default cubes. Using the **Card** button, you can open a new window that you can use to define a new cube. The next screenshot shows that window for the default cube **Job Ledger Entry**:

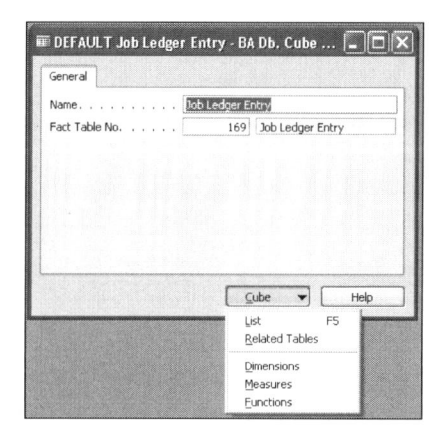

The **Cube** menu button allows managing the definition of the **Dimensions**, **Measures**, **Functions**, and **Related Tables** of the cube. After you have defined the cube layout, you can click on the lookup arrow in the textbox containing the **DEFAULT** cube, as shown in the next screenshot:

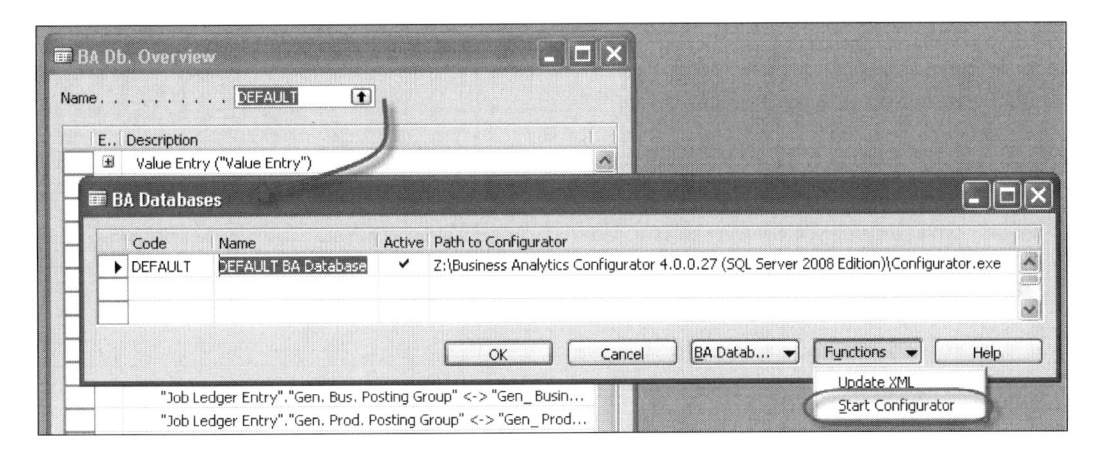

The system will export the cube definition in an XML file and feed that to the **Configurator.exe**. This executable will then launch a batch process that will start by creating a small data warehouse in SQL Server. Next, it will create and start the required ETL scripts and .dtsx packages in SQL Server Integration Services. These scripts will then create a SQL Server Analysis cube, and launch the data export and process the cube. After that, the cube is ready to be used for reporting and analysis purposes. A schedule will be created that will refresh the data every two hours. This time period can be changed according to your requirements.

The advantage of Business Analytics is that the cube will be created automatically, based upon what you define in Dynamics NAV. No knowledge about SSIS or SSAS is required. You can then use for example Excel to connect to the cube and start creating reports.

Other Reporting and Business Intelligence Tools

There's also an advanced BA module that you can purchase that comes with a BA report generator and Enterprise manager. This Business Analytics reporting tool is presented in the following screenshot:

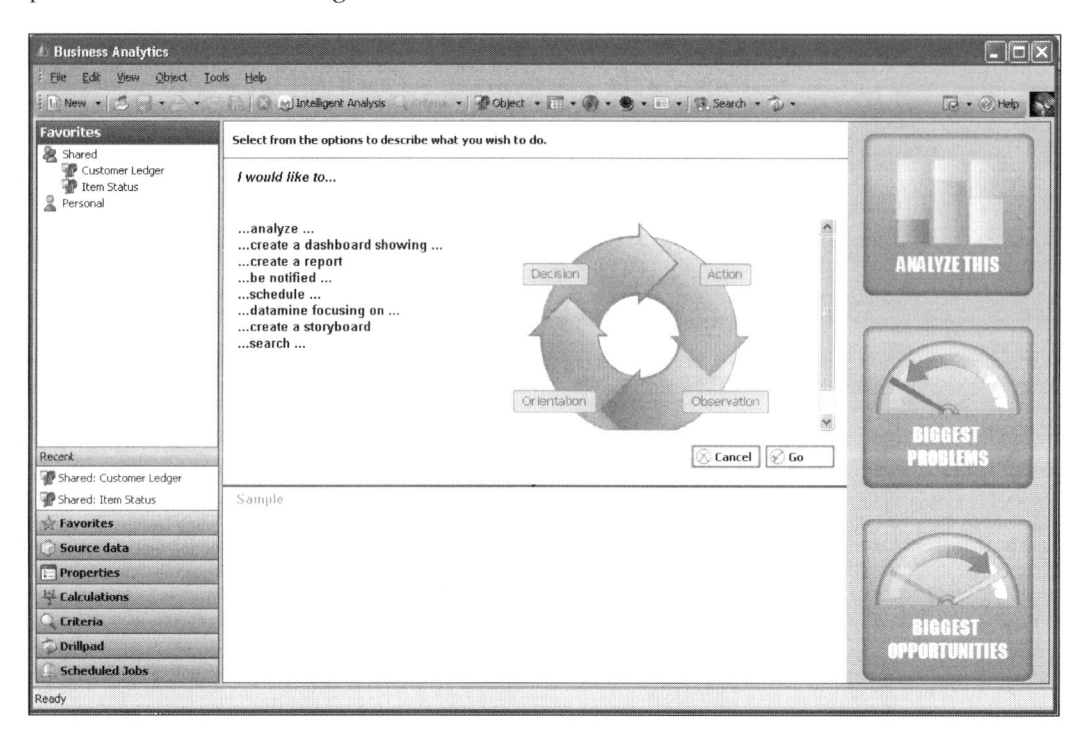

This is a very good and intuitive reporting tool that allows for the creation of BI reports, including KPIs, charts, maps, and many other data visualisations. The tool can also be used to analyse the cube data and create dashboards.

There are also a couple of disadvantages of using BA, and that's why I would not recommend implementing it.

A first restriction is that the cube can only contain data from one company. In most Dynamics NAV databases, there are multiple companies and any BI solution probably has the requirement to be able to report over multiple companies. With BA, that is not possible out of the box.

Secondly, because of the fact that the ETL scripts and analysis services database is created automatically, they are difficult to customize. There's no documentation on the structure of the data warehouse, ETL scripts, and cube. It is possible to find out, but will require time. Then, if you start customizing the data warehouse, ETL scripts, or Analysis services cube, making changes is not so straightforward anymore.

To summarize, Business Analytics can be a great solution for your business, as long as you are happy with its capabilities and restrictions as they come out of the box. As soon as you want to customize it to fit your needs it can get very complex. In that case, I would advise to look for other tools that can help you or to even build the cube from scratch. Business Analytics can be your first, easy to make, step into the world of BI, but be aware that it is not a scalable solution.

The advantage of having a BI solution

Because your ERP reports are developed directly on top of the ERP application, in our case Dynamics NAV, these reports usually contain the most actual information. In BI reports, because of the cube data model and ETL process, it is possible to include information from multiple data sources. For example, you might want to combine information that resides in Excel workbooks, legacy databases, CRM applications, and Dynamics NAV. Because it takes time to process all of this information, the information contained in the cube is usually older, from a couple of hours up to several days, depending of your ETL process. That might seem like a disadvantage, but there are some very interesting advantages of using cubes.

First of all, there's performance and ease of use. Connecting to a cube from Excel is very easy, just as it is to connect to the Dynamics NAV database. But the data model of a cube is self-explaining. Star (and snowflake) schemas are easier to understand compared with the Dynamics NAV data model. So, users less familiar with the Dynamics NAV data model will be able to create reports on top of the cube.

Secondly, because the cube can contain information coming from multiple sources, this data can be compared and directly used in the BI reports. A BI solution has, in many cases, scalability built into its data model. For example, if you want to include an extra database, you only have to modify the ETL part of the BI solution. The design of the cube and reports should not be impacted or can be prepared to manage that. A similar example is being able to report over multiple companies.

The cube also allows for more types of data analysis and trend detection. You can define a number of KPIs in a cube and measure how your business is doing.

Summary

In this chapter, we took a look at the database behind your Dynamics NAV application. How are the tables organized, how can you create an ER model to be able to create and develop reports more quickly?

Then, we had a look inside Reporting Services and what added value it has to offer. Reporting Servicescomes free with any SQL Server license and was used to integrate RDLC reporting into the Role tailored client. In the next versions of Dynamics NAV I expect to see a lot more of reporting services incorporated into the role tailored client. That's why I believe it is very important to start learning about this technology right now.

All companies use Microsoft Office Excel. I have never had a customer who has not used it. Understanding how you can use Excel in combination with Dynamics NAV is very important, and this chapter provided you a good overview of what's possible in that area.

Last but not least, we had a look into Business Intelligence tools available in SQL server. We did not go into much technical detail, but the information in this chapter about BI is meant as a starting point. You should now have a better view on what's available out there and the data model all BI solutions are based upon.

If the methods or tools explained in this chapter are too difficult or too expensive to implement, you should consider looking if there are no add-ins available that fit your requirements. There's no point in reinventing the wheel and there are many very good add-ons out there.

In the next chapter, we will have a look at what the future might bring to Dynamics NAV, from a reporting point of view.

7
A View of the Future

This chapter is about the future enhancements that are expected in Dynamics NAV version 7. Besides Dynamics NAV, there's also SQL server that is about to release a major new version called SQL Server Denali.

The goal of this chapter is not to provide in-depth knowledge about these two releases, but to provide you with enough information so you will get an idea of what to expect.

For Dynamics NAV users, developers, and functional and technical consultants, a lot of changes were introduced in Dynamics NAV 2009. A new way of working in the Role Tailored client combined with many new technical possibilities like enhanced reporting, web services, .NET add-ins, .NET variables, and so on.

I would like to say in this chapter that this is only the beginning of our voyage into new technologies and possibilities. Expect everything to evolve, more rapidly than you are used to in the past. Microsoft products like SQL Server, SharePoint, and Office are all evolving and integrating and this will have an impact on the Dynamics products.

Being aware on what's happening and keeping an eye on the new products that are coming out will help you in the process of seeing the trees in the forest as we like to say in Netherlands.

Dynamics NAV 7 and beyond

Microsoft has announced a couple of very interesting improvements and new features in the next release of Dynamics NAV, version 7. At this moment, no test or community pre-release of Dynamics NAV version 7 is available to the public. There are versions out there, but under a very strict NDA agreement. I will try to highlight some of the changes that were already mentioned at Microsoft conferences and blogs.

Jet Reports Express

Jet Reports is a product that at this moment I don't have a lot of experience with. But nevertheless I have heard many great things about it and it is already widely spread at many Dynamics customer sites. In the next version of Dynamics NAV, we will get a Jet Reports Express edition for free. That is if you are on a Business Ready Enhancement Plan.

The reason why Jet Reports are a logical choice is its integration with Microsoft Excel. Jet Reports is in fact an Excel-based reporting solution.

The advantage of this over regular Excel is the capability to leverage flow fields, dimensions, as well as normal fields. You can have report templates. You can export to PDF and even schedule to receive reports automatically.

Combine this with the power of calculations and the Excel charting and pivoting engine and you have the building blocks of a very good and user-friendly reporting tool.

A disadvantage of Jet Reports seems to be performance. When you create a Jet Report containing a lot of data, performance will decrease and you are better off using the existing Dynamics NAV reporting tool.

A question right now still is, which of the set of features that are currently available in Jet Reports will be included in the Jet Reports Express edition?

I think it is a good idea, because now that RDLC reporting is introduced in Dynamics NAV and is here to stay, end users might feel less capable of creating and developing their own reports. Now you can use Jet Reports Express as your self-service reporting tool on top of Dynamics NAV.

RDLC mandatory and 2008 integration

In Dynamics NAV 7, the Classic client will disappear. We will still use it for development, but no longer as a Classic client for end users. Because of this, Classic reports will no longer run in the Role Tailored client and so you will need to have an RDLC layout for all your reports. But this is true only for new reports. Existing reports imported from older versions will still work in the Classic client, until you click a button to convert it. Once it's converted, you won't be able to run it using the Classic client. However, if you don't click on that button to convert the report, it'll still work in the Classic client in NAV 7. At Convergence in the US, Claus Lundstrom (who is in charge of reporting) presented a session about reporting, and he went into some of the things that they had decided for NAV 7. The two big things were as follows:

- NAV 7 will not ship with any Classic reporting capabilities. There will be no more section designer, and ALL Classic features will be gone. It will not be possible to run Classic Reports, because the sections will be removed from the objects altogether. There will be one way and one way only to create reports and that is using RDLC (and he confirmed that we'll get RDLC 2008).
- The NAV report object will become the Dataset Designer (which looks exactly like XMLPorts, with fields indented under tables). We'll have direct control over what is included in the dataset right in the report object. You manage the dataset in C/SIDE, and the actual report in Visual Studio.

> Claus is an active blogger; he regularly posts little bits of information on the NAV team blog: http://blogs.msdn.com/nav.

Dynamics NAV 7 will support the RDLC 2008 specification. This means we will now have more controls in the toolbox in Visual Studio for data visualisation, more global variables and constants and functions in the expression designer and no longer the limitation of data bound information only allowed in the body of the report.

This means that a lot of the workarounds that we now apply in document reports might no longer be necessary, and so report design will become easier with more possibilities on data visualisation and interactivity.

Any investment you make at creating RDLC reports will not be lost. Moving from Dynamics NAV 6 to 7 from an RDLC reporting point of view should not be difficult. Reports can be transformed seamlessly, without any complication or user interaction.

If you want a sneak peak in the improvements RDLC 2008 has to offer I would advise you to try out Report Builder version 2 or 3. We have covered Report Builder briefly in the previous chapter. The difference is that the dataset will now be generated by Dynamics NAV and the design environment is BIDS.

Section designer replaced with an extended data item designer

The way that we now create the dataset for an RDLC report in Dynamics NAV is by using the section designer. The fields that you drop on the section designer will become the fields in your dataset in Visual Studio.

Now, many of the properties of fields in the section designer are of no use anymore. Also, C/AL code in the section triggers has no effect and even some sections (transheader and transfooter) also have no effect on the dataset. This makes it very difficult to detect what still works and what does not, making it difficult to predict what the dataset will look like.

In Dynamics NAV version 7, the section designer will be replaced with something else that will be easier to use. It will look and behave more like the page designer, and be an extension of the data item designer, where you drop the fields as they should appear in the dataset. The reason is that Classic reports will be discontinued, so sections are no longer required in the report designer.

Dynamics NAV and SharePoint

One very interesting announcement that Microsoft has made public is the Dynamics NAV SharePoint client, called **NAV Portal**.

Reporting Services, Project Crescent, Excel, and many of the other Microsoft tools in the BI tool stack are all beginning to be very well integrated on the SharePoint platform.

When Dynamics NAV provides a full client on SharePoint, you can imagine how much more will become possible. For example, imagine having the possibility to create an integrated sales dashboard in SharePoint, displaying customer cards and lists, with access to orders straight from the ERP application (and even entering and posting orders), but also linking to full on BI reports that are published on the same SharePoint site, integrating documents, workflows, web parts, and so on.

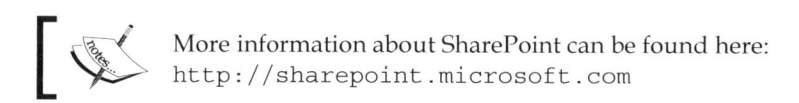

> More information about SharePoint can be found here:
> http://sharepoint.microsoft.com

Dynamics NAV in the cloud

Microsoft has announced that Dynamics NAV will be the first Dynamics product on Azure and integrated with Office 365; combined with the NAV Portal this is a huge step forward.

Moving Dynamics NAV to the cloud could have huge advantages and reduce the costs of implementation projects. One of the principles of cloud computing is that it is very scalable and you only pay for what you use, like your electric bill. You don't have to worry anymore (or a lot less) about maintaining IT infrastructure and staff. For small and medium-sized companies in particular this could cut costs and reduce overhead, allowing companies to focus more on the core business. Also, because of the way the cloud is set up, you don't have to worry anymore about implementing complex backup systems and securing your data can become a lot easier. Of course, a lot of the advantages that the cloud offers have to be analysed further and fine-tuned to your requirements, but it is a very interesting concept that is becoming more and more a reality instead of a concept. Since Microsoft has announced that Dynamics NAV will be amongst the first ERP applications they will port to the cloud; I believe that is a very good indication of the maturity of both products. Combined with the integration on SharePoint and other Microsoft products, this could prove to be a very big step forward.

> More information about Windows Azure can be found here:
> http://www.microsoft.com/windowsazure

What will SQL Server do?

At the time of writing, CTP3 of SQL Server Denali was just released and promises to be an exciting release. That is important for us Dynamics enthusiasts because Dynamics NAV runs on SQL Server and the power of SQL Server and the new possibilities capabilities that SQL Server Denali will bring us will in the end also become an added value for Dynamics NAV and even one day might end up in the Dynamics NAV product itself.

SQL Server Denali will bring some new possibilities capabilities on high availability solutions. The idea is that a database should always be available, even when it's down. In the current and previous SQL Server versions we had database mirroring, log shipping, server clustering, replication, and similar options to achieve this goal. In SQL server Denali high availability will be available more out of the box and should be less complex to implement.

The BIDS environment as we are used to today will also evolve into a new tool. BIDS and SSMS will be merged into a new development environment.

A View of the Future

> There are many new features in SQL server Denali, and the best place to look for information is here: http://www.microsoft.com/sqlserver/en/us/future-editions.aspx

In the following sections, I will focus on the exciting new technologies and products that are coming with SQL Server Denali related to BI and Reporting.

Project Crescent

Project Crescent is the working name of a new reporting tool that Microsoft is working on. It is meant to deliver a very highly visual design experience when creating reports. It can create very interactive reports using familiar office design patterns and multiple visualisations.

Very interesting is that it will be fully integrated with PowerPivot and SharePoint. PowerPivot is all about the data and pivoting the data, Project Crescent can be a layer on top of that used to visualize this data.

Project Crescent will also have integration with PowerPoint. PowerPoint is still the tool we use to communicate with management but it lacks interactivity. This is where Crescent will come in very handy.

Visualisations are based upon Silverlight. The demos that I have seen also show the capability to design while you preview or run a report.

The difference with Reporting Services is that it is meant directly for end users to use. It should be very easy to use. In terms of self service business intelligence, Project Crescent will be the self-service reporting tool. Project Crescent works in SharePoint with Reporting Services installed in SharePoint mode. There are no property boxes or context menus. Everything can be achieved with a minimal number of mouse clicks.

It combines the functionality, interactivity, performance of Reporting Services and PowerPivot, with a lot of intelligence and algorithms that try to detect what you are trying to do and help you in a visual way.

For example, you drop some fields from a dataset into a bar chart and then create a second bar chart, created via copy paste, in which you change some fields. The visualisations are connected to the same underlying dataset(s) and interact. For example, you click on a bar in the bar chart, representing the Sales value from a particular customer, then that customer becomes highlighted in all other visualisations in your report.

You can compare it with a rolecenter in the Role Tailored client. It consists of different parts that visualize different types of data in different ways, but in Project Crescent it is more interactive, more visual, and with more intelligence.

A very nice feature is the **play axis**. For example, you create a bubble chart representing sales figures on a chart by country of department and you drag the time dimension to the play axis, then you can actually play your report and see the bubbles moving in time. If you have seen the TED talks from Professor Hans Rosling about **The joy of stats** (http://www.gapminder.org), which are actually fantastic, then now we can create these kinds of visualisation ourselves in Project Crescent.

I just cannot wait to see Project Crescent released. It looks like the kind of reporting tool you always dreamed of but thought would never become real and affordable.

The following are screenshots of Project Crescent, taken from this website: http://blogs.msdn.com/b/sqlrsteamblog/archive/2011/07/12/sql-server-codename-quot-denali-quot-ctp3-including-project-quot-crescent-quot-is-now-publically-available.aspx

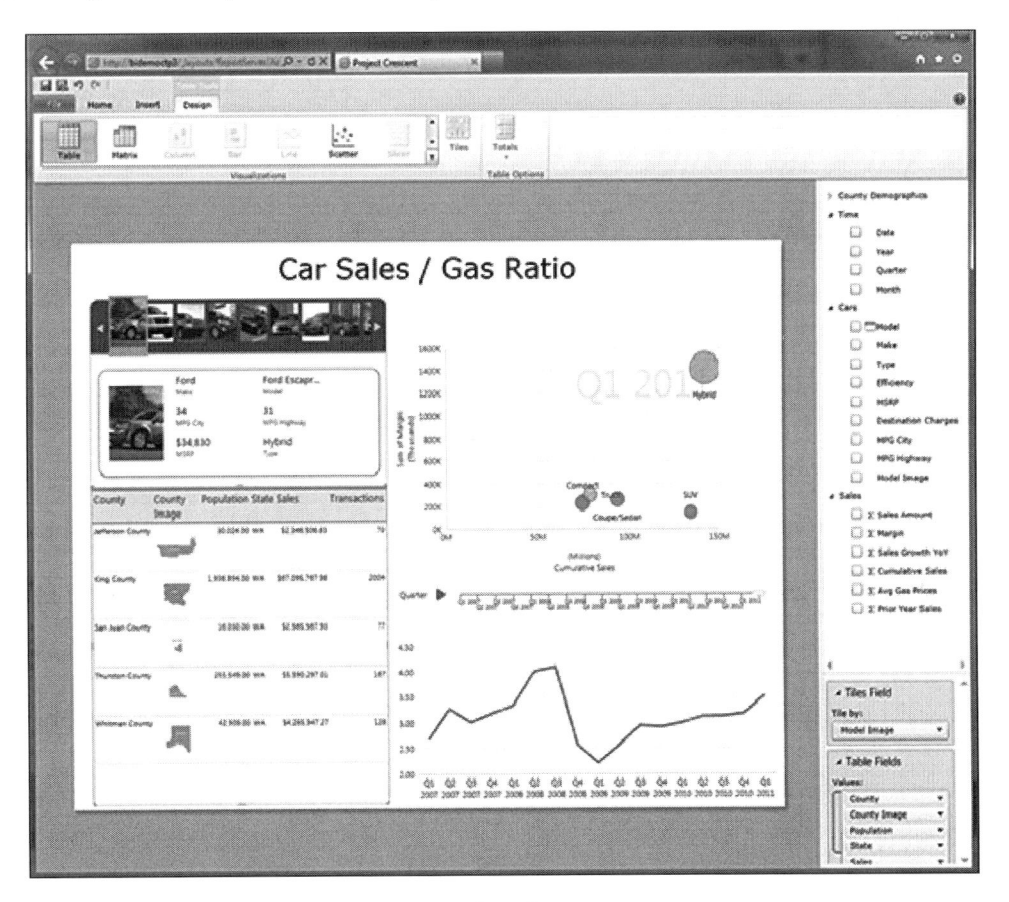

The next screenshot shows other types of visualisations and interactivity available in Project Crescent:

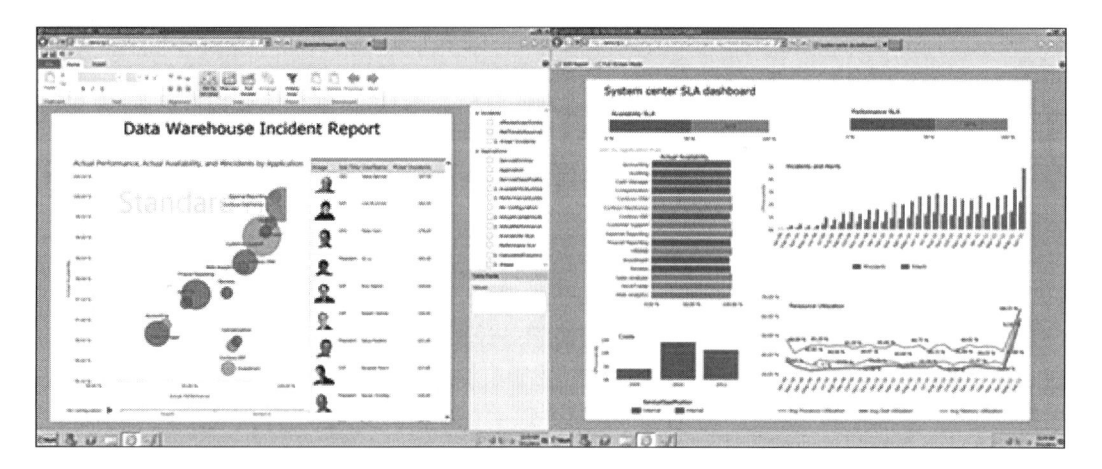

This is where you can see a teaser video of Project Crescent: http://blogs.msdn.com/b/bi/archive/2010/11/09/data-visualization-done-right-project-crescent.aspx

You can see more information on the technet wiki page for Project Crescent here: http://social.technet.microsoft.com/wiki/contents/articles/3734.aspx

BISM

BISM is the new Business Intelligence Semantic Model for SQL Server Analysis Services.

In fact when UDM was developed, it was meant to be the Unified Dimensional Model containing building blocks for all kinds of BI data models. The problem is that the UDM model is sometimes too complex to be used in simple projects. Also, reporting in cubes requires knowledge of MDX and DMX and in the world of relational databases we are used to SQL as the query language.

That's why Microsoft has now developed the BISM. BISM has a lot of the same principles that you find in PowerPivot. For example, in PowerPivot you just create your model by adding in tables, create relationships and calculations. You can then use DAX to query your data. That is a lot easier and faster than MDX or DMX. DAX actually combines SQL and MDX in a new expression language. All new BI tools from Microsoft will support BISM: Reporting Services, PowerPivot, Project Crescent, and Excel…

Basically, UDM has failed to become the unified model for the relational and multi-dimensional world. BISM is a new attempt to reach this goals and it seems like it will be successful this time.

Right now, there's a lot of confusion and discussions going on, on the roadmap towards the BISM. SQL Server Analysis services will not be discontinued, and neither will MDX and DMX be discontinued. BISM will support them all and gradually evolve into a new unified model for relational and non-relational data.

> **Start Learning DAX!**
> One very good piece of advice I can give you is to now start learning DAX. I believe DAX will become more and more important and will end up being used in many Microsoft products like SQL Server, Excel, Analysis services, Reporting Services, and so on. There are even rumours that DAX might become a new standard query language replacing SQL, MDX, and DMX. We will have to wait and see if that really will be the case, but there's no harm in starting to prepare by learning DAX.

Summary

This chapter gives an overview, based upon the information that's available at this moment and on what is to come in the near future. Dynamics NAV 7 and SQL Server Denali are coming and it's better to be informed and understand what to expect.

We have seen that Jet Reports will be available in an express edition and that the new RDLC 2008 standard will be used in Dynamics NAV 7. The section designer will disappear and with it the classic client.

SQL Server Denali has some great enhancements on high availability and reporting. The new BISM model might be a revolution in the Microsoft BI world and might become the standard in all BI and reporting tools in the future. It could even find its way into the Dynamics NAV application.

PowerPivot and project Crescent, based upon Silverlight and running on SharePoint, will become a very user friendly, interactive, and visually compelling reporting tool allowing for self-service BI. And because it's very easy to connect to Dynamics NAV it might also have a deep impact on the way we think about reporting. Don't forget, even Dynamics NAV will be running on SharePoint soon. SharePoint is becoming the platform that will integrate them all.

A View of the Future

In the Microsoft product stack until now it was a bit confusing because there were so many products and tools to choose from. Finally, we will now start seeing it all coming together.

A lot of the currently existing third-party tools and Dynamics NAV add-ons address the lack of reporting features in the older Dynamics NAV versions. But Dynamics NAV version 6, with the new RDLC enhanced reports gives you, at no additional cost, the possibility for a more powerful and efficient reporting tool. So, please invest a little time to get the features explained in this book; I promise you will not be disappointed.

Many companies, developers, and entrepreneurs are looking for new reporting tools that can be of use for small and medium-sized businesses. While there are a lot of very good tools out there I believe you should not discard the Microsoft tool stack, especially with what's coming out in the near future.

Index

Symbols

'(comment) sign 222
+/- sign 226
.xsd file 16
– sign 226

A

About this Report feature 101
ABS function 207
aggregate functions, datatypes
　Avg 193
　Count 193
　CountDistinct 193
　CountRows 193
　First 193
　Last 193
　Max 193
　Min 194
　RowNumber 194
　RunningValue 194
　StDev 194
　StDevP 194
　Sum 194
　Var 194
　VarP 194
applied filters
　showing 234
array variables
　CompanyAddr 224
　CustAddr 224
　ShipToAddr 224
AS IS situation 309
automation 83
AVG function 194

B

BA 310
BackGroundColor property 257
BISM 322
budget dimensions 34
Business Analytics. *See* BA
Business Intelligence
　advantage 313
　and Dynamics NAV 306-309
　BA 310-312
　BA, advantages 311
　BA, reporting tool 312
　OLAP data model 307
　SSIS 308
Business Intelligence Semantic Model. *See* BISM

C

C/AL Code button 206
CalcPct2 function 243
CalcPct function 243
Caption fields 213
cells, merging 233
cells-in-cells technique 161
chart
　areas 162
　data regions 161, 162
　layouts 13
　subtypes 163
　types 163
chart, operators
　count 13
　sum 13
chart, types
　column 13

point 13
chart creation
  limitations 13
chart definition
  example 13-15
Chart Generator Card 15
Chart Generator Tool 15
Chart Panes
  about 9-11
  enabling 10
  limitations 11
Chart Parts 9-16
chart performance 18
chart security
  about 17
  record level security 18
Chr(177) 226
Classic Client (CC) 13
classic report
  colour, adding to 77
  sections 68
Claus 317
Codeunit (Format Address) 224
Colour property
  about 135, 138
  assigning, to 136
combination restriction fields 41
conditional formatting
  adding 240-243
  appropriate colors, selecting 260
  implementing 257, 259
  report, testing 260
  report code 258
  using 257, 258
controls, List report
  images 70
  labels 70
  picture boxes 70
  shapes 70
  text boxes 70
CreateBook function 82
Create Layout Suggestion option
  using 118-123
  using, examples 120-122
CreateTotals() function 59
Ctrl+Alt+F1 shortcut 211
Ctrl-R 58

CurrReport.BREAK function 84
CurrReport.CREATETOTALS function 85
CurrReport.PAGENO function 85
CurrReport.PREVIEW function 85
CurrReport.QUIT function 85
CurrReport.SHOWOUTPUT function 86
CurrReport.SKIP function 84
CurrReport.TOTALSCAUSEDBY function 85
Customer table 55
Customize This Page feature 12

D

data 264
data-bound information display, in header
  about 209-224
  copy number, displaying 226, 227
  current page, displaying 226, 227
  issue, solving 219
  process, at runtime 219
  report addresses, working with 224, 225
Data Analysis Expressions. *See* DAX
database 264
database design, Dynamics NAV
  about 265-268
  managing 265-269
  Properties window 267
  schema 265
  Table Designer window 267
Data Connection Wizard 295
Data Item 55, 209
DataItem Execution Flow
  visual representation 73
DataItemLink property 64
DataItemTableView property 66
DataItem triggers
  OnAfterGetRecord 71
  OnPostDataItem 71
  OnPreDataItem 71
DataItemVarName property 206
DataItemView property 61
DataPerCompany property 267
data region control 204
Dataset Designer 317
DataSetFieldName property 183

Data set name property 221
DAX 305, 323
default dimensions
  about 42
  specifying 42, 43
Design button 62
dimension-based reports 49
dimension combinations 40, 41
dimensions
  about 31, 36
  default dimensions 42, 43
  financial information, analysing with 43-48
  performance issues 37
  setting up, in Dynamics NAV application 32
dimensions, types
  budget 34
  global 33
  shortcut 33
dimension setup
  accessing 37
  locations 34-36
dimension value 37, 39
dimension value combinations 41
Dimension Value Combinations Matrix page 42
dimension values 37
document map
  using 172-175
Document map label property 173
document reports
  about 23, 203
  data-bound information, displaying in header 209
  examples 23
  global variables, defining 206
  number of copies option 204-208
DSN Name 297
Dynamics NAV
  about 315
  and Business Intelligence 306-309
  and SharePoint 7, 318
  cloud computing 319
  database design 264
  Jet Reports Express 316
  Microsoft Excel. using with 294-297
  moving, to cloud 319
  RDLC mandatory 316, 317
  section designer, replacing with extended items 317, 318
Dynamics NAV 2009
  about 8, 87
  Classic report design, workflow 52
  reports 203
Dynamics NAV application
  about 7
  dimensions, setting up in 32
  dimensions types 33
  role centers 8, 9
Dynamics NAV database
  creating, in SQL server 269-273
Dynamics NAV database, creating in SQL server
  foreign key 274, 275
  relations 274, 275
  rules 269
  SQL Server database, managing 270
  steps 269-273

E

EnableExternalImages property 165
EnableHyperlinks property 183
enhanced report design, in Dynamics NAV 2009
  about 128
  limitation 128, 129
  RDL schema versions 128
examples, document reports
  Report 116, Statement 23
  Report 206, Sales-Invoice 23
  Report 405, Order 23
examples, list reports
  Report 101, Customer - List 21
  Report 301, Vendor - List 21
examples, other reports
  Report 1012, Jobs per Customer 23
  Report 113, Customer/Item Sales 23
  Report 313, Vendor/Item Purchases 23
examples, test reports
  Report 1005, Job Journal - Test 21
  Report 2, General Journal - Test 21
examples, transaction reports
  Report 1007, Job - Transaction Detail 22

Report 104, Customer - Detail Trial Bal 22
Report 4, Detail Trial Balance 22
Excel-like layout, report
 controls, overlapping 79
 creating 78, 79
 look and feel, disadvantages 80
 report to Excel, printing 80, 81
 ShapeStyle property, values 79
Excel Buffer table (370)
 automation 83
 features 81, 82
ExcelBuf variable 81
expressions
 about 188
 defining 188-191
 Fields collection 191, 192
 ReportItems collection 192
 User collection 193

F

Field Menu button 56
field picker 57
Filter tab 231
financial information
 analyzing, dimensions used 43-48
First() function 144
first enhanced report, creating
 chart, data region 103
 filter, setting 111
 filtering, to report 108, 109
 format options, adding to report 107, 114
 format strings, list 114
 list, data region 103
 matrix, data region 103
 page breaks 111
 report creation workflow 115, 116
 sorting options, adding to report 108-113
 steps 91-107
 table, data region 103
 zero rows, filtering out 113
FontFamily property 138
foreign key 274
Form type report, report wizard 52, 53
format property
 about 113
 cons 115
format strings

 custom numeric format strings 115
 standard date and time format strings 115
functions
 aggregate functions 193-195

G

GETFILTER() function 234
GETFILTERS() function 234
Get function 223, 226
global dimensions 33
Globals collection
 ExecutionTime 192
 PageNumber 192
 ReportFolder 192
 ReportName 192
 ReportServerURL 192
 TotalPages 192
GroupHeader option 60
GroupNumber() function 159
Group parameter 224
GroupTotalFields property 66

H

Hidden property 146, 167, 214, 218, 232
hyperlinks
 about 181
 enabling 183, 184
 page, filtering 182, 183
 report, filtering 182

I

Iif() function 236
image data textbox
 hiding 218
images, adding to report
 about 164-168
 MIMEType element, values 164
 properties, setting 164
 value elements 165
Indent Dimension Values function 40
InScope() function 156
Insert New Section window 56
interactive sorting
 specifying 171, 172
international properties

Padding 135
intOutPutNo variable 207
int prefix 205
ioOfCopies variable 205

J

Jump to bookmark property 180
Jump to URL property 183

K

Key 61, 62
KPI's
  adding 240-243
  data bars, simulating 244-248
  spark lines, simulating 251-257
  table, recreating 248-250

L

Language property 114
Label Type report, report wizard 54
List data region
  border, adding 143, 144
  defining 139
  document outline 147-149
  List control, using 140, 141, 149
  List properties 141
  properties, grouping 142, 143
  properties, sorting 142, 143
  Redo 150
  steps, summarizing 144, 146
  Tab, including 142
  Undo 150
List report
  about 21
  classic report, section 68-70
  classic report color, adding to 77
  controls 70
  creating 55-59
  data, grouping 60-68
  data, sorting 60-68
  examples 21
  triggers 71
localhost 282
lvar> "" 223
lvar parameter 222

M

Maintain relationships property 274
  Entity Relationship (ER) Model, using 275-277
matrix box
  about 151-153
  advanced techniques 154, 158-161
  colours, using 155-158
  green bar matrix 158-161
  matrix, dragging to 154
  subtotal, adding to 154
Message() function 222
meta data 32
Microsoft
  website 269
Microsoft Excel
  using, with Dynamics NAV 294-297
Microsoft Excel, using with Dynamics NAV
  about 294-297
  custom query, creating 302
  Excel Data Mining Add In 298-300
  PowerPivot 301-305
  PowerPivot, advantages 301, 302
  tables, creating 302
MsgBox() 222
multi-column reports 184-186
  print previewing, Print Layout using 186
multiple data items, using 117, 118
MyVarX variable 221

N

NAV Portal 318
NODBC driver
  advantage 264
  using 264
NoOfCopies variable 205
No PictureBox control 217
NoRows property 199

O

Object Designer 266
OLA
  references 240
OLAP data model 306
OnAfterGetRecord() trigger 207

online reports
  versus printed reports 90, 91
Online transactional processing (OLTP) 306
OnPreDataItem trigger 207
OnPreReport() trigger 210, 216
optional enhanced layout
  optional enhanced layoutabout 88
Options tab 204

P

Page break at end
  property 226
Page break at end property 208
page footers 186, 187
page headers 186, 187
PageSize property 200
Parent property 200
pk 62
PlaceInBottom property 70
posted dimension information
  viewing 43
Posting report
  about 21, 22
  examples 22
PowerPivot
  about 301
  advantages, over Excel 301
  using, with Dynamics NAV 301-305
Preview & Filter button 302
primary key. *See* pk
printed reports
  versus online reports 90, 91
printer
  selecting, for printing reports 27-29
PrintOnEveryPage property 70
PrintOnFirstPage property 187
PrintOnLastPage property 187
PrintOnlyIfDetails property 118
print report settings
  determining 26, 27
ProcessingOnly property 78
ProcessingOnly report
  about 77
  advantages 78
Project Crescent
  about 320

screenshots 321, 322
PromotedCategory property 127
property, report items
  BackgroundColour 135
  BackgroundImage 135
  BorderColour 135
  BorderStyle 135
  BorderWidth 135
  Padding 135
property, data item
  CalcFields 76
  DataItemIndent 76
  DataItemLink 76
  DataItemLinkReference 76
  DataItemTable 76
  DataItemTableView 76
  DataItemVarName 76
  GroupTotalFields 76
  MaxIteration 76
  NewPagePerGroup 76
  NewPagePerRecord 76
  PrintOnlyIfDetail 76
  ReqFilterFields 76
  ReqFilterHeading 76
  ReqFilterHeadingML 76
  TotalFields 76
property, report
  BottomMargin 75
  Caption 74
  CaptionML 74
  Description 75
  HorzGrid 75
  ID 74
  LeftMargin 75
  Name 74
  Orientation 75
  PaperSize 75
  PaperSourceFirstPage 75
  PaperSourceOtherPage 75
  Permissions 75
  ProcessingOnly 75
  RightMargin 75
  ShowPrintStatus 74
  TopMargin 75
  TransactionType 75
  UseReqForm 75
  UseSystemPrinter 75

VertGrid 75
viewing 74
property, section
  PlaceInBottom 76
  PrintsOnEveryPage 76
  SectionHeight 76
  SectionWidth 76

R

RDL
  about 89
  advantages 292, 293
  comparing, with RDLC 292, 293
RDLC
  advantages 292, 293
  disadvantages 292, 293
  viewing 246
RECORDID function 183
record level security 18
Refresh button 297
Relative option 17
RelativePct option 17
REM function 227
Repeat report item with data region on every page property 220
report.rdlc visualisation 96
Report | Page Header 213
Report Builder, SSRS
  @ Sign, using for parameter creation 287
  about 278, 279
  blank report 280
  data source user 289
  downloading 278
  parameters, using 288
  report, using 279, 280
  Tablix data region 286
  three tabs 280
  using 280, 283, 284
  visualized/hidden areas 280
report definition language. *See* **RDL**
report designer
  about 52
  report wizard 52
report functions
  CurrReport.BREAK 84
  CurrReport.CREATETOTALS 85
  CurrReport.NEWPAGE 85
  CurrReport.PAGENO 85
  CurrReport.PREVIEW 85
  CurrReport.QUIT 84
  CurrReport.SHOWOUTPUT 85
  CurrReport.SKIP 84
  CurrReport.TOTALSCAUSEDBY 85
Reporting Services
  about 88
  RDL, differentiating with RDLC 89
  RDLC, differentiating with RDL 90
report items
  about 134
  data regions 134
  options, using 137
  properties 135
  static report items 134
Report properties, Layout tab 185
reports
  about 18
  creating, without development tools 31
  Excel-like layout, creating 78
  filtering 182
  functions 84
  groups 19
  need for 20
  other reports, examples 23
  printing 24, 25
  properties 74
reports, Dynamics NAV 2009
  conditional formatting 240
  conditional formatting, implementing 257
  document reports 203
  KPI's, adding 240
  TOP X reports 227
reports, types
  document 23
  list 21
  posting 21, 22
  test 21
  transaction 22
report sections
  body 70
  collapsing 168-170
  expanding 168-170
  exporting, to Excel 171
  footer 70

GroupFooter 70
GroupHeader 70
header 70
TransFooter 70
TransHeader 70
Report Selections table
  about 30
  advantages 31
reports linking
  bookmark links 176-180
  types 175, 176
Report triggers
  OnCreateHyperlink 71
  OnHyperlink 71
  OnInitReport 71
  OnPostReport 71
  OnPreReport 71
report wizard
  Form Type reports 52, 53
  Label Type reports 54
  Tabular Type reports 54
  using 52, 53
Role Center
  about 8
  example, for Order Processor role 8
  example, for small business 9
Role Tailored Client (RTC)
  about 8, 51, 87
  Chart Panes 9-11
  Chart Parts 9-16
  chart types 9
  reports 18-20
  report, making available 127
  using 13
Role Tailored Reports
  Create Layout Suggestion option, using 118-123
  enhanced report, creating 91
  multiple data items, using 116, 117
  optional enhanced layout 88
  template, changing 123-127
RowNumber function 158
Run command 92, 94
RunningValue function 159
RunObject property 127

S

section triggers
  OnPreSection 71
security filter 18
SETCURRENTKEY 228
Set functions 223-225
Setup | General | Business Analytics Setup 310
SharePoint 318
Shift+F12 265
shortcut dimensions 33
Sizing property 168
Snowflake schema 308
Sort tab 229
SourceExpr property 183, 210
SQL server
  BISM 322, 323
  DAX 323
  Project Crescent 320, 322
  SQL Server Denali 319
SQL server Denali
  about 319
  features 320
SQL Server Integration Services. *See* **SSIS**
SQL Server Option 18
SQL Server Reporting Services. *See* **SSRS**
SSIS 308
SSRS
  about 277
  BIDS, using 289-292
  developing, tools used 278
  Report Builder, using 278-289
Star schema 308
Start button 92
static filters 13
static report items
  image 134
  line 134
  pointer 134
  rectangle 134
  textbox 134
Sum functions 105
Switch() function 231

T

TableRelation property 268
Tablix data region 286
Tabular-Type Report Wizard 238
Tabular Type Report, report wizard 54
template report 239
test report
  about 21
  examples 21
textbox
  about 138
  as data region 139
  expression example 138
TextBoxX, naming 216
The joy of stats 321
tips
  applied filters, using 196
  blanking properties 199
  dummy report 196
  empty datasets, checking 199
  ExecutionLog 197, 198
  images, using 197
  lines, using 197
  page headers/footers borders 197
  page numbers, using 196
  pagination 200
  proper name, using 200
  rectangles, using 197, 200
  report border, adding 197
  report layout setup table, using 199
  report usage, tracking 197
  SQL monitoring tools, using 199
  testing 200
  title, using 196
TO BE situation 309
Toggle Item property 146
Toggle Table/Matrix
  implementing 256
toolbar, report viewer
  buttons 100
  Document Map 100
  Print button 100
  Save As button 100
  Zoom button 100
Tools | Create Layout Suggestion 239
TOP X reports
  about 227

chart, creating 234-238
performance 228
sorting 228
Sort on window 229
table, creating 229-234
TotalFields property 59, 66
totals, running 69
Transaction report
  about 22
  characteristics 22
  examples 22
triggers, list reports
  Data Item processing 73, 74
  DataItem triggers 71
  Report Execution Flow,
    visual representation 72
  report triggers 71
  section triggers 71
  using 72

U

unique keys 63
User collection
  Language 193
  UserID 193
UseReqForm property 25

V

View | Layout option 213
Visible property 97

W

Windows-Key + R 92
Windows Azure
  URL 319
wizard
  using 238, 239

Y

Y-axis Max value 248

Z

zero error
  dividing by 233

[PACKT] enterprise
PUBLISHING
professional expertise distilled

Thank you for buying
Microsoft Dynamics NAV 2009: Professional Reporting

About Packt Publishing

Packt, pronounced 'packed', published its first book "Mastering phpMyAdmin for Effective MySQL Management" in April 2004 and subsequently continued to specialize in publishing highly focused books on specific technologies and solutions.

Our books and publications share the experiences of your fellow IT professionals in adapting and customizing today's systems, applications, and frameworks. Our solution based books give you the knowledge and power to customize the software and technologies you're using to get the job done. Packt books are more specific and less general than the IT books you have seen in the past. Our unique business model allows us to bring you more focused information, giving you more of what you need to know, and less of what you don't.

Packt is a modern, yet unique publishing company, which focuses on producing quality, cutting-edge books for communities of developers, administrators, and newbies alike. For more information, please visit our website: www.packtpub.com.

About Packt Enterprise

In 2010, Packt launched two new brands, Packt Enterprise and Packt Open Source, in order to continue its focus on specialization. This book is part of the Packt Enterprise brand, home to books published on enterprise software – software created by major vendors, including (but not limited to) IBM, Microsoft and Oracle, often for use in other corporations. Its titles will offer information relevant to a range of users of this software, including administrators, developers, architects, and end users.

Writing for Packt

We welcome all inquiries from people who are interested in authoring. Book proposals should be sent to author@packtpub.com. If your book idea is still at an early stage and you would like to discuss it first before writing a formal book proposal, contact us; one of our commissioning editors will get in touch with you.

We're not just looking for published authors; if you have strong technical skills but no writing experience, our experienced editors can help you develop a writing career, or simply get some additional reward for your expertise.

[PACKT] enterprise
professional expertise distilled

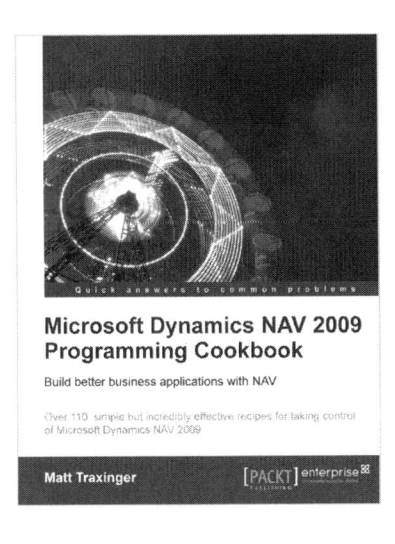

Microsoft Dynamics NAV 2009 Programming Cookbook

ISBN: 978-1-849680-94-3   Paperback: 356 pages

Over 110 simple but incredibly effective recipes for taking control of Microsoft Dynamics NAV 2009

1. Write NAV programs to do everything from finding data in a table to integration with an instant messenger client
2. Develop your own .NET code to perform tasks that NAV cannot handle on its own
3. Work with SQL Server to create better integration between NAV and other systems
4. Learn to use the new features of the NAV 2009 Role Tailored Client

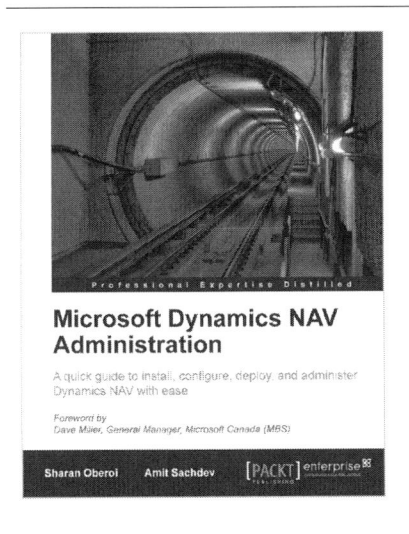

Microsoft Dynamics NAV Administration

ISBN: 978-1-847198-76-1   Paperback: 190 pages

A quick guide to install, configure, deploy, and administering Dynamics NAV with ease

1. Install, configure, deploy and administer Dynamics NAV with ease
2. Install Dynamics NAV Classic Client (Dynamics NAV C/SIDE), Dynamics NAV Role Tailored Client (RTC), and Dynamics NAV Classic Database Server on your computer to manage enterprise data
3. Connect Dynamics NAV clients to the Database Server in the earlier versions and also the latest Dynamics NAV 2009 version

Please check www.PacktPub.com for information on our titles

Printed in Great Britain
by Amazon.co.uk, Ltd.,
Marston Gate.